I'M THE MAN

I'M THE MAN

THE STORY OF THAT GUY FROM ANTHRAX

SCOTT IAN

WITH JON WIEDERHORN

Da Capo Press
A Member of the Perseus Books Group

Designed by Jack Lenzo
Set in eleven-point Caslon by The Perseus Books Group

Library of Congress Cataloging-in-Publication Data

Ian, Scott.
  I'm the man : the story of that guy from Anthrax / Scott Ian with Jon
Wiederhorn.
     pages cm
  Includes index.
  ISBN 978-0-306-82334-3 (hardcover) -- ISBN 978-0-306-82335-0 (e-book)
1. Anthrax (Musical group : U.S.) 2. Ian, Scott. 3. Rock musicians--United
States--Biography. I. Wiederhorn, Jon. II. Title.
  ML421.A515I26 2014
  782.42166092'2--dc23
  [B]
                              2014015428

Published by Da Capo Press
A Member of the Perseus Books Group
www.dacapopress.com

Da Capo Press books are available at special discounts for bulk purchases in
the U.S. by corporations, institutions, and other organizations. For more information, please contact the Special Markets Department at the Perseus Books
Group, 2300 Chestnut Street, Suite 200, Philadelphia, PA 19103, or call (800)
810-4145, ext. 5000, or e-mail special.markets@perseusbooks.com.

10 9 8 7 6 5 4 3 2 1

For Pearl and Revel...

I know what I am and I'll always be, your reality, is better than I could dream
All my fears turn from black to white and I'd stand and fight
the whole world for you...

CONTENTS

ACKNOWLEDGMENTS

I have to start with my family, without whom the last fourteen years of my life would have been drastically different.

Pearl, you make me feel like a superhero every day. Like a bizarro Hulk, "The happier Scott gets, the stronger Scott gets!!!" The power of my love for you is unequaled. We are the *betters*. I am in love with you. And to Revel, my beautiful boy, my cool dude, my bumblebee (thanks, Pearl) . . . your daddy is so proud of you. I love you. Keep kickin' ass my man! We are 3, it's a magic number.

To Mom, thank you for always caring (aka Jewish mom), and thank you for working your ass off to raise two great kids.

Dad, you have always been my rock and I wouldn't be where I am today without you. To Rhea, I couldn't have asked for a better step-mom and I'm lucky to have you.

To my brothers, Jason and Sean, you two are the definition of the word *mensch*. You have always had my back. I love you bros.

Thank you to my Uncle Mitch for having great taste in music and comics. You opened the door . . .

To my Aunt Paula and Uncle Stu, real life Mad Men. Your creative/artistic sensibilities definitely rubbed off, and thanks for designing the first Anthrax logo!

Thank you to the first dudes I ever really jammed with, Neil Stopol and Dave Weiss.

A million years ago at Bayside High School I heard about a kid who could figure out any song on guitar note perfect. People called him "Beethoven" aka Danny Lilker, and it was with him that our shared dream became a reality. There is no Anthrax without Danny.

To my other brothers Charlie and Frankie. We are the nucleus, by definition: *the central and most important part of an object, movement, or group, forming the basis for its activity and growth.* Through all the ups and downs, triumphs and tragedies and peaks and valleys that we've faced in our lives together as a band for over thirty years, you have been my Constant. Wow, this is way too serious! I am one lucky motherfucker to have been in a band for over thirty years with you. Look what we fucking did!!! I love youse guys.

And to my brother, the voice of Anthrax, Joey Belladonna. You opened your mouth in 1984 and with Charlie, Danny, Frankie, and I set the world on fire!!! And the mark we made cut so deep we were able to do it again in 2011 with *Worship Music.* Nothing but love and respect for you. Here's to tearing shit up for twenty more years, my friend!

Rob Caggiano, you gave your blood and sweat just like the rest of us. I am so proud and happy for you. Blow it up, brother!

John Bush. Thinking back on those times in NYC while writing this book put a huge smile on my face. Sometimes it felt like we were in the trenches but being there with you always made it okay. And to my man Paul Crook, you, sir, are Metal.

By the way, Jonny Z, thank you for believing. You are truly the godfather of Thrash.

Huge thanks love and respect to Missi Callazzo, Mike Monterulo, Ed Trunk, and Maria Ferrero for not only being my friends but for going above and beyond.

To my friends and MVPs who have stepped in and kept the machine running; Joey Vera, Andreas Kisser, Jon Dette, Jason Bittner, Gene Hoglan. Life savers, each and every one of you.

Respect, thanks and gratitude to all of the crews who have busted their asses for us since 1984. And to our first ever roadie, Joe Allen. Thanks, Doe!!!

Metallica, Black Sabbath, KISS, Iron Maiden, Ozzy, Motörhead, Dio, Pantera. Playing shows with you was and is our privilege. Thank you.

Who needed drugs when I had Stan Lee, Gene Simmons, and Stephen King. Directly responsible for opening my mind to other worlds than the one I grew up in. I chose this path because of you. Thank you.

Chuck D. You made a dream come true for me. What we did together will eternally krush. Respect, my brother.

Thank you to Rick Krim, Bruce Gillmer, and Erik Luftglass for believing in me and giving me a job when I needed it!

I had so much fun working on this book with Jon Wiederhorn and my editor, Ben Schafer. Thanks, guys! And thank you to Jim Fitzgerald for kicking ass and to everyone at Da Capo for being so into it.

To my lifers: Andy Buchanan, Mike Tempesta, John Tempesta, Dominick DeLuca, Zach Throne, Mark Johnson, Marc Paschke, Rich Ross, Whit Crane, Tim McGlinchey, Brian Posehn, David Karon, Matt Hanrahan, Corey Taylor, Joe Trohman. I have to thank Anthrax for putting me in the right place at the right time to meet each of you.

Thank you to Kirk Hammett for thirty one years of friendship. And for writing the foreword to this book. And for teaching me that no matter how successful you are in life you can still be a nice guy.

To my friends Cliff, Darrell, Ronnie, and Jeff. I miss you and the honor was all mine.

I am writing these acknowledgments on Anthrax's 33rd anniversary. *Thirty-three* years! In my professional life the fact that I have had this career is the single most important thing to me. I have been able to do what I have always wanted to do with my life, and I get to keep doing it for one reason and one reason only . . .

You. The fans. All of you. Whether you've been with us since day one or you just saw us for the first time playing the *Among the Living* record at Knebworth, it's because of you. You, my friends, the kind of people who are willing to look a little deeper and work a little harder to find the music they love. Everything is better if you have to sweat a little bit for it.

> Thanks for sweating with me.
> I love you maniacs.
> Cheers,
> Scott
> Los Angeles, CA
> July 18, 2014

Thanks to: my parents, Sheldon and Nancy Wiederhorn, my wife, Elizabeth Kaplan, my children, Josh and Chloe, Scott Ian and Pearl Aday, Hap and Miriam Rust, Ben Schafer, Carolyn Sobczak, Lissa Warren and the whole Da Capo team, Al Jourgensen, James Fitzgerald, Matthew Oppenheim, Chris Steffen, Jillian Locke, Katherine Turman, Ian McFarland, Amy and Albert Wilk-Sides, Ken Micallef and Jeff Perlah.

—Jon Wiederhorn

FOREWORD

ENTER THE PIT
By Kirk Hammett

It all happened in a place so far away from where I had grown up. I was in San Francisco playing in Exodus when I got a call to come out to the East Coast to audition for Metallica. The word was that James and Lars were unhappy with Dave's drinking and overall performance and wanted him out of the band. Mark Whittaker, who was Exodus's manager, also happened to be Metallica's sound guy, so when Mark got wind of Dave's inevitable exit, he played Exodus's demo for Lars and James, who both deemed the guy playing the leads on that cassette worthy of an audition. That guy was me.

When Mark picked me up from the airport I was mortified. There was snow on the ground and I was wearing a denim jacket. Up to this point, I had never been out of California. I only knew that there were other places in the world through movies, maps, and pictures. So what I saw on the way to seedy Jamaica, Queens, was eye-opening to say the least. In San Francisco back then, it was rare to see whole swaths of neighborhoods that bore the decades of crime and filth and waste, but I had never seen such a used-up piece of humanity as I did when we finally got to the place called the Music Building. Don't get me wrong, it wasn't some den of iniquity or sleazy hellhole or anything amusing like that. It was just so rundown and in a totally dilapidated state and boring that the only thing one could do with the building was to rent out whole office spaces to bands, and then proceed to let them do whatever they wanted to do, as long as they paid their rent.

There were broken windows everywhere, piles of drywall here and there, concrete and rebar sticking out at eye level. Mark told me there were a bunch of Top 40 cover bands and a few metal bands practicing in the building. He said one of the heaviest groups was called Anthrax, and they were a cool bunch of guys. "They gave us a fridge!" he said.

The space we were renting was on the fifth or sixth floor, and our room was huge, dirty, and empty. There was a smaller, closed-off room in the corner. The only things in the main area were sleeping bags, a bunch of British metal magazines, a scrap heap of egg-carton foam, suitcases, and boxes of booze and food. And a refrigerator. There was broken glass on the floor, of course. And it was cold, thanks to the broken furnace somewhere in the bowels of the building. Mark told me that everyone slept out here in the open space and rehearsed in the room that was closed off. I asked where the other guys were, and Mark pointed in the closed-off room and said, "They're in there, sleeping." I looked at my watched and saw that it was 7 p.m.

Soon after, Cliff walked into the room and I said hi. He said, "Hello, very glad to meet you," in such a way that immediately revealed how confident he was. Then James and Lars appeared and we exchanged greetings. I had met them both before, but I wasn't sure if they actually remembered me, due to various circumstances involving alcohol. We talked about my flight, and they asked if I brought any equipment. I had an amp and guitar with me. This was back in the days when you could check anything with the airlines—and I mean anything. I gave the porter $20, he taped a Fragile sticker to my Marshall cabinet, and away it went with me to NYC. It was hilarious watching the cabinet get stuck on the baggage carousel when Mark and I went to pick it up!

The first time we ever jammed together in the practice room, we spent an hour playing a few Mercyful Fate and Metallica songs. Lars and James kept smiling at each other, which I thought was kind of strange. I figured they either really liked what they were hearing or maybe they were really close in a SF kinda way. But things pretty much clicked from that moment on.

After we played, we all walked to the liquor store down the street and bought 40-ouncers because it seemed like a good deal economically.

This was waaay before 40s became popular. When we got back to the Music Building, the guys showed me how to put egg-carton foam under my sleeping bag to create a lumpy cushion that was a bit more comfortable than sleeping on the cold, bare floor. Not only was there no heating in the place, there wasn't any hot water, only cold. We drank and tried to stay warm. We listened to metal, talked about metal, and I told them how much I enjoyed playing their songs. Then we passed out.

The next morning we were awakened by the dull vibration of some band playing in the room down the hall. At first I thought I had died and was in purgatory. Then I opened my eyes and remembered I was at the Music Building with a bunch of guys I barely knew. I looked over at Cliff and saw that he was reading a *Dungeons & Dragons Call of Cthulhu* role-playing book. Being a big horror fan and well-read in the works of H. P. Lovecraft, I said, "I know that book!"

He said, "Oh yeah?" which was what he said when he was interested in something.

I discovered that we could talk in detail about Lovecraft. I was relieved we had something in common besides music. He loved horror movies as well. His all-time fave was George Romero's *Dawn of the Dead*.

After struggling to put on my shoes in the chest-heaving cold, I wanted to see what this place looked like during the day. I wandered out to the main hall, figuring that one of those metal bands that Mark was talking about was responsible for waking me up. So I went in the direction of the music. As I drew closer, what I heard was definitely metal. It was loud and fast, and the guitar sound was really great! After listening through the door for a while, I headed back down to our room. As I was talking to Cliff, these two guys walked through the door. One was incredibly gawky in a Joey Ramone kind of way, and the other looked like a Jewish version of a wannabe Glenn Tipton. Cliff said, "Hey, these are the guys from Anthrax—this is Scott, and this is Danny."

And that was the first time that I heard that gravelly, throaty, slightly devious and mischievous-sounding New Yawk voice of Scott Ian: "Hey, we brought youz guys a toaster oven!"

That was April 8, 1983, thirty-one years and one day ago as I type this.

A lot has changed since then. But what hasn't changed is my relationship with Scott. From meeting him that cold morning in the Music Building to hanging out with him very recently at Fear FestEvil in San Francisco, I've always appreciated and marveled at our friendship. Even though we grew up on opposite sides of the country, we share a lot of the same sensibilities and interests. We also happen to share the same sick sense of humor that we still bond over all these years later.

From the very beginning I could see that Scott has a humongous, Godzilla-sized heart. He always has time for everyone, whether you are friend, fan, or foe. In a sense, to me he emulated some of the heroes he read about in those comic books we use to read way back in the eighties. He was definitely a people person, in direct contrast to myself being quite introverted. It was healthy for me to hang out with him. I observed how confident he appeared, and he was always very welcoming in social situations. I'll never forget, after many days with no access to hot water in the Music Building, how he convinced these girls he knew to let us take advantage of their health club account so we could use the locker rooms to shower in!

Scott helped me come out of my shell a little bit. I was so shy back then, and watching Scott in action in social situations taught me how to conduct myself a little better when I found myself in similar circumstances.

It was good to have Scott as an ally on the East Coast. Actually, all the guys in Anthrax were quite friendly, and we hung out a lot. Every time we were in their area, you could count on all of us meeting up, and craziness would ensue. What's funny is that back then those guys weren't fully realized drinkers like we were. When we came around with various bottles of vodka in tow, we never really noticed that they drank maybe one drink to our four or five! But they were entertained by our belligerent antics and were glad to join in when it looked fun. Sometimes I couldn't tell if Scott was drunk or just high on life, which I think he often is. I admire his state of mind; I envy it, to be honest.

Scott was always so supportive of us and the kind of metal that Anthrax and Metallica and a whole generation of new metal bands were playing. There was no bitterness or sour grapes. It was exciting. We were forging through uncharted musical territory, and it was a brave new world for everyone. When it came time for our first US tour, Scott was very helpful. I'll never forget asking him if I could borrow his Rockman (an analog device you could plug your guitar into and play into headphones) because I did not have a practice amp. It was the eve of the Metallica/Raven *Kill 'Em All for One* tour, and he said, "Sure!" I still have it somewhere, thirty-plus years later, and I still mean to get it back to him sometime. The fact that he was so willing to help all the time was not lost on me.

When we were recording *Ride the Lightning*, Scott came to London to do press for Anthrax's first album, *Fistful of Metal*. One particularly crazy night with Cliff and Scott culminated with Cliff unable to get off the floor and onto his bed, and Scott and I laughing and trying to help the poor guy. But he was just too tall and skinny, and that's what made it sooo hilarious! Then Scott turned around and grabbed a teapot full of water and poured it into a rented Marshall amp I was using, laughing and screaming, "Oh, it's tea time!" That set the precedent for decades of similar behavior, which we still kind of engage in today.

Scott often came to see us during the *Master of Puppets* tour. We saw Ozzy backstage for the first time, and we were both in total awe of him. Anthrax came out on tour with us in Europe that fall, which was really fun—until the Cliff tragedy.

I'll never forget how upset Scott reacted when he heard the news. I'll never forget how he, Frankie, and Charlie roamed the streets of Copenhagen with James 'til about 3 a.m. I was thankful they were giving him support when I could not. I was totally incapacitated with grief and in too much of a state of shock to even leave my bed, let alone my room. When Scott came to the funeral, I insisted he stay at my place, which was actually my mom's house.

Scott has always been there for me, emotionally as well as physically.

He has turned me on to so many cool things over the years, and I like to think I've done the same for him. He was always a kind of cultural barometer for me. I would ask him what new comics were worth checking out. I turned him on to certain books, and we always had a shared love for musical equipment. It was Scott who told me about this really cool company that made great, quality guitars; they were called ESP. He hooked me up with their people in New York, and the next thing I knew I was in the warehouse grabbing bolt-on necks and saying to the ESP guy, "No, this is too thin. No, this is too wide." So I have Scott to thank for our twenty-seven-year relationship with ESP.

But really, if I were to try and chronicle all the amazing and not-so-amazing times I have shared with Scott, it would take another book. Our friendship spans three decades and counting, and we've had an amazing time throughout. Scott's birthday is on New Year's Eve, so I've had the pleasure of spending many New Year's/birthday celebrations with him. It's funny how those celebrations always became adventures more than anything. You can come to your own conclusions on those while I roll out a couple more anecdotes.

We have matching tattoos…don't jump to conclusions. We decided to get them one night after watching a Van Halen rehearsal show in LA. We were so blown away by the band and by hanging out drinking Jack Daniels with David Lee Roth that we both came to the conclusion that the best way to immortalize that particular evening was to get matching tattoos. And everyone who was with us that night got the same tattoo. No, it's not "VH." It's something more symbolic that shows his commitment to his friends and events that are important to him.

I'll close with one not-so-amazing time I shared with Scott, just to put our friendship into perspective. Three years ago, Scott and I were in Hawaii with our lovely wives, Pearl and Lani. We were enjoying downtime until we learned that a massive tsunami had hit Japan and that all of Hawaii was under a tsunami warning. I'll never forget how pale Scott's face went when he heard the news. My wife and I explained to him that tsunamis from the west have a tendency to lose all their destructive force once they get close to the islands, but that didn't stop him from staying up all night staring out his window in anticipation of imminent destruction, preparing to evacuate his pregnant wife at the first sign of peril. By the time the tsunami hit Hawaii, it was barely a foot tall. The next day we congratulated Scott and Pearl for living through their first tsunami! (By the way, tsunami warnings are a fact of life in Hawaii. I have experienced four of them.)

The most important thing I've learned about Scott is that he's an amazing human being. Sure, he has fallen for some of the same trappings we all fell for in our younger years and later learned to circumvent. But while we have both changed in our own ways over the decades, the core elements that made us friends exist to this day. I still consider Scott one of my closest and dearest friends. What we experienced as friends separately and collectively has informed us and shaped us into who we are today.

He's sharp, funny, amusing, lovingly sarcastic, loyal, charming, and a great schemer in the best possible way. He's flexible, a great musician with great instincts, and he's a man of wealth and taste. He's also engaging, has a vivid imagination, is a natural leader, has a dark side that I admire, and looks great on all those TV shows. In addition, he has an amazing ability to locate free stuff, and he is an excellent poker player, somewhat of a media whore, serious about his food and drink. I consider Scott a visionary, an honorary San Franciscan, a fighter when he needs to be, a great riffy guitar player, a fellow drinker of Fernet-Branca, a great father and husband, a fellow lover of horror movies, and an overall celebrator of life and art, with a sense of New York awareness that has never faded, even though he's been on the West Coast for twenty-plus years.

He's my pal.

I'd take a bullet for this guy. Probably more than one...

This is his story, written by "The Man" himself.

PREFACE

I f I was sober, maybe it wouldn't have happened. But I was as wasted as I'd been since my eighteenth birthday when I got stupid drunk on countless glasses of Popov vodka and orange juice, and let's just say my judgment was irreparably impaired. I had been a New York Yankees fan since I was eleven years old. My dad took me to my first game in 1972, and I've followed the team religiously through the years, even when they sucked. So when I had the chance to break into their spring-training park, Legends Field in Tampa, Florida, and take the on-deck circle as a souvenir, I was too tempted to resist.

I flew into Tampa on August 18, 1997, for a guitar show at Thoroughbred Music. There was a lot of time to kill between appointments, so I got really drunk with Zakk Wylde and then hung out with my friend Ed, who was putting me up while I was in Florida. He was sober and I was with him, my friend Angela, and her sister Heather, both of whom I had known since the late eighties. They were the only girls that came to Anthrax shows back then. We drove past the ball park at two in the morning, and I shouted, "Oh my God, Legends Field! I read in the paper that there's a Thurman Munson monument here. I have to go see it. He's my favorite Yankee of all time!"

We were at a red light so I started to get out of the car. "Whoa, whoa," my buddy Ed said. "We'll go tomorrow when it's open to the public. We'll walk around and you can see it then."

In my ego-fueled haze, that wasn't going to fly. I could see the monument from the window. If it could have spoken, it would have called my name and invited me over. Ed knew I was out-of-my-mind drunk, so he clicked the door-lock button in the front, which locked the whole car. It was probably a good move for him, but I've never taken no for an answer. When I was a kid and my mom told me I couldn't do something, I either talked my way into doing it or I simply ignored her. When every label on the planet told us Anthrax wasn't a marketable band, I told them all to fuck themselves. When everyone said the band was done because grunge and alternative rock had wiped out metal, we found a way to persevere. The word "no" just isn't in my vocabulary, which is why as a teenager I earned the nickname Scott "NOT" Ian.

On the ride back from Legends Field, I plotted how we were going to get back to the stadium to check out the monument. I decided that when we got to Ed's we'd get Heather to take us back to the park. She didn't drink either, but she was more adventurous than Ed.

By the time we got to Ed's it was well past 2:30 a.m., and he went right to bed. I convinced Heather, who wasn't doing anything anyway, to take us back to Legends Field without Ed knowing. She saw how much I wanted to go, so she agreed to drive us back there. She parked her car by a fence outside the stadium and stayed there, while Angela and I hopped the gate and walked into the grounds. I went right to the monument. It was bathed in silvery moonlight that made Munson look like a deity. He had a private audience and looked way cooler than he would have by day with the regular sunlight and a bunch of gawking tourists with cameras. I was sure Munson would have been honored that one of his biggest fans had gone out of his way to share such a personal moment with a hero and a friend. Of course, I was also drunk. I took some pictures then convinced Angela to come with me to check out the stadium.

We went in and walked down the aisles to the lush, green, grassy field. I stood at home plate and pictured myself in a pinstriped uniform with a bat in my hands, facing down Orioles pitcher Jim Palmer. I could almost see the ball leave his calloused hand and zip toward home plate. I swung and connected. The ball rocketed past first baseman Eddie Murray and into the outfield. I took off, for real. I ran around the bases and slid into second. Safe!

I ran around the field, shouted, "This is amazing!" and urged Angela to join me running the bases. We went from base to base laughing like kids, and there was no one there to stop us. I circled third base and slid headfirst into home plate. It took me a minute to recover from that brilliant move. I slowly got up and brushed myself off and then I saw the on-deck circle. It was made of thick, heavy rubber and had a big Yankee logo on it—the bat with the hat. I thought it would look amazing in our studio in Yonkers right in front of all my amps, and I could record all my guitar parts standing on it, showing off my Yankee pride.

"I gotta have this thing!" I slurred, not even thinking how I would get this two-hundred-pound piece of rubber into the airport and on a plane back to New York. I picked up one side of it, but it was so heavy I could only lift it halfway off the ground. I tried to roll it up. The grass was wet and I was slipping and falling down. After a few minutes of wrestling with the thing, my arms were tired, so I gave up and put it back where it was.

"Let's get out of here," I said. We walked back out and in the distance I saw cop lights flashing where Heather was parked waiting for us. I was so wasted I didn't think we did anything wrong. What did we do? We ran around the bases a little bit. We didn't break anything. I didn't actually steal anything.

It didn't once occur to me that maybe we should go a different way, hop a different fence, and get the fuck out of there. So we walked straight out the front. The gate we had hopped was open. There were golf carts, security guards, and three cop cars there. Heather was sitting on a curb. We came walking out and I waved to her and said, "Hi!" with a big smile on my face. A cop grabbed me, slammed me over the hood of a car, arms behind my back, and handcuffed me. Another grabbed Angela and cuffed her. I was in shock. I said, "What the hell?!?"

"Shut the fuck up!" snapped the cop.

"What did I do?" I protested. "I didn't do anything."

They threw me down on the curb and said, "Yeah? How about breaking and entering, asshole? How about burglary?"

"Burglary? What burglary? I didn't take anything."

Then one of the cops told me they had a video of my inept attempt to steal the on-deck circle.

I was still buzzing with liquid courage, so I said, "Yeah, but I didn't! I left it there! I'll write you a check, I'll get you money. Tell me how much it costs. I'll give you whatever it costs right now, and you can still keep the on-deck circle!"

The cops laughed and walked away. I sat there cuffed and totally confused. I looked at Angela and she just said, "Fuck, we're in real trouble."

They didn't arrest Heather because she never went into the park. They told her to go home. She said she'd wake up Ed and they'd get us a lawyer. Then she took off.

Angela and I were sitting there helpless when one of the cops walked over to me and said, "Hey, aren't you the guy from Anthrax?"

"Yeah, yeah I am!" It's sometimes kind of a bummer to be recognized in public. This was a godsend.

"What's going on, dude?" he said.

I told him I was an insane Yankees fan and I got stupid drunk and wanted to see the stadium because I heard there was a Thurman Munson monument in it. Then one thing led to another and I decided to run the bases. "Is there anything you can do to get me out of this? I've never been arrested in my life."

He told me he'd see what he could do. He talked to the other cops. One of the cars left. I thought that was a good sign. The Anthrax cop was talking to the Legends Field security guys. Twenty minutes later the Legends guys took off in their golf cart. "Yes!! Go, Anthrax cop!" I figured he had gotten us out of this mess and I'd send him a bunch of band merchandise to thank him. Then the security guys came back. The good cop walked over to me and said, "Alright, I have good news and bad news. What do you want first?"

"The bad news?"

"I talked to my fellow officers and they were all fine with me driving you back to your friend's house. They truthfully don't give a shit. It's less paperwork for them. I told them you were a guy in a band."

"That's bad news? I can go?"

"No," he explained. "Because the Legends Field head security guy said, 'We have to call management. We can't just let this go.'"

Here's the bad news. They called the Yankees owner George Steinbrenner, who lived in Tampa. It was five in the morning, and if you know anything about Steinbrenner, you know he had a reputation for being a fucking hard-ass. He wasn't called the General, *Der Fuhrer*, and the Kaiser for nothing. My heart fell. I fucked with the wrong dude. They told Steinbrenner I was a guitarist in a popular band and I was just pulling a prank, and the former Yankees owner said, "I don't give a fuck who he is. He's going to jail."

I said to the Anthrax cop, who I was rapidly losing faith in, "Okay, what's the good news? Can you just drop us off somewhere and we'll sort it out later?"

"No, I can't," he said. "It's on the books. I'll get in big trouble. They called the cops. They filed a report. You're under arrest."

Up to that point it had been like a bad dream, and suddenly, as the alcohol was wearing off, reality was starting to set in. So far, there hadn't been any good news. Then the cop filled me in on my good fortune. He was supposed to drive me downtown and put me in a cell with thirty deviants—from murderers to rapists. He was basically saying, "You and this pretty young girl will be in a jail cell with hardcore criminals, and you'll probably end up getting fucked up the ass if you're lucky."

"Look, I'm not going to take you downtown," he said. *That* was the good news. He drove us to some small town out in the boonies of Hillsborough County twenty-five minutes away that was basically a big drunk tank where people were sleeping off DUIs. The place looked like a high school cafeteria with tables and chairs and a few harmless-looking dudes passed out. They booked us and, as much better as it probably was than city jail, it sucked. Once you're in the system, you lose all your humanity. The people who work there don't give a fuck about you or your story, and rightly so. Maybe if they were Anthrax fans, they might have cared, but none of the people I talked to knew who Anthrax were. To them I was just another troublemaker. The cop who dropped us off wished us good luck and left.

I sat there for a while then they brought me into the office, finger-printed me, and took my mug shot. They told me to strip and gave me an orange jumpsuit that said Hillsborough County Jail on the back. Angela had one, too, and from that point on we were there to be ignored.

"When do I get a phone call? How do I post bail? What do I do?" I asked. Nothing. I didn't know what to do and no one would talk to me. Finally, one lady was nice enough to say, "You'll get your phone call."

She told me there was a phone in the jail that inmates can use anytime they want as long as the call was collect. I thanked her for helping me. I swore to her that I had never been arrested and I wasn't an asshole. I just wanted to get back home. But she'd already said all she was going to say to me. She acted like she had broken the rules by even telling me that much.

The thing is, they hear that shit all day long. They're numb to it. I started to think about Angela. I was bummed that I brought her into this situation. She could give a fuck about Thurman Munson, and now she was in jail because I was an idiot. I kept saying, "I'm sorry, I'm sorry." She was totally cool about it. "Hey, I didn't have to go," she said. "I chose to run around like a jackass, too."

By that time it was 6:30 a.m. and I decided to call my dad. Before he even heard my voice, a recording came on that said, "You are being called by an inmate in a correctional facility. Do you accept the charges?" I could tell that threw him a little. He said, "Hello?"

"Dad, it's me . . ."

"Scott?!?"

Then the voice came back that said, "Do you accept the charges?" Dad took the call, and I explained to him that I was in jail in Tampa. I told him that I had to get a lawyer to fill out a stack of paperwork and file for bail and it had to be done by 11 a.m. or I'd be stuck in jail another day.

He asked me why I was arrested, and I told him I broke into Legends Field.

"How old are you?" he said.

"Dad, I need paperwork filled out and . . ."

"How *old* are you?" he repeated.

I sighed. "I'm thirty-four years old. You know that."

"Well, maybe you need to start making some better decisions in your life," he said. But he agreed to call his lawyer right away. It turned out that wasn't necessary because Heather had gone back to Ed's house, woken him up, and told him we got arrested. So he had already gone through the process of getting the paperwork taken care of, and bail was being posted. When I got off the phone with my dad, Angela called her sister, and Heather told her we'd be out by 11:30.

Before we left, they wanted us to have TB shots because there had been an outbreak of tuberculosis in the jail and if we didn't get the shot they wouldn't take responsibility if we got sick. Knowing I was getting out made me cocky. I told them I wasn't getting any shot. The nurse said, if I didn't get the shot, I wasn't getting out for at least another day. We got the shots. Not long after, I got an upset stomach. I don't know if it was the injection, the unbelievable amount of booze I had in my system, or the stress I had been under since we got arrested, but I realized I had to take a shit right away—a fucking bad, insane booze shit. I didn't see any bathrooms except for one toilet in the middle of the room in front of everyone. I poop-walked to the infirmary where I got the shot because there was a door in there that looked like a bathroom. It was open. I saw the toilet. Thank God!!!

I told the nurse, a heavyset older woman, that I needed to use the toilet. I asked politely if I could go.

"Go ahead," she said and pointed to the stained, wet toilet in the main room.

"No, that's why I came in here," I groaned. "Can I please use the toilet to have some privacy?" She looked right through me and said, "Ain't no way you're using this private bathroom."

I went back and sat next to Angela. I didn't tell her what was going on. Instead, I experienced an award-winning episode of mind over matter. The mental concentration I had to exert to avoid completely soiling myself was mind-blowing. There was no way I was going to sit on the filthy toilet in front of forty or fifty people, some of whom were Anthrax fans sweeping up the jail. These guys were prison inmates who had to clean up the drunk tank every day. They heard I was in there and were happy just to glance over, smile, and nod. I couldn't possibly take a shit in front of them. I sat there with my cheeks clenched and my stomach in knots for three fucking hours. The pain was insane, but I acted like everything was normal.

Finally it was 11 a.m. and they called our names and processed us out. Ed and Heather were waiting for us. They asked us what we wanted to do and I said I really wanted to go back to Ed's to take a shower right away and get something to eat. By then the news of what had happened was public. Ed turned the radio to 98 Rock in Tampa and the DJ said, "Scott Ian, if you're still in town, call us. We want to know what happened."

I almost crapped myself right there, but I held it in and didn't say a word. We got back to Ed's and I went straight into the bathroom, turned the shower on, slid onto the clean, shining toilet seat, and took an Incredible Hulk–sized dump. I can't believe the porcelain didn't explode and the toilet didn't overflow. Everything poured out of me; it was a huge relief. I felt well enough afterward to go to Universal Studios to check out the rides. The last thing I expected was for people to point at me and yell, "Hey you stole home plate!" but word travels fast.

I'll get into more detail about how I expunged my criminal record and cleared the air with George Steinbrenner later. Everything has its place. Just note that the incident at Legends Field was an anomaly for me. It was the only time I've ever been arrested, and it'll definitely be the last. See, I've never been an attention-seeking, drug-snarfing metal dude with a death wish. I have plenty of friends who are, and I love drinking with them and listening to their stories. But that's not me. I've never shot up, never done blow, and I haven't even smoked pot since 1995.

I didn't get into music for pussy. I got into it for music. Sure, there were girls along the way, but not like there were for those '80s hair bands. For the longest time, thrash metal was a dude scene; if there were any chicks at the show, they were usually dragged along by their boyfriends. Basically, I'm a guy who made a name for myself by working my ass off. There have been plenty of ups and just as many downs, and through it all Anthrax have persevered. We've been rewarded for our efforts and grouped as one of the Big 4 along with Metallica, Slayer, and Megadeth. But my story is very different, as much respect as I have for each and every one of those guys. I don't have tragic tales about being abused, abandoned by my parents, sleeping in the streets, choosing between my next fix and my next meal, or getting into gang fights and cracking guys over the head with empty 40s. As my mom likes to say, at heart I'm a good Jewish boy.

I grew up in Queens, New York, got good grades, and geeked out over comic books, horror, and sci-fi. Then I discovered rock and roll, and everything changed. In that respect I was like a lot of aspiring musicians, but I always had inextinguishable drive. From my early teens, I was motivated to find musicians to play with, write songs, get signed, play shows, and grow and grow and grow. I was persistent as hell, a tenacious prick if there ever was one. Every time an obstacle came up, I used my laser-beam focus to figure out how to get around it and move on. Keep moving forward. Overcome problems, deal with changes. Singers and guitarists came and went and sometimes came back. I carried on. My story in Anthrax is one of determination, dedication, and sometimes luck, both good and bad. It's a story filled with triumphs and challenges, but it hasn't all been drama and struggle. I've had a hell of a lot of fun, and I've come to the realization that the music business is the craziest, least predictable enterprise on the planet. Literally anything can happen. Having spent more than thirty years releasing albums and touring, I've accumulated a boatload of funny and fascinating experiences regarding my band, friends, peers, and people I met from the time I first picked up an acoustic guitar to the moment I stepped foot onstage at Yankee Stadium for the Big 4 Festival. When it comes to Anthrax, I'm the man and this is my story.

I'M THE BOY

I was born in Jamaica Hospital in Queens at 7 a.m. on New Year's Eve, 1963. It was an auspicious beginning, sort of. Oddly enough, that's where the legendary Music Building was located, which is where Anthrax, Metallica, and other bands made history writing and rehearsing some of the earliest and most memorable thrash songs. Metallica even lived at the place for a while. And man, it was a slum. When I went there with Anthrax, I used to think, "God, this neighborhood is such a dive. It must have been so much different when my parents were living here." But maybe it wasn't, and that was one of the hardships they had to face. If so, it was one of many.

My parents never had it easy. They were second-generation immigrants, and when I was growing up my father, Herbert Rosenfeld, was working in the jewelry business and my mom, Barbara Haar, was a housewife. I think that was part of why she was so unhappy. She didn't want to be a happy homemaker. She wasn't cut out for it and didn't have the patience. My parents came from working-class families and got married way too young. My dad's father, Harold Rosenfeld, was born in 1908 in Worcester, Massachusetts, and my grandmother Sylvia was born in 1912 in Manhattan. They met in the south shore of Brooklyn while he was driving a Good Humor truck. They got married in 1938 and he continued to work in the summer. Then in the winter before my aunt and dad were born, my grandparents would drive to Florida every winter in a Model-T Ford and live there with the money he made selling ice cream—like they were on vacation.

My dad and his sister were raised in a tenement house in a fourth-floor walkup. They never had any money even after my grandfather got a job as a shoe salesman to earn some extra cash. He was a good, hard-working man, but they could never afford any luxuries, and he kept a diary of every penny he spent in a day.

My grandmother on my mom's side, Lena, was from Russia, and her husband, Moe, was born in 1902 in a tiny Polish village called Nisko, which is no longer on the map. During World War I the Germans occupied the village and started killing all the men. So, when he was seventeen, his parents smuggled him out of the country. He lived in Amsterdam with a family who hired him as a grocer. Once he saved up enough money to buy counterfeit identification papers, he stowed away on a ship to New York and got all the way to Ellis Island. He got off the boat and waited in line with all the other refugees, but, when the people at immigration saw that he didn't have the right papers, they turned him around and put him on a boat back to Amsterdam. He spent another six months or so working and then he was able to get the proper paperwork. Then he got back on another ship, came back to New York, and this time immigration allowed him in.

My grandpa Moe was a smart guy but he was broke. So he went to the Lower East Side where there was a community of Jews that sort of looked after each other, and he got a job as a grocer. He hustled his ass off and climbed the ladder really quickly. By the time he was in his early twenties, he had his own grocery store in Rockaway, and when he had made enough money, he brought his parents over. They were strict Orthodox Jews, which was weird for my mom because she grew up in Queens in a household that wasn't religious. They even used to have a Christmas tree around the holidays before her grandparents moved in. Then suddenly she was in this house with her dad's parents, who only spoke Yiddish and wouldn't even try to speak English. They were hardcore Jews. They hated Moe's wife and my mom because they thought Moe deserved better. And they really weren't good with children. When they made everything super religious, my mom rebelled and tried to run away, but they always got her back. And then her father whacked her with a belt.

It was a different time back then. Basically, you beat your kids when they didn't behave. It wasn't abnormal. It was just accepted. You got hit. It's hard for me to believe because my grandparents never had anything but love for me and my brother Jason, but both of my parents took a lot of abuse growing up. My dad once told me a story about yelling to a friend through an open window when he was a kid. His mother got so mad she picked him up, flipped him upside down, held him by his underarms, and dangled him out the window four stories in the air. And when my uncle got caught stealing her cigarettes, she held his hand against a hot stove. They didn't fuck around when it came to discipline. There were no time-outs or positive reinforcement. It was all spare the rod and spoil the child.

Even though they had a difficult upbringing, my parents didn't pass that on to Jason and me. They were not hitters. Maybe once in a blue moon if one of us really got out of line, we'd get a slap. But, when I was a kid, just the sound of my dad's raised voice was enough to scare the shit out of me. I'd like to say I had a well-adjusted home life, but that wouldn't really be true. My dad was twenty-two and my mom was twenty when they got married. And then my mom immediately got pregnant with me. That wasn't the plan for either of them, but back then if you got pregnant, you got married. No one from a good Jewish home got an abortion. It was unheard of—lucky for me!

Soon after I was born, my mom cheated on my dad with the love of her life, who had previously spurned her, Lenny Chumsky, and my dad found out. They split up for a while. During that time my mom started drinking heavily, and her father, Moe, shamed her into begging my dad's forgiveness. He accepted her apology, and they got back together. This was 1964, and people really weren't getting divorced back then. Maybe it would have been better if they had made a clean break. I feel like their marriage was doomed from the start.

We moved to Florida when I was three because my dad was unjustly accused of stealing diamonds from the company where he worked, Harry Winston Jewelry. He failed a polygraph test because he's untestable—meaning he'll fail no matter what—so they fired him even though he hadn't taken anything and no one had any evidence that he had. He got another offer from a family in Florida to work at Mayer's Jewelers in Miami to do repairs and sizing for rings. My parents thought a change of scenery might be good for the family. I don't remember most of our time in Florida, except for my first vivid memory in July 1966.

Maybe it was an omen or a metaphor for the trauma that was about to strike our family—okay, it was nothing that dramatic. I was stung by a bee. I wasn't allergic or anything, but it hurt like hell and I'll never forget that day. We were living in this apartment complex, and the back of the place had sliding glass doors that led outside. There was a grassy area near the pool, and I was walking through the grass barefoot. The bee was resting on a small piece of clover, and I stepped right on him. He didn't sting me right away. He flew up and I ran. I remember thinking, "I'll jump in the pool to escape the bee," but before I got there the bee stung the inside of my ear. It was really loud, and I screamed because of the noise and the pain. That began my lifelong hatred of most stinging and biting insects. I hate spiders, and I can't look at a wasp without feeling murderous. Bees and I have a grudging respect for each other nowadays. Fortunately, they removed the stinger and it didn't cause any serious damage because it didn't sting my eardrum. My ear just swelled up and hurt like a motherfucker.

My mom hated Florida and longed to get back to New York. My dad loved it. But, as fate would have it, someone at my dad's company stole a bunch of jewelry and the boss made everyone take a polygraph test. My dad explained what had happened to him in New York. They polygraphed him anyway, and of course he failed again, so the boss—who dealt with the mafia buying and selling hot jewelry—fired my dad and told him that if he found out he was the thief he was going to find himself at the bottom of the ocean with cement shoes. My dad was indignant and stormed out. Later, his boss discovered his private secretary and her daughter were on heavy drugs and they were the thieves. But my dad never got an apology.

As soon as he lost his job, we moved back to New York, and for nine months my mom had to work in a bagel shop to help pay the bills. My dad got another job in the jewelry business with Gimbel Brothers as an appraiser, and then he became manager of the production department and a buyer of stones at Aaron Perkis Company. We were still far from rich, but at least he had some income flowing in.

My dad would do anything he could think of to make my mother happy, but she always had something to complain about. That's when I first noticed that my parents didn't like being together. By the time I was four or five, my mom seemed weird and distant. She did all the things she felt she had to do as a mother taking care of two kids, but, even at that age, I could tell there was no joy there. When I got a little older, I understood that she didn't want to be a housewife and she didn't like being with my father. Then I realized she drank.

All I knew back then was that there was alcohol in the house. She drank a lot of scotch and it was a problem for her. Later on, I found out she was also taking pills—Quaaludes, Valium, diet pills, anything she could get a prescription for to help her escape. She was miserable because she never wanted to be with my dad. She wanted Lenny Chumsky, but she compromised. It was a fucked-up position for my dad to be in, and from the time I was four years old up until I was eleven and my parents split up, there was a lot of tension in the house. I don't think they ever loved each other. But for some reason they thought having another child might make their relationship better, so three and a half years after I was born, my mom gave birth to Jason, who became both my responsibility and my right-hand man all through childhood.

As difficult at it was to be with my mother, there were some good times. When I was four years old she used to read *MAD* magazine to me. When she was a kid, she had every issue, but my grandmother would clean her room and throw them out. Who knows what they'd be worth today?

My mom was also a big horror fan. She loved scary movies. In New York on Saturday and Sunday mornings, there used to be Chiller Theater on WPIX and Creature Feature on WNYC, channel 11 and channel 5 back before cable. A lot of times, instead of watching cartoons on Saturday mornings, we'd watch horror movies with my mom. Mostly, it was the old black-and-white Universal classic monster movies—*Frankenstein, Wolfman, Dracula*—and I loved them all from the time I was four or five.

When the original version of *The Thing* came on, my mom said, "When I was your age this was the scariest movie ever made. This is the movie that terrified everybody." We started watching it, and I was prepared to jump up and run out of the room in fright—only it wasn't scary. I said, "Mom, it looks like a walking vegetable. How is that scary? Wolfman is much scarier than him," and my mom said to me, "Scott, in the 1950s that was scary."

The thing is, I was never scared by horror movies. I loved them and I still do, but I always knew they weren't real. To this day, movies don't scare me. Books, however, sometimes scare the shit out of me because the action and dialogue are all in my head. It's a different type of reality. You create your own images and your flesh tingles or your heart sinks when something bad happens. That's why Stephen King has always been one of my favorite authors. *The Shining* scared me so much that all these years later I still can't walk down hotel hallways without thinking some fucked-up ghost twins are going to grab me.

If anything, I felt an emotional connection with the monsters in the classic movies. Not Jason in *Friday the 13th* or Michael Myers in *Halloween*. They were just mindless, immortal psychopaths. And of course awesome. But Frankenstein's monster—what a sad dude. He was already dead, he's brought back to life, then he's just persecuted and hated, and he's ugly and scary. All he wants is to be left alone and everyone fucks with him. I always felt bad for those kinds of monsters. Lon Chaney Jr. in *The Wolfman* gave off such emotions with or without the makeup. He played Larry Talbot, who gets attacked by a werewolf and kills it, but he gets bitten during the fight. So he turns into a werewolf every full moon. He elicits so much empathy because he didn't deserve his fate. He didn't want to murder people as the Wolfman; it was completely out of his hands. Dracula was a different story. You didn't really feel bad for Dracula—he was a vampire doing his thing. Dracula was my least favorite of the original Universal monsters.

We didn't know it at the time, but on a psychological level my brother and I related to characters who were thrown into a life they didn't ask for. Growing up, we tried to shield ourselves from our parents' unhappiness as much as we could. Like Frankenstein, we just wanted to be left alone.

We lived in Bayside, Queens, in Bay Terrace until I was eight years old. It was a very Jewish, upper-middle-class-to-rich part of the city. We were certainly not in the upper middle class. We lived on Bell Boulevard in an attached two-family house. We were on one side and some other family was on the other side. But there were giant houses right down the street from the house we lived in. So in the wintertime we'd get snow shovels and walk around and offer to shovel people's driveways for twenty bucks. We made a fucking fortune—by preadolescent standards. I had tons of friends on that block and the next block over. Everyone knew everybody else. The rest of Bayside was Irish, Italian, German, and it ranged from very lower middle class to filthy rich—a mishmash of wealth and ethnicity.

In around 1972 we moved out of Queens, which sucked because I was leaving all my friends right after third grade. We moved to Seaford, Long Island, and I started fourth grade at a new elementary school. As bad as it was for me, it was way worse for my mom. My dad had good intentions. We had been renting in Queens, and suddenly he was able to buy a house in Long Island, so hey, we were following the American dream. We had a backyard and a driveway. But my mom didn't want to move out of Queens and leave her friends any more than I did. My dad did it to put her in a new environment where she might be happier. The effect was just the opposite. She was even more depressed in Seaford, and that's when her life started getting really dark. She was not a *Stepford Wives* mom. She drank more, took more pills, and even became suicidal. The strongest memories I have from that time are of her in hysterics, crying or screaming at me and my brother. She would fly off the handle and we would just try our best to stay out of the way. Sometimes no matter how careful I was, and I was one careful eggshell-walking motherfucker, I'd get caught in her crazy tornado and then I would literally just run for my life. I can remember one of these delightful occasions when she was screaming at me for something and I turned and ran from her, out of the living room and into the hall, head down in a full-on sprint, hoping to make it to the relative safety of my room, when suddenly I got hit in the back with something hard. I went sprawling forward and was lucky to break my fall with my hands. I got up quickly, clutching at my back, trying to figure out what hit me, and saw my mom at the end of the hallway crying. I was crying as well, my back was killing me, and I realized that she had thrown something at me. She was shrieking in hysterics and apologizing and I saw the ceramic Exxon coffee mug (free with a $5 purchase!) lying broken on the floor. I just beat it to my room and slammed the door. My mom stayed away, and I avoided her until my dad came home and we sat down for dinner. She told my dad what she did and how sorry she was and that was fuel (no pun intended) for another screaming match later that evening after Jason and I went to bed. I was okay physically; mentally I was fucking pissed off, and looking back on it now this was probably the beginning of me figuring out how to get the hell out of that house and away from all the dysfunction.

Jason and I spent most of our time in Seaford in the basement playing with our GI Joes and reading comic books, hiding from our parents, who were always fighting. The basement was our Fortress of Solitude, our Sanctum. My mom was miserable and crazy, always freaking out, and my dad would go to work every day and come home and then we would have a tension-filled dinner. After that, they would fight, and my brother and I would play and go to bed. The time from 1973 to 1975—when my parents finally split up and my mom, my brother, and I moved back to Queens—was the most turbulent part of my childhood. The kids I was hanging out with when I left the house were my age and a little bit older. And already some of the fifth graders were starting to drink and smoke weed. Some of them stayed out past midnight on Friday and Saturday nights. I was too young for that. I went out with them one time, and there were young kids drinking this stuff called Tang-O, which was a ready-made screwdriver—orange drink with shitty vodka. I tried it and it tasted gross. But ten- and eleven-year-olds were getting wasted on it every week.

These kids used to say, "Are you coming to hang out?" and I usually said, "Nahhh." Some of them replied, "Quit being a baby. What are you gonna do, go home and play with your GI Joes?"

I wouldn't say yeah, but that's exactly what I was doing. I totally escaped into this fantasy land in my head because everywhere I looked there was turmoil. Kids were getting wasted and I wasn't ready for that yet. Then I'd turn around, and my mom and dad were screaming at each other, and my mom was throwing glasses and dishes. I felt much more secure in the basement with my brother.

My parents definitely loved Jason and me, but we were not nurtured and coddled—not even close. My dad worked in the city even when my parents were together. So we'd only see him at dinner and on weekends. And my mom was at home pissed off when we came back from school. Sometimes she'd get drunk and angry and shout about how her life didn't turn out the way she wanted it to and it was all our fault. Sometimes she'd have these full-on fits and start throwing our toys. We had the GI Joe Apollo mission capsule. Either my brother or I did something that upset her, and she screamed, "Wait 'til your father gets home!" Then she took this thing and flung it across the room; it hit the top of the living room wall and crashed to the ground in pieces. "You're fucking buying me a new one," I remember thinking. "You broke my GI Joe toy!"

Chapter 2

MUSIC IS THE MESSAGE

The only time there was peace in the house was when my parents were listening to music. No one from my family played music for a living, but my dad used to sing, and at some point in the fifties he sang doo-wop on the street with Paul Simon and Art Garfunkel (before they were *Simon & Garfunkel*), who went to the same high school as he did. Both of my parents had stuff like the Woodstock soundtrack, Neil Diamond, Elton John, Carole King, the Doobie Brothers, Bob Dylan and The Band in their record collections. I loved that stuff, but I didn't know anything about aggressive music until I was seven and I discovered Black Sabbath.

My dad had a younger brother who was only ten years older than me, Uncle Mitchell, and I thought he was the coolest guy in the world. When I was six or seven, we'd go to my grandparents' house, and I'd go into Uncle Mitch's room. He had all these posters of Zeppelin and other rock bands, cool black-light posters, a big vinyl collection, and lots of comic books. I'd sit there and look at his records for hours. I thought, "This is the coolest place ever. This is the kind of stuff I'm going to have when I'm a teenager."

One day I was flipping through his collection—the Beatles, Dylan, the Stones—and then I saw the first Black Sabbath record. I looked at the cover and thought, "What is this?" There was a creepy witch standing in the woods. I asked Mitch, "What am I even looking at?" He said, "That's Black Sabbath. They're acid rock." I said, "What's acid rock?" I didn't even know what acid was yet. And no one was using the term "heavy metal" to describe music.

He put on the record. It starts with rain, thunder, and an ominous ringing bell. And then there's this super creepy and heavy Tony Iommi guitar riff that I later discovered was the first famous tritone in rock. I definitely was scared—but also elated. The posters of black panthers with glowing eyes glared at me, and evil wizards stared me down. Then this guy with a nasal voice who sounded like a warlock started singing about Satan and screaming for God to help him. I was like, "I'm not sure what's going on here." But at the same time, I wanted to hear more.

Uncle Mitch also had tons of comics so whenever I was in his room I sat there and read. He introduced me to the greats from Marvel and DC: *The Incredible Hulk, Fantastic Four, Spider-Man, Captain America, The Avengers, X-Men, Thor, Conan, Batman, Superman, Flash, Justice League.* I would lose myself in these worlds created by Stan Lee, Jack Kirby, Steve Ditko, Neal Adams, Jim Steranko, and all the great silver-age comics and artists. Back then, comics were twelve or fifteen cents, so every week I'd go to the candy store and use my allowance to buy my own.

Fortunately, when my mother was flipping out my father was always there for my brother and me. Hanging out with my dad was pretty cool. He had the opposite temperament of my mom. He was even-keeled, solid, and calm. He only raised his voice if he really, really needed to. He was a rock, and I give him all the credit for that part of my personality, how I'm able to be calm and roll with stressful situations. If my dad had been neurotic like my mom, I'd be a lunatic in an asylum somewhere. Whenever he could, my dad took Jason and me skiing and to baseball games.

We started going to the original Yankee Stadium in 1972, and we saw a bunch of games after that. It's odd, because, living in Queens, we should have been Mets fans. My dad wasn't even a Yankees fan. He was a Dodgers fan. The Yankees were his enemy. I think that's why I became a Yankees fan. I got sick of hearing about the Brooklyn Dodgers, who were, of course, the LA Dodgers by that point, so I gravitated to the Dodgers' rivals.

Everyone thinks of the Yankees as a world-class team: they've been in the World Series forty times and won twenty-seven of them, which is more than any other team in the Major Leagues. But when I was a kid the Yankees sucked. They were horrible right up until 1976. Still, going to baseball games was amazing. It was another world. Every time there was a crack of the bat, thousands of people cheered for the team wearing pinstripes. What a cool uniform. The Mets had goofy colors. The Yankees had class.

I didn't just love to watch baseball. My friends and I also loved to play. We started out with stickball, which we'd play with a broom handle and a tennis ball. When I was in PS 169 in Bay Terrace, I used to play all the time after school, and I was pretty good. There was a stickball field set up there with the boxes painted on the wall. So it was a natural step for me to go into Little League, which I played for years. I usually played second base or shortstop. One of my role models was Freddie Patek, who was on the Kansas City Royals and was only five foot five. There were still a lot of guys who were actually normal-sized humans playing sports back then, so it gave a kid like me hope.

As pivotal as hearing Sabbath was, Elton John also had a big effect on me growing up. We had all the records in the house, and in 1974, before my parents completely split up, we all went to see Elton at Nassau Coliseum during the *Goodbye Yellow Brick Road* tour. The power went out during the show, but it was still amazing. He did all these costume changes, and it taught me how you can be entertaining with more than just music. The songs were great, but he was so theatrical and really played to the crowd. We saw Paul Simon in 1975 and that was amazing, too.

Although it's hard to fathom, I had a lot of friends who didn't care about music. They didn't give a shit about going out and buying records. All they cared about was baseball and comic books, which I was definitely into. But I wanted to take my love for music to the next level. My dad always had an acoustic guitar in the house. He rarely played it. I think he knew about three chords, but I knew it was lying around somewhere. I had seen the Who on television. I knew the band because they had some of the best songs on my parents' Woodstock record. So I'm watching them, and Pete Townshend starts spinning his right arm around like an airplane propeller. It looked really cool, and that's when I asked about the guitar and said, "I want to do that. Can I have guitar lessons?"

They said sure, but they wouldn't let me start on an electric guitar. My dad insisted I begin on an acoustic, and if I could prove to him that I was serious about the instrument, I could switch to electric. My guitar teacher was this tall guy with long hair who was probably nineteen or twenty. His name was Russell Alexander, and I thought he was the coolest dude in the world. He had a Stratocaster, and I had my stupid acoustic. Not long after, he told my dad, "He's really getting good. He's really into this." And I was. I practiced every day and learned all the basic chords. I learned how to read, how to play scales, and rudimentary theory. A few months into the lessons, Russell started giving me guitar homework. I'd have a lesson once a week and have to practice and write out charts, which I hated because that wasn't fun. I just wanted to play.

Every time Russell came over, I would say, "Teach me 'Whole Lotta Love.' Show me how to play 'Pinball Wizard.'" All I wanted to do was learn songs. I didn't care about writing out scales on pieces of paper. He would get frustrated and say, "Look, you have to learn this stuff to be able to . . ." And I said, "You mean to tell me every guy in every band knows all this stuff and knows theory?"

"Yeah, they do," he said.

"I don't know about that," I said with the skepticism of a bratty kid. It didn't seem possible that all these cool rock stars spent years sitting around and doing homework to learn how to play.

I kept taking lessons from Russell for a while, and he taught me some songs on acoustic. In third grade I played Bob Dylan's "Blowin' in the Wind," Jim Croce's "Bad, Bad Leroy Brown," and the Surfaris' "Wipe Out" at my elementary school talent show on Long Island. It was just me, my acoustic guitar, and a mike in the auditorium. Everyone clapped. I was a little kid. What were they going to do, boo me? But I knew the songs. I totally knew the songs.

So, when I had been playing acoustic for six months, Dad made good on his promise. He took me to this music store in Queens on Union Turnpike and bought me a used Fender Telecaster Deluxe, 1972. It was coffee-table brown with a black pick guard. I wish I still had it—it would be worth about nine grand. I sold it probably around 1978 because I really wanted a Fender Stratocaster. I didn't know much back then, and to me a Tele didn't look cool. A Strat was cool, a Les Paul was cool. Nobody I liked played Teles. Also, I liked the shape of the Strat better. It was sleeker and less folkie. I saved up some money and went back to the store where we got the Tele, and they had a natural wood Strat that I really wanted. So I traded in my Tele and gave them another two hundred dollars. That's how I acquired new gear for years, even into the formative days of Anthrax in the early eighties. I was always buying and selling gear, trying to get more and better stuff and find good deals.

Once I got that first Tele, I told my parents that I didn't want lessons anymore. I wanted to learn on my own. I had enough foresight to say, "I don't want to learn guitar to sound like my teacher. I want to sound like me," because I was afraid they'd take my guitar away otherwise. It worked! They agreed to let me do my own thing.

I knew how to play basic chords really well by then and I had a good ear, so I would put records on and figure out the guitar progressions—pretty much everything except the solos. From there I was like, "I need a better amp." Back then I had a small Fender Deluxe. I wanted the Twin Reverb because it was bigger, but it was too expensive. And I got a fuzz box, the Electro-Harmonix Big Muff pedal. I plugged that into the Fender Deluxe, and I'm sure it sounded atrocious, but back then it seemed amazing.

My dad had a first cousin, Eddie, in Long Island who, like Mitch, was only ten or twelve years older than I was, and he lived about two miles away so I saw him a lot. He was a biker, and he shared a house with a bunch of other bikers. They had a jam room set up in the basement with a drum kit and a bunch of amps, and they'd all go down there and play. I'd follow them down when I was eight or nine to watch. They had Les Pauls and Gibson SGs and Strats and wah-wah pedals and fuzz boxes. They'd plug in, and all of a sudden there were all these dudes with long hair and beards and leather vests rocking out. It was the coolest thing I had ever seen, and it made me want to play guitar even more.

As much as I loved the Beatles, Elton John, and Simon & Garfunkel, I definitely viewed them as entertainment, like comics or horror movies. It wasn't until September 1975 when I heard "Rock and Roll

All Nite" from *KISS Alive!* that I thought, "Oh my God, this is something else entirely." I took to it like a moth to a flame. We were in our yellow Ford Torino station wagon right around the time the album was released, and the song came on the radio. I didn't know what it was. It wasn't announced and I had never heard KISS before. But I was singing along by the end of the song. My parents were yelling at me to shut up because they didn't know who the band was and it was too loud for them. Afterward I was like, "Who was that?!?" But the DJ just went on to the next song. I thought, "Oh man, I'm never going to know who that was! That was the greatest song I ever heard in my life and I'm never going to know who played it!"

Then around Halloween I was watching TV during the day, flipping through all five channels we had back then, and I stopped on a talk show that featured these four guys in makeup. I had no idea who they were or what their story was. Then the announcer said, "And now, to play their hit single from their new album, *KISS Alive!,* here's KISS with 'Rock and Roll All Nite.'" It's funny because sitting there at eleven years old, I didn't like the way they looked. I said to Jason, "This is stupid. Who do they think they are? They look like idiots. That's a band? Why do they look like that?" I just didn't understand. Elton John was flamboyant, but he didn't dress up like he was going trick-or-treating. The Who didn't wear makeup and platform shoes.

A second later, KISS started played the song I had heard on the car radio, and my jaw dropped. I turned around and said, "We have to go to the record store right now! I have to have this album! KISS, KISS, KISS!"

I'm sure four million other eleven-year-olds right at that moment were doing the same thing. It projected into our fucking nerve center and we were plugged in. It made sense. We were programmed and that was it. I was a KISS maniac for three years, from '75 to '78. I loved other music, too, but for those three years, it was all about KISS.

They were larger than life. Other bands sang about being famous, touring, and scoring chicks. Zeppelin sang about—who knows what the fuck Zeppelin sang about, wood nymphs and sprites—and the Stones and the blues guys wrote about how bad chicks were and how rough life could be. I already knew how rough life could be, and I hadn't discovered chicks yet. KISS was all about escaping, blasting to another planet, and never looking back.

The night in 1975 when my parents sat us down in the house in Long Island to tell us they were finally splitting up is as memorable to me as Anthrax's first sold-out show. I recall them saying, "It's not you guys. We both love you very much. But we're not happy and we need to be apart." I felt a huge sense of relief and was actually happy. Jason wasn't any more upset than I was. "Well. Who's going to give us allowance?" was all he had to say. Our main concern was whether we were still going to see our dad much. I had the greatest sense of relief knowing they weren't going to be screaming at each other 24/7. My mom, Jason, and I moved back to Queens, literally six blocks from where we lived before. It was the best. All of a sudden I was going to seventh grade with all my friends from first, second, and third grade. Long Island was like this weird other world, and now I was back in the city and I knew all these people! I was thirteen and riding the bus to school—and smoking weed and drinking and listening to rock and roll. Everything changed for the better. My mom was working nine to five. She wasn't around, so I was looking after my brother. We had total freedom. It was amazing. At the same time, I knew I had to do whatever it took to get out of the Boroughs. I didn't want to be in Queens the rest of my life. I wanted to escape and make my own mark on the world.

The same year, my maternal grandmother died of cancer. It was too much for my mom and she had a breakdown. There was lots of crying, yelling, and door slamming. She started drinking more. One night Dad went to pick her up from a friend's party where she had gotten completely wasted. On the drive home Mom opened the door and tried to jump out of the car and kill herself. Dad kept hold of the wheel with one hand, leaned over the seat, and in one fluid motion yanked her back into the car and punched her in the face as hard as he could. She slumped over unconscious, and he was able to close the back door. Though it's not what my mom wanted at the time, he definitely saved her life that night. Instead of driving her home he took her directly to a mental hospital and checked her into rehab.

While my mom was away, my dad came to live with us. We didn't know the details. All we knew was that she was sick and my dad would stay with us while my mom was in the hospital getting better. I was going on twelve, and those six weeks my mom was away were pretty great. My dad left early in the morning to go to work and didn't come home until seven o'clock, so my brother and I would go on a fucking tear. It was like the inmates were running the asylum. I'd empty small Scope and Listerine bottles and fill them with my mom's vodka so my friends and I could drink it on the ten-mile bus ride to school every day.

Also, I'd steal my dad's weed and spark up between classes. He kept these rolled pin joints in a tin of Sucrets. I would have thought he would have seen that some were missing and confronted me, but he never did.

My friends would giggle like idiots when they smoked, but it never affected me. It seemed like I was immune, but that was great because everyone thought, "Fuck, Scott can handle his high." That was good for some street cred.

When my mom got back to the house, things changed but not that much. She saw a therapist every week named Dr. Rice, and she thought he channeled the word of God. She applied everything he said to her, and I guess he was good for her because she became a lot more mentally balanced and only screamed at us for no reason half as often. She went right back to work to support the three of us, which must have been a chore. When you're a kid, you don't realize how much your parents sacrifice to put food on the table. While we were outside having fun, she was working her ass off doing secretarial work and hating life. But my mom's long hours meant more freedom for Jason and me. Some people who grew up latchkey kids become insecure and depressed later in life. I never understood that. Being on our own gave me a feeling of independence, developed my self-confidence, and most importantly meant there was no one there to tell me what I could and couldn't do.

We would get up and go to school then we'd come home and make sure the dishes were done and the apartment was clean. As long as that happened, we could go out and play unsupervised until dinnertime. I got into a little trouble, but I could never do anything really bad because I always had my brother to look after. I knew I'd be fucked if I got dragged off by police somewhere and he was left by himself on the playground. I loved my brother and I think that's what kept me from ever going too far with alcohol and drugs. I'd drink enough to get a buzz, but I always had my wits about me. And I felt cool and rebellious, like I was one of those tough kids in a TV after-school special about how to stay out of trouble and avoid temptation. I loved temptation, but I knew where to draw the line. With a few exceptions that became my MO. Having Jason to watch over didn't just keep me in line; it gave me a sense of responsibility and helped mold me into the person I would become. I had this very important role and I didn't want to fuck up.

Some kids I hung out with were already getting in trouble with cops, whether it was shoplifting or vandalism. Granted, many had way worse lives than I did. Their parents would beat the shit out of them. A lot of them were poorer than we were and were getting shitfaced all the time at age thirteen. They'd drink beer in cans out of paper bags and look for fights. I thought, "That doesn't seem like fun to me. I can already kinda see where it's going. They're just going to become their parents."

Many of those people still live in Bayside; they never got out. They became firemen or did construction. There's nothing wrong with that, it just wasn't what I wanted. And most of them became alcoholics. I'm not judging them. A lot of rock stars are alcoholics. I just knew early on that wasn't going to be me. I heard some of the problem kids who got busted by cops for fighting, stealing, or vandalism ended up in reform school. I didn't know what that was, but I knew because of the way people talked about it that I didn't want to end up there. I was like, "Fuck all that shit, I'm already having fun." I didn't need real trouble to get my kicks.

Most of the really screwed-up kids we hung out with knew where I stood and that I wasn't going to break store windows or put lit firecrackers in anyone's pockets. I'd egg cars with them, steal comic books and sodas from the Grand Union to prove myself, but I never committed any real vandalism or violence. When I learned how to sneak in and out of the store undetected and what the best route of escape was, I'd rip off six-packs of beer, which definitely kept me in with the cool crowd. I had my purpose. And I was always a smart-ass. I could bust balls as well as anyone, which kept me off the wedgie and beatdown list that kids my size usually wound up on. Even the biggest fuckups liked me. I never judged them, and even though I was a little, tiny kid, no one fucked with me because I was always friends with the real crazies.

There was a guy named Kenny who used to beat the shit out of kids who looked at him the wrong way. But Kenny thought I was cool because I made him laugh. I think I lived vicariously through him and some of his screwed-up friends. When other kids from the neighborhood who weren't part of our cool gang would try to ride their bikes through the shortcuts in the shopping center back lots, these delinquent kids would knock over their bikes, fuck with them, and shake them down. If you didn't pay the twenty-five-cent tax to ride through, they'd cut your tires and rough you up. The day after Kenny fucked with some of these kids, I'd see them in school, and even though they were way bigger than me, they'd look at me and run away. I was always the shortest kid in class. I couldn't have hurt a fly, but I was friends with all the right people, always. No one laid a finger on me.

Since we didn't want to be at home, my brother and I practically lived in the streets. When my mom would yell at us and tell us we were turning into juvenile delinquents, I'd say, "Why can't we just go live with Dad?" because my dad was always calm and centered. Also, he didn't judge us like she did, probably because we didn't live with him and he wasn't working two jobs to make ends meet. We saw him twice a month on weekends and every Wednesday for dinner, which we were visibly excited about. That bummed my mom out sometimes because she was an unbelievably stressed-out single woman working her ass off for us, and we didn't give a shit. We just wanted to hang out with Dad. The rest of the time we did what we needed to do around the house and then stayed out of her way to go do what we loved.

Chapter 3

ROCK AND ROLL ALL NITE

When summer came and school let out, we went to a sleep-away camp in Honesdale, Pennsylvania, called Camp Cayuga. That was great because it got me away from the friction of being at home and I got to hang out with other kids and play sports and go swimming. I also had my first experiences with girls. Where I grew up in Bay Terrace, most of the girls I knew from seventh to twelfth grade were rich Jewish brats, stereotypical JAPs. My family was barely even middle class and we lived in a very small two-bedroom apartment, so there was no dating for me. Those girls wouldn't look my way twice. But at Camp Cayuga, everyone just partied and fooled around. It almost didn't matter what you looked like as long as you weren't radically deformed. And the counselors didn't give a shit. They'd all get high as soon as they were done for the day, so we ran around like maniacs. I hooked up with a lot of girls while I was there. I never went all the way with any of them, but there was a lot of kissing and, in the parlance of the time, heavy petting.

I was twelve and a half the first time I had an orgasm with a chick. Her name was Julie. We were both young and didn't have a clue what we were doing, but nature took its course and we figured out what to do, short of fucking. None of the girls there would have sex, including Julie, because they were worried about getting pregnant. And everyone knew that we were just having fun and nothing would get too serious. Once Julie said, "Are we boyfriend and girlfriend?" And I went, "Well, I live in New York and you live in Pennsylvania. Probably not."

Even after camp, I was a happy kid. Some people are devastated and depressed when their parents separate, but when my folks went their separate ways in 1975 I had so much music to listen to and I was playing baseball and hanging out with friends and skateboarding—I couldn't have been happier. Without question, 1977 was the golden year of my youth. I was thirteen, the Yankees won the World Series, and I had my Bar Mitzvah, so I got all these presents and checks. I totally cheated my way through the ceremony. I didn't know Hebrew because I didn't go to Hebrew school. I could have gone, but my friends who went all hated it so much. And I went to enough of their Bar Mitzvahs to know I didn't want to be up there singing for three hours. I was like, "I'm not going to more school. I'd rather ride my skateboard and play baseball."

The thing is, it was really important for my grandfather that I have a Bar Mitzvah, so my parents got me a tutor and he wrote my Torah portion out in English. *"Buh-ruch-ah-tah, Ado-nay . . ."* It was phonetically transliterated on a paper for me to read. It took about seven minutes, but that was good enough for my grandfather. He was happy and that's really all that mattered. The timing of my Bar Mitzvah was perfect. I had just gotten really into skateboarding. The sport was in its second wave of popularity. The initial era was in the sixties when everyone had these tiny little wooden decks with wheels that were made out of rock. It was really primitive. With the advent of the urethane wheels in the midseventies, it turned into a completely different sport because you could maneuver the boards with greater precision and perform stunts that required real skill.

I got a board from a mail-order place called Val-Surf that advertised in the back of skateboarding magazines. I ordered a G&S Fibreflex board with Road Rider 4 wheels and Tracker trucks. That was a big deal back then. I traded up the Road Rider wheels when Kryptonics came out. My brother and my friends all had skateboards as well, and we would do whatever we could to emulate the pictures of skaters in the magazines. There were no videos back then. You couldn't see skating on TV. You'd just see a photo of a guy doing a trick and try to figure out what the hell he was doing. Most of the time, we'd ride down the hills in Queens as fast as we could like maniacs, destroying ourselves, falling off our boards after hitting potholes at thirty miles an hour and tearing up our arms and legs. We'd wear elbow and knee pads and we'd have jeans on, but if you fell at top speed you could rip straight through a thick pair of jeans. Skateboarding took a front seat to baseball at that point in my life. Every day as soon as school was over, that's all I was doing, and then when school was out I was doing it all day.

After my Bar Mitzvah I took all the cash I made, about $1,100, and bought flights for my brother and me to Los Angeles, where we rode our skateboards all summer. My mom's friend Bobbie Zuckerberg let us stay with her in Laguna Beach because there were no skate parks in Queens in 1977, and they were really popular in LA. We were a few blocks from the ocean, which was amazing for two kids from Queens. My only concern was that I didn't know how I was going to be able to follow the Yankees while we were in California. I solved that little dilemma one of the first nights we were there. I sat on the porch with a transistor radio and listened to the Angels games because every thirty minutes or so they gave scores from around the league.

As much as I cared about the Yankees, being in LA was all about the skating, and there was plenty to be had. Bobbie was a nurse, so every morning on her way to the hospital where she worked, she dropped us off at this skate park in Irvine, and then she picked us up again in the afternoon when her shift was over. That was our day care. I was thirteen, my brother was ten; I couldn't think of a better way to spend the summer. We learned so much about riding in pools and on these banks because we saw what kids in California were doing. We were figuring out all these street tricks, and we couldn't wait to show our new skills to our friends back home. Then on our last day there, I broke my wrist.

I had ridden six or seven feet from the ground up the wall of this bowl, and when I went to turn my 180 to come back down the wall, my back foot slipped off my board. I somehow landed sideways on top of the board and my left arm was underneath me. I heard an audible pop, saw a blinding red flash, and felt an intensely sharp pain in my wrist, which was already starting to swell. My brother ran up to me, and I said, "Find my board!" because when I landed on it, it kicked out from under me and went rolling away. He found it, then we called Bobbie at work, and she picked us up and brought us back to the hospital. They x-rayed my arm and saw I had a fractured wrist. They decided not to set it since I was flying back to New York the next day and they were worried about swelling. They wrapped the arm and splinted it and told me I had to go to the doctor to get it set as soon as I got back to New York.

The flight home really sucked. My arm was killing me and I just had to gut it out. The next day we went to the doctor to get it set, and he looked at me and said, "Take a deep breath, this is going to hurt." Then he grabbed my arm and pulled it. For about fifteen seconds I was in agony, and then the pain passed and the doctor put a cast on my arm. I was in the cast for six weeks, and that's when I realized skateboarding wasn't my priority anymore. The idea that I couldn't play guitar for six weeks was more unbearable than the thought of not skating.

When the cast came off, the first thing I did was pick up my guitar. I kept skateboarding but never above my pay grade. As much as I loved guitar, though, I still hadn't made the connection that it would be the tool for my future livelihood.

That defining moment came at the end of 1977. On December 14 I saw KISS at Madison Square Garden. I got the tickets at the Ticketron at Moonshine Records, right inside the Bay Terrace shopping center across from where I lived. You couldn't order tickets online or even over the phone back then. You had to wait in line along with all the other fans, some of whom had camped out all night. We got up really early in the morning and went right over to buy KISS tickets for all three shows. Even so, our seats were kinda crappy—the back of the floor behind the sound desk. I still have the tour program and the shirt I bought the first night. Of course, the shirt doesn't fit anymore but it's a great souvenir. Tickets were $6.50. I paid for them myself, and it was the first time my mom let me go to a show with my friends without my dad or uncle chaperoning me. Being off the leash only added to the excitement.

We took the train in. The spectacle of the whole show was completely insane. We were surrounded by 18,000 screaming maniacs. It seemed unbelievably loud, and it took me a few songs to even understand what I was hearing. But I was still losing my mind, jumping up and down with my friends. Once my ears adjusted to the volume, I was completely blown away by how great the band sounded. Gene blew fire, which I could see, but they didn't have video screens back then, and we were too far back to see him spit blood. But just being in that room with that energy was a life-affirming experience.

I left the arena with my friends to take the steps down to the Long Island Railroad back to Queens, and I said out loud, "This is what I'm gonna do. That's it. I'm gonna be in a band like KISS."

I knew I wouldn't necessarily be spitting blood and blowing fire and wearing makeup, but I wanted to do what those guys were doing. I wanted to write and play music I loved, be onstage, rock out on guitar, and have thousands of people cheering. It just seemed like the greatest job in the world. I was fourteen that month, December 31, and I already knew, for sure, what I was gonna be when I grew up.

I started spending a lot of time in Manhattan after that. It only took fifteen or twenty minutes to get into the city on the subway, so after school I'd escape to Greenwich Village. For a fourteen-year-old kid into rock and roll, the Village was like Disneyland. I was out of the grip of Queens; the chains were broken and nothing was holding me back. I knew that when I got a band together that was worth anything, we'd go to Manhattan. I was already looking forward to being part of that bigger, better world. It seemed like I was on a mission and I was on the right path, hanging out at record stores and guitar shops. I was going to get out and travel around the world. I used to think about that all the time.

There was a big disco scene in the seventies in New York, with places like Studio 54, which I was way too young and uncool to get into, but the music was everywhere. Chic, the Village People, and Donna Summer were on the radio all the time and the streets were lined with disco trendies. In reaction to the craze, a lot of longhairs and rockers launched this "Disco Sucks" movement. They had T-shirts and signs. It was almost like a political campaign. I jumped on the bandwagon because the people I hung out with hated disco. I even had a Disco Sucks shirt. But I secretly loved disco. Nile Rodgers, who fronted Chic and produced some of the greatest disco songs of all time—like Sister Sledge's "We Are Family" and Chic's "Le Freak"—was an amazing guitarist. And the Village People were huge, theatrical pop stars.

I fucking loved *most* of that music. The grooves were great, the guitar lines were funky and immediate, and the beats made you want to shake your ass—but I drew the line at the "YMCA" thing. I loved disco; I fuckin' hated dancing. The idea of doing the boogie all night long was about as appealing to me as a root canal. I was way too self-conscious to enjoy dancing, which is one of the reasons I was a closet disco fan. But I was always open-minded about music. My criterion was simple. Either I liked it or I didn't, and just because I didn't like one thing didn't mean I wouldn't try listening to something else from that same band or genre. I was open to anything.

I was also opinionated as fuck. If I didn't agree with someone, especially when it came to music, I'd let them know. The funny thing is I was a quiet and introspective kid overall. I lived in my head most of the time, thinking of the future. I knew that if I wanted to play guitar and be onstage I'd have to be extroverted and fearless. So I weaned myself into that mind-set. From the start, I was willing to struggle and be uncomfortable, do whatever it would take to be up on that stage with those lights shining down on me. There's no room in that world for fear.

I'd think about rocking out in front of crowds every day, almost every hour—even more than I'd think about girls. None of the girls I knew were into rock and roll anyway, so it wasn't like I was missing out on any chicks. Girls came back into my life when I went back to sleep-away camp at age fourteen. (Today, as the parent of a little boy, I'm already filling out the camp application for when he's thirteen—have at it, Revel.)

In 1978, when I was fourteen and a half, I went to an overnight camp in New Jersey filled with cute, horny girls. They were getting their first taste of freedom, and they could do whatever they wanted. Did I mention they were horny? All these chicks wanted to do was fool around, even more so than the girls at Camp Cayuga. Only, the same basic rule applied—no fucking. I was okay with that since no one had touched my dick besides me since the *last* time I was at summer camp. Again, I did everything with these girls but have sex, and I did it a lot more than I had two years earlier. Plus, I sorta knew what was going on this time, so it wasn't awkward, but it was just as exciting.

Summers in New York were pretty great because I didn't have any home-work, so I had no reason to be home. Then I started seventh grade at IS 25 in Queens and after school I wanted to stay out with my friends until late at night. I was hanging with some older kids, and it was nor-mal for them to be out until 11 p.m. on school nights. On weekends there was no curfew. We went to the baseball field or the park down the street or someone else's apartment to listen to records and drink. Sometimes we went into the city. I wasn't out of control. I never did anything *too* stupid. But that didn't matter to my mom. Suddenly, since I was back in school, she decided I needed a 9 p.m. curfew.

I said, "Fuck this shit." There were parties going on and chicks to try to score with. I said, "I'm not a fuckin' baby. I'm not coming home at 9 o'clock."

So I would get home whenever, and my mom would scream at me. I'd talk to her for a minute and then go to bed. It was always the same thing: "I don't understand why I have to be home so early. All my friends . . ."

"I don't care what your friends are doing," she'd scream loud enough to wake my brother. "This is my fucking house and my fucking rules!"

Apparently, swearing was okay, but staying out late was forbidden. I told her I had people to hang out with and a life to live, and I wasn't going to have a curfew. She grabbed me by the arm and said, "You're coming to see Dr. Rice. You're fucked up. I fucked you up. It's my fault. But you have to change."

She made an appointment for me to see the magic doctor, and I have to admit I was kind of nervous. I could have refused to go, but I figured I'd play along. I mean, I didn't have to listen to the dude. We walked into his office in Great Neck, New York, and I saw a kind, quiet man in his sixties. He asked my mom to step out of the office, and I sat in one of those psychiatrist chairs. My jitters were unfounded. We talked for thirty minutes. He asked me about school, my friends, my aspirations in life, what I liked to do, and why I had a problem coming home early. Then he asked me what my grades were like in school. I told him, "I get great grades, mostly As and an occasional B." And he said, "Well then I really don't understand what the problem is. Are you drinking or taking drugs?" I told him I smoked weed once in a while and I drink beer and vodka and orange juice sometimes, but that was the extent of my partying. I barely ever got drunk enough to have a hangover.

Dr. Rice called my mom back in and asked her to sit down. "Look Barbara," he said. "I'm going to keep this short because I think you have to look at the fact that Scott has great grades, and until his grades are affected by what he's doing with his friends and staying out late, I see no problem with his schedule."

I looked at Dr. Rice like he was some kind of superhero. Here was a total figure of authority and someone my mom completely trusted. She dragged me there thinking Dr. Rice was going to straighten my ass out. And he took *my* side! I said, "Y'see! Y'see, Mom! I told you I wasn't doing anything wrong." And she said, "Okay, but the rule from now on is that if your grades slip, if your next report card comes and it's not as good or better than the previous one then the curfew goes into effect. Are these the rules?" I told her I was fine with that. It was a total revelation.

Suddenly, I knew the game. All I had to do was maintain my grades, and I could do whatever the fuck I wanted. That was it! Dr. Rice had explained the secret of life to me. Whatever the rules are—whether they're to keep your grades up, keep your boss happy, write good songs, be a great live band—keep the people that enable you to do what you want to do happy, and you can do anything you want in life. Thanks to Dr. Rice I was like, "That's it, man! I've got life by the balls now."

It was a breeze because school came easy to me. I was a smart kid. If I did the absolute bare minimum I would get Bs, and if I applied myself in the least I'd get straight As. So it wasn't hard for me to maintain my grades through junior high. With my social life taken care of, there was only one thing severely lacking—money. We got five dollars for allowance every week, which I knew wasn't going to last for comics, records, and concert tickets. My mom was really stoked about the idea of me having a job. If I was ever lying on the couch, watching TV, not doing anything, she'd scream, "Get off your ass and get a job!"

She didn't need to say *shit*. I always wanted to make money so I'd be independent and not have to ask other people to buy me things. As a kid, you're at the mercy of your parents when it comes to finances.

I wanted that to end as soon as possible. Aside from shoveling snow, the first time I made an effort to make my own money was when I was twelve. We were still living in Long Island and I got a job delivering the *Long Island Press*. I'd wake up at 6 a.m., and there would be big bundles of papers waiting for me to pick up. I'd fit as many as I could in a basket on my bike and ride around the neighborhood throwing papers at people's houses. Sometimes it would be pouring rain, and I'd have to put the papers in these little baggies that were like newspaper condoms. The brakes on my bike would get wet and barely work. I almost got sideswiped by a car a few times. Pretty soon I realized this newspaper delivery thing wasn't worth risking my life for. I hated it and the pay was terrible. The end of the week would come, and I'd go to the guy in charge of the routes, and he'd hand me about ten dollars.

The shittiest job I ever had was cleaning a fish store in a shopping center across the street from our house. That paid better than delivering papers, but I'd come home smelling like fish, which was fucking disgusting. I'd shower with really hot water and wash my hands for, like, ten minutes, but it still didn't totally get rid of the smell. No one else seemed to notice, but I felt like Lady Macbeth trying to wash the blood off her hands. The only good thing about that job was I got to bring home free shrimp. My mom liked that. I just got sick of them after a while, so I quit and went on to the next shitty part-time job I could find.

I had a basic foundation in rock and roll from my parents and my uncle. I loved Elton John, the Who, and KISS. I knew about Black Sabbath. But it wasn't until I was in junior high at IS 25 that I really learned about hard rock and heavy metal. There was a small crew of eight to ten longhairs who would sit together at lunch and talk about music. Whatever my friends and I heard, we were always looking for something louder, faster, or heavier. We wanted to find the craziest drummer, the wildest singer, and the guitar player who made the craziest sounds. Our obsession was beyond geeky. We made charts and wrote in the names of all these players: Ritchie Blackmore, Ace Frehley, Jimmy Page, Joe Perry, Rick Nielsen, Ted Nugent, Tony Iommi. Then we'd walk around the lunchroom and get people to rate the guitar players from one to ten. For two years, Ritchie Blackmore won as best lead guitar player until we heard the first Van Halen record, and then we stopped making the lists because no one thought there could ever be a better guitar player than Eddie Van Halen.

One kid, David Karibian, started bringing in a tiny boom box every day, and we'd listen to different tapes. He was actually the guy who introduced us to Van Halen. One day he came in with a tape queued to "Eruption," this amazing Eddie Van Halen guitar solo that was like a concerto from another planet. When we walked over to the table he said, "Guys, wait until you hear this!" Then he hit play and eight or nine of us sat there with our jaws on the floor, not having any idea what we were even listening to and how it was possible. Then the super-guitar-saturated version of the Kinks' "You Really Got Me" started, and we were like, "Holy shit, who is this?!?"

I went straight to the record store after school and bought *Van Halen*. Another kid, Zlotko "Golden" Novkovic, also came in with bands no one else had heard of. One day he asked me, "Have you heard AC/DC?" I said, "No, what's that?"

"Oh man, they're great! They're from Australia, they're really, really hard rock, they're probably the heaviest band I've ever heard!" He played *Powerage* at lunch. I remember thinking two things: "Wow, the guitar sounds so cool," and "I've never heard vocals like *that* before." Bon Scott was like no one else. His voice was so ballsy and it dripped with attitude. It was almost like he was laughing at you while he was singing. All I could think of was, "Wow, he sounds like a fucking pirate." I loved their guitarist Angus Young even before I knew he wore a schoolboy outfit, rolled around the stage, and rode on Bon's shoulders during shows. "Riff Raff" was so fast. I was like, "Jesus Christ, how do you play a song like that?" It was like someone had kicked Led Zeppelin in the balls and told them to man up. AC/DC quickly became my favorite band because KISS had already put out *Love Gun* and had lost some steam. I was getting much more into heavier stuff.

Between 1976 and 1979 I listened to two hundred bands for the first time because every day someone brought in something new: Aerosmith, Rainbow, Thin Lizzy, Judas Priest. Then came 1980, the best year for hard rock and heavy metal, ever. Ozzy Osbourne did *Blizzard of Ozz,* Judas Priest put out *British Steel,* Black Sabbath released *Heaven and Hell* with singer Ronnie James Dio, who kept the band alive after Ozzy was kicked out. Iron Maiden released their debut record, and Motörhead's *Ace of Spades* came out as well. Holy crap!

I would go to the Music Box every week with my friends and buy three to four metal records, and we would have to fight over them. Eventually we discovered Bleeker Bob's in the West Village on 118 West Third Street. One time I was there I literally tried to rip the first Iron Maiden album out of the hands of a friend of mine. I saw Eddie— the band's mascot—on the cover, and I thought, "That zombie horror artwork is cool. That's gotta be good."

I was having a tug-of-war with this guy over who was gonna buy it. After some well-chosen words, and maybe because my friend didn't want to spend six or seven dollars on a band he didn't know, I won the battle. If I hadn't won, I would've gone home and gotten my shitty little tape recorder that you used to have to use two fingers to push play and record on, and I would've brought that to my friend's house and held it in front of a speaker to tape the record so I'd have something to listen to until I could find another copy. Yeah, it'd sound terrible but so what? We didn't know anything else. When I hear people say, "I hate MP3s, they sound like shit," I'm like, "Fuck you, you have no idea, you first-world-problem-having motherfucker."

When I got an album, I took it home and carefully slit the cellophane on the album jacket. I never wanted to damage one of the covers because they were like pieces of art. That's one thing that's been tragically lost in the transition from albums to CDs, and now MP3s. Most kids don't know what they're missing. I peeled the plastic off the Iron Maiden album jacket and pulled out the record, which was housed in a white paper sleeve. I carefully reached in and removed the black twelve-inch disc. Taking care to hold it by the edges, I placed the gleaming, grooved slice of vinyl on the turntable and lowered the needle. The staccato guitar riff and wah-wah countermelody of "Prowler" began, and right away I thought, "Holy fuck! Best band ever! I can't wait to tell my friends about it."

The next day I was all excited. "Guys, guys, guys! Have you heard Iron Maiden yet?" And four people in our clique went, "Duh! We got that last month."

One time, though, I was first to the table with something special. I was at the Music Box, and I saw *Ace of Spades* by Motörhead. I had heard of Motörhead, but I didn't know their music. So I bought it and went home, excited to put it on. The first song, "Ace of Spades," started. It was so fast and the bass was rumbling. The guitars ripped my head off, and the vocals came in and they were raspy and harsh but still kind of melodic. I had never heard anything like it. In 1980 they were playing the hardest, fastest, and most aggressive music on the planet, hands down, and broke my brain! I looked at the cover again and thought, "Who are these three Mexicans and how do they play so fast?" I had no idea they were English! They looked like banditos, all dressed in leather with cowboy hats on, and they were standing in the desert. It looked like they were ready for a gunfight. Naturally, when I played it for my friends, everyone loved it, and, bang, Motörhead became one of our favorite bands. As a guitar player, they were a huge influence for me and early Anthrax.

But AC/DC were still my favorite, which is why my son's middle name is Young. After I heard that *Powerage* record, I went out and bought their back catalog—*High Voltage, Dirty Deeds Done Dirt Cheap, Let There Be Rock*—they were all amazing, full of bluesy-grit, sleaze, and power. The band came to New York in '78 and headlined the Palladium. I desperately scraped together nickels and dimes, but I had already spent my allowance money to see Cheap Trick, so I didn't have enough for AC/DC. That's the same reason I never saw Thin Lizzy. I had one more chance to see AC/DC when they headlined the Garden in 1979 on the *Highway to Hell* tour. But, once again, I was broke. I figured I'd be able to see them when they came back the next time.

Tragically, Bon Scott died the next year. He passed out after a night of heavy drinking and a friend left him in a car, where he choked on his vomit and died. I found out at school from a friend. At first I didn't believe him and thought he was either misinformed or fucking with me. Then I heard the report on the radio, and I felt like I had been punched in the stomach. Bon's death hit me hard, maybe in part because I never got to see him live but also because he was my first real rock and roll hero who didn't make it to thirty-five. Jimi Hendrix died when I was seven, and I remember my parents talking about that, but it didn't really affect me. Bon was my favorite singer, and I couldn't believe that he could have drunk himself to death. He seemed invincible. I still kick myself that I missed those two New York shows.

Chapter 4

THE BIRTH OF ANTHRAX

By the time I started high school, my only goal was to play with other people and have a band. I was never one of those kids who sat in their rooms practicing lead guitar for eight hours a day. I couldn't do that. I needed to be with other musicians jamming real songs, whether they were covers or originals. Sitting in my little shitty six-by-six room practicing would have driven me crazy. I was persistent and tenacious, and it didn't matter that I couldn't solo like Eddie Van Halen. I figured the only way I was going to make it is if I got out and played gigs in Manhattan.

I used to read *Rock Scene* magazine and see pictures of the Ramones hanging out at Gildersleeves and CBGB in '76. I wanted to hang out there, but I was too young to get in. So I had to wait until CBGB started doing hardcore shows when I was a little older. Even so, the Ramones were a big influence on me because they were in Forest Hills, which was at most five miles from where I lived. They were a bunch of longhaired dudes with Levis and leather jackets and T-shirts, and I looked just like them. I was like, "Look at these guys! They're on TV. They tour the world. And they're from Queens!" At that point in time, I didn't know KISS were from Queens, too. Back then, no one knew anything about KISS that the band members didn't say in interviews. Their early history was a mystery. But the Ramones were proud about being from Queens. I went to go see them at Queens College, and I thought, "If they can do it, I can do it. They're the same as me."

That was the cool thing about bands like the Ramones and the Sex Pistols. They introduced the DIY spirit to rock music. All of a sudden you didn't have to be a trained musician with amazing skills. As long as you had willpower and tenacity, you could get a band together and go onstage. I had that shit in spades.

I'd find other musicians through flyers they posted in music stores, and we'd jam out songs by Black Sabbath, Deep Purple, Thin Lizzy, AC/DC, and even Judas Priest. It didn't seem like things could be any cooler. Then, I lost my virginity.

It happened on Fire Island in this share house that my mom rented with some other people. Every other weekend we went out to the beach there. One time I met a girl named Susie who was a couple years older than me. We were there for three days, and she was all over me right away. I barely said a word. I was fifteen. I didn't have any game—no moves whatsoever. But the first night we were sitting on the couch together, she started kissing and grabbing me. It was like something from *Penthouse* Forum.

"Dear *Penthouse*, you're not going to believe what happened to me." We didn't fuck that night, but the next evening she put on the soundtrack for *Saturday Night Fever*. Like I said, I never hated disco, but I was *loving* the Bee Gees *that* night. Everyone had gone to sleep; all the parents were in bed. And right there on the couch, Susie totally attacked me. We were just a few feet from the bedrooms. My mom could have walked through the living room at any time.

I asked her if she was a virgin, and she said she wasn't. I pretty much figured that by how forward she was. I was nervous so I said, "Uh, I am." And she went, "Don't worry about it."

She kissed the shit out of me, stuck my hand down her pants, ripped her shorts off, undid her bra, and whipped her boobs out and unzipped my jeans in about three seconds. She was Ali-fast, and foreplay be damned, she hopped on top of me and guided me into her. I took it from there. Some things come naturally, even for geeks who play with GI Joes and love the Fantastic Four.

I was like, "Wow, you rule! Can I take you home with me so I can show you off to all my friends? No one is going to believe I'm fucking this hot seventeen-year-old chick." It was a pretty great way to lose my virginity. But even though I was staying out at night, hanging with older kids, and trying to get my music career off the ground, it would be another two years until I got laid again. And that would be with the girl who became my first wife, Marge Ginsburg.

Before that, I hooked up with my first semiserious girlfriend, Kim Eisenberg. She had long brown hair and was only a little taller than I was. I met her in Florida because her grandparents lived in the same development as my grandparents. We hit it off and continued the relationship in New York when I was a junior in high school. She lived in Coney Island and I wasn't driving yet, so I had to take a two-hour subway ride on the F train to see her. We didn't see each other all that often, but we stayed together for about a year. She was nice to me, and I liked telling my friends I had a girlfriend. In the end, the commute proved too difficult, so we broke up. Another reason it ended was because we didn't sleep together. I obviously wanted it, but she said she wasn't ready.

One time we actually tried. We were at a party at my friend Richie's house on the first floor of the building we lived in, and she came in from Coney Island. After my mom went to bed, we snuck into my room and I tried to make it happen, but it was just a complete failure. She wasn't really into it, and I'd never even tried putting a condom on before. I was frustrated because it wasn't going on right, so I said, "Fuck this rubber. I can't use it. It's not working." And she said, "I'm not doing it without one!"

"Apparently I'm not doing it with or without one!" I snapped back. We returned to the party, and two days later she called me and gave me the "maybe we should see other people" line. At that point, I didn't care. All I wanted to do was play music.

It had nothing to do with that experience, but my first band, Four-X, was named after the condom. We just took the *e* out and added a dash so we wouldn't get sued. The band was composed of me and a bunch of my friends: Dave Weiss—who I knew from the neighborhood—on drums, Paul Kahn on bass, and Neil Stopol on vocals and guitar. Neil was one of the first people I met after my parents split up and my brother and I moved with our mom back to Bay Terrace. We became friends immediately. Four-X played a talent show at Bayside High School. At the time we just did covers, but I thought we were really good. It was fun and we played well. But Four-X didn't last very long because we didn't have the right chemistry. I thought Dave was a great drummer. I'm still friends with Neil, but honestly it didn't feel right with him, and I think he felt it, too. It wasn't until I met Danny Lilker, who was a grade behind me, that the elements started to come together for Anthrax.

Danny was a tall, skinny kid with curly hair, which he was growing out. He always wore rock or metal T-shirts and seemed like the kind of guy I would get along with. His nickname in high school was Beethoven, because he had perfect pitch and he could figure out anything. All he had to do was listen to something, anything, and he'd instantly figure it out, regardless of genre. I met him in 1979 when I was a junior and he was a sophomore and we were in this after-school project called Sing Band. This group of actors would do these sketches and sing, and we'd play music as the band for their songs. It was the kind of stuff you'd hear in Broadway musicals, and I've always hated that crap, but it gave me a chance to play for an audience.

I found out that Danny lived just a couple blocks from me and I would pass his home every day on the way to school, so I'd stop off, pick him up, and we would walk to school together. We started hanging out and became really good friends. We talked about our families, and it turned out his was messed up as well. His sister was a pretty heavy drug addict. Once, she shot up in a van in front of me. Seeing that scared the shit out of me. I was like, "Oh my God, I've only heard about this on TV." Danny took it all in stride. I could tell it upset him, but he didn't want to interfere. We both had other priorities.

At the time he was in a band called White Heat, which played gigs in Manhattan, including Great Gildersleeves, and they performed originals. I was in awe and pretty jealous. Their guitarist, Peter Zizzo, was the first guy I knew who could play all the Van Halen licks. He was a shredder and had equipment I could only dream of: a Charvel guitar, a killer Marshall amp. I used to tag along with Danny to their rehearsals like a total groupie. White Heat's singer, Marco Shuhan, was a tall dude with long hair who lived in Manhattan. To me, that was the dream. Oh my God! To get out of Queens and move into the city. I had no idea how to accomplish that. Even back then the city was expensive. To be in a band and live there, you had to have gigs and a record deal, and all of that was way beyond me. I just wanted to form a great band.

White Heat weren't great, but they had some good songs and they could draw a crowd, even in the city. Every day when we were walking to school, I would say to Danny, "Hey, when White Heat break up, we're going to start a band together." He'd laugh and we'd keep walking. Before Danny and I had a band, we had a name. He had learned about the bacterial disease anthrax in science class, and one day he turned to me and said, "Have you ever heard of anthrax?" I said, "No, what's that? It sounds cool."

It turned into this thing. I'd say to him, "When White Heat break up, we're going to start a band called Anthrax." Back then, nobody knew terrorists would eventually use it to wage biological warfare. Few people even knew it was an infectious ailment that usually affects wild animals. It just sounded metal. Danny would say, "We're not breaking up. What are you talking about? We just did another demo and we're playing shows." And I would say, "Yeah, whatever, but if you guys break up, me and you are going to form a band and tour the world."

That was my mom's worst nightmare. In her mind, I was going to be a doctor, a dentist, or a lawyer. That's the Jewish sign of successful parenting, and it's why you find so many Goldbergs and Finkelsteins in those professions. I can't count how many times my mom said, "Who do you think you are that you're going to make it in the music business? Everybody wants to be in a band. Everyone wants to be on television, everybody wants to be famous. Why do you think you're going to be able to?"

"Because, Ma, I'm going to do it," I said. "I'm going to try. I have to at least try."

"You're wasting your time," she'd say. "You have to go to school. You have to go to college. You have to have a real job and make money."

It all went in one ear and out the other, because I knew what I wanted and I didn't give a shit what she said. Mom had a point, but there was no way I was ever going to let that slow me down, not once. "Mom, what's the worst that could happen?" I'd say. "I try, and if I fail, you say, 'I told you so.' I could always go back to college later. I could always get a job, so I've got to try for a few years. I *have* to try."

As much as I crushed her perception of what a good son does, she tried to shatter my dreams and wouldn't accept my argument.

"No son of mine . . . ," she'd begin. I'd sigh and think, "Here she fuckin' goes again." The only worse thing I could do to her was leave to be a race car driver. When I was a little kid, that's what I wanted to do, and she would shout, "Over my dead body!" I always thought she should have been happy I just wanted to be a musician and not pursue a *really* dangerous career.

From 1980 on, I was determined to launch Anthrax and play gigs. There was no such thing as failure. I was already out of comic books by that time. I wanted to be Steve Harris; I wanted to be Glenn Tipton or Lemmy. Those guys were my heroes, and while they seemed completely untouchable and unreachable, I felt a kinship with them. "I play metal, they play metal," I figured. "They started somewhere and now look at them. I just need to find the right dudes to play with. I have to try harder."

My mom turned a blind eye to anything I did in music. Honestly, I didn't expect anything different, so I didn't care. I had my friends, my dad, and my brother, and I had the support of the first real girlfriend who would actually have sex with me. I met Marge at a party through a mutual friend. It was early 1981 just a few months before I graduated high school. She was wearing a tight green sweater and jeans and had kind, warm eyes and a nice smile. We talked and got along pretty well, but I wasn't hitting on her or anything. I couldn't pick up a girl if she weighed thirty-five pounds and jumped into my arms.

Then I heard she liked me. That gave me the confidence to ask her out. We started seeing each other, which was great because she was cute and I could tell she really liked me. Any girls I had been with before looked at me as someone to fool around with, not someone they really enjoyed being with. She wasn't a big music fan, but she thought it was cool that I played guitar and was putting this band together. And it didn't hurt that we were both Jewish. She was a year behind me and was a student at the Bronx High School of Science, which is where the smart kids went. She spent a lot of time on her studies, so we only saw each other once or twice a week, which was good for me because I was happy to be in a serious relationship, but I had the space to concentrate on music and not be dragged down. The band was more important than my relationship, my family, school, everything.

The spring of 1981 brought the moment I had been waiting for. White Heat broke up because of musical differences, just like I said they would, so Danny and I formed Anthrax, both of us on guitar. It made sense. We were best friends. We literally hung out every day and had the same taste in music. Dave Weiss and Paul Kahn came over from Four-X with me, and vocalist John Connelly, who also went to school with us—and later formed Nuclear Assault with Danny—sang for us.

John used to walk around the halls of Bayside High with a saxophone around his neck and always had a thirty-two-ounce bottle of Pepsi in his hand. A lot of times he would wear black jeans, black shoes, black shirt, and a priest's collar. John was weird but in a good way. Danny was friends with him before I knew him, and he brought him into the band. Our first jam session was July 18, 1981, and everything seemed to click. It went so well and we thought it sounded so good; right then, we agreed to form a band and call it Anthrax.

History's a funny thing. We get called one of the Big 4 thrash bands, which is a huge honor. Metallica, Slayer, and Megadeth are composed of some of the most creative and talented metal musicians ever. And when the thrash scene was at its peak, these guys played with more speed and agility than anyone else. Anthrax also grew into a band that strived to play faster than anyone else. But at first the crazy speed came from the fact that we weren't very good as players yet. Our adrenaline would be pumping, we'd get out there, and suddenly Dave was speeding along, and we were strumming away trying to keep up with him. We even played covers way too fast.

The first show we ever did was in Flushing, Queens, in the basement of St. John's Episcopal Church. We sold tickets to friends for three dollars, and there were maybe thirty people at the show. The church had a piano, so we opened with Danny Lilker sitting at the piano playing Judas Priest's "Prelude," which is the intro for *Sad Wings of Destiny*. The piano wasn't miked, but people could hear it because nothing else was on. Then Danny jumped off the piano seat, ran onstage, picked up his guitar, and we broke into Judas Priest's "Tyrant." Most of the show was covers, but we also played a couple of Danny's original songs from White Heat, "Hunting Dogs" and "Satan's Wheels." It was terrible, looking back at it, but also a shitload of fun, and our friends were sympathetic and supportive.

After I finished high school I went to St. John's University, but I quickly figured out that a college degree wasn't going to help out my music career, and studying for classes would only hold me back. Plus, I needed cash to upgrade my equipment. My dad supported my music dreams by giving me a part-time job at the jewelry company where he worked. I'd go to school from 8 a.m. until noon, then I'd get on the subway and work as a messenger from 1 p.m. to 5 p.m. In January 1982 I stopped going to college entirely. I woke up in the morning as if I was going to school, my mom would leave, and I'd go back to bed and sleep for another two hours. Then I'd get up and go to the city. I'd go to Forty-Eighth Street and hang out at the guitar stores, then show up at my dad's office at one o'clock to work for him. I did that for about a month, just dicking around. I finally got up the balls to tell my father that I'd stopped going to class. He asked what I was doing all that time. I told him I was sleeping in and then hanging out at Manny's and Sam Ash, then coming over to his office.

"Does your mother know?"

"Oh God, absolutely not, of course not."

He understood why I hadn't told her, but he felt I couldn't keep such a big secret any longer. He told me to tell Mom and then start coming to his office at 9 a.m. to work full-time for him. I was ecstatic because I knew if I was working full-time I could make more money and I could buy equipment and finance our recordings. At the time, I had shitty gear, and I felt that was holding me back from being a professional musician. I used to go to the guitar stores in the city and play their guitars, but I didn't have money for anything, so I'd always walk out. Once I started working full-time for my dad, I had some cash and it was great, and my mom didn't have to know . . . until four months later my dad said, "You really *do* need to tell your mother that you haven't been going to school. What are you going to do? You have to be honest and tell her."

So I did. I went home that day and during dinner I told her I wasn't going to school anymore and I was working for my dad to support my music habit.

The noise that came out of her mouth was louder than what I would have heard if armed gunmen had suddenly showed up in ski masks. The sounds she made are still moving through space, through solar systems and galaxies somewhere. That scream has kept alien invasions at bay and is going to end up on a planet millions and millions of miles away and destroy all life because it was so bloodcurdlingly loud and frightening. It was like I had stabbed her in the heart with a butcher knife. Every hope and dream she ever had for her firstborn Jewish son was thrown into a volcano.

I sputtered, "I'm working. I'm working! I'm making money! I have a job, it's not like I'm doing nothing!"

"I don't fucking care! You left school and you lied to me and . . ." She went on this maniacal tirade, screaming about how I was a failure and would never do anything with my life and how she had tried to raise me and had given me everything. She was shouting and crying the whole time. My brother was cowering to the side, glad that he wasn't bearing the brunt of her anger.

"Get out! Get out now!" she shouted and threw me out of the house. I packed a bag, walked to the pay phone at the Exxon station across from where we lived, and called my dad at his place in Merrick, Long Island. I said, "Well, I told her."

"How did it go?" he replied.

"She threw me out. Can I come stay with you?"

"Yeah, of course. She threw you out?" he said, stunned, even though he knew more than anyone how irrational and emotional she could be.

"I've got a bag packed. I'm coming there now."

I had a shitty old car, so I drove to his house, and I lived there for about four months. I'd take the Long Island Railroad in to work with him every morning and hang out in the city at night before returning to his house. After a few months, my dad talked to my mom and told her I wanted to be in Queens with my friends and she should take me back. At first, my mom was not into it, but she finally relented though she still didn't support my rock and roll dreams.

The main problem with Anthrax at the time was we had all the wrong players for a lasting band. John was a great guy, but he couldn't sing. He had a fierce screaming voice but couldn't carry a melody, and we knew we wanted to be a big, powerful band like Judas Priest or Iron Maiden that had a singer who could belt it out. We *tried* to get John to sing, but it didn't work so we asked him to leave. That was the beginning of Anthrax's vocalist woes.

We tried out a guy named Jimmy Kennedy, but he wasn't right, either, so my brother Jason joined the band. He was fourteen, so he still had a high voice, and he could actually carry a tune. He played a few shows with us, including a club in Long Island called My Father's Place, which booked a lot of big bands, but we wanted to tour and Jason was still in high school. My mom would have had an aneurysm if he dropped out, and as much as she busted my balls I still loved my mom, so there was no way that was gonna work.

There were other lineup problems. We had to get rid of Paul Kahn 'cause he couldn't play the new, heavier stuff we were writing. Kenny Kushner replaced him for a short while. He was another guy we went to school with and knew from the neighborhood. He was a good bassist, but he wanted to play guitar and sing in more of a hard rock band, so he also left.

That's when Danny moved over to bass, and we went through a couple of guitarists. Greg Walls joined, which worked out pretty well for a couple years. He had a great personality and was quick witted. He reminds me of Satchel from Steel Panther; he was a lot of fun to hang out with, which was one reason I was bummed when he left a couple years later to pursue a more stable line of work. Bob Berry replaced him for a short period. He could play pretty well, but knew nothing about metal.

But without question our biggest problem was that we still couldn't find the right singer. The upshot was we had a place to write songs and practice until we found one. We were renting a room in Bay Terrace at a place called the Brewery, which was right across from my mom's house, but our friend Paul Orofino (who owned the place) closed up shop to open a bigger and better version of the Brewery Studios up in Millbrook, New York, and turned it into a successful business.

I found another place in 1982 after I picked up a weekly New York music paper and saw an ad for rehearsal rooms for $150 a month, which was way cheaper than the hourly rate we were paying at the Brewery. A guy named Andrew Friedman was managing the building. He had previously been the conga player for Kid Creole and the Coconuts, so he knew the music business and helped us out for a while. We checked out the place, which everyone called the Music Building, and it was a hellhole in the worst part of South Jamaica, Queens, but bands could practice there around the clock. All the rooms used to be offices, but the businessmen were all scared off, probably at gunpoint. So the owners started renting these spaces to bands. You could put a lock on the door and tape posters and flyers on the walls. You could insulate the place, bring in a rug, whatever you wanted. And there was a guard at the front door all night long so as long as you were in there no one would get shot. When you exited the building, however, your life was in your own hands.

There's no question that the place was gross, cold in the winter and boiling in the summer. And it was filthy, infested with mice, roaches, and god knows what else. But the rehearsal rooms were much larger than what we were used to. We could easily fit all our stuff in there, plug in, turn up the volume, and pretend we were Judas Priest. I liked having a big place because I felt like I needed all my shit with me at all times. Hey, I had twelve Marshall cabinets and I was going to use them, Goddamm it! We actually splurged for the extra-large $300-a-month room. Considering we were rehearsing in there five nights a week, it was a great deal. The place became our clubhouse. We'd hang there all the time. I was still living in a tiny room in my mom's apartment in Queens. So our jam room at the Music Building was really more like my *own* apartment. As soon as I'd get off work, I'd go straight there, stay late, go home, and sleep. Then I'd get up, go to work, and do the same thing again. And on the weekends I'd go straight to the Music Building and dick around with my gear and jam.

Chapter 5

REPLACING OLD PARTS

One day I was sitting in one of the offices of the Music Building and I found out Guy Speranza had left Riot. I fucking loved Riot and I thought Guy had a great voice. I figured maybe we could get him to sing for Anthrax. I got his number through Andrew Friedman, who was still well connected and was sort of managing us. I called, he answered. I said, "Guy?"

"Uh huh, who's this?"

"Um, my name's Scott, I have a band called Anthrax."

We weren't anybody at the time. So he said, "How did you get my number?"

I lied, "Oh, from the label."

"Oh, Okay . . ."

"I'm just calling because we're a band, a new band, up and coming, and we've got a lot of shit going on. Andrew Friedman who was in Kid Creole and the Coconuts manages us and . . . "

I spewed a bunch of bullshit at him. I've always had a gift for that. I said, "We've got all this shit going on and we need a singer and you would just be so perfect. You'd put us over the top."

Guy (who sadly died in 2003 of pancreatic cancer) was actually super cool, considering I was cold-calling him out of the blue. He thanked me for thinking of him then explained that he quit Riot because he was fed up with the music business.

"I'm done. I will never, ever play in a band again," he said.

"Really, why?"

"If you stay in it long enough, you'll understand. I hated it. I'm working as an exterminator now in Brooklyn and I'm way happier."

I thanked him for talking to me and hung up. Then I thought about what he had said. What could be so bad that would make Guy quit a great rock band to become an exterminator?

Since Guy Speranza wasn't going to join Anthrax, I decided to call Neil Turbin, who I knew from Bayside High. We had met in TV studio class, where we got to make our own films. The teacher was Arnold Friedman, who years later was arrested and convicted of child sexual abuse. Director Andrew Jarecki shot a documentary called *Capturing the Friedmans* about the investigation. It's funny that the teacher of a film class wound up the subject of a critically acclaimed movie. Somehow, I don't think Friedman appreciated the irony. The rest of the world might have known Arnold as a pervert, but I just remembered him as a cool teacher. Neil and I used to hang out in the school film studio and play music. We'd bring guitars, jam, and film ourselves. Neil was really into UFOs and knew everything there was to know about them. He also loved Judas Priest. We liked a lot of the same bands. And Neil hung out in the city. He used to go to CBGBs and Great Gildersleeves, and he had connections at clubs.

He was singing in some other band at the time, which is why I didn't approach him sooner. When I heard he was free, I called and asked him if he wanted to sing for Anthrax. By that point, we had enough going on to pique his interest, but he wanted to hear our songs. We showed him what we had been working on, and he said, "I'm not singing these words. I'm writing my *own* words."

We were fine with that, so he wrote his own lyrics and some of them were pretty silly. One song, "Soldiers of Metal," had a verse that went, "Blasting the cannons, shaking the ground / Hacking and killing, we're not fooling around." But whatever. We felt like we finally had a real singer, a real front man. What we actually had was a real problem.

Neil viewed himself as the *front man*, and he was not going to listen to a fucking word that anyone else had to say about anything. That didn't sit well with the rest of us. Anthrax was a democracy. I tolerated Neil's ego to a point. I thought, "Okay, I get it. We need you. You're a singer. But you're not the boss here, motherfucker."

There's never been a dictator in Anthrax, but in the early days I was certainly the most involved in making the machine run as smoothly as possible. Through the years, a lot of people have wondered why I'm *still* the focal point of Anthrax. It's a good question. I've never played lead guitar or sung for the band. I might not be the most handsome member, :-)>. I credit my status as Anthrax's mouthpiece to two words—pushy Jew. If there's one thing I got from my mom, it's that. When it came to the band, I was always fucking confident and tenacious, and I had a lot to say. That's just who I was and who I still am. Even though Danny started the band with me, he didn't have that personality. He was laid-back and somewhat lackadaisical. Not me. I was a total pit bull.

I looked at Iron Maiden as role models. Steve Harris was the front man even though he was surrounded by amazing players and vocalists. He wrote the lyrics and a lot of the music, and he called the shots. I fucking lived and breathed Iron Maiden. That's what I wanted to be from 1980 to 1985. Whatever we did, we looked to Iron Maiden because they did it the best. So, yeah, I was determined, but I was a strong leader. I took everyone else's opinion into consideration before I made any band decisions.

Neil wasn't happy about that. He wanted to call all the shots, which is why we had problems with him from the start. For some reason, he was usually respectful to me. We never really got into bad arguments. Sometimes he'd get pissy and say, "Yeah, why don't you get your brother back in the band if you don't like me? Let's see what Jason can do." I'd just laugh and say, "Whatever, dude."

But he treated everyone else like shit, especially Lilker. But Neil looked cool and had long hair. And Danny and I both agreed he could sing, which was more than we could say for some of our past members. So we put up with his shit. Neil seemed good for the band at first and sounded good on demos, but we weren't looking at the big picture. All we wanted to do was get signed and tour.

In September of 1982, Danny and I saw a flyer at Bleeker Bob's for a show featuring Anvil, Riot, and Raven on October 30. Fuck! Raven were coming in all the way from Newcastle, England, for the concert, which seemed absurd to us. We knew them from our independent record hunts. They were a really fast New Wave of British Heavy Metal group that featured the amazing Gallagher brothers on bass and guitar and drummer Rob Hunter, who called himself Wacko. The guy wore a hockey goalie helmet onstage and definitely earned his name, smashing his head into his cymbals, mike stands, walls, and anyone he was having any sort of dispute with. Then there were Anvil, who came from Canada and whose front man, Lips, played guitar solos with a vibrator and was responsible for a lot of really cool pre-thrash stuff. Hell, you probably saw that movie. Finally, we loved Riot, who were from New York and just kicked ass. Their second singer, Rhett Forrester, was still with them at the time. Tragically, Rhett was shot and killed on January 22, 1994, when he was carjacked and refused to give up his vehicle.

The concert was billed as the Headbanger's Ball and it was in Staten Island at the St. George Theater. We had never heard of the place but it didn't matter. We were going. These were bands we fucking loved, and we were wondering who even knew enough about them to book them. I asked around and found out it was a guy named Jonny Z, who sold records at a flea market in New Jersey and apparently also promoted concerts. The day of the show we were in line and there was a guy handing out flyers for other Anvil and Raven gigs. I asked him, "Are you Jonny Z from Rock and Roll Heaven?" and he said, "I'm Jonny Z, who are you?" I said, "I'm Scott Ian, I have a band called Anthrax," and I handed him a five-song demo tape with "Howling Furies," "Evil Dreams," "Satan's Wheels," and a couple of our other early songs and a flyer for a show we had coming up in Queens.

"You have to come to my store and check it out," Jonny said. "We're open on the weekends."

"What do you mean?" I said.

"We're in a flea market and we're open Saturday and Sunday." He gave me and Lilker backstage passes for the Headbanger's Ball show, so we got to go in early and hang out. Lips and Anvil drummer Robb Reiner and Raven vocalist and bassist John Gallagher were just walking around. It felt like we had made it and were suddenly part of the inner circle. In reality, we had a long way to go, but that was the moment when I felt the first real spark that Anthrax would tour the world someday.

Danny and I were hanging out in our leather jackets, trying to be cool and not get in the way. I had brought some Anthrax shirts we had printed up, and I was giving them to people. I handed one to Lips, and he actually put it on backstage to help promote us, which was unreal. He didn't wear it onstage because he performed shirtless with bullet belts, but getting that affirmation from Lips that we *were* somebody was like Bon Scott floating down from the heavens, giving me that smarmy smile, and saying, "You're doing alright, kid."

The next weekend, Danny and I drove down to Rock and Roll Heaven and saw a treasure trove of metal imports and hard-to-find albums. They had picture discs and fanzines, and it was virtually all metal. From then on we were regulars. We'd come in on Saturdays and sometimes we'd stay overnight. There was a group of metalhead bikers who called themselves the Old Bridge Militia who were always there. They'd have these big parties Saturday nights at this guy Metal Joe's house. We'd go to the party and crash on the floor and drive home Sunday morning. While we were in Old Bridge, we learned about this place called Club 516, which had metal night every Tuesday. There weren't any bands, but there was a DJ who would play metal, and they had all these cutout cardboard guitars that people would use to air guitar and headbang to their favorite metal songs. It was so nerdy, but it was a blast. It's a tradition that came from the Soundhouse club in London, where Iron Maiden, Saxon, and other NWOBHM bands got their start. Jonny's shop carried the British magazine *Kerrang!*, which was a metal bible, and they wrote about everything that went on at the Soundhouse.

During this whole time, I was working full-time for my dad in the day, then Anthrax would get together at night. Every couple of weeks Danny and I would write another song. Then I'd use the money from my day job to pay for studio time, and we'd record it. We always wanted to try new shit, better shit. We redid recordings because we wanted our tapes to represent us at our best. Whenever we made a new demo, I'd give it to Jonny. We were friends at this point because we were at his store all the time. We'd come in and he'd go, "Oh, it's the Anthrax boys, the boys from Queens!" Danny and I would give him a tape; he'd listen to it and critique us. He'd tell us to keep plugging away. Then we'd come back the next week and give him another tape, and he'd say something like, "You know, I thought this was okay, but I don't like the lead guitar. The lead guitar's not good. And the drummer's gotta go."

He hated Greg D'Angelo—thought he was a terrible drummer. I'd say, "No, he's really good," and Jonny would counter, "He's not a metal drummer." Sometimes we'd make changes in the band based on Jonny's advice because we thought that if we listened to him maybe he'd book us some shows. He wasn't signing anyone at that point yet, but we had a feeling that he was going to make things happen for us.

One Saturday in late 1982, I showed up at Rock and Roll Heaven, and Jonny said, "Scott, don't give me a tape yet. I can't wait to play you this demo tape *I* just got. It's this band called Metallica from San Francisco. It's called *No Life 'til Leather*, and it's the greatest thing I ever heard in my life."

Of course, part of me was already jealous because Jonny went and found some new band he liked and didn't want to hear our band. He put on the Metallica demo, and I sat there and listened to it. I was eating my heart out because it was so good but, at the same time, loving it undeniably. "This is fucking awesome!" I said afterward. It was like Motörhead with these crunchy guitars mixed with the riffs of Judas Priest and Iron Maiden and all this other cool shit. I thought, "Oh my God! This is what *we're* supposed to be doing! How did *they* do it? How did they get this sound?"

It was—way better than the crappy demos we were making.

"This band's amazing. They're amazing!" Jonny enthused. "I'm going to bring them to New York and we're going to make an album!"

"Really? How? You don't have a record company."

"I'm going to start one, they'll be on it, and I'll manage them."

It sounded crazy since Metallica were in San Francisco. I said, "But that's what *we* want to do and we're right *here*!"

Jonny was always brutally honest: "You guys aren't ready yet." That was always his line. "Metallica. *These* guys are ready!"

We were pretty deflated. A part of us knew Jonny was right and Metallica were the shit. On the drive back to Queens, Danny and I were sitting in the car, silent. What do we have to do? Everything we were doing sounded great. We thought we had it—then Jonny basically tells us we sound like crappy Iron Maiden. It was so frustrating. And now he had this new band he was fawning over.

I turned to Danny and said, "Fuck Jonny! He's never going to do anything with us." Danny just shrugged. Then the superhero-like unstoppable force of my will took over. "Fuck Jonny," I said again. "Someone just set the bar. We just have to be better." It was a rude but necessary awakening because by late 1982 we knew we weren't the American Iron Maiden. Before that, Maiden were always special to us—first because they were so fucking good. Even when Paul Di'Anno was singing for them, they were musical role models. But we also revered them because in the beginning of their career they seemed like a band that had the kind of success that was within our grasp, which gave us something to strive for. Then they went from opening for Priest to headlining. And when Bruce Dickinson joined they became a different animal altogether. Within three months they went from playing shows for 2,000 people to selling out Madison Square Garden. By the time they released *Number of the Beast*, Maiden was already out of reach.

Coincidentally, we had our first brush with greatness when Iron Maiden played the North Stage Concert Theater on Long Island about six months before they blew up. Lilker and I went down there with my brother and all of our friends. Someone who knew us was working the show and handed us passes to be in the photo pit. Kids were getting crushed in the first few rows, and we were standing in the pit watching Maiden tearing it up two feet in front of us.

Originally Anthrax were booked to play the same venue that night with about fifteen other bands, but the gig got postponed because Maiden took the date. Before the show, we printed up all these flyers with the logo we had at the time and the new date of the show, which was about a month later. We snuck in all these flyers under our shirts and between songs, while the lights were out, we threw them into the air. When the stage was lit again, Bruce Dickinson was standing in piles of paper that had fluttered to the stage. He didn't see us toss the flyers, lucky for us, because we probably would have been thrown out. And magically, none of the security guys saw us either. So we stood there with these sheepish grins on our faces.

Bruce looked down at the ground, and the band went into the next number. Once they finished the song Bruce reached down and picked up one of our flyers. "Someone's thrown a bunch of paper up here. I'm assuming they want me to read it," he said. "It's something about a band called Anthrax, and they're playing here in about a month's time. So yeah, that's what all this stuff is up here on the stage."

We couldn't fucking believe it. It was totally a *Wayne's World* moment. The singer of our favorite band had just mentioned our name onstage. We were losing our minds, thinking, "Holy crap! The place is going to be packed for our show!" A month later, there were maybe 150 people there in this 2,000-seater. But still, it was so amazing to us that Bruce Dickinson read our flyer. Who could have imagined that six years later we'd be opening stadiums for Iron Maiden all over Europe? Definitely not us. We had just come to the realization that they were way out of our league. And now there was this new band from San Francisco that was in the same ballpark as us. They had already achieved what we were striving for, but they weren't light-years ahead of us. And we sounded different. My guitar tone was different than James Hetfield's. We did our own thing. In the beginning, we were more Maiden, they were more Motörhead.

I won't say Metallica didn't influence us. Hearing *No Life 'til Leather* was mind-blowing. But at the same time, riff-wise and beat-wise, we never sounded like Metallica. You can put on any Anthrax record, and I don't think you could listen to a song and say, "That sounds like a Hetfield riff." At the same time, we knew right away that Metallica were good—really good. To me at least, that just meant digging in our heels and pushing extra hard.

It sucked that we couldn't try to compete with them right away because we were about to change half our band. Berry, who never belonged in Anthrax, moved on, and later formed Hittman with our ex-singer Jimmy Kennedy. More significantly, we finally decided to fire Greg D'Angelo. I still think he was a solid drummer, but we would try to get him to play double bass, and he couldn't do it. Me and Lilker were like, "Dude, listen to motherfucking Motörhead. Check out that song 'Overkill' and just do that!" But he couldn't. I don't know if he didn't want to or if it was physically too difficult for him to manipulate both feet like that. Before we got the chance to let Greg go, he quit. It was May 7, 1983, right after we opened for Metallica at Willie's in Sayreville, New Jersey. Out of the blue, he said, "I'm leaving. I'm joining Cities."

Cities were the up-and-comers in the New York scene. They had originals in the vein of Van Halen, and they could headline L'Amour for a thousand people. They had this shredder guitar player with long, cool, straight blond hair, Steve Mironovich, who looked awesome. The bass player, Sal Italiano, is in Anvil now, and he looks exactly the same. They were *the* hot band, and they wanted Greg. I was jealous but also angry. Even though we probably would have fired him anyway because he couldn't play thrash, I felt betrayed. "You're joining Cities?!? Dude, they're not going to go anywhere, they're just local bullshit. They think small. They'll never play outside New York."

"Well, they really want me and they promised me . . ."

"You're an idiot!" I was yelling at him in the dressing room, "Go ahead and play with your fucking Van Halen wannabe nobody rockers! Have fun!!!"

There's no question I let my emotions get the better of me. I was envious that he was joining a band that was bigger than Anthrax, and I took my anger out on him. We were pretty close before, and that kind of ended it. It was stupid because not only did I no longer have a drummer, I lost a friend.

Chapter 6

WATCH THE BEAT!

As it turned out, losing Greg was the best thing that could have happened to Anthrax because, to this day, Charlie Benante is the greatest drummer I've ever played with, hands down. He can do anything, and he has a second sense for what you're thinking before you play it so he can intuitively do something complementary. And he can play in any style with any musicians. He can hold a beat as well as Phil Rudd from AC/DC, go crazy on the kit like Keith Moon, or play unfathomable time signatures with the precision of Neil Peart, and it's all filtered through his own incredible style. On top of that, he's totally chill, no pretension whatsoever. He just loves to play. And he loves Anthrax as much as I do.

We met in May 1983 through a mutual friend, Tom Browne, who I'd see at shows all the time. After he found out Greg left he came up to me and said, "You guys need a drummer, huh? I know this guy from my neighborhood, Charlie, and he's amazing. Everyone says he's the fastest double-bass drummer there is."

I said, "Really, faster than Robb Reiner from Anvil? Faster than that guy from Accept?" The German band Accept had just put out *Restless and Wild,* and the opening track on that album, "Fast as a Shark," set the bar. Hearing it for the first time was one of those moments when I lost my mind for a minute and thought, "How is that even possible? Am I really hearing what I think I'm hearing?"

Of course, there are drummers who can play way faster than that today, but back then it was pretty groundbreaking. We called Charlie, and he asked us if we would come to his house in the Bronx, which is where his drums were set up. Danny and I schlepped out from Queens to his place, a three- or four-story attached two-family house. He had a small room at the top with this giant Gretsch kit set up. There were eight toms and tons of cymbals, so there was barely enough space in the room to maneuver around the drums. We squished into the room with him and set up our amps, then we auditioned him, though it was more like an awesome jam session. We played "Invaders" and "Phantom of the Opera" from Iron Maiden and some songs from Judas Priest and Motörhead, and he nailed them all.

Afterward, Danny Lilker and I were marveling at how good and fast Charlie was. I don't know if it's because he was excited, but the Maiden covers were faster than Maiden played them, which made them sound almost like thrash. Then Charlie said, "You guys aren't going to ask me to play 'Fast as a Shark,' are you?" Apparently, Tom Browne had told Charlie that we were in awe of that song. I said, "No way. No one can play that except Accept. Can you do it?"

"Uh-huh."

We didn't know the whole song. I knew the opening riff and enough to get into the verse, so we started playing and Charlie burst in, and, holy shit, he was playing it faster than the album—straight-up double bass faster than Accept! We played it for a minute, just fucking around, and then Danny and I looked at each other and everything clicked. Here was the missing piece of the puzzle. This is what we needed to make Jonny Z shit his pants.

I said, "Well, hey man, do you want to be in the band?"

"What does that mean, 'be in the band'?" answered Charlie.

"Do you want to join and write songs with us and play shows? We know this guy Jonny Z . . ."

"Yeah, I know him. I saw you guys at the Headbanger's Ball show. I always see you guys around. Lemme think about it."

I wondered why he suddenly seemed so blasé. So I told him I thought we had real chemistry and that we'd work really well in a band together.

Charlie said he thought we sounded good as well. Then he told us he was friends with this drummer Armand Majidi, who eventually joined Sick of It All and had played in the hardcore bands Straight Ahead and Rest in Pieces. Armand was from Queens, like us. Charlie paused and told us he didn't want to offend us or anything, but Armand had said we were just "these rich kids from Queens that get whatever they want."

"What the fuck, man?" I said. "Do we look like rich kids from Queens? I live in a shitty two-bedroom apartment with my mother and brother. Who's rich? 'We get whatever we want?' Man, I work full-time and then hustle to rehearsal."

Charlie was immediately apologetic. "Yeah, I thought it sounded kind of weird," he said. "And even if it was true, who cares? What would be the problem with that?"

Yet he still wouldn't commit to being in the band. He said he'd jam with us and maybe do some gigs, but he wasn't sure about joining Anthrax full-time. He could draw really well and was planning to go to drafting school. He was afraid his mom would flip out if he didn't go and joined a band full-time instead.

I decided to take it slowly and not throw the baby out with the bathwater. We needed Charlie, and he said he'd play gigs. That was a start. We came back and jammed again, and it sounded really good. We played more Maiden and Priest as well as some Sabbath and Motörhead. Then he learned our songs and they had never sounded better. Getting Charlie to commit to the band was a war of attrition. I was persistent and eventually wore him down. I won. I wanted him as my drummer, and that was it: "You're drumming for Anthrax." Next thing you know, Charlie's our drummer.

As soon as he was in the band we wrote "Soldiers of Metal." The song revealed a new side of Anthrax. It was more up-tempo, it had barreling double bass, and it trumped anything we had ever done. Now, all we needed was a new lead guitarist.

Jonny used to tell us that all the time, and he was kinda right. We needed someone with real firepower and stage presence.

A month before we fired Bob, I met Danny Spitz, but the thought didn't even enter my mind to have him join the band. He was this cocky little fuck who worked at a guitar store on Forty-Eighth Street called We Buy Guitars. I used to go in there all the time, and he once said to me, "I've heard about your fucking band. I'll blow away your lead guitar player. You should hire me and fire that guy." I was like, "Uh, dude. I just came in here to check out an amp. We're not looking for another guitarist." A month later we were looking for another guitarist. I called Spitz. Again, he was a totally arrogant prick, but at the same time he was kind of endearing because he was this tiny little dude, all five foot two of him—he was smaller than me. But he had these five-pound balls that gave him this overwhelming confidence and attitude. And he could play really well. He was much more skilled than Greg or Bob. Aside from that, he had his own gear. That was cool because I was getting tired of always having to share my shit with our guitarists. I had twelve Marshall cabinets and a bunch of heads, which I bought with the money I made working for my dad. But every time we'd play out, I couldn't perform with six stacks when Greg or Bob only had one, especially since they were the lead guitarists. So I always split my stuff up, and I hated doing that. "It's my fucking shit! Go buy your own gear," I'd tell them. Greg was even cheaper than Neil, and Neil was cheap. Greg never chipped in for rent at the Music Building, he wouldn't pay for studio time, nothing. And he always expected to get paid for playing gigs and recording.

Spitz shoved it in my face in the way only he could do. "I heard your old guitar player didn't have his own gear."

"He didn't."

"Sheesh. That's lame. How many cabinets do you have?"

"Twelve," I replied.

"Yeah, I have twelve cabinets, too. They're Wachuwan custom-built 4 × 12s. And I have five guitars and six amps." I'm sure Danny got a good deal on gear since he worked in a music store, but he also came from money. His dad was a lawyer. I didn't care about that. I was just excited he had so much equipment.

I pictured having twelve cabinets onstage, four wide, three high. That's what Manowar had at the time, and it looked so cool. So partially based on the amount of gear he had, I said, "Why don't you come down and audition?"

He said, "Pfft, audition! I'll fucking play anything you want. Give me your fucking songs. I'll learn them."

I gave him "Across the River" and "Howling Furies," and he called me a couple days later and said, "I know the songs. When are we doing this?"

We set up a date to audition Danny at the Music Building. While he was tuning his guitar and getting his gear ready, I warned the rest of the guys about his attitude. "He's really arrogant, but if you take it in stride it's kind of funny," I said.

Right then, Spitz walked into the room where we were set up. Tom Browne was there and Danny, oozing with hubris, took his guitar out of his case, removed his strap, and threw it at Tom. "Shorten this for me. It's too long," he said like Tom was a paid guitar tech. "Who the fuck is this guy?" Tom asked.

Spitz totally aced the audition. He knew all the songs and he ripped on the solos. After Neil left, Charlie said, "He's a little weird, but he played really good." Neil Turbin did not want him in the band and seemed threatened by Danny's strong personality. I said to him, straight up, "Well, we're taking him."

Neil said, "Really? You really want that guy in this band? There's nobody else?" I said, "We need a good guitar player now. We're going to make a record and we're not waiting. He's in the band."

There was nothing Neil could do. I put my foot down, and Neil wasn't at the point yet where he could tell us, "It's either my way or the highway." That would come soon enough.

I called Spitz the next day and said, "Do you want to . . ."

He interrupted me. "Yeah, I'll be in your fucking band. We're going to take over the world."

That's who Danny was back then. A decade later he quit and started a new career making and repairing delicate watches. But in the beginning he was dead serious about being a rock star. Even though he could be obnoxious, I liked his attitude. We shared the same hunger for success. I never cared about the rock star cliché; I just wanted to make records and play shows. But Spitz *knew* he was going to be a "rock star." And we needed that because Charlie was so shy back then he barely spoke a word. The only place he exploded was behind the kit. And then you had Neil, who bitched about everything, and Lilker, who was this mellow musical virtuoso.

Around that time, we found out Jonny really *was* bringing Metallica to New York—into our 'hood! These dudes we had never met were coming into our backyards where we were trying so hard to become the big men on campus. Even though Jonny had never managed a band or put out a record, he sent Metallica $1,600 and said, "Get to New York and I'll take care of things." He was totally determined to manage them, start a label, and put out their record. It seemed like a stretch. He had never managed anyone or put out anything. He was flying by the seat of his pants. But within weeks of that conversation, Metallica were packed into a U-Haul truck driving to New York. The guys switched off between who was in the passenger compartment and who was in the back where you're only supposed to store your belongings. I can only imagine how uncomfortable that must have been.

But it prepared them for what lay ahead. They were literally driving blind, putting an awful lot of faith in a guy they didn't know, who promoted shows and sold records at a flea market. That's the amazing thing about it. It didn't make any sense. It shouldn't have happened, and if it did, New York should have eaten these guys alive. But this was Metallica. They were as determined as we were, and they were a great band from the start. Maybe they got lucky, but they made their own luck, too, grasped every opportunity that came their way.

And Jonny was confident. He didn't know what he was doing, but dammit, whatever happened he was behind it 100 percent. While Metallica were on the road from California to New York, Jonny called me up and said, "When they get here, do you think you guys could meet them and help them out, make sure they're okay?" By then my bruised ego had healed. "Sure, where are they staying?"

"At the Music Building. We got them a rehearsal room."

"Oh, cool. They'll be rehearsing here," I said. "But where are they staying?"

"At the Music Building. They're staying at the Music Building," Jonny said, like I didn't understand him the first time. I guess I didn't. *No one* stayed at the Music Building.

"We can't afford hotels. There's no money," he said. That much was true. Metallica had no cash and Jonny had spent his last $1,600 to get them to New York. He had to pay for everything with credit cards and refinance his house. It was a sucker's gambit. "You realize there's no place to sleep and there's no showers and no hot water," I said. "It's a fucking shithole."

"I know, I know. They're aware of that."

Lilker and I were there the day Metallica showed up in New York for the first time. We all hit it off immediately and became fast friends. We were both in the same boat; we were no-name bands trying to do something real. Granted, they were actually in a *worse* boat back then than we were. They didn't know anybody except us, and they were about to see the place they'd be calling home until they went on tour.

We did everything we could to help them out. They could barely afford to eat. We had a refrigerator and a toaster oven in our jam room. We gave those to them after I walked in and saw their bassist Cliff Burton with a pack of Oscar Mayer hot dogs. He was eating them cold because they come precooked. I said, "We have a toaster oven downstairs. We'll give you the toaster oven so you can at least heat these things and have a bun. Use our fridge and keep stuff in it."

I have a picture of James with a piece of bologna on his hand, because they couldn't even afford a loaf of bread. We called it the "loser's lunch": bologna on hand, hold the bread. We'd drive Metallica back to our houses to shower because Lilker's parents would go to work, and my mom still worked. So during the day we'd head over to the Music Building, pick up Metallica, come back home, and let them shower. Then we'd all go back to the Music Building. Some of our other friends started helping out, too. Some guys we knew in Queens let them crash at their houses. Sleeping on the floor in someone's house was better than being on a flea-ridden mattress in the Music Building.

My initial jealousy of Metallica melted away as soon as we met. I pretty much lived at the Music Building 24/7, although I slept at home. So I felt like we were brothers. I used to sit in their room night after night and listen to them jam. Whenever I had seen any band rehearse before, they set up like they were playing a show. The drums were in the middle, the amps were on stage left and stage right, and everything faced out. Anthrax practiced that way, too. Metallica were the first ones I saw that set up the drums and then put all the amps around them. Lars Ulrich was in the middle of a semicircle, and everyone else was around him, facing in. Soon after we met I saw them setting up their gear and I said, "What are you guys doing?"

"This is how we jam," Lars said. I didn't know what to make of it. . . . And then they started playing, facing the amps, and once again, I had that feeling, "This is the best thing I've ever heard." The tone that Dave Mustaine and Hetfield had was like a dual chainsaw symphony. Sitting in that ten-by-twelve room, surrounded by their amps, listening to Metallica play those *Kill 'Em All* songs in late '82 before the album came out, were definitely some of the coolest moments of my life. It's especially amazing, realizing what Metallica went on to become and knowing that I was literally sitting there when they were putting all the pieces together to start their domination. They were on fucking fire; it literally seemed like flames were coming out of their fingertips. They were so ready to seek and destroy. Every time I heard them, I was totally inspired. And although they were already notorious drinkers and I was around them all the time, I always abstained. I was completely sober back then because I got alcohol poisoning on my seventeenth birthday and I couldn't touch alcohol for years after that.

Chapter 7

SOLDIERS OF METAL UP YOUR ASS

t was New Year's Eve 1980, and we had a big party at my friend Richie Herman's house. He lived on the first floor of our building, and his dad was always out of town, so we had fifty or sixty people at his house to celebrate my birthday. I went nuts. I'd been drinking before, but now I was almost legal. I was seventeen, and I drank so many screwdrivers made with that ultrapremium vodka, Popov. It's right up there with Grey Goose and Tito's, if they tasted like used Russian bleach. I must have had twelve. I have vague memories of making out with this girl, and we stopped kissing because I was getting queasy. I felt the vomit come up my esophagus, and I pulled away and puked all over her and then proceeded to puke all over Richie's bathroom.

I crawled up the stairs one flight back to my mom's apartment, crashed out, and woke up the next day still throwing up. I was sick for two or three days. Just the smell of booze nauseated me for years. Looking back, that was an advantage because I didn't drink much during all the formative years of Anthrax, and that helped me maintain focus. I'd go to bars and have a beer or two, but I was not part of the Alcoholica team. Metallica had a totally different dynamic back then. Their music was strong enough to hold up even when they were sloppy drunk, and even when Dave Mustaine was in the band they really were the Four Horsemen. They just all had very strong, different personalities. James Hetfield was actually the wallflower. He was quiet like Charlie with a good sense of humor and hadn't developed his rock star persona yet. He looked awkward around people, but when he was holding his guitar and screaming into the mike he was right at home. That was where he belonged, even though he never said anything onstage.

Mustaine was the real front man of the band. He did all the talking onstage and he had that rock star personality. He was also an out-of-control, mean drunk, but he had a sharp sense of humor. Lars could be funny, too, and he could talk a ton of shit. He actually couldn't really play when they started. He learned by jamming along with James's songs and just got better as they went. It would be hard to imagine Lars in any other band, but he's the right drummer for Metallica. He was also the voice of the band from day one.

If I were to single any of them out as someone who looked like he didn't belong, it would be Cliff. Anthrax and Metallica had a certain look: tight jeans, high-top Nike or Converse sneakers, metal T-shirt, leather jacket, or denim over leather. And then there was Cliff in his bell bottoms, cowboy boots, R.E.M. T-shirt, and jean jacket decorated with Lynyrd Skynyrd and Misfits pins. He was definitely an oddball, but in his own way, he was the most metal of all of us because he flew his own flag and he was the most talented musician—possibly the best I had ever met—even better than Lilker. He was a virtuoso bassist, and he understood music and theory. Compared to him, we were cavemen. He was very aloof but not standoffish. He was cool, laconic. He almost resembled a character from the fifties, like the Fonz from *Happy Days*, if the Fonz played in Molly Hatchet. Cliff would stand there with a cigarette, give you a squint-eyed Clint Eastwood grin, and say, "What's up?"

We were into the same movies, books, and TV shows, and we liked all of the same bands, so we became instant friends. I was a Skynyrd fan from growing up, but I had never heard R.E.M. I asked him who they were, and he said they were this killer band from Georgia. Then he gave me a tape with *Murmur* on one side and *Reckoning* on the other. I took it home and checked it out, and, yeah, he was right. That early R.E.M. stuff was cool. Cliff was an awesome, awesome dude and everyone knew it. He had this aura. They all did. At first, there seemed to be no dissension between them. They were all drinking buddies and they did stupid shit. But Dave was a little stupider. And when he was really drunk, he could be a total asshole. Late at night he would dump piles of trash in front of other bands' rehearsal room doors, so when they'd show up the next day their whole front door would be covered with a mountain of garbage. And they'd know which band did it because Metallica were the only ones sleeping there. So all these musicians would knock on Metallica's door, wanting to beat them up.

I was with them on April 9, 1983, when they were playing L'Amour with Vandenberg and the Rods. Vandenberg were onstage in the middle of the afternoon sound checking, and Mustaine was already hammered. He was in the middle of the floor of the venue, and as soon as they ended a song he started screaming at them that they sucked and they should get the fuck off the stage. Jonny Z pulled him away. But I didn't think any of that shit was enough to get him kicked out of the band. The guy is arguably the godfather of thrash metal. He wrote a lot of the riffs on *Kill 'Em All* and even some of *Ride the Lightning*. Without Dave Mustaine, maybe thrash metal never would have happened. At least in the beginning, he was the driving force, artistically.

A day or two later, I woke up, drove to the Music Building, and saw Cliff standing outside having a smoke. "What's up?"

"Nothing. What's going on?" I answered, figuring it was just another day.

"Not much. We fired Dave. He's on a Greyhound back to San Francisco."

I laughed because Cliff was always being sarcastic and busting balls.

"Yeah, that's funny," I said. "Look, I have to go work with my amp. I'm not real happy with the tone. I'll see you upstairs."

"I'm totally serious," he said. "Go upstairs to the room right now and talk to James and Lars."

I went upstairs, looked around, and didn't see Dave anywhere. "What's going on?"

"Didn't Cliff tell you?" James said.

"Yeah, but he's lying, right?"

"No, we fired Dave this morning,"

I still figured that was impossible and they were playing a trick on me. "You're fucking serious?"

"We're totally serious," said Lars.

I said, "Holy shit. You have gigs coming up and you're making an album next month. Does Jonny Z know?"

"Yeah, we told him a couple days ago," Lars continued. "We made him promise not to say anything. We didn't want Dave to find out. We didn't know what he would do."

They had the whole operation planned out with the precision of a military air strike. It turned out that L'Amour show with the Rods was Dave's final straw. They purchased a one-way bus ticket back to LA and waited for a night when Dave got really drunk, which they knew wouldn't be long. There was a Greyhound station almost next door to the Music Building; they woke him up while he was still mostly incoherent and fired him. He had passed out in his clothes, so they didn't have to help him get dressed. They just collected his stuff, which they had mostly packed in a bag already, and literally put him on the bus before he understood what was happening. Then they made plans to send him his gear.

I was standing there with my jaw open, speechless, and Cliff walked back in. "See, I told you," he said.

"Well, what are you going to do about your shows and the record?"

"We have a guy coming in from this San Francisco band, Exodus," Lars said. "He's flying in and joining the band. He already knows most of the songs, and he's learning the leads."

When he got there, Kirk Hammett was a fucking trouper. Everyone's attitude in Metallica and Anthrax at that point was, "Fuck, put me on a park bench with a newspaper on top of me. I don't care. We're making a record."

I was nineteen. Everyone else was around the same age. We didn't give a fuck about anything except making music, whatever it took. But adapting to that lifestyle was harder for Kirk than for any of the other guys. He was certainly the most sensitive of the four of them. Sometimes the stress of living like that would show. Back in San Francisco, he was in a band that was starting to happen, and he had a place to stay. He wasn't living in a filthy rehearsal squat. But he never complained or got angry. He was probably the nicest guy I'd ever met, and he never, ever changed, even with all the money and fame. He's still the same sweet kid I met the day after he arrived from SF.

Once I got done helping Kirk acclimate to the luxuries of South Jamaica, it was time to focus again on Anthrax. We decided "Soldiers of Metal" would be the song to introduce us to the world because it had that barreling double bass that delivered a knockout combination along with the guitars, bass, and vocals. But the demos all sounded flat. We needed someone to produce it properly. Tom Browne was a huge Manowar fan, so he introduced me to their guitarist, Ross the Boss. I didn't know much about Manowar, but I kind of liked the first album. It was cool that they had Orson Welles narrating "Dark Avenger." I thought the image of them in loincloths holding swords was a bit gay, but Ross was in the Dictators, and I was a big Dictators fan. I told Ross we wanted to make a quality demo, and he said, "Let me produce it for you; I've been doing it for years."

So in early 1983 I used $1,500 that I saved up from work to go into this really good studio in Long Island, Sonic Studios, with Ross and record five songs. Like I said, I was always paying. Neil Turbin was a cheap motherfucker, Lilker never had money, and even though Spitz had some cash he never wanted to spend it on Anthrax. We recorded "Soldiers of Metal" along with some old songs we had already recorded with Greg but that had a different feel with Charlie playing. We tracked the music in two days, and Neil sang his vocals on the third day. It was a solid five-song demo, the best thing we had done.

We went to the flea market to give it to Jonny, and someone there said, "Oh, Jonny's at the IHOP down the street on Route 18." So Danny and I went over there and literally walked up to the table where Jonny and his wife Marsha were eating breakfast. He said, "Oh, it's you guys. What's going on?"

"We have a new demo, a new drummer. Ross the Boss produced it." We were so amped up each sentence practically ran into the next.

"Oh, really? Wow." That was what Jonny said when he was impressed by something. Then he said, "Okay, we'll check it out. But can we finish eating breakfast?"

We went back home, and the next day Jonny called me all excited. I had never heard him talk about our band like this before: "This is great, this is great! You've got it now. You have it! This is great!!"

He said it was the best thing he'd ever heard from us and he wanted to sign us to a record deal, and if we wanted him to, he would manage us as well. Jonny made good on every word. He printed up the single of "Soldiers of Metal" and sent it all over the world. All 2,000 copies they printed sold out. A couple of months later we were in the studio recording *Fistful of Metal*.

In April and May 1983, before we started working on the record, we played about five shows around New York and Jersey with Metallica. In the inner sleeve of their *Kill 'Em All* album, there's a live photo of them, which was actually a staged shot taken at a sound check. In the foreground of the picture, in front of the stage, there are these KISS road cases lined up to extend the stage out. Those were ours. I bought a bunch of them for our gear. Most of the backline they used was mine, too. Then in early 1984, Metallica were scheduled to play The Channel in Boston, but all their equipment was stolen from their van, including James's prized guitar amp. In a state of despair, he sat down with an acoustic and wrote "Fade to Black," their first big metal ballad.

Metallica had just released *Kill 'Em All* and they were about to go to Europe. Suddenly, they had no gear, so we lent them tons of stuff, basically our entire backline, to play the shows. At one point, Jonny Z offered me a point on the Metallica record as payment for helping them out and lending them a ton of gear. I told him I didn't want it and that I'd feel sleazy taking money from them. I was just glad I could help. I would have done that for anybody. I would only expect they'd have done the same for us. And Metallica definitely paid us back in full by taking us on tour with them and breaking us in the UK.

We wrote about half of *Fistful of Metal* before Charlie was in the band. And after he joined we came up with faster stuff like "Deathrider," "Metal Thrashing Mad," and "Subjugator." The album is a really good representation of what we were listening to at the time: Maiden, Priest, Motörhead, but also other NWOBHM stuff like Raven, Accept, and old Scorpions (even though those last two bands are German). In addition, we were into British punk, including GBH and Discharge. It was all part of that process of discovering the next heavy band. We heard

Venom and went, "What could be more extreme than this?" Then we listened to Discharge's *Hear Nothing See Nothing Say Nothing* and went, "Okay, this is the heaviest record ever made! Let's do something even heavier!!"

The first time I saw slam dancing and stage diving was when I went with Neil to check out the Exploited at Great Gildersleeves. At that point, I had never been to a punk show in my life. We were sitting up in the balcony, and I was looking down at the kids in the crowd as they smashed into each other and climbed on top of one another's heads, crawling to the stage and diving off. "Dude, that looks fun. Let's go down there," I said. Neil seemed alarmed: "No man, you'll get killed. They'll beat our asses. Punks and skinheads hate metal dudes."

I didn't believe him and thought he was being a pussy, but I found out later it was true. When the punk, hardcore, and metal scenes started to cross over in '84/'85, there were so many fights between longhairs and skinheads in the crowds at thrash shows. Even so, slam dancing soon became a really big thing in metal. The West Coast–style circle pit was suddenly everywhere, and that evolved or devolved into moshing, where people in the crowd formed a much more violent circle pit that was less about actual slam dancing and expressing yourself and more about making aggressive physical contact with other moshers. There were always a few assholes in the pit, but most of the fans were there to have a good time, not to hurt anybody. There was an unspoken rule that if someone got knocked down, you weren't allowed to trample him. You had to help him get up and make sure he was okay. It was civilized anarchy most of the time.

Lilker was into the most extreme hardcore and metal as well as great, melodic rock, and he was the main songwriter in Anthrax back then. He wrote about 75 percent of the riffs for *Fistful of Metal*. But we all worked on the songs as a team. We'd be writing a song, and we'd say, "No, we should play that one faster. That's how fast Motörhead plays. We should go even faster than them." We could, so why not? Charlie could play faster double bass than Philthy Animal Taylor, and we could play the riffs faster, so we did because we thought it was a blast. It felt so good to play that fast and bang our heads to the beat of Charlie's double-bass drumming.

Jonny originally arranged to have us record *Fistful of Metal* at Barrett Alley Studios in Rochester, where Metallica did *Kill 'Em All*. So we drove there in October 1983, ready to record the album with Metallica's first producer and engineer, Paul Curcio and Chris Bubacz, only to find out that the mixing desk was gone, and they had ordered a new one that wouldn't be there for at least three weeks. We had a truck full of gear and nowhere to record. The studio let us crash there for the night, then we called Jonny back in New Jersey, and he said he didn't know the studio wasn't ready. Since we couldn't record in Rochester, Jonny called Carl Canedy of the Rods, because Carl lived up in Cortland, and asked if Carl knew any other studios in upstate New York.

We unloaded the truck, and Danny Spitz and I took the U-Haul and went on a road trip while everyone else stayed at the studio. We checked out two places. The first was in Elmira, and it was just a crappy room on top of a store. They had no gear and it sucked. The second was Pyramid Sound in Ithaca. It was a real recording studio with a control room, a ton of gear, and a big live room. We met Alex Perialas, who ran the place. They were way more expensive than Barrett Alley, but they were awesome, and Danny and I decided this was where we had to do the record. We talked to Jonny Z, who worked out a deal with Alex. He told them he had a record label and he would have all of his bands come record at the studio.

They were happy with that, so we drove back to Rochester, got the truck, and went back to Ithaca to do the record with Carl producing and Chris engineering. The album was a combination of anger and aggravation from the two years of crap and member changes that led up to the lineup that's on there, combined with the uncontained excitement and youthful energy of finally being able to get into a real studio and make a whole record. At first, we were a little intimidated, but we were prepared. We had rehearsed five nights a week for two years, so we knew our shit and we were tight. And we were pumped. We had a shoestring budget to work with, but we made the most of it. Plus, we were good at nailing songs on first or second takes. We were in Ithaca for three weeks, and we stayed at the Rock and Roll Hotel in Cortland, which was really a crash pad run by two sisters. We also spent some time in a fleabag motel in Ithaca. Even though we were still

Mom and Dad,
January 1964.

Herb Rosenfeld sees his
son for the first time.

Baby metal.

I was into Angus very
early on.

Even at four years old
I knew this was creepy.

Happy kids.
Jason and I circa 1969.

My best child-
hood memories
are from going
to Disney World.

Ten years old and haven't
heard of KISS yet.

I was a fan even
when they sucked!

Me and Neil Stopol, Four-X at the Bayside High talent show, 1980.

Four-X, Bayside High talent show, 1980. From left to right:
Paul Kahn, me, Neil Stopol, Dave Weiss.

That's my first Strat.
Battle of the bands at
Bayside High, 1980.

High school graduation with Mom, Grandpa Moe, and Jason.

First Anthrax gig in the St. John's Episcopal Church basement, Flushing, NY, 1981.

Me and Danny Lilker on the twin Charvel attack.
First ever Anthrax gig, 1981.

My Father's Place gig with Jason singing, Dave Weiss drumming, Kenny Kushner on bass, and Danny Lilker on guitar. April 1982.

At the Iron Maiden gig at the Northstage Theater, August 1982. Jason is holding some of the flyers we threw on stage. Left to right: Jason, Jimmy Kennedy, Dave Weiss, don't know, me.

ANTHRAX

At

Great Gildersleeves

331 BOWERY (Bet. 2nd & 3rd Street)

Info: 533-3940

9:00 P.M. AUG 1 9 1982

Our first gig
in Manhattan.

Early 1982. Greg Walls, Greg D'Angelo, Danny Lilker, Neil Turbin, me.
I am extra metal.

Air guitar at the 516. That's Charlie choking me.

Recording *Fistful* at Pyramid Sound, late 1983. I still have that Strat.

Outtake from the
Fistful of Metal
back cover shoot.
Four of us hated
the pics so much
we went with no
photo.

My twentieth birthday,
December 31, 1983.
Shirts optional.

Fistful is certified vinyl and my first magazine cover! I made it!

My first passport. That's the sweatshirt I was wearing when I met Lemmy.

A couple of ex-cons fresh out of jail in London, March 1984.

X-mas 1984 at Jonny Z's house.

The infamous *Fistful of Metal* tour vest.

Recording *Spreading the Disease* at Pyramid, late 1984.

Joey blowing us away. *Spreading the Disease*, early 1985.

About to have a pirate attack, early 1985 on our East Coast tour.

S.O.D., July 1985.

My pal Fred.

This was an EPIC show.

Recording
I'm The Man,
Miami 1986.

Tracking *Among* with Eddie Kramer.

an unknown band and weren't making any money, we felt like we were living the dream—making a real album, going to bars, and hooking up with local chicks who were impressed we were in a band, even though they didn't know Anthrax from Aerosmith.

We worked at Pyramid Sound for three weeks. In addition to tracking our songs, Neil and Jonny convinced us to record a cover of Alice Cooper's "I'm Eighteen." Around that time, Quiet Riot went to number 1 with their cover of Slade's "Cum On Feel the Noize," so Jonny thought we needed a cover song as well to help propel our album sales. Neil was way into it. I didn't want to do it. I didn't think "I'm Eighteen" made any sense in the context of the rest of *Fistful of Metal*, but that didn't matter. To protest, I didn't play rhythm guitar on that track. Spitz played all the guitars. It's the only song in the history of the band that doesn't feature me. I flat out didn't want it on the record, and it certainly didn't take us to number 1, so I guess I was right.

Chapter 8

FISTFUL OF HEADACHES

At the same time as I was living out my rock and roll fantasies, I was still dating Marge. After she graduated from high school, she went to Northeastern University in Boston, so she was gone for four years. We were supposed to be exclusive and have this long-term relationship. I visited her about once a month in Boston and would hang out for a few days, so when she was in class or was busy with her studies I'd check out who was playing in the area and go to local punk and metal shows. I hung out a lot at the Paradise, this small club on Commonwealth Avenue. It was really small and narrow but a lot of cool bands played there. Another club that booked metal shows in Boston was the Channel, a big warehouse on the water which was demolished in the late nineties to make way for some major highway construction. And if there was no one good at either of those places, there were always punk shows at the Rathskeller, which everyone called the Rat, probably because that's what ran around the place besides people. It was kind of like the CBGB of Boston but even grimier. There was a doorman outside named Mitch who got cancer. So he had a laryngectomy and could only talk with one of the mechanical devices you hold up to your throat. When he spoke he sounded like a grumpy version of one of those really old Speak & Spell learning toys.

After I got back home, I talked on the phone with Marge a lot, but I realized pretty quickly that seeing her once a month wasn't satisfying my libido. It's a shitty thing to say. I could have jerked off and stayed faithful, but there were girls at clubs who were digging us, and when we were hanging out at L'Amour or 516 trying to promote the band, there were always chicks around and some of them were really hot. I thought, "Well, Marge is away in Boston. It was her choice to go to college there and leave me in New York."

That's a fuckin' selfish attitude. Shit, I was nineteen, and these girls we'd meet were available and eager. You didn't have to be terribly smooth to hook up with them. There was no Facebook or Twitter, so there was no chance of getting caught. There were way more ways *not* to get caught back then. If you got busted cheating, you were basically an idiot.

In my brain I thought I was in love with Marge, but the monogamy option just wasn't going to cut it. The other option was to be with Marge for the rest of my life and realize that I'd only ever had sex with her and one other girl. That couldn't happen. It's not like I was hooking up on a nightly basis. It was really only an occasional thing, but cheating is cheating, and I kept the charade going on for years. Marge thought we had this great relationship because I'd come see her once a month and we'd go see a museum exhibit or something and have sex. And then I'd listen to her talk about all of her classes while I nodded and smiled and thought about Anthrax.

In some ways, the joke was on me. In Boston I had Marge and in Ithaca there were girls that made me feel like a rock star. After we were done with the album, I went crashing back to reality. I was back in my cell in my mom's apartment, and I had all my gear in there because we'd left the Music Building by then. We weren't there every day and didn't want to pay the rent anymore. That left us with no place to rehearse or leave our shit. I had to stack all these Marshall cabinets and guitars and pedals to the ceiling. There was just enough room for a single mattress on the floor next to the windows. I slept and lived there for almost three years. I'd come back from a show and load my own gear back into my mom's apartment. There were no roadies or techs. Just me. It didn't matter. Whatever needed to be done, I was fuckin' gonna do it.

Soon after Ithaca we were back in New York with the finished album. That was Anthrax circa 1984 and I still like it for what it is. At the time, of course, I loved it, but I always hated the mix. And I hated the cover art way more. That and the title were Neil's idea. Back then, Neil had this chain-mail metal glove he'd wear onstage, which he made himself. He used to sit in his apartment and weave these metal links with blacksmith tools for hours on end. Maybe he should have been a renaissance fair craftsman and not a singer. He saw that Judas Priest were wearing all this metal and he figured we had to look more metal than them—hence the glove.

"We've got to have a guy on the cover of the album who's getting punched by a guy wearing my metal glove through the back of his head and it comes out his mouth!"

That was Neil's idea of "metal." It was my idea of crap.

"We'll call it *Fistful of Metal* because I wear a glove and it's fuckin' metal!" Neil enthused.

Nobody else had any ideas. We had one other piece of art done for us that tied in with the song "Death from Above." The chorus was, "Jet fighter, jet fighter. Turbo jet engines ignite." So someone did this art based on a photo of a fighter pilot in an F-14 with a helmet and the oxygen mask. It was cool and sleek. But it reminded me of Black Sabbath's *Never Say Die*. Also, it didn't look very metal.

So we went with Neil's idea and had an artist friend of Danny Spitz named Kent Josphe create the image. We didn't know what else to do. We looked at Metallica's *Kill 'Em All* and said to each other, "That's a terrible cover. Let's not use that guy." Jonny Z was using him for all his stuff, and it was terrible. Exciter's *Violence and Force* is the worst-looking record of all time. So by default, we ended up with a rush job done by Danny's friend. We were pretty shocked it was so bad because we had seen the guy's portfolio and he had lots of cool paintings and drawings. Plus, he's the one who did our logo for the "Soldiers of Metal" single. He sent us six or seven logo ideas, and that one stuck out. Slam dunk. That's Anthrax right there. The logo was killer. So we figured we'd let him do the artwork based on Neil's idea.

Then we saw the finished art for the album cover. The first thing I said was, "Wait a minute. It makes no sense. There are two right hands on the cover!" It was the same hand holding the guy's head as it was punching him through the face. I couldn't figure out if there were two people, one guy holding him and the other guy hitting him, or if this guy was born with two right hands. The cover was all wrong, but we didn't have the budget to do anything else. It was either use that or have nothing on the cover but the band logo and the words *Fistful of*

Metal, because we had already agreed on the title. To make matters worse, on the first printing in the States, our fucking name came out pink, not red. Nothing is less metal than a pink band logo, but we were helpless to do anything about that, either. Megaforce wasn't about to dump thousands of copies of the record just 'cause the band's name was pink. Everything was wrong with the album except the music.

I kind of look back at it more fondly now just because it's so goofy, but man did we hate it back then. The thing is, if you look at all the big thrash debut albums that came out, they all had terrible covers: *Fistful of Metal,* Exodus's *Bonded by Blood,* Metallica's *Kill 'Em All,* Megadeth's *Killing Is My Business . . . and Business Is Good,* and Slayer's *Show No Mercy* were all pretty bad. I wouldn't even say ours was the worst. I'll take *Fistful of Metal* over *Killing Is My Business . . .* or *Kill 'Em All.* But I would say *Bonded by Blood* took the cake. Whatever that thing is on the cover of that Exodus album is atrocious. At the same time, it's so great because bad cover art was a big part of early thrash metal. It's almost as if everyone was thinking, "Alright, we can't have artwork as good as Iron Maiden because we're not as big as Iron Maiden, so we're just going to do our best and this is what you get."

As soon as we started touring to support *Fistful of Metal,* Neil got ultra-cocky. He felt like he was the boss man, and he became inflexible. His attitude was "I'm the singer and it's my way or the highway." He thought we'd be dead without him. The shitty thing is, he was right. We were on the fast track. Jonny Z was managing us, and he was bringing Raven back in the summer of 1984 to tour like they did the year before with Metallica opening, and this time we were scheduled to open all the dates, starting May 30. Everything was already announced and planned, and if we lost our singer, we'd have had to cancel. Jonny wasn't going to wait around for us. There were other bands he was talking to like Overkill and Legacy (which became Testament). We had to strike while the iron was hot, and that gave Neil the ability to pull all these power plays.

He decided what we were going to look like and what we were going to wear. He made this chain-mail belt for me that was six or seven inches wide all the way around. It weighed twenty pounds, and he wanted me to wear it onstage. I liked to run around when we played, and the belt weighed me down. But he said, "Scott, you're going to fucking wear that belt! Lilker, turn your bass down and never step in front of me." Whenever we opposed any of his ideas, he threatened to quit. We hated his guts, but we were powerless to do anything about it.

The biggest dick move Neil ever pulled was when he fired Danny Lilker behind our backs after *Fistful* came out in January 1984. The main reason he did it, in my opinion, was because Danny is taller than him. He honestly didn't think someone should be taller than the front man onstage. He thought it made him look bad, so he tried to stand as far away from Danny as possible, which was hard when we were playing stages the size of Ping-Pong tables.

But I have to admit there were issues with Danny. He was lazy. He was getting into weed and the rest of us were clean. And he was forgetful. We were rehearsing at a studio in New Rochelle by then. It was thirty minutes from Bayside, so I'd pick up Lilker, and we'd drive over the Throgs Neck Bridge to New Rochelle. Twenty minutes after we'd left, Danny would say, "Oh, I forgot my bass."

"Dude, I figured you'd left it at rehearsal."

"No, it's at home."

"Man, we'll be there in ten minutes. If we turn around we'll be late. We'll have to borrow a bass from another band."

Stuff like that was constantly happening. Danny was laid-back and lackadaisical, and I was always that guy—bam, bam, bam, gotta move forward—but that was no reason to kick him out of the band. Danny was the guy who was there from the beginning. It was me and him. We started Anthrax, and he was the main riff writer at the time. Charlie hadn't started writing songs yet, and the stuff that I had written before wasn't good enough anymore. It still kinda sounded like Iron Maiden, whereas Danny's writing got so much better as we progressed. The first time he played "Deathrider," I almost peed myself. It was amazing. But Neil didn't like Lilker and felt he was holding us back. We finished *Fistful* in October 1983, and in November we had a show at a roller rink in New Jersey called Skateway 9. Talas, which were Billy Sheehan's band, were headlining, then came Exciter, then us. We thought we should have been in the middle of the bill, but Jonny said, "Exciter are coming from Canada. We can't make them open the show. They're an international act." International? Fucking Canada? But we liked Exciter, so we relented.

We had a great set, and about six hundred kids lost their shit because we were the local favorites. Exciter were cool and tore the place up as well, and Talas were nuts. Seeing Billy Sheehan play bass was insane and still is. He's incredible. Things just got better. *Fistful of Metal* came out in January, and we were thrilled to finally have a record out that people could buy in stores, even if we never got used to that shitty artwork. I was still riding a natural high from having a record out when I got a call from Lilker. He sounded strange.

"Dude, what's going on? Neil just called me and told me I'm out of the band," he said.

"What are you talking about?"

"Neil just called me and fired me."

I figured he must have been confused. Neil didn't tell me anything. We didn't have a band meeting. I thought maybe there had been a mistake, and I told Danny I'd figure out what was going on and call him right back.

I called Neil and said, "Dude, what the fuck! You fired Danny?"

"We talked about it. You knew this . . ."

"No, we've talked about Danny's problems and that I would talk to him and we would get him back on track. No one fucking told you to call him and fire him, that's . . . you can't just fire Danny, it's not . . ."

"Well, he's out," he interrupted. "It's either him or me. I can't be in a band with that slob anymore. He's an embarrassment onstage. He's not a professional musician. He doesn't look like he belongs in Anthrax."

I would wear leather pants onstage, Neil had his whole Rob Halford–meets–Rhett Forrester look, and Lilker would have jeans and a black leather jacket on with some metal T-shirt. I never had a problem with the way he looked. Cliff didn't look like the rest of Metallica, and no one cared. It just didn't matter.

"You can't fuckin' do that, man . . ."

"That's it. It's either him or me."

I hung up and called Charlie and Spitz, and everyone came to the same conclusion. We couldn't lose our singer. We had to go on tour and support our album. It was sickening knowing our hands were tied and we were backed against the wall. We felt like if we lost Neil the band would be done. We'd be held up for months trying to find someone else to sing for us.

I got off the phone with those guys and sat in my room in my mom's house and cried. I was sick to my stomach, throwing up. I had gone from a state of elation from having just released our first record to feeling like I had lost a loved one, and in a way I had. I called Danny back and explained the situation: "Neil said it's you or him. I called Charlie and Danny, and I can't believe. . . . I don't want to say this to you, but this is what we're doing, this is what we have to do if we're going to move forward. We can't lose Neil. As much as we hate him, we just can't."

Danny was silent for a moment. And then he just went with it. If I didn't know any better, I wouldn't have thought he was angry, but I knew he was devastated. Telling Danny that I was going with Neil's decision was probably the worst moment for me in the history of Anthrax. It was fucking brutal. I hated Neil before, mostly because he was such a douche, but he was laughable because he was an idiot. Now, I genuinely hated him because he was a tyrant and he made me lose my best friend. I'd dream about the day when Neil wasn't going to be in the band, either. I'd look at him with his smug expression, and I'd think, "Dude, this is not going to happen for you. You're never going to be what we're going to be—not while you're in the band."

We bided our time until we could make good on that promise, which was hard at first because everything was taking off. People across the US and Europe were discovering thrash, and a movement was definitely forming around us. We were psyched, but it wasn't something we felt responsible for. And I don't think Metallica did, either. The funny thing about a movement or a scene is it seems to happen when a certain type of band just happens to tap into a certain sound at the right time and the public feeds off it like wild wolves. It's nothing you create. Yes, you make the music, and when the fans get the scent of it they come flocking, but it's definitely something that's out of your control.

Maybe you can mold what you do once you sense something happening, but we were writing these songs before anyone knew what thrash was. Critics called it power metal or speed metal at first. Then someone coined the term "thrash."

In March 1984 I went over to England to promote *Fistful of Metal*. The British press had taken to us, and I was doing one interview after another. While I was there, Metallica passed through London. They were scheduled to play some European shows with Exciter and the Rods as part of a break they were taking from recording *Ride the Lightning* in Denmark. But the tour was canceled because of—believe it or not—lack of ticket sales, so they were stuck in London for a while. The people who ran the studio they were using in Denmark thought they were going to be gone for a couple weeks, so they booked another band to record during that time. Metallica's European label, Music for Nations, put the band up in an apartment on Gloucester Road with a lot of bedrooms and invited me to stay there as well, because we were on the same label. I was supposed to be there for a few days, but I ended up staying almost three weeks since it was my first time in the country and I had somewhere to stay.

One Sunday afternoon Cliff wanted to buy a new Walkman, because his had broken, so we went to an area called Tottenham Court Road, where all the electronic shops are. We took the tube down there, which was usually pretty easy. Even though it was March, it was still cold, and all I had was a black leather jacket. Cliff had a big winter snorkel coat with a fur-lined hood. We walked to the station near Gloucester Road, paid our fare, and went into the station. We stood on the platform waiting for the train when two cops came up to us.

"Can we help you?" I said.

"Well, yes," replied a cop with a moustache and a bent nose. "If you admit to carrying illegal substances up front, we'll make things easier on you."

"Excuse me?" I said and almost laughed because it seemed like a Monty Python sketch. "We're not carrying anything illegal. What are you talking about?"

"All right, that's it then. Come with us," replied his beefy partner. "You're under arrest."

"For what?"

"For suspicion of carrying illegal substances," said Crooked Nose.

We walked with these two cops to a police station inside the train station. They had us remove our jackets and they searched them. Mine was empty, but Cliff had a cold so he had some Sudafed pills loose in his pocket. The police didn't believe it was cold medicine and said they'd have to send them to the lab to be tested. They brought us to the back of the station and separated us. Then they put me in a six-by-six cell, with a sliding window instead of bars. It was a concrete room with a space to sit. They had me remove my clothes, so I was standing there in my boxers, freezing. They shut the door and walked away. Nobody read me my rights or said a fuckin' word, and they didn't say how long they thought I'd be there.

In England if they feel like searching someone for anything, you have no recourse whatsoever. Apparently, they don't share the Fourth Amendment right to privacy. I knew I was gonna be okay because I didn't do drugs, but Cliff was a big pothead, and I was thinking, "Jesus Christ, if he has a joint on him we're fucked." My New York, Jewish paranoid brain immediately flashed to the scene in *Midnight Express* when Brad Davis, who plays Billy Hayes, is caught with drugs, gets thrown in a Turkish prison, and is beaten by guards. I was thinking, "This is it. My family is never going to see me again. I'm going to be in some fucking weird prison, and the next time I see my girlfriend, she's going to put her boob on the glass like in the movie, and I'm going to have to kill a guard and bite his tongue out."

I started banging on the door. "Hey, is someone out there?" Finally, a guard slid the door open. "What do you want?"

"What's going on?" I asked as innocently as I could.

"We're bringing your mate back to the flat to search the place." My stomach dropped into my testicles because I knew Cliff had a big bag of weed back at the house. Out of the corner of my eye I saw him shrug his shoulders as Crooked Nose, Beefy, and four other cops led him out the door. I remained in the cell for another two hours with nothing to do but replay possible scenarios in my head of having to call my parents and explain to them why I might never see them again. Time ticked by at the speed of gridlock traffic, but my mind continued to race. I figured we'd get a chance to talk to a lawyer, and maybe we could plea bargain a reduced jail sentence. But I was convinced I was going to be thrown into a jail somewhere in London, and who knew what a bunch of pervs were going to do to a short, skinny, longhaired American Jew. Finally the door opened and it was one of the cops. He handed me my clothes and said, "Get dressed. I'm going to take you to the captain's office."

I thought, "This can't be good." I wondered if my cell mates would just beat me up every day or make me their bitch and gang rape me. I walked into the captain's office with the cop, and Cliff was already sitting there with a half smirk. Immediately, the captain started apologizing. "Sorry, you know. But we have a lot of problems with drug dealers, especially on the days of football matches. You have to understand, my officers suspected that you were carrying."

I lost my mind and started screaming at the guy. "You're apologizing? I just spent six hours of my life in a jail cell in my boxer shorts because you thought we looked like drug dealers? You're fucking out of your mind. What kind of a country is this?"

I went nuts—Cliff was punching my leg to get me to shut up—but I was on a tear.

The guy said, "I understand you're upset . . ."

"Upset? I'm going to get a fucking lawyer and sue your police department for wrongful arrest!" So Jewy of me. I couldn't believe that they were allowed to do this. I was beyond control. "You backward-ass motherfucker. I was freezing in there. No one offered me anything to eat or drink. You treated me like a fucking convict, and I didn't do anything wrong."

I couldn't stop myself. I just kept yelling. "You don't have anything better to do than torture American tourists? We fucking told you we didn't have anything, but you pulled us aside and treated us like shit just because of the way we look."

I didn't stop to think that maybe the captain could have arrested me for swearing at him. Fortunately, he didn't take any further action. I think he actually felt bad. The cops escorted us out of the station, and we headed back to the apartment. With all my rage vented, I wanted to know how we managed to pull the get-out-of-jail-free card. I asked

Cliff, "What the fuck, dude? What happened back at the house? How did they not find your weed?"

"Where's the first place you would look if you were searching for someone's stash?" he said.

"I dunno. Under the mattress??"

"Exactly. And what's the one place they never looked?"

These dumb cops never even checked under the bed. Six bobbies combed the place. Kirk was just a little surprised sitting in the living room practicing guitar when they all walked in, and they turned the flat upside down. But all they found were empty beer cans because they never looked under Cliff's mattress, where he had a big bag of weed. Odin himself must have been shining his light down on us that day.

I looked at my watch and said, "Too late to get your Walkman," and Cliff said, "Fuck it, let's go get drunk."

We went back, picked up Kirk, and got wasted. The evening ended with the three of us wrestling in somebody's hedges on the front lawn of their house and getting yelled at as we went running down the street. What were they gonna do, call the cops on us?

Chapter 9

TURBIN FAILURE

When I got back from England, it was business as usual—only worse. Neil was in a rage about everything. He thought he was all-powerful and had no idea he had signed his death warrant by firing Lilker. Unfortunately, he had a stay of execution while we were on tour. He became a straight-up dictator telling us what to do all day. We'd travel in a van with a couple rows of seats. There were two people in every row except the back row, which Neil had to have entirely for himself. We all put our personal shit in the truck with the gear. Neil insisted on having his suitcase in the van; otherwise, he wouldn't come on the tour. He needed to receive special treatment because he was the singer and he had us by the balls. The rest of us would share the driving. Neil would never drive. He'd never let anyone borrow anything. If I'd forget my shampoo and ask if I could borrow his, he'd say, "No man. It's a special shampoo. It's from Israel and it's the last one made."

All of Neil's possessions were the last one made and came from Israel. They were impossible to get again so he had to make them last. It was incredible how selfish he was. We told Jonny Z that we couldn't go on anymore with this guy, and if we were going to make a second record, we had to find a new singer. It's pretty risky for a band to switch singers on its second record, so we expected Jonny to flip out. Fortunately, Jonny hated Neil almost as much as we did because Neil used to talk shit about him to us and it would get back to Jonny. Neil would say, "Fuck Jonny Z, we have to get a real manager. He doesn't know what the fuck he's doing."

"I don't know, man," I'd say. "Look at Metallica. Things are going pretty well for them."

"Fuck them. What are they ever going to be?" Neil replied. "Who are they? Nobody. We have to be like Judas Priest, that's who we have to be like."

The way Neil saw it, you were either Priest or you were nobody. He was above this speed metal shit we were playing. He wasn't into thrash. He loved Rhett Forrester and Riot and Priest. That was it. He felt like he was slumming by being with us. But he wasn't about to quit, no matter how many times he threatened to. That was alright. By the time we hit the road with Raven, we knew his time with Anthrax was running out, which gave us the freedom to stop feeling like we were under his control. We were untethered and ready for revenge.

We replaced Lilker with Frank Bello, who started out as one of our roadies. He just stepped in, and it was so easy because we were friends, he could play, and he already knew the songs. Frank hated Neil too and was an active participant in our Turbin torture tour. When we were out with Raven, we bugged the shit out of Neil at every opportunity. He was furious and couldn't understand why he wasn't in control of every situation anymore. "Ghostbusters" was the biggest song on the radio that summer. You could flip through the stations in any city and hear it six times in a row, probably. Neil despised that song, so every time "Ghostbusters" came on the radio, we'd crank it no matter how late it was. Everybody else in the van would sing the chorus as loud as we could, and Neil would freak: "Shut the fuck up! "Shut up, shut up! I'm trying to sleep! You have no consideration."

That was always his line, "You have no consideration, I'm a singer, I'm a singer, you have no consideration." Eventually, he gave up. "Ghostbusters" would come on, and you'd hear, "Fucking dicks!" from the back of the van as we all sang along. It was great. He'd threaten to leave, like usual, and this time we called him on it. "Fucking leave! Who gives a fuck? Quit, quit the band! Who cares?" That just made him angrier.

On the tour with Raven, we were driving long distance in a rickety van, and we had a tour manager, who was supposed to give us our ten-dollar per diem once a week. A week went by and none of us got any money. We asked Tony, Jonny Z's partner, who was also out on the tour, where our money was, and he said to get it from the tour manager. So I went, "Hey, man, I didn't get a per diem."

He told me he gave the per diems out Monday, and since I didn't pick mine up when he handed them out, I wouldn't get it that week. I thought maybe that's how it worked on big tours. What did I know? But it seemed weird. I asked Wacko if I had to pick up my per diem the day it was issued, and he said, "No, when you want it just ask for it." I said to him the manager told me otherwise, and he said the dude was probably pocketing my money.

Now, I'm not a huge, muscular guy or anything, but I'm a New Yorker, and I don't like being taken advantage of. I went back to the guy and said, "You motherfucker! Give me my $70 right now or I'm going to hit you in the head with a bat!" I got my money.

At the end of the tour, Raven felt sorry for us being in a van and invited us to ride on their bus. It meant I didn't have to drive anymore, which was good, but we didn't have bunks, so we had to sit up, which sucked for sleeping. The tour routing looked like it had been put together by a blind man throwing darts at a map of the US. We played Los Angeles at the Country Club in Reseda on a Thursday night then drove 1,200 miles to play Seattle Saturday night. We stopped at some shitty pay-by-the-hour motel to get some rest. We checked in. I pulled the covers back and there was blood all over the sheets. I don't know if some chick with a heavy flow had her period there or if someone had been killed, and I didn't want to know. It was disgusting and I needed to sleep, so I took a hundred dollars that I had saved from my per diems, checked into a Holiday Inn, and crashed for seven hours. I was broke, but I had my first sound sleep in months. After we played Seattle, we drove back to LA to play a second show there on Monday. It was stupid. But we were fuckin' metal warriors. We were like, "If this is what you gotta do to make it, we'll do it. Whatever it takes."

Neil made realizing that possibility harder and harder. He was losing his voice onstage because we were playing so many shows and he wasn't pacing himself. "All the more reason to fire him," I thought. We'd open the show with "Deathrider," he'd scream, blow his voice out, and not be able to sing the rest of the show. As much as we wanted him to fail, we didn't want to play bad shows. I told him he might want to hold back a bit on the "Deathrider" scream and pace himself so he could get through the whole song without losing his voice.

"Fuck you!" he screamed. "Don't tell me how to fucking sing. I don't fucking tell you how to play guitar! You don't know what the fuck you're talking about!"

Charlie's cousin Dennis had a video camera back then, and he'd film the shows. We played one back to Neil and said sarcastically, "Well, what's going on here? What note was that? Three songs into the set and there's nothing coming out of your mouth."

He still thought he had the upper hand. The last concert of the tour was at Roseland Ballroom in New York City. That was the famous show where Metallica got signed to Elektra, Raven signed to Atlantic, and Island came and scouted us and we ended up signing with them. The venue was sold out, which was unheard of. For these three then–relatively unknown bands to sell 3,500 tickets at Roseland was a sign that something big definitely was about to happen. You could feel it in the venue. The whole place buzzed with excitement, and when we took the stage, the anticipation turned into this tsunami of energy. We opened with "Deathrider," and right away every fucking kid in that crowd was headbanging and punching the sky. We'd never seen anything quite like that, and we could really feel the connection they had with the music. It was the right songs at the right time. It was like when I first heard AC/DC and this shock wave passed through my entire body like I had been hit by lightning.

These kids had been waiting for this to enter their lives, and now we were there. Neil surely wasn't 100 percent that night, but he seemed to have taken our advice and didn't blow out his voice. He might have missed a note or two, but any flaws were overcome by the enthusiasm of the crowd. After the show, we were all riding high, even Neil, until he got into a huge screaming fight with Jonny Z.

Megaforce had tour jackets made for us. They were old-school satin vests with the words "Anthrax U.S. Attack Tour '84" embroidered on the back. I think Jonny did it on purpose, but somehow Neil's was the wrong size, and he fucking lost his mind. He said, "You fucking big, fat fucking nigger thief."

We were laughing. "Huh? Why does he think Jonny Z is black?" Neil was shouting, we were all cracking up, and Neil screamed, "I'll never fucking play for you again, you fucking fat fuck!"

Later that night, Neil and I were walking to my car because I had to give the fucking asshole a ride back from Roseland to Queens. On the way he said, "That's it, Scott. I respect you and I respect what we've done, but I have no respect for that fat fuck. I can't be in this band one more minute if he's still the manager."

Once again it was "It's him or me," and this time it backfired for poor Neil, who ended the conversation with, "We're firing Jonny Z, or I'm out."

I dropped him at his house and said goodnight to him and smiled a grin that silently said, "Goodbye, motherfucker!" The day after we got home from that tour, I drove over to Charlie's in the Bronx. We had been waiting for this day for ages. It was like, "Light the fucking candles on the cake, dude. Call Neil's house."

It took a week to get him on the phone. Who knows what the fuck he was doing during that time? I'd go to Charlie's every afternoon, and we'd call Neil every couple hours, or even every twenty minutes, to fire him. Finally, *RING, RING* . . . "Hello."

"Neil, it's Scott."

"Hey man, what's up?"

"Listen, I've got good news and bad news. You'll never have to play a show for Jonny Z again."

"Did you fire Jonny?" he excitedly asked.

"No, *you're* fired."

"What?!?"

"You're out of the band, Neil. You're done, it's over. You've made our lives miserable and that's not going to happen anymore. We're moving on. We're finding a new singer . . ."

"You'll never do anything without me! I'm the only reason this band's done anything. You'll never find a fucking singer as good as me, you'll never get . . ."

This time it was my turn to interrupt *him*. "Yup, thanks, Neil. Bye."

He was still yelling at me as I hung up. Charlie, Frankie, and I high-fived and laughed. We called Jonny Z and told him the news. He sounded as happy as we were. In the wake of firing Neil, there was a minute I thought of suggesting we get Lilker back in the band. Maybe I could have salvaged my friendship with him, but Frankie had been with us for eight months at that point. I very well could have said I wanted to give Danny another chance because he was unfairly ousted. But Danny was in the rearview mirror. I was more consumed with finding a new singer and moving forward, and Frankie played with his fingers like Steve Harris and no bassist was better than him onstage. Plus, he had become family.

When I say Frankie's family, I'm not talking about an intense bond between unrelated band members. Frankie actually *is* family. Charlie is Frankie's uncle, and their relationship can sometimes be an insanity unto itself. The two guys are both talented stubborn Bronx-born Italians, and they grew up in a house together like brothers. Charlie is five years older than Frankie, and when Frankie was really young his parents split up and he moved back into Charlie's mom's house because Frankie's mom is Charlie's older sister.

They hung out together all the time, jamming, listening to KISS, and fighting. As calm, cool, and collected as Charlie is, Frankie is the opposite. He's as volatile as nitroglycerin. Charlie's got a long fuse, but when Frankie burns it down to the wick, they both explode and leave collateral damage.

One time we were working at Top Cat rehearsal studio in New York, when Frankie started yelling at Charlie about something and Charlie shouted back. Before I knew what was happening, Frankie grabbed a skateboard and whipped it at Charlie. It missed him and bounced off the wall. Charlie picked it up and threw it back harder. Then Charlie stormed out, and Frankie yelled that he was gonna kick his ass. Family!

We went back to Ithaca, New York, to record our second album, *Spreading the Disease*, in November 1984 with Carl Canedy, since he did a good job with *Fistful of Metal*. We had already written most of the songs. Musically, it was a real collaboration between me, Charlie, and Lilker. The only thing that wasn't written yet was "A.I.R.," and that came way later, after Joey Belladonna joined the band. Charlie brought that in toward the end of the recording session, and it really showed how much he was coming into his own as a songwriter. It also showed where our heads were musically and is pretty much a bridge between *Spreading the Disease* and *Among the Living*.

Once again, we had songs, but no singer. That little snafu could have derailed a lot of bands, but we were on fire and nothing could stop us. It was just another obstacle we'd have to overcome. We had lineup changes before; this was just another bump in the road. I never for a minute doubted that we'd come back stronger.

We started off by hiring this guy, Matt Fallon, who used to sing with guitarist Dave Sabo (who hadn't yet formed Skid Row) in Steel Fortune. I met him when we played with Metallica and Steel Fortune in Sayreville in 1983. The guy sounded good onstage. So, when we were looking for a new singer, some mutual friends recommended him, and I checked out Matt again at a Steel Fortune show in New Jersey. He was commanding and his voice was powerful. Afterward, I asked him if he would audition for Anthrax. He was totally into it, he sounded good at the audition, and we all figured we were set.

But when Matt started singing in Ithaca, we realized he was green and was in way over his head. When he sang, it was like he suddenly lost his voice. He did a lot of takes and nothing sounded good, so it became pretty clear right away that he wasn't going to last. He had way more attitude than experience, and he had a big mouth. While we were in Ithaca, we got an offer to open a show for the Scorpions in New Jersey, and we were all pumped about it. Then Matt said, "We can't open for the Scorpions."

"What are you talking about?" I said.

"We can't be on the same stage as them. They'll fucking blow us away."

That was the last straw. It only took two months for us to tell we weren't happy with this guy anyway, and after that comment Charlie, Danny, Frankie, and I decided to send him packing. If you don't have confidence in your own band, you might as well work in a car wash. Within hours of that conversation, we pulled a Mustaine on him. We literally went and bought him a bus ticket back to New York, gave it to him, and said, "Sorry man, this isn't going to work."

Chapter 10

JOEY BELLADONNA: TAKE ONE

When Jonny Z found out we fired Matt Fallon, he was livid. We were already over budget, and he was waiting for us to come out of the studio with this finished album. The last thing he knew, we were done with the guitars, bass, and drums, and all we needed was the vocals, and suddenly he heard we fired Matt. We were so desperate, we considered putting out the record as a four-piece. We'd have two singers like KISS. Frankie would be Paul and I would be Gene, because Frankie had a clean singing voice and I could sing in more of a hardcore style. We figured we'd split up the songs and plow through them because we couldn't sit in the studio twiddling our thumbs for much longer. Nobody was thrilled with the idea, especially me and Frankie, but we figured we'd do it if that was what it took to finish the fucking record.

We were about to start tracking vocals when Carl said, "Look, I know this guy from around here who was in a band called Bible Black. They used to play around upstate New York. He's a great singer. He's got long black hair. He looks the part, and he has a great voice. I know his name is Joey. I just have no idea how to get hold of him."

Carl made a bunch of calls and was able to track down Joey Belladonna through a guy who promoted club shows. Joey was living in Plattsburgh, New York, and didn't know who we were, but he was looking for a gig so he drove to Ithaca two days later. He knew nothing about thrash. He didn't know Metallica, Megadeth, Slayer, Exodus— he was into more classic rock. He arrived to audition wearing really,

really tight jeans and leather boots that weren't Doc Martens or anything. They weren't cowboy boots, either. They were somewhere in between . . . rock boots. One of them had a chain on it. And he was wearing a sleeveless tiger-striped shirt that was cut too short. It looked like he had put on a costume, dressed up to meet us like he thought this was what a singer should look like. For some bands it would've been great, just not Anthrax.

I was standing there in an Agnostic Front T-shirt and ripped Levis with suspenders, thinking, "What the fuck? At least he has long hair." I have to admit I was judging him by what he looked like. Maybe he was doing the same thing to me. I tried to put my biases aside and give him a chance since he was already there. Maybe later we could teach him how not to dress. We had a mike set up in the studio, and we asked him to go in and sing something without any backup, just so we could get a feel for his voice.

He shuffled up to the mike and started singing "Oh, Sherrie," by Journey, and "Hot Blooded," by Foreigner. The songs he chose wouldn't have made my top 10 list at the time, but he sounded great and we had never worked with a real singer before. Joey sang with vibrato, knew how to breathe properly, and had technique. He enunciated what he was singing and sustained notes like Rob Halford. Instantly, Carl said, "That's your golden ticket right there. Listen to that guy's voice. You guys will be unlike any other band out there. This is going to put you miles ahead of anybody."

We were thinking the same thing, but we didn't know how Joey's voice would blend with the thrashy music we were playing or if he'd even be into singing along with it. We asked him if he'd hang out for a week and jam with us. He was into it. He had a bag with him, so he came prepared to stay for a few days. We decided to go out to dinner and hang out. I actually said to him, "Um, do you have any other clothes because we don't dress like you're dressed."

"Oh, yeah. I don't dress like this, either," he said. "I heard you guys were a metal band, so I got some stuff to wear to hopefully look like what I thought would be cool, but I can see it's not."

He changed into jeans and a T-shirt and looked like a normal guy, which made us all more comfortable. We laughed with him about the idea of having to look a certain way to be "metal" and talked a lot about music. He liked stuff like Rush, Deep Purple, and Black Sabbath and had albums by Iron Maiden and Judas Priest. So we figured he'd eventually fit in.

We started working with Joey in late fall of 1984. He didn't have a huge ego like Neil or Matt, and was open to advice. We jumped right into teaching him stuff from *Fistful of Metal* and some of the new songs. There was a learning curve, but pretty soon he caught on to what we were doing. He didn't ask too many questions and let it all sink in. He was eager to learn but didn't want to take control. It seemed like good chemistry after all. Every day, he'd sit there with headphones on in the studio, and he just absorbed our style and took in the songs. I sat and worked with him to help him sing with the right attitude and aggression. He caught on quickly, and once he learned something, he made it his own and sang the shit out of it.

In early '85 we decided that before we recorded anything with Joey, we should do some shows. We had never seen him onstage, and he had no idea what thrash concerts were like, what a mosh pit looked like, and how intense the crowds were. We booked an East Coast run of dates and told him to think of the shows as an educational experience. I said, "Look, this will be good because you'll be able to feel what is going on out there with this kind of music, and then you'll come back with a new appreciation for how energetic and explosive it can be. You'll have experienced it, and you'll have it in your gut."

He was into that, so we played New York, Providence, Boston, and a couple other cities, traveling around in an old rented RV. Billy Milano was our driver, so Joey got to see pretty quickly the kinds of people we called friends that were hanging around the metal scene. There were other surprises as well.

Fans were diving off the stage, landing on top of each other. Some leapt feet first and caught fellow moshers in the face with their boots. Fights broke out. There was blood, there was chaos. It was anarchy in the USA. And Joey loved it.

Removing the training wheels and taking him on tour turned out to be a good move, one that definitely helped his performance on *Spreading the Disease*. Joey took direction really well and sang the songs as if he had been there from the start. It took a while, but by working on one song at a time and carefully going over every verse and every chorus—letting it all sink in—he delivered some amazing vocals. He learned from our guidance but also added his own ideas for note choices, and his innate sense of melody greatly contributed to the overall picture. To me, the work he did on *Spreading the Disease* was his best in Anthrax up until he came back for *Worship Music*.

One thing about Joey that was initially a blessing—but eventually became a curse—was that he didn't write his own lyrics. He was perfectly happy singing my words and never questioned the content. That was cool with me for years because I enjoyed the new creative challenge and nobody else in the band wanted to write lyrics. But it added extra time to the recording process—time we didn't have. Obviously, I'd have to finish the words to the songs before he could sing them.

There were some leftovers on *Spreading the Disease* from the first album. Neil wrote the lyrics for "Armed and Dangerous" and "Gung-Ho," and I wrote everything else. The main theme that comes across on the album is the idea of being an outcast and fighting for survival. "A.I.R." stands for "Adolescence in Red," and it was my wordplay on George Gershwin's "Rhapsody in Blue." I thought I was clever for coming up with such a highbrow title. Everyone thinks "Madhouse" is about being in a mental institution, but it's actually a metaphor about us trying to make our mark in the world. "Medusa" is about the character in Greek mythology, a woman with snakes for hair who turns men into stone with a mere glance. It became a metaphor for having a shitty wife or girlfriend, but that's not what I wrote it about. The Medusa just seemed so metal.

"Aftershock" is my description of a nuclear apocalypse, and "The Enemy" was my first socially conscious tune. It's about the Holocaust. Being Jewish, I learned from an early age about Hitler and the Nazis and how they killed six million Jews, and I felt it was something I should write about. Call it an ethnic obligation. "Lone Justice" was about the character Roland Deschain in the Stephen King book *Dark Tower*. It was my first foray into the world of Stephen King, who I discovered in the late seventies after I saw the movie *Carrie*. I thought the film was really intense, so I checked out the book. I was a pretty avid reader by that time, and after reading *Carrie* I was hooked. King released *The Stand* in

1978, and I got way into that. I also wanted the character in "Lone Justice" to be like Clint Eastwood in *The Good, the Bad and the Ugly*.

I wrote most of the lyrics for *Spreading the Disease* in early '85 because that's pretty much all I had to do. We had already been in the studio for almost eight months, the guitars were all tracked, and I was still in Ithaca so I could work with Joey and make sure he had the right inflections and emotions for the songs. He started recording his vocals in March. By the time April or May rolled around, things started getting weird with Carl. He would stroll into the studio midday, we'd do stuff for a couple of hours and then Carl would look at his watch and say, "Oh, I gotta go. I've got some stuff back at my house that I need to take care of." This started happening every day, and when he was gone he didn't want us doing anything with Alex Perialas, who was engineering the record. He just wanted us to wait until he came back, and usually that wasn't until the next day.

Joey and I were getting really frustrated, so we asked Carl what was going on and why he wasn't staying and working with us longer. He actually said, "If you could come out to my place and cut the grass and help around the house then I would be able to spend more time producing the record."

I called Jonny and told him what Carl had said, and that was the last thing he wanted to hear because we were getting more over budget by the day and he was having some major problems at home at the time with his wife Marsha and their other partner Tony Incigeri. Tony basically handled Raven, and Anthrax were Jonny's baby. Our album was costing so much to make that Tony and Marsha wanted to pull the plug, mix whatever we had, and just release it, even though the vocals weren't done. To Marsha and Tony, Anthrax were a liability. They wanted to focus all of their efforts and finances on Raven, who had signed with Atlantic and were making a record that was going to be more commercial and had radio potential. They thought Raven would be huge. Of course, that didn't happen. But Tony was arguing that Megaforce was wasting its time and resources on us and Anthrax could never be commercially viable.

Fortunately, Jonny still believed in us, so he took the money he had left in his bank account—about $29,000—and he moved out to

Ithaca. He took off from Jersey and stayed with us in our apartment, because he was determined to get the record done. That's when the studio hours became more regular. If Carl wasn't there, we worked with Alex, which was a pleasure because he was totally capable of producing great records, as he proved many times over the years, and he was engineering the whole thing anyway. Finally, all the vocals were done, and it was time to mix the record, which should have taken two weeks, but took a month because Carl was stringing the process out again. But I have to say on June 30, 1985, when we were officially done mixing *Spreading the Disease*, I was happy with the way it sounded—way happier than I had been with *Fistful of Metal*.

Chapter 11

SGT. D IS COMING!

Most of the time in Ithaca I was alone, and I was trying to think of things to do besides writing lyrics. I almost shaved my head, but Billy Milano talked me out of it. Instead, he shaved "NOT" in my chest hair. He said, "You shouldn't shave your head, that's bullshit. That's not who you are. You're into hardcore, that's cool, but keep your long hair." I already had the nickname Scott "NOT" Ian. It didn't come from *Wayne's World*, either. In my neighborhood in the '70s everyone would say "NOT" in that same sarcastic way as Wayne and Garth did later, and that became part of my lexicon.

I didn't shave my head, but I kept listening to hardcore UK bands like Discharge, GBH, Exploited; NYHC groups including Agnostic Front, Murphy's Law, AOD, Cro-Mags, the Crumbsuckers; and West Coast stuff such as Suicidal Tendencies and Black Flag. It didn't matter where it was from. I loved Corrosion of Conformity (COC), who were from North Carolina, D.R.I. (Dirty Rotten Imbeciles), who were originally from Houston, and this German band Inferno.

At the same time, I started drawing cartoon strips of a zombie character I named Sgt. D. It was kind of my weird take on World War II comic hero Sgt. Rock combined with my love for horror. Sgt. D is dead and he smokes a cigar and he's really right-wing and angry—like a cross between an undead Rush Limbaugh and Rambo. He lives to hate. He's not racist; he hates everyone living. I'd draw these comic strips and hang them up around the studio. In one, Sgt. D was coaching a Little League team full of zombies, and one of his kids slides into first base, and the ump calls him out, so Sgt. D cuts the guy's head off.

It was stupid shit, but I'd hang them up around the studio, and Joey, Carl, and Alex would read them and laugh.

While we were playing the hurry-up-and-wait game recording *Spreading*, Charlie, Frankie, and I did a quick hardcore demo with me singing and sent it to Jonny to give him an idea of what a hardcore project from us might sound like. It included the Agnostic Front covers "United Blood" and "Last Warning" as well as a version of Discharge's "Hear Nothing See Nothing Say Nothing." We didn't know what we were going to call it at the time because although I had this comic book character, Sgt. D hadn't transformed into a musical project yet. Jonny loved the idea of us doing a hardcore band and thought we should call it the Diseased as a play on Anthrax. The more I thought about the hardcore band, the more I started thinking about merging it with my comic book drawings. I'm not a good artist, so they were pretty shoddy looking, but they were funny, and after I did a bunch of them I started writing songs from the perspective of Sgt. D. That's when I came up with the name Stormtroopers of Death (S.O.D.).

I thought it would be funny to make the S.O.D. songs super-fast, heavy, and short. So I wrote riffs which were kind of hardcore but from a metal perspective because that's what I knew. The songs were mostly sixty or ninety seconds long, with some joke tunes that were only three or four seconds. In no time, I had about nine or ten songs done.

But I kinda hit a wall. Everything started to sound really similar. So I called Danny Lilker to help me out. I contacted him out of the blue and I half expected him to tell me to fuck off. We hadn't had much contact in the last year and a half since Neil kicked him out of Anthrax. We had bumped into each other, but we never had much to say to each other and we definitely didn't hang out.

He answered the phone, and I told him I was up in Ithaca recording Anthrax stuff, and during some downtime I started writing these really fast tunes that were a blend of hardcore and metal, and I thought he would be the perfect person to work with. I knew Danny was into hardcore because I'd sometimes see him at CBGB Sunday hardcore matinees. He said he'd come up, and a couple days later he got on the bus from New York to Ithaca and spent a few days at the studio. We clicked immediately and plowed right into the material. Unfortunately, that caused some friction with Frankie because suddenly he wasn't involved in this thing that Charlie and I were doing with our former bassist.

Frankie was understandably angry because he played on these other hardcore tracks. Now we were moving forward without him, and he was out in the cold with Joey and Spitz, who weren't exactly his buddies. There's no question that a schism had developed, the first of many in the history of Anthrax. Jonny was caught in the middle trying to keep the peace. He explained to Frankie and the other guys that we weren't doing S.O.D. when we were on the Anthrax clock. It was never a question of one or the other. Anthrax was always the priority. There was just this time off, but when I got Lilker back into the picture, it felt like it was meant to be. I only ever thought S.O.D. was going to help Anthrax because if we got hardcore kids into the band, it would create a natural bridge for these guys to check out what we were doing with Anthrax.

The friction that ensued actually inspired Danny Spitz to start a side project as well and try to get Joey and Frankie involved. Fans of English pop might remember when a couple of guys in Duran Duran went off and did Power Station, which was huge, and then some of the other Duran Duran dudes did a side project they called Arcadia that nobody cared about. Charlie and I used to joke that we were going off to do Power Station and they would be Arcadia—which never happened, anyway.

As much as I hated leaving Frankie out, I knew Lilker was the right guy for S.O.D. because he's a great writer and his underground sensibility matched the music. We wrote the next ten songs while Danny was in Ithaca, and then S.O.D. was done. It was like Anthrax, but different. Eventually, it would be termed crossover. There were some great metal riffs, but it was definitely rooted in hardcore, and it was all about fun. That's it. If it didn't make us laugh then it wasn't S.O.D. The band was one big inside joke and that's what made it great. Even though Danny and I wrote all the songs (except for "No Turning Back" and "Pi Alpha Nu," which Billy Milano wrote), S.O.D. would never have been what it was without Billy.

I met him at an Agnostic Front / Murphy's Law show at CBGB in early '84. He came up to me and said, "Oh, aren't you in Anthrax?

I heard you come to shows here." Then he told me that he overheard some skinheads who hated longhairs talking about beating me up, so he suggested I come backstage to hang out with him and Agnostic Front.

I said, "Sure, I'd love to." Aside from appreciating being saved from a possible beatdown, Agnostic Front was an NYHC institution. We loved the music, but they *lived* it. They'd get into fights all the time, and their singer Roger Miret eventually went to jail for almost two years on drug charges. I was thrilled to meet him and guitarist Vinnie Stigma. Afterward, I hung out with Billy, who was the bass player in a hardcore band, the Psychos. He was a huge, intimidating guy, and he was a swarming beast onstage, so he had developed a bit of a reputation in the NYHC community. It was pretty cool that Billy befriended me like that because back in those days there was clearly still a strong divide between headbangers and hardcore fans. Longhairs definitely were not welcome at the CBGB Sunday matinees. Skinheads and punks didn't like each other, but the one thing they agreed on was that they *hated* the longhairs. Thanks to Billy, I was accepted into that scene pretty quickly. I even said to Billy, "I've never had an issue here with people wanting to fight me," and he said, "That's because you know me! Because if they fuck with you, they fuck with me."

I definitely appreciated that since I was five foot six and not terribly well built. Billy used to say, "We're going to hire Jacques Cousteau to find your sunken chest." Billy was great for S.O.D. He looked the part, and he dug into the spiteful, apolitical subject matter without hesitation or remorse, like a shark planting his teeth into the flank of a seal.

Some of the shit he was singing was pretty rough, too. Like the title track, "Speak English or Die": Nice fuckin' accents, why can't you speak like me? / What's that dot on your head, do you use it to see?" Then there was "Fuck the Middle East": "They hijack our planes, they raise our oil prices / We'll kill them all and have a ball and end their fuckin' crisis." Now those are some ridiculous lyrics.

It felt great to work on those songs after the painstaking, endless procedure that *Spreading the Disease* had become. We finished mixing *Spreading* on June 30, 1985, and all our gear was still set up in the studio. Even the drums were still miked. That enabled us to dive right into *Speak English or Die* and record it quickly and cheaply. Carl knew we were gearing up to work on S.O.D., and he said to me one day that he'd love to produce it for us. There was no way that was going to happen after all the time it took to make *Spreading*. We planned to make the S.O.D. record in a week tops, so we hired Alex to do it, and he did an amazing job.

We had one rehearsal the night of July 1. It was me, Charlie, Danny, and Billy, and we tracked the album on July 2. We did the vocals on July 3 and had a barbecue to celebrate America's 209th birthday the next day. On July 5 we mixed it and it was done. And although the music is totally different than *Spreading the Disease*, you can play that and the S.O.D. record back to back, and they sound just as good.

When we listened back to *Speak English or Die*, we knew we had created something great. And it felt special, knowing that we'd done it in a mere three days—pulled it out of our asses, basically. At the time, there was nothing heavier. We had blast beats, and it was faster and more brutal than anything else we had heard. We were all really proud of it.

When people heard this stuff, though, they immediately thought Billy was racist. What they didn't understand was, there was this fucking Jew behind the curtain. No one bothered to dig into the motivation behind the subject matter; they just reacted, and they dug into Billy big time.

"Scott, you motherfucker!!" he once said. "I get all this shit about being a racist and everybody's up my ass, and it's all your fault! You're a sneaky little fuck. It's all you, and you just get to stand there and smile and play guitar."

Billy wasn't a racist, a xenophobe, or a homophobe, but he totally went with it and owned the Sgt. D character. Plus, he looked like the type of guy who might actually believe the things Sgt. D was saying. Sgt. D hated everybody: black, white, Asian, Arab, Christian, Jew, male, female, child, adult. He lived to hate. Billy was a skinhead, but he totally wasn't racist or a Nazi. I used to have to say to people all the time, "I'm a fucking Jew. You really think I would be in a band with a Nazi?"

It seemed so ridiculous to me that anyone would ever take what we were doing as anything but comedy. The music dripped with sarcasm; we had three-second songs and a number about milk. Yeah, it was extremely politically incorrect before its time, but that was my sense of humor and I'd been like that since I was a kid. I've never had any sacred cows when it comes to comedy, and obviously I'm not a racist, I'm not homophobic, I'm not jingoistic, I'm not any of those things. I just hate political correctness, especially in music. If you're going to play aggressive music, the idea of pussifying it, to use one of my favorite George Carlin words, takes the power out of it.

I hated the straightedge attitude. I didn't drink much, but I hated the idea of punk rockers who made loud music preaching about not drinking, not doing drugs, and not having sex. There were straight-edge dudes who told their fans to stay celibate until they were married. I was like, "What the fuck? This isn't Catholicism. It's rock and roll." Those three words have been a euphemism for fucking since the days of Chuck Berry. So from the start, I went into S.O.D. with a few simple goals: to make the stupidest record ever written, to make the heaviest record of all time, and to have the whole thing be tongue in cheek, from the sexism of "Pussywhipped" and "Pre-Menstrual Princess Blues" to the viciousness of "Kill Yourself."

What was so fucked up about the backlash we got was that anyone who knew anything about Anthrax was aware I was Jewish, yet people would write reviews saying we were racists. When we played live, Nazi skinheads would come to the shows and *Sieg Heil* us. Billy would say, "Put your fucking hands down, you fucking assholes. I'll come out there and fucking break them off."

This whole mythology has built up around *Speak English or Die,* which people now consider a groundbreaking crossover album. The truth is, when it came out practically nobody knew it existed. It wasn't until after *Among the Living* blew up that fans went back and discovered S.O.D. When the album came out, we only played seven gigs in New York and New Jersey. We opened for Suicidal Tendencies at L'Amour, and then we did some shows with Overkill. Our last gig was at the Ritz on December 21, and that was with Motörhead, Wendy O. Williams, and Cro-Mags.

The shows were pretty memorable, though. Billy frequently got into fights with Nazi skinheads. Whenever someone tried to preach hateful messages at us or say they considered us part of their "team," we were very clear that they pegged us as the wrong guys and they were idiots. We'd tell them to leave the show and fuck themselves. Most of the people in the crowds were into the music and got the joke, but there were always morons and some of them paid the price.

At one of the L'Amour shows with Suicidal, some punk kid in the front row was spitting on Billy. I kept seeing arcs of spit landing on Billy's back whenever he turned around, but I couldn't see who did it. Then, I finally saw the guy. It was one of those people we used to call "peace punks," who supported bands like Reagan Youth. They were dirty and crusty and had this almost Rasta-ish vibe. They hated Billy because he was a loudmouth skinhead, and that was the antithesis of what they stood for. When I saw the face of the guy who was spitting, I stopped the show, got on the mike, and said, "Billy, that fucking crusty-looking dude right there, he's been spitting on you for four songs."

Billy reached down and pulled this guy up on the stage and started punching him like he was holding a rag doll. After he got a bunch of blows in, he grabbed the guy's arm. I figured he was going to escort him out of the club. Instead, he jerked the kid's arm up so far and hard, the guy let out this sickening scream. Then he winced and gritted his teeth because he was in so much pain. His nose and mouth were bleeding, and there were tears streaming down his cheeks, diluting the blood. There was too much noise in the room to hear a crack, but his arm was dangling at an absurd angle, so Billy must have broken it. No one checked to see, and Billy just turned him around and threw him down the stairs, and then the club security opened the door and tossed him into the street. I was a bit shocked. I didn't mean for it to go that far, but at the same time, Billy got his point across. Don't fucking spit on us. If you get caught, you're going to pay the price.

After the seven shows, Charlie and I had to go back and work on Anthrax, Billy formed the similarly themed M.O.D., and Danny returned to Nuclear Assault. Aside from feeling like I was part of a really killer album, it was great to work with Lilker again. While it didn't erase what happened in Anthrax, it felt like we were finally able to move past our impasse. I liked knowing that the most recent memory I'd have of Danny was doing S.O.D., not trying to explain why we couldn't keep him in Anthrax. That was good for me mentally, and I think it was healthy for him as well.

Between '85 and '88 we saw each other more than we had. We crossed paths, me in Anthrax and him in Nuclear Assault. But still, we were never friends the way we had been growing up. Those days were definitely over. It's hard enough to maintain relationships with anybody from your past, especially when you're in a band and you're traveling ten months out of the year. But to completely forgive a major incident like being kicked out of a band you started, well, that was wishful thinking. If the shoe was on the other foot, I would have been the same way. Some things just can't be forgotten. We still bump into each other from time to time, usually at festivals, and there's no animosity. It's never awkward. We hang out and it's cool. It's just not what it was and it never will be.

In addition to freaking out over hardcore with S.O.D. in '85, Charlie, Frankie, and I were listening to rap all day long. That was actually nothing new. Back in the day, when we weren't listening to Maiden, we'd be cranking Run DMC, LL Cool J, and Eric B. & Rakim, all that shit that came out from '81 to '85, even before Public Enemy. I loved it as much as I loved metal. One night my friend and guitar tech John Rooney and I were sitting in my tiny bedroom in my mom's house, and my gear was out. We started writing rap lyrics about being in Anthrax. "We're Anthrax and we take no shit / and we don't care for writing hits."

Neither of us was a rapper, but we rapped these verses back and forth and cracked each other up. I plugged in my guitar and played the Jewish folk song "Hava Nagila" while John continued to rap. I said, "This is fucking ridiculous! This is the stupidest thing ever. I can't wait to show it to the rest of the band. They're going to die!" Little did I know we were planting the seed for one of Anthrax's most popular songs, "I'm The Man."

Chapter 12

A LESSON IN VIOLENCE

When John and I started writing "I'm The Man," I just thought it was funny. I didn't think it was something we would do on a record. A few days later, we were rehearsing in the city, and John and I showed Charlie and Frankie what we had come up with. They loved it, and suddenly it wasn't just a funny joke. It was something funny that we actually could do. The song is a rap-metal hybrid—possibly the first one ever recorded. Run DMC were sampling guitars; we were actually playing them and drumming and rapping. So if I'm not wrong, we were the first metal band to mix hip-hop in their music.

Although we were really serious about our love for rap, the song is a total joke. Each verse starts like an actual rap song, but with super-dumb lyrics, and then Charlie flubs the last line. We correct him and then the song breaks into this thrash part that ends with Frankie doing an impression of Taylor Negron's character, Julio, in the Rodney Dangerfield movie *Easy Money*, saying, he's "the man" and is "so bad he should be in detention." Stupidly awesome, right?

Here's a snippet: "Charlie, beat the beats, the beats you beat / The only thing harder's the smell of my feet / So listen up close or you might get dissed / Go drain the lizard or take a . . . chair! / It's piss! Damn . . . watch the beat!"

We split up the lines between the three of us. Danny and Joey didn't listen to rap at all, so we didn't include them, although when we played the song live starting in 1986, Charlie would come off his drum kit, and Joey would play the drums while Danny held down the guitar parts, freeing up the three of us to live out our Run DMC fantasies. We had the song completely written and the parts divided up. We knew we could do a really good job with it in the studio, but then we thought it would be even cooler if we had the Beastie Boys come in and rap with us.

This was before they put out *Licensed to Ill* in 1986 and blew the lid off everything. We knew the Beastie Boys from hanging out in New York. They were a punk band before they started rapping. So we got hold of them and asked if they'd do this rap-metal hybrid, "I'm The Man," with us. They were totally into it. Ad-Rock said, "Just tell us when. We'll come to the studio and we'll do it. All good."

We planned to work on it some more later, but we had to change focus because our agency booked us a tour opening for W.A.S.P. and Black Sabbath. We hated W.A.S.P. We didn't like their music, and their singer, Blackie Lawless, was an arrogant prick, though the rest of the guys in the band were pretty cool to us, especially guitarist Chris Holmes—the guy best known for chugging a bottle of vodka in front of his mom during an interview for the movie *The Decline of Western Civilization II: The Metal Years* while reclining on a flotation device in a swimming pool. But Black Sabbath—holy shit! Going on the road with Tony Iommi, the man who literally invented metal and the first heavy thing my uncle played me way back when I was a kid—that was mind blowing.

There was just one drawback. The Black Sabbath of 1986 wasn't the Black Sabbath that made *Paranoid* or even *Born Again*. Iommi was the only original member. Bassist and lyricist Geezer Butler left the band after the *Born Again* tour and didn't come back until Sabbath reunited with Ronnie James Dio on *Dehumanizer* in 1992. When we went out with Sabbath, the band was supporting the album *Seventh Star*, which was commercial and critical flop. The cover was just a picture of Tony in the desert, and the record jacket had to say "Black Sabbath Featuring Tony Iommi," since it didn't feature Geezer. Iommi was backed on the tour by vocalist Glenn Hughes, bassist Dave "the Beast" Spitz, and drummer Eric Singer. In other words, audiences didn't exactly flock to the shows. We were supposed to be out for a month, and they canceled the tour after five dates because the ticket sales were weak.

Still, we had fun while it lasted. Glenn Hughes was out of his mind back then. He was really drunk and silly all the time, and even though Sabbath didn't sound like Sabbath, we felt like we were in the company of rock royalty—at least from the headliners. As we might have expected, Blackie was a total asshole. He wouldn't talk to us, did extra-long sound checks so there wasn't time for us to sound check, and acted like a total diva. But whatever. We got to meet Tony Iommi and play five arena shows before the tour went belly up. To be able to perform for 3,000 people in an arena felt like a good omen, even if most of those people didn't know who we were. We thought, "This is it. We made it. We're in the big leagues. We're only ever going to do this now."

Of course, as soon as we were done with the tour, we were back in the clubs, but we didn't care. We had a taste of the big stage, and it whetted our appetites for more. We were going to work as hard as we needed to in order to get back there. Our agency scrambled for us when the Black Sabbath tour ended, and in four weeks we were out on a head-lining club tour. We had our own bus and we did well, playing for three to four hundred kids everywhere, meeting promoters, radio station programmers, and journalists all over the country and reconnecting with people we met two years earlier when we came through with Raven.

The record was selling well, people were buying T-shirts. It felt like we were back on an upward arc. We didn't make a dime because we were still recouping all the money the record label spent on us when we were in Ithaca, but we had a blast, and we all got along well because we had great chemistry. We felt like we needed each other to be Anthrax. Danny was still as cocky as the day I met him, but he was doing a great job onstage, and he had become the rock star he always wanted to be, so he was happy.

Joey had come into his own as the front man of the band, owning it every night onstage. Offstage he was different from the rest of us. We'd say, "Joey, you're from another planet. It's called upstate New York."

He was from Oswego and we were all from the city. Danny lived across the Tappan Zee Bridge, but that was close enough to the city to be considered a New Yorker. Joey was kind of hickish—not in a bad way. He was just different from us because of his upbringing upstate. He couldn't help who he was, and I think that's what made him stand out and made him special. No other band had a guy like him. He was a fish out of water, but he was a fish out of water who learned to breathe. It worked because he loved what he was doing even though the kind of music we played was still sort of foreign to him.

Being a singer was all he ever wanted to do, and now the band was blowing up worldwide; he loved it. Joey has that indescribable thing that great front men have. He's able to get up there and control the audience and keep them in the palm of his hand. There's a duality there because Joey's a total rock star even though he's totally *not* a rock star. He's the nicest, kindest, and most gentle human being, but when he gets onstage he's a fucking lunatic.

Even though we only played about a hundred shows between the fall of 1985 and the summer of 1986, touring for *Spreading the Disease* was really important in establishing us as a band that was going to stick around and that could bounce back after the departure of its lead vocalist.

The wildest show we played on the *Spreading the Disease* tour was April 26, 1986, at the Olympic Auditorium in Los Angeles. The place was notorious for crazy violent punk and hardcore shows, and the gig was promoted by Suicidal Tendencies singer Mike Muir. The bill his promotion company put together was Anthrax, D.R.I., COC, Possessed, and No Mercy, which was one of Mike's side bands. Billy Milano flew out and came to the show, and it's a good thing he did because it was a chaotic mess. There were 3,000 people there, and they were a volatile mix of skinheads, punks, metalheads, and Suicidal gang-looking dudes. Can't we all just get along? Fuck no!

The Suicidals were running security for the show, which made about as much sense as the Hells Angels handling security at Altamont, and everyone knows how well that turned out. Skinheads were getting onstage just to fight with the Suicidals. By the time we got onstage, the audience was a sea of brawls. About thirty minutes into our set, someone jumped from the seats behind the stage and ran through Charlie's drums, knocking over part of his kit. Not long after that some big biker-looking dude got on the stage, and one of the Suicidals smashed the guy's head in with the bottom of a mike stand. He was lying unconscious and bleeding on the stage. We said, "That's it. We're out of here," and we got the fuck off the stage. We went straight to our dressing room and saw that it had been completely trashed. Everything was destroyed, so we made a beeline for our bus. We locked the door and sat there waiting for our crew to show up so we could leave.

A few minutes later, Billy came stomping onto the bus. His shirt was torn and he was filthy. There was blood all over his hands, shirt, and pants. We thought he had been stabbed. "Don't worry. It's not my blood!" he growled.

"What the fuck happened to you?" I said.

He laughed. "Every skinhead in LA thinks he's a fucking tough guy. Every skinhead in LA wants to fight the guy from New York. So I fucking had at it."

He beat up ten guys in the crowd that started shit with him. He looked like it, too. There was so much blood, it looked like he'd been next to someone who stepped on a land mine.

The skinheads weren't always the ones causing trouble. A lot of times the security was just as bad. They didn't know what to do with cross-over crowds, and they usually targeted hardcore fans as the trouble-makers. When the skins entered the mosh pit and started jumping the barricade, security got freaked out and sometimes started pounding fans for no reason. We stopped plenty of shows on the *Spreading the Disease* tour to scream at security to stop beating kids up. When we played Albuquerque, New Mexico, a few days before the LA show, a bunch of kids with shaven heads were dancing at the front and scurrying over the barricade. Instead of pushing the fans back into the crowd, the security guards grabbed them and threw them out of the venue. When I saw that, I stopped the show and said, "C'mon, these guys aren't hurting anyone. If you don't let them back in here right now, we're done. We'll just leave. We're not playing another fucking note until that happens."

The crowd went nuts, and all these security guards crowded together to confer. Then this guy with a different colored T-shirt joined them. He must have been their boss. Next thing we knew, eight of the dudes who were kicked out were back in the venue. We started playing again, and the security all gathered tight together at the barricade. One of them was beating on a kid. I leaned over and punched the guard in the back of the head.

"You big, fat fucking Nazi," I said. "Stop beating up these kids. There are a thousand of them. What if they all rushed the stage and started beating the fuck out of you?"

The guard jumped up on the stage and rushed at me. I took off my guitar and swung it like a baseball bat. The guy jumped back. Then our Hulk-like security guy, Billy Pulaski, pulled the guitar out of my hands, grabbed me, and threw me behind him. He got between me and the guard, and the security guy stopped and went back into the crowd. The audience went wild. They loved it.

After the show we were in our dressing room, and our tour manager came up and said there was a gang of security guards waiting outside to beat us up. They were between the door and the bus. We didn't know if we should call the cops or make a run for it. Suddenly, two of the skinheads who were kicked out that I got back into the show came up to me: "Hey, we can help. Just hold on." They left and came back five minutes later. One of them said, "Alright, let's go. We have a bunch of people outside and we're going to get you to your bus." Sure enough, we went out, and there were a dozen or more skinheads and other dudes between where the guards were waiting for us and where we were. The skins circled us and walked us to our bus. We didn't say anything, but these guys were yelling at the guards: "Yeah, you think you're fucking tough now, you fucking assholes! Let's go!" Since there were a lot more skinheads than security guards, we were able to walk right to our bus and drive away.

Another great moment on the *Spreading* tour came the night we played the Arcadia Theater in Dallas. That's where we recorded our performance of "I'm The Man," which we used for the live version of the *I'm The Man* EP. More significantly, that was the night I met the guys in Pantera. This was back when Terry Glaze was singing for them, before Phil Anselmo came in and they became the Pantera that would shake the world. They were a different band back then and they looked totally glam, but under the hairspray they were awesome dudes.

They weren't actually at our show, but Dimebag Darrell's girlfriend Rita Haney was there in the afternoon. She was a skinny little punk rock girl with purple hair, and she was all excited: "After you guys play, you have to come to this club and see this band, Pantera. They're awesome," she said. "They play their own songs, but mostly covers. They even play Anthrax songs. They fuckin' love you guys. They'd be so jazzed. They can't come to your show because they have to play, but if you came to their show it would mean the world to them."

We used to get invited to see bands we didn't know all the time, and we usually politely declined or just didn't go. But we had nothing else to do in Dallas, so a bunch of us went. There was a big crowd there, about a thousand people, because they were the big local band. During the show, we got onstage and played "Metal Thrashing Mad" with them. Afterward, I got stinking drunk because that's what you do with Pantera. The next night Pantera opened for us down in Houston and the partying continued. Dime and I joked around, talked about gear, and laughed our asses off. I mentioned to him how I thought he killed it on guitar and I'd love to do some stuff with him in the future. I'm sure I meant it, but I had no idea it would actually happen on three of our future albums.

Every day on tour was a blast and *Spreading the Disease* was selling. Megaforce shipped around 19,000 copies and they sold out right away. One day Jonny called us and said, "We're up to 50,000 copies!" That was a big deal for a metal band on its first major-label album. Next thing we knew, we had sold 100,000! The bigger we got, the crazier the crowds got. And the more resentment built up from the people who thought we had turned into big major-label sellouts, even though everything we had done was heavy as fuck and our next album would be one of the fastest, heaviest thrash records ever released.

As much as I loved hardcore and CBGBs matinees, I eventually stopped going because I started receiving threats. I don't know if kids were jealous or suddenly thought I felt like I was above them. I totally didn't, but all it took was one misunderstanding for everything to go belly up. For the *Spreading the Disease* tour, we printed up a T-shirt featuring the old-school "NOT" man on a skateboard, and there was the NYHC logo on the sleeve because I had been going to CBGB Sunday matinee hardcore shows since 1983 and the music was a big part of my life, regardless of the fact that I played in a metal band and had long hair. To me, the hardcore scene was all about individuality. It meant doing whatever you did and being yourself. That's one of the things so many of the bands at the time were preaching, and I took it to heart.

Then at some point the scene started to change. By 1986 there was new blood. And a lot of the kids who probably a week earlier were listening to Ratt and Dokken decided to shave their heads and start going to hardcore shows because they were pressured into thinking it was cool. It really seemed like they were trying to distance themselves from their past. Inevitably, someone with an axe to grind saw the shirt we printed with the NYHC logo and started a rumor that Anthrax tried to trademark the design. There was absolutely no truth to that, but kids started making a big stink.

One Sunday around the fall of 1986, I went to a hardcore show. There was no one of note on the bill, but I had nothing better to do. I was living in my apartment in Forest Hills, and a few of these sixteen- or seventeen-year-old kids with freshly shaven heads followed me on the subway home from the city, got off the train when I got off, and trailed me on Queens Boulevard onto Union Turnpike. I knew they were behind me, and I was weighing my options. Finally I turned around and said, "What's your problem, motherfuckers?"

"Fuck you, poser," one of them said. "We're going to kick your ass."

"Fine. Three of you on one, pussies! Let's go. One of you's getting knocked out, that's all I'm gonna say. So let's go, right now!"

I stood my ground against these three punks wearing their brand-new Murphy's Law shirts, trying to represent. They stood there and shouted, "Fuck you, faggot. You're not hardcore."

"I'm not claiming to be anything," I said. "I'm just a guy going home from a show at CBGB. If you have a problem with that, let's go. I'm not afraid."

Finally, they turned around and walked away. But I stopped going to shows at CBGB after that for a while because, who knows? The next guy who had a problem with me might be holding a knife or a gun. I didn't want to put myself in that position down on the Lower East Side, where a bunch of assholes were just waiting to beat me up so they could say they took down the dude from Anthrax. That could have very easily happened and it just wasn't worth it.

Chapter 13

THE HORROR OF IT ALL

hen we were done touring for *Spreading the Disease*, we were excited to go into the studio with the Beastie Boys to make the real version of "I'm The Man." But before we could get to that, we had to finish writing *Among the Living*, which we had started on tour. A lot of people still consider that our quintessential record; it was definitely the right album for the right time—fast and thrashy, pissed off and energetic as fuck. Everything we learned as a band from recording *Fistful of Metal* up through *Spreading the Disease* went into the songs. If Anthrax were an education in heavy, *Among the Living* was our master's thesis. It was a product of its environment, bred from the excitement and aggression of being a major part of an ever-evolving thrash scene. We didn't need amphetamines or blow to make songs that ripped; we were riding high on the thrill of our experiences playing with bands we respected and making the music we loved.

The springboard for the whole record, the song that set us directly on the path of no return, was "A.I.R.," the last track we wrote for *Spreading the Disease*. We had actually finished recording *Spreading* and were gonna start mixing, and Charlie said, "I have one more song we need to get on the record. We have to work on this." At first we were like, "C'mon, we're already late. We've got the album. Let's go." Then he played me the riff and I thought, "Holy shit, this will totally *make* the record. It's different from most of the other songs, but it's complementary. It's got a lot of energy and it's catchy." So he came back to Ithaca and we all worked on that one song. To me, that was the beginning of our true identity as Anthrax. If that song didn't make it onto *Spreading*, it would have been on *Among the Living*. From there, we were on fire and nothing was going to stop us.

While we were supporting *Spreading*, we wrote "I Am the Law." Charlie played us these anthemic riffs and the Judge Dredd connection just clicked in my brain. The music just sounded like Mega-City One to me. For those unfamiliar with the story line of the British comic book, Dredd lives in a postapocalyptic world where the cops (judges) arrest criminals and sentence them on the scene, and the punishments are severe. Judge, jury, and executioner, Dredd is the biggest bad-ass of all of the judges. Another song I wrote was "Indians," which was an effort to be more politically relevant. It's about the plight of Native Americans who were rounded up and forced to live on shitty reservations. The idea for the song came to me because the riff sounded like American Indian music and Joey's mother was part Iroquois (so I was told), so it was perfect. We tested out "I Am the Law" and "Indians" on tour, and they both went over well, so they made the cut early.

We were so used to how each other worked at that point that the rest of the songs poured out of us. We had a style, a particular sound we all knew was Anthrax, and we wrote to fit that format. We knew from S.O.D. that we could play as fast as anybody, so when we wrote a thrash part, our attitude was, "Let's make that even faster." And from experience we knew exactly when to inject a slow mosh part for maximum effect. Some of the lyrics were about ridiculous experiences we underwent as a touring band. "Caught in a Mosh," for instance, is about our guitar tech Artie Ring.

We were playing at the Rainbow Music Hall in Denver, Colorado, in '86 and a kid climbed onstage and fucked up my pedal board. Artie ran out to push this kid offstage, and the two got tangled up, fell into the crowd, and got sucked up by the pit. One second Art was there, the next he was gone, like something flushed down a toilet. Eventually, Artie climbed back onstage. We finished the show and got on the bus. The next morning Artie came crawling out of his bunk, and he could barely move. He was holding his back hunched over, and when I asked him what was wrong he said, "Oh, man, I got caught in a mosh." We thought that was the funniest thing we'd ever heard, because Artie was my height and skinner than me. The last place he'd ever want to be was in a mosh pit getting trampled. Immediately a lightbulb illuminated over my head. "That's a song title, right there!" I wrote all the verses about being stuck in places you wouldn't want to be in life.

I wanted to have a couple of socially relevant songs on the album as well, so I wrote "One World." If "Aftershock" from *Spreading the Disease* was about the result of a nuclear conflict between the US and Russia—the endgame—"One World" addressed the steps man could take to avoid total annihilation: "Russians, they're only people like us / Do you really think they'd blow up the world, they don't love their lives less / America, stop singing "Hail to the Chief" / Instead of thinking SDI we should be thinking of peace." Hey, I was young and still thought I could change the world with the power of metal!

"Efilnikufesin (N.F.L.)" is about John Belushi, a hero of mine. It's about what a waste his overdose was because he was so fucking talented and had so much more to offer the world, and it was kind of my way of warning kids to stay away from narcotics. That was a big thing for me. I wasn't preachy about it, I just hated that shit.

Whenever I smoked the pin joints in school, I never got high. Weed never did anything for me. So I had virtually no interest in drugs, and that carried over into Anthrax. Blow became all the fashion in the eighties, and even at our level, we'd see friends in bands who were always wasted on the stuff; they would get it for free because no one could actually afford it. I hated when people I hung out with were on blow. None of them would shut up. They'd just talk bullshit for hours and hours. Worse still was the antisocial aspect of it. No one wanted to do it in front of you, so they went into the bathroom to snort it. Then they'd come out sniffling, and it was obvious what they'd been up to. That shame factor made me hate it even more. I thought, if you wanna do it, just do it. Don't fucking hide away like a rodent. And if you don't want to share it with people, then just wait until you get home. Everything about cocaine turned me off. Just the idea of putting something up my nose was unappealing. I have to admit I was kind of scared of it, too. Some people overdosed and died on cocaine, not to say anything about heroin. I've always stayed away from all that shit.

I had other ways to escape besides drugs, and I wrote about them on *Among the Living*. Two songs on the album come from Stephen King stories. He was such a big part of my life. His books were so creative and inspiring, especially *The Stand,* which "Among the Living" is based on. And then "A Skeleton in the Closet" was about the King novella *Apt Pupil,* which is about a teenager who discovers a Nazi war criminal and blackmails the guy into telling him detailed stories about his horrific crimes. Stephen King stories became such a major part of my life at that point that they were really all I knew. I didn't understand much about the real world when I was twenty-two. Most of my life was spent in fantasy land.

Anthrax were getting ready to head into Top Cat rehearsal studios in New York in July 1986 to finish writing and rehearsing *Among the Living.* I was sitting in my mom's house with all my gear when the phone rang. It was Kirk Hammett and he seemed frazzled. He was calling from Evansville, Indiana, and he sounded out of breath. "So, James was riding down a hill on a skateboard and he fell off and broke his wrist. He can't play guitar and we don't want to cancel any shows so we need someone to come out and play guitar and James will just sing. Can you possibly do it?"

He was speaking so quickly I didn't think I understood what he was saying at first and asked him to repeat himself. Yeah, what I heard was right. Metallica wanted me to come out and play rhythm guitar for them on the *Master of Puppets* tour. I was stoked. "I'd love to. Of course I'll do it!" I told Kirk.

All I would have to do was learn the *Master of Puppets* stuff. I knew everything else. Then reality hit me. We had an album to make, and we were supposed to be in the studio in three days to finish writing and rehearsing before we started recording. I told Kirk that, and he asked if there was any way to push it back. I told him I'd check with Jonny Z, and he gave me the number of the hotel where they were staying. I called Jonny at 11 p.m. and said, "Dude, I just got a call from Metallica. James broke his arm and they're asking me to come out and learn the songs and finish the Ozzy tour, and I really want to do it."

Jonny immediately dashed my hopes. He told me we had deposits on the studio and we were on a deadline. "You can't just take a month off because you want to," he said. "This will fuck up your whole schedule going into the next year."

I already knew the answer before I called him. I was just hoping he'd do some magic and make it happen like he did when he got Metallica to New York to record *Kill 'Em All*. I called Kirk back and explained the situation. I apologized, and they ended up getting James's guitar tech John Marshall to fill in. That was a major bummer for me, but I was being totally unrealistic when I originally told Kirk I could do it.

We saw Metallica soon enough when they invited us to tour Europe with them in the fall of '86. The first date was September 10 in Cardiff, Wales. There were six weeks of shows booked and they were all sold out. We both went over so great every single show. And Metallica were incredible even though James still wasn't playing guitar because of his broken wrist.

A tip for new bands hitting the road: it's okay to have a friend be your guitar tech, but make sure he's someone who can play well so in the event of an emergency you have a fill-in right there on hand. It benefitted Metallica, and it didn't hurt us any when Lilker left the band. At that point in their career, Metallica were in a bus and our gear was on their truck. We were in a cargo van with luggage. We had a driver because none of us wanted to attempt to drive in the UK on the wrong side of the road. We had one crew guy to help us out. He helped set up the drums, and Metallica's crew helped with our guitars. There wasn't much in the way of amenities. We got a dressing room every day but we weren't getting a per diem, so we had no money. Metallica had catering for the tour, but there was a mix-up the first few days, and the catering company didn't know that we were supposed to be getting fed, too.

For those days we all dug into our pockets for change to buy shitty snack foods like sausage rolls and English pizza. Now that's *real* torture—forcing a bunch of New Yorkers to eat the English version of pizza. It's all dough with lumps of cheese and kernels of corn.

The first day of the tour, our driver offered to run down the road and get some pizzas for us. We gave him a bunch of money to come back with four pies. He returned thirty minutes later holding the pizzas sideways and had no idea he had done anything wrong. When we opened a box all the cheese and sauce had slid into a mushy pile decorated with corn niblets. We had nothing else and no more money, so we were stuck in this cold dressing room pulling chunks of cheese from the edge of the box, replacing them on the warped, slimy slices of pizza crust and trying to avoid the corn niblets. I thought, "Fuck this. Take me home now. I hate it here. I don't know how Iron Maiden survive in this country."

Then we started the show, and I *really* wished I was still at home in my mom's house. We played great and the crowd loved it, but during the entire set we got showered with saliva. We started with "A.I.R.," and it began raining spit—not just on Joey or me, but on all of us. I thought, "Oh no, they fuckin' hate us!" Then we ended the song and everyone screamed and applauded. So we started the next song, and sure enough the fountains of phlegm started again. It happened every song. We wondered if it was some kind of joke they played on opening bands. Halfway through the set, one of the guys in Metallica's British crew told us, "They're spitting on you because they fucking love you! It's an old punk rock tradition called gobbing."

I was thinking, "I wish they didn't love us so much."

We had played the Hammersmith Palais, our first UK show, in May of 1986, and there wasn't any spitting and they loved us that night as well. Apparently, gobbing was a semi-recent phenomenon that started with English punk audiences in the mid- to late seventies. In metal it was short lived, thank God, but we happened to be there right when it was at its prime. It's a good thing Billy Milano wasn't there. He would have killed everyone in the crowd. Metallica got it twice as bad as we did.

During Cliff's bass solo the spotlight was on him. He was throwing his head up and down and his hair was flying everywhere. The spit that spattered him looked like swarms of bugs flying around a street lamp in the summer. Hundreds of gobs landed in his hair. It stank like bad breath. It's a good thing they had showers at those venues. We were only gobbed one other time, in Ireland in 1989 when we were headlining. We adamantly told the crowd, "If you spit on us we're leaving." We actually left a show in Omagh, Northern Ireland, after two songs because they wouldn't stop spitting.

The last night of the UK tour with Metallica was in London at the Hammersmith Odeon, and Music for Nations threw a big aftershow party for us at the Forum Hotel. We were having a blast, thinking, "Wow, look at us! We just played a sold-out UK tour. Everybody loves us." We were high on adrenaline, drunk on beer, and about as rational as kindergarteners.

Cliff and I ran into a room that had chutes for the laundry, and we unzipped our flies and pissed down them. At one point, there was a circle of us standing there, me, Kirk, Cliff, James, Charlie, and Frankie. We all had drinks and made a stupid metal pact like, "Headbanging bros forever!" We toasted and drank. Then all of a sudden Cliff and Kirk got serious.

They told us that when they got home from the tour they were going to fire Lars. They said they couldn't take being in the band with him anymore and were done putting up with him. I knew there were issues between him and some of the other members, but every band has its problems. They usually work themselves out.

Cliff explained the plan: "The three of us have agreed. When we get home from this tour, we're gonna get rid of Lars, even if it means we can't use the name Metallica anymore." Somehow Lars owned the name at that point, or at least they thought he did. I looked at James and said, "This is crazy but you are Metallica. Everyone is going to know who you are even if you use a different name. At this point, everyone already knows you. It doesn't matter what you call yourself. It's still gonna be you guys and your music."

It was weird to think of Lars being out of Metallica, and I hoped they'd be able to work things out with him and that it wouldn't be the end of the band, but I wanted to back my friends, and Kirk and Cliff were always the guys in the band I was closest to. We were all basically nerds who liked the same things: music, horror movies, and comic books.

I didn't ask why they were gonna kick Lars out. I figured it was because they wanted a better drummer, but apparently there was also a lot of business-related stuff going on behind the scenes they weren't thrilled with. That conversation ended the UK tour on a sobering note. We had a day off, and then we were scheduled to play twenty-seven more shows in Europe with Metallica.

The first date was in Lund, Sweden, on September 24, and that was a good gig because no one spat at us and everyone loved both bands. The next day we played Lillestrom, Norway, for about 4,000 people, which was also great. Then we went back to Sweden to play Solna, near Stockholm. That was Cliff's last show.

It was at a big gymnasium-type place that held thousands of kids. Normally, we'd stick around for Metallica's show and then hang out and goof around when they finished, leave at the same time, and head to the next city. We were on a bus now, which made traveling easier, but that night we decided to leave early because the roads were icy. There had been a storm, and our driver wanted to head to Copenhagen as soon as possible to avoid the streets freezing up. We figured we had another month on the road to hang out with Metallica, so no big deal. We saw the guys after we finished our set, and I said, "We're going to take off. We'll see you tomorrow in Denmark."

We got into Copenhagen and stepped off the bus around 9:30 the next morning. We had a hotel that night because we had the next day off. We were pretty groggy as we walked into the lobby to the front desk. I saw our tour manager talking to some guy, so I waved and said, "Hey Mark, what's up?" He had a look of total shock on his face. There was no color in his cheeks. He looked scared. Something was not good.

"The promoter for the show tonight says there's been an accident," he told me. "Metallica's bus crashed on the way here." Then he paused, and when he started to speak again he had to force the words out— almost cough them into existence. "Cliff was killed in the accident. Everybody else is okay. Lars had some minor injuries and was taken to a hospital."

My brain started spinning like a gyroscope. I replayed the sentence over and over: "Cliff was killed in the accident." After what seemed like five minutes but was probably only ten seconds, I shook my head and said, "Really? Really? You believe that?!?" I was in complete denial. "There's no way. I'm sure they just got too fucked up to make bus call and they made up this crazy story. We'll all laugh about it later."

Anything seemed more plausible than the thought that their bus had crashed and Cliff was actually dead. I had never heard of anything like that before. I'd never ever heard of any band's bus crashing let alone killing a member. It seemed completely unreal. When you're in this tour bubble and things are going great, you feel invincible. Something

like this happening was out of the realm of possibility. I asked the promoter, "Are you sure?"

"Yeah I'm sure," he said.

I didn't know what to say, didn't want to believe it. Then reality hit me like a sucker punch. People around us started talking about
what had happened. Fans showed up at the hotel to show their support.
Somehow everyone found out where we were staying and eventually
there was a big crowd in the street. Mark got a call that James and Kirk
were on their way to the hotel. Lars had checked out of the hospital.
He broke a toe but would be fine. He had family in Denmark, so I figured he was going to see them.

Mark asked if we would stay at the hotel to be with James and
Kirk when they arrived. Of course we would. Our friend was dead and
our other friends were grieving. It was insane. A couple hours later
James and Kirk showed up. James was heavily sedated and drunk at
the same time. Kirk said doctors had given James a bunch of sedatives
because he was freaking out, but they didn't put him to sleep so he kept
drinking. We were all in a room together, and James kept pounding
beer, vodka, whiskey—whatever was within his reach.

Kirk was pretty drunk, too, but stable. He told us what happened.
He wasn't awake when the bus crashed. All he knew was he was suddenly getting thrown around like a rag doll in a dryer. Then it stopped
and he got out of the bus and everyone was screaming. It was pitch
black. Everyone was trying to account for everybody else, and no one
could find Cliff. And then they saw his legs sticking out from under the
side of the bus, and they fucking lost their minds. I can't even imagine
what that was like, and I never want to know. Even to this day it's hard
for my brain to wrap around that image.

James started crying and screaming, "Cliff!!! Cliff!!" Then he became destructive. He kicked over lamps and threw bottles of booze.
Frankie and Charlie looked at each other and, without saying a word,
mutually decided to get James outside before the hotel had him arrested.
The hotel management wouldn't care that Cliff was dead. They'd just
want to prevent their place from getting trashed. The two of them took
James outside for a walk figuring maybe he'd calm down. I stayed inside with Kirk. We could hear James down the street screaming Cliff's

name over and over. I was completely heartsick. I hung out with Kirk a little while longer. He was finally passing out. He said, "I'm going to sleep, I don't think I'll see you in the morning." They were leaving super early to fly back to San Francisco.

We didn't know what we were doing. People were scrambling to try and get us flights, but we were supposed to be on the tour for five more weeks. Now, we had to try to change flights and no one had any money to buy new tickets. We were stuck in Copenhagen the whole next day, then Jonny Z figured out the cheapest way to get us home. We flew to London, stayed there for a day, then got a flight back to New York. As soon as I got home I showered, packed my bag, slept, then got up to fly to San Francisco.

I stayed at James's little apartment in the city and at Kirk's mom's house for a few days, hung out with Metallica, and then went to the funeral. I met Faith No More drummer Mike Bordin for the first time and their guitarist, Jim Martin; they were good friends with Cliff. We all hung out at Kirk's mom's house for hours every day drinking beer and talking. Those guys were already figuring out what to do next. I asked James what was happening with the Lars situation.

"We're not going to do that now," he said. "We can't lose two guys, we can't do it. We're going to find a new bass player. The last thing Cliff would want would be for us to not play music. That's the last thing that guy would want. We'll start looking soon and figure it out."

Within a couple of days, we were sitting around Kirk's house, making jokes. Someone said, "Get Lemmy." I suggested Gene Simmons. We were just throwing stupid names out there to keep the tone as light as possible, so we weren't all completely depressed. We drank and told stories about Cliff. It was so surreal. I half expected him to walk through the door and say, "Ha, ha. I got you guys!" It seemed like something Cliff would do.

Then Metallica were auditioning people. I thought Armored Saint's bassist Joey Vera was going to get the gig. He seemed like the obvious candidate. He's a great player and they were already friends. But he decided to stay with his band, which was doing pretty well on its own. Armored Saint had two records out on Chrysalis and were just about to record *Raising Fear*. Next thing I knew, they offered the job to

Flotsam and Jetsam bassist Jason Newsted. Michael Alago, who signed Metallica to Elektra, is the one who told me. I had never heard of Flotsam and Jetsam. I said, "Jason who?"

I finally got hold of Kirk, and he said, "Yeah, Jason is a great dude. He's ripping it up. He fits in really well and we're getting along great. I think we're going to go back to Europe and try to make up some of the shows, and hopefully you guys can come with us."

I hoped that would work out and it did. When Metallica made up the shows that were canceled when Cliff died, we went back out with them, and they were absolutely triumphant. It felt like snatching victory out of the jaws of defeat.

Chapter 14

MUBLANIKCUFECIN

The last song we wrote for *Among the Living* was "A.D.I. / Horror of It All," which is about Cliff's death: "Say goodbye, it's such a horror / My memories, there's nothing harder / Anger and hatred fill the page, so smash the walls, it's time to rage."

Cliff was the first person I really cared about who died. I had only lost two grandparents at that point—my dad's father, who I barely knew, and my mother's mom, who I did know and loved, but I was still very young (eleven) when she passed away. So Cliff's death hit me hard, and if nothing else, it filled me with fury and determination. Knowing a good friend could die in such a crazy way emphasized how frail, precious, and sometimes unfair life is. If anything, it made me more dedicated to do things our way because if we didn't, we might not get another chance.

We knew we wanted Eddie Kramer to produce *Among the Living* because he's a legend. We couldn't believe it when Island said they'd ask him and he said yes. He had worked with Jimi Hendrix, Led Zeppelin, David Bowie, the Rolling Stones. But the real reason we wanted him was because he produced some of the best KISS albums in the 1970s, *Alive!* and *Rock and Roll Over*. We loved the live feel he got from the bands he worked with. When you played a record he worked on, it sounded like the band was right there in your room. That's what we wanted with *Among the Living*. We didn't think *Fistful of Metal* or *Spreading the Disease* captured the power of our live show. We always felt like when we were at our best onstage and rehearsing, there was something transcendent and indescribable about our sound. We told Eddie that, and he was cool with it because that's how he had worked with some of his biggest bands, recording them in a live environment to capture them at their best.

It seemed like we were on the same page and we were psyched. There was a major buzz about our band, and we were working on what we felt were the best songs of our career with one of the best producers in the world. It was pretty much Anthrax in a live room with everything miked then Eddie hit record. Everyone had their parts down, and Joey had figured out how to best blend his muscular melodic vocals with our crushing riffs and trampling rhythms. While we were tracking, there was as much energy in the studio as in a sports arena during a critical playoff game.

I felt like we had the world by the throat and we were about to unleash this total monster that would flip the thrash metal scene upside down. After we finished recording at Quadradical Studio in Miami, we flew to Nassau, Bahamas, to mix the record at Chris Blackwell's Compass Point Studios, where Iron Maiden had worked. We thought, "We're finally doing what Maiden does." We knew we weren't nearly as big as Maiden, but we felt good that everyone was behind us. The label was happy because *Spreading the Disease* was successful, and they had huge hopes for *Among*. Back then labels still believed in building bands. They signed groups for five- to seven-record deals because they figured that's what it would take for a band to break. We were right on track, and we felt like we were in control of our own destiny. The new music we had was undeniable and would hit people like a brick across the face. From experience, I knew metalheads love that feeling.

But if we had let Eddie Kramer have his way, listening to *Among the Living* would have felt like being hit with a wet sponge. When it came to recording the album, Anthrax and Eddie were peas in a pod, but our philosophies couldn't have been more different when it came to mixing. At that point in time, the biggest album in the world was Def Leppard's *Hysteria*, which featured Mutt Lange's game-changing production. It sounded huge, and everything was layered and bathed in reverb. But that had nothing to do with Anthrax, and everyone knew it—or so we thought. We started mixing in the Bahamas, and toward the end of the first day Eddie said, "Come in around dinner time. I should have a rough for you guys to listen to."

We couldn't wait to hear it. We had played so well, with so much anger and energy, we were sure Eddie was going to make the album sound like a ferocious live show. We ran into the studio like children waiting for the ice cream truck. Then Eddie hit play, and everything we had done was completely drowned in reverb. It sounded washed, echoey, and artificial.

I said, "Eddie, it kinda sounds like there's too much reverb." I was really careful about what I said because it was Eddie Kramer and we had a great experience working and recording with him up to that point. I had nothing but respect for this man. But the mix sounded nothing like Anthrax. I said, "I'm not sure what's happening. What am I hearing?"

He said, "Well yeah, I have some reverb on this and I boosted the delay. I envision this as a very modern-sounding record."

I said, "Well, I don't know how that makes it sound modern, it just sounds like a big wash of sound. I can't distinguish anything. I can't make anything out. We're playing very fast and this kind of production doesn't work with music being played at this speed. It needs to be live, tight, and very dry."

He said, "Scott, that's already been done. You need to do something different!"

He was excited but I was getting mad.

"Eddie, this is different, but it's not right for Anthrax. It doesn't make sense. This doesn't work at all. You can't understand the song. Everything is washed out."

"The most successful album in the world right now is Def Leppard," replied Eddie. I could tell he was getting irritated. "Listen to that production. It's so modern."

"We're not Def Leppard. You can't just put that kind of production on Anthrax. It doesn't work."

He was being as stubborn about his position as I was about mine. There was no way in a million years I was going to let our album sound like this. It would have been the end of us. So I said, "Eddie, you need to take all that reverb and delay off."

"Don't tell me how to mix a record," he snapped. "I've been producing since before you were born."

I put my foot down. "Look, man, you're a great producer. I love your stuff. But this is our album. This is Anthrax's record. You're going to go on and make five hundred more records with five hundred different bands, but this is *our* album. We'll live or die by this. Maybe we don't get another chance after this record, who knows? It's gotta be the way we want it."

I thought that would do it, but he kept at it. "That's not the fucking record I'm making."

"Then we have a big problem here," I said. I couldn't believe I was being so stubborn and forceful with Eddie Kramer, but our career was on the line. "We need to hear this without all the reverb. Will you take all the fucking reverb off and dry it up and make it sound like something you did in the seventies?"

He slammed a fist on the control board. "Do you think your fucking opinion is God? Who made you God?"

"My opinion is not God, Eddie, but about Anthrax, it is." At that point, I didn't care if one of my heroes thought I was a whiny asshole. "Either pull the fucking reverb or don't mix the record and we'll call the label and get someone else to do it."

"Fine, fine! Come back in two hours."

He tried to make the record sound bad by yanking every bit of reverb and delay off *everything*. Bands usually have some reverb on the vocals at least. But he pulled it all to be a dick. Maybe he thought we wouldn't like it and we'd see things his way. That wasn't the case. It sounded fucking great, like we were getting pummeled in the chest. We were ecstatic and totally effusive about how great we thought it was. This was the sound we had in our heads that our other two records failed to capture. I think our enthusiasm won him over. He saw how excited we were about how our music was sounding, and he dropped his attitude. We had crossed the line in the sand and everything changed for the better. From that point on, we got along amazingly. He put a little something on a snare or vocal to give it extra punch, and we were fine with that. We were working together. I only wish I had a copy of what Eddie originally envisioned so I could play it for people and say, "This is the record Eddie wanted to make." Mutt Lange definitely changed the fuckin' game with *Hysteria,* but we didn't want to be any part of it.

We finally recorded the studio version of "I'm The Man" during the *Among the Living* session. When we listened back to it, we thought it was cool, funny, and original, but we wondered where we were going to put the Beastie Boys. All the lines were taken. Either someone had to give up their part, or we had to go without having the Beasties on it. None of us felt like we should cut out anything we did because it sounded really good.

Months later we bumped into the Beasties at a show in New York, and Ad-Rock asked, "Hey, whatever happened to that song?" *Licensed to Ill* was out but hadn't blown up yet. I don't know if that would have made a difference, but I said to them, "Oh, we did it ourselves and it turned out really good. I can't wait for you guys to hear it." They didn't care. It's not like they were sitting around waiting for the phone to ring to come do "I'm The Man" with Anthrax. Of course, it might have been really cool to have them on it, but it did great on its own even though we never expected anything to come from it.

We couldn't put it on *Among the Living* because it would have been totally out of place with the other songs. That was a really dark, angry record, and we didn't want to interrupt the flow. Plus, we certainly didn't think that anyone who liked our band was going to like that song. Our UK label put out a twelve-inch single for "I Am the Law," and I asked them, "What if we throw 'I'm The Man' on there as a B-side? If people hate it, it will go away quick. It's a B-side. It's a joke. Who cares? Ha, ha, it was funny, we'll never do it again."

They did it and to everyone's surprise it became the biggest thing we'd ever done. Within months it went from the B-side of "I Am the Law" to being its own EP, featuring two studio versions (one was censored for radio), a live version, live recordings of "I Am the Law" and "Caught in a Mosh," and a cover of Black Sabbath's "Sabbath Bloody Sabbath."

We played "I'm The Man" in 1987 at the Castle Donington Monsters of Rock festival in front of 80,000 people, and they sang along with every single word. It made no sense, yet at the same time it made perfect sense because it reiterated that we were not just one thing. We were a thrash band, but we could fuck around with rap, insert "Hava Nagila" in the middle of a song, and cover Black Sabbath all in the same breath. Still, I wondered, "Don't people realize this is a fucking joke that my friend John and I wrote in my bedroom? I'm playing 'Hava Nagila,' which is fucking Bar Mitzvah music that a DJ plays when everyone gets in a circle and dances the hora, and the family of the kid getting the Bar Mitzvah puts him on a chair and lifts him into the air. Does anyone have any idea what's going on here?"

It didn't matter. People ate it up, couldn't get enough of it, and to this day it's probably our most requested song. We still bust it out every once in a while. We'll do two verses and two choruses and then go into another song while the crowd loses its shit. One thing I've always loved about Anthrax is that we have few parameters. When Slayer play, they have a certain image. There's no smiling in Slayer. It's all rage and ferocity. Even Metallica and Megadeth have always looked and acted a certain way onstage. It's not a façade; it's more like who they are when they're all playing together. Anthrax never felt the need to fit into a certain mold, and that has allowed us to experiment. We did "I'm The Man," and then we came back a few years later with Public Enemy and played a metal cover of "Bring the Noise," and our fans loved it. I think our attitude comes from the fact that we're all New Yorkers. We're not from San Francisco or LA. Ever since Neil Turbin left, our attitude was, "We are who we are and we're just going to be ourselves."

Sometimes we're brutal, sometimes we're silly. We are our audience. I think we learned that from the Ramones. We're just a bunch of dudes playing in a band and writing songs and going on tour, and there's no reason for us to ever have to put on a game face or a band face. If something's funny, we're going to laugh. If we're happy, we're going to smile. If we're pissed, we're going to sound angry. Why only have one emotion in your art? I don't feel the same way all day long. People's moods change and so should their music.

That's why I started wearing shorts in concert. When Neil was in the band, I wore jams all day long until I had to put on my stupid leather pants to be in Anthrax, and I was like, "Fuck, now I can't move around." I had to wear a metal belt and leather pants. It was fucking idiotic, like asking a basketball player to wear boots and tight Levis.

I believed strongly in having integrity and showing people who I was, at least in Anthrax. When it came to my home life, that was a different story. The whole time I was fucking around, Marge had no idea our relationship was a sham and I was living a lie. When she graduated from college, she left Boston and came back to New York. We moved in together because that's what was expected from Jewish kids who grew up in Queens. We were supposed to get married and have babies and raise our kids with all the other Jewish people in the neighborhood. Marge graduated with a fancy degree from Northeastern and got a job at IBM that came with a good salary. So it didn't matter that I was broke. She supported me.

The whole time I ran around like a maniac, touring and making records, there was this part ingrained in me to get married and do what was expected. It almost seemed like part of the programming in my DNA. So, against my better judgment, Marge and I got engaged and started making wedding plans. I knew it was a huge fucking mistake, but I figured everything would somehow work out. I had cheated on her from time to time, and I didn't know if that was going to change. There are lots of guys who are unfaithful to their wives. Maybe I was just one of them. At that point, living a lie seemed easier than breaking up. There was too much baggage that would come along with that. It was terrifying just to think about.

It's not like I hated her. We got along fine, but I wasn't attracted to her anymore and more importantly I wasn't in love with her. It wasn't like I was out there looking to cheat on her, but when I was on tour and doing stuff, if the situation arose, I would go for it. I was twenty-two years old and I was having fun. I didn't stop myself. So on November 27 we got married. We had a big fucking Jewish wedding at a temple. My whole band were there, James and Kirk were there and they were all wearing suits. Her parents were more religious than mine, so it was important to them to have a long religious ceremony. There was a cantor who sang and a rabbi. At one point I looked out during the service, and James was sleeping because the rabbi was droning on and on. I stood there the whole time thinking, "What are you doing?" It was such a façade, such an act. At least it was a great party and everyone got drunk.

Anthrax went on tour right after we got married, so we didn't have a honeymoon until later, when we went to Disney World. Romantic, huh? That kind of foreshadowed what a dream come true this marriage was going to be. Anyway, I made a promise to myself that I would try to stay mostly faithful, and that lasted about a year. Then, of course, I started fucking around again. It's not like I was sleeping with Marge. I know a lot of people get married and suddenly they're not having sex anymore. Usually it's because the wife isn't as interested as she used to be. In this case, it was me. I made every excuse I could think of.

She'd make a move and I'd say, "I can't. I have to have enough energy to play later." Once I even told her I had a headache. I actually said that. The sad fact was I wasn't attracted to her anymore. She had put on a lot of weight and was turning into her mom. Her mom was a large woman and her dad was big as well and I couldn't tell her she was fat and needed to lose weight. I was an asshole, but I wasn't *that* much of an asshole. Maybe I was, but I was just a little more subtle.

I got her a gym membership as a birthday present one year. My genius idea was that it would be a hint that she needed to lose weight and maybe she'd go on a diet even if she didn't actually go to the gym. When I gave it to her, I wasn't trying to hurt her. But, understandably, she started crying. It sucked because she never did anything to me. She was always sweet, kind, and loving, and I was twenty-two and I wasn't in love with her. I should have broken up with her when she went away to college, but I was too much of a pussy.

Fortunately, so much was happening with Anthrax, I wasn't often at home. We started with a short headline tour in Japan. I didn't hook up with anyone there, but Danny Spitz sure did. Once I came out of my hotel room to go down to the lobby, and there were four girls standing in the hallway in a line. His door opened and a girl came out and he was standing there in a towel. He smiled at me and said, "Next," and the first girl in line walked in. I was like, "Damn, I didn't know Spitz had such game!"

Chapter 15

DEBAUCHERY & DESTRUCTION

Even though I was married and I had hooked up with chicks on the road, I still had *no* game. A few times on tour, I'd look for a girl at an aftershow party, and it was easy enough to find one I was attracted to. Everyone knew I was the guitarist of Anthrax: "Hey, uh, you want to come see the bus?" But if they said yes, it seemed so lame to me that I'd just take a picture with them and go read a book in my bunk.

Some girls would come on the bus and have sex, and then they'd say, "I have to go. My boyfriend is waiting outside." That never happened to me, but I've seen that go down so many times, usually with guys from the crew. It didn't matter to them. They'd just say, "Alright, tell him you'll be out in twenty minutes." Guys in bands might get laid sometimes, but the dudes in the crew get most of the action. They're the ones who ended up in threesomes and orgies and have all these stories to tell later.

Artie Ring, the tech I wrote "Caught in a Mosh" about, heard that some bands kept photo books of naked groupies, so he got a Polaroid camera and started making an album. He'd get girls on the bus, ask them to take off their clothes, and have them make these weird faces or poses. The albums got pretty good. They weren't erotic, but they were really funny. There's a part of me that wishes I would have taken more advantage of the decadence back then, but most of the time I couldn't be bothered. The whole thing seemed so stupid. I was like, "Really? This chick just bent over and stuck a cigarette up her ass for a fucking Polaroid, and now she wants to have sex with me? No thanks."

After a while Artie got bored of taking regular nude photos so he got creative. He painted faces on girls' butts and threw deli meat at their privates and took photos long before Howard Stern or Marilyn Manson ever did it. I'm sure he didn't do anything Led Zeppelin didn't do first. And we never got a girl to get it on with a red snapper or a mud shark. We wouldn't have known where to get them even if we had wanted to.

Once, Artie got a bunch of girls to pose in shapes that formed the letters of the alphabet, and they'd all have carrots, celery, Sharpies, bananas, you name it, sticking out of every orifice. That was definitely good for a laugh. They were all legal age and nobody got hurt, and it kept the crew happy.

The first show on the *Among the Living* tour was May 26, 1987, with Metal Church opening at the Penny Arcade, a five-hundred-seat club in Rochester, New York. During the spring and summer, we played midsized venues, then we went to Europe from September to October and did a big headlining tour. In no time, we went from playing five-hundred-seaters to places three times as large.

On August 22, 1987, we played the Castle Donington Monsters of Rock show in England (now called Download Festival). It was the biggest show in our history at that point. There were 80,000 people there, and we were on a bill with Bon Jovi, Dio, Metallica, W.A.S.P., and Cinderella. I'm sure it chewed away at Blackie's fucking balls knowing that we were higher up on the bill than he was. At some point during the day, we found out that Gene Simmons and Paul Stanley were in London doing promotion and were coming to the show to see Bon Jovi. When Blackie found out, he took off because he was talking shit about KISS, and Paul Stanley found out.

People in W.A.S.P.'s camp told us that Blackie was afraid to face Gene and Paul. I was thinking, "Like those guys would even fucking bother to confront you. You're not even a piece of dog shit on Gene's boot."

Kirk and I were equally excited that we might get to meet Gene and Paul since we were both big KISS fans. Later that night Bon Jovi were onstage, and there was a tent set up backstage with a monitor to watch the show. We were both pretty buzzed, so we decided to watch Bon Jovi for the hell of it. We went into the tent and saw Gene and Paul standing there in front of the monitor. We hid behind a pillar at first because we were freaked out. Then we thought, "Fuck it. How many times do you get the chance to see Gene Simmons and Paul Stanley in person?" It was so lame. We walked over to where they were standing watching the TV and sidled up into their sight line until they looked at us.

I said, "Hey, Gene, Paul. We just wanted to say hi. We're huge fans." And before I could finish my sentence Gene pointed at me and said, "*You* are Scott Ian from Anthrax." Then he pointed at Kirk. "And you're Kirk Hammett from Metallica, and I hear you both had fabulous shows today."

"Peeeeeeee" went my wiener in my pants. Kirk and I were both speechless. Finally I sputtered, "How do you know? . . ."

"You guys are doing wonderful," said Gene like a beloved uncle. "We see you in the magazines. It's great. You're kicking ass. It's awesome."

He knew damn well what big KISS fans we were because we talked about them in interviews. So he said, "I know you guys are KISS fans and I thank you for that. Of course without *us* you wouldn't exist."

It was total Gene, but I had no problem with that. I told him, "Damn right I wouldn't exist! It was 1977, I saw you at the Garden, and that's the only reason I'm standing here right now!"

We shook hands with both Gene and Paul, and then Kirk and I ran out of there like two eleven-year-olds flipping out. We were so psyched. "Can you believe he knew who we were?!?" I said.

"I know!" Kirk said. "Dammit, we didn't get a picture. Fuck!"

Before we knew it, Anthrax went from playing 1,500-seaters to performing for 7,000 people a night. The bigger we got, the more ridiculous we became. There wasn't a hotel that was safe from our shenanigans and practical jokes. We didn't stay in hotels when we were touring for

Spreading the Disease. But things changed when *Among the Living* took off. When you're twenty-three or twenty-four and you're riding around in a luxury bus goofing around all the time, it's easy to lose perspective. Your food is cooked for you, you've got guys to set up and move your gear, and you're treated like a celebrity. Everyone wants to hang out and party or sit on your bus and listen to tunes. It's an amazing feeling, but if you don't keep yourself in check, life can quickly spin out of control. A lot of it is just youthful stupidity.

One of our favorite hotels was the Biltmore in Providence, Rhode Island. It's a classy, beautiful old place that has a huge lobby with chandeliers and long creepy hallways that reminded me of the Overlook Hotel from *The Shining*. The stairs were lined with patterned rugs, and the rooms had big, fluffy mattresses and more pillows than you could possibly prop under any part of your body. It seemed way too nice for us. We were used to Motel 6s, and this was the kind of place corporate CEOs stay. Somehow Jonny knew someone and was able to get us a special rate.

Even though we loved the hotel, once we were in our rooms, we were degenerates—completely disrespectful and destructive. Whenever we played Providence we had a lot of our East Coast friends with us from Rhode Island, New York, Boston, and Philly. A lot of people would take the train to see us because they knew we would have a massively insane party at the hotel after the show. Before long, we were launching what we called pirate attacks. One or two people would fill a garbage can with water, bust into someone else's room, and dump the trashcan over the other guy or all over the floor and the bed. Then people would take sides and these battles would go on for hours with water flying and everyone slipping all over the floor. This didn't just happen at the Biltmore—we pulled this shit wherever we stayed. And we never got caught. We destroyed these rooms, soaked everything, ruined beautiful carpets and bedspreads.

One of my favorite moves was the "band meeting," which only worked until people caught on. You'd call someone in the crew and tell him we were having a band meeting in a certain room in five minutes and he had to come. As soon as he left his room to attend this "meeting," every other door in the hallway would open and ten guys would run out and deluge him with buckets of water.

If your room got trashed, you had to call downstairs and somehow figure out a way to change rooms. We'd say, "Oh, the toilet's not working," or "The heat's not on. Can I come down and get the key for another room?" You had to make sure no one would come up because if someone did, he'd see the place was trashed and we'd get thrown out. We usually had six rooms, and by the time we were done it looked like the place had been in flames and firemen doused the rooms and hallways with a hose.

We always wondered, "What happens when the maids come in the next morning and nothing's dry?" It's amazing these places let us come back. It's just as amazing none of us ever got arrested. The more we got away with, the more we pushed the envelope. One time, I thought I was going to be the victim of a pirate attack and I really didn't want my room trashed, so I filled up liter-sized water bottles with piss. Every time I had to pee I'd use these bottles. So then when someone came at me with water I'd say, "Don't fuckin' do it! See this. It's piss." They'd throw the water anyway, so I'd let fly with these urine bombs. It was disgusting but fucking hilarious. And once you elevated the battle to flying piss projectiles, where is there to go? Poop!

We were flinging around shit like monkeys in a zoo. It wasn't always so crass. Sometimes we'd be slightly more clever. One trick was to get someone's key when they were out and sneak into their room and shit in their garbage can. Then you'd fill the trash with hot water and turn the heater on full blast. Whoever your target was—and we were all victims at one point or another—would come back to their room six or seven hours later and open the door to a hot, nauseating wave of human excrement. The smell would get into your clothes and your belongings. It never went away. You pretty much had to throw away your stuff after you'd been targeted. It was so wrong and we were so vile. We'd never do that today, but back then we didn't think about what minimum-wage-earning, hardworking maid or custodian was going to have to clean up our mess. We just didn't care.

We even pulled stunts that no one benefited from, like upper-deckers. That's where you shit in the top of a toilet tank and replace the lid. Or we'd shit between the mattress and the box spring of a bed and then put the mattress back. Who would do that? It's horrible. We never had the satisfaction of seeing someone's reaction to our handiwork. We could only imagine the aftermath. On top of that, we smashed lamps, bashed holes in walls, broke windows. Why? Because we could.

I can't even say I was drunk when I did that stuff because I didn't party much back then. I'd drink heavily on rare occasions, but I always stuck to beer so I was never too wasted. I was so focused on what we were doing with the band. Every day, even if we did one little thing, it was one tiny step forward. And if I was hungover that wasn't going to happen. Charlie and Frankie didn't party much, either. But Joey raged pretty hard. And he was a bad drunk. He would get a few beers in him and suddenly turn mean and nasty; he'd want to fight everybody.

In addition to dealing with Joey's beer muscles, I started getting more flak from the new NYHC community, which was still convinced I tried to corrupt their scene by trademarking the NYHC logo. I started getting threatening mail and phone calls and ugly messages waiting for me at venues. I ended up sitting down with metal old-timer Michael Schnapp, who since the eighties has worked for metal bands in every capacity across the country, and explained what was going on. He was good friends with Jimmy Gestapo from Murphy's Law. I had known Jimmy since the first CBs show I went to, which was Murphy's Law and Agnostic Front. I said to Schnapp, "Dude, I need to bury this shit. I'm tired of having to look over my shoulder and worry that if I'm at a show somewhere, someone's gonna stab me."

Schnapp organized a sit-down with Jimmy Gestapo. It was like something out of a fuckin' mob movie except we weren't drinking espresso and anisette. We were already friends; it's not like we had a problem. Jimmy knew I didn't do anything and that all the accusations were bullshit. But he was a respected elder statesman of the hardcore community.

He looked at me like the Godfather and said, "We're playing in a couple of weeks. You're going to come to that show. I'm going to bring you onstage. I'm going to say some shit to the crowd. We'll play 'Crucial Bar-B-Q together, and that's it. It'll be buried. Anyone who has a fucking problem with you will know they have a problem with me."

So that's what we did. I went to the show. Jimmy said, "You see that guy right over there? Don't believe all the bullshit. He was part of this scene years ago and he's cool. He's always been cool." I got up onstage, and we played their song "Crucial Bar-B-Q," and nobody ever bothered me again. Thanks Jimmy!

Aside from Castle Donington, we had done all headline shows for *Among the Living* until we got a phone call in early 1988. KISS wanted us to open up for their *Crazy Nights* tour. Even though I wasn't a fan of the record—or any eighties KISS—it was mind blowing that they were interested in touring with us. We went over well but the best memories weren't onstage. I'd sit with Gene in catering for hours every day, and he told me everything I ever wanted to know about KISS from 1975 to 1978. He would eat his dinner or sip his coffee and let me ask anything a superfan would want to know. I reminded him that I went to all three shows at the Garden in 1977. He said, "Where did you live in Queens?"

"I lived in Bayside, Bay Terrace."

"Where were you going to school at the time?" he asked.

"IS 25," I answered, not sure where he was going with this. Maybe he was going to take credit for building my junior high school.

"Interesting," Gene continued. "What bus did you take to school?"

"I'd take the 28."

"Okay, of course you wouldn't have known this then, but each night at the Garden, as soon as the show was over, I got right into a car and had the driver take me to my mother's house because I wanted to get away from the chaos." He told me his mother's address, and it was practically across the street from Bayside High School. He said, "On those days, when you were on your way to school, I was probably sitting in my mom's kitchen, reading the paper and drinking coffee, and you passed right by me three days in a row on your bus on the way to school. I might have even seen your bus go by."

It was hard to fathom—the winged demon of KISS catching a glance at my bus while my friends and I took swigs of Scotch from a Tupperware bowl. During our catering chats Gene and I also talked about Anthrax. He was really complimentary. "You guys have created your own sound, and now that you've reached this level, you have gold albums," he said. "You'll only ever have gold albums now. You've made it." He was straight up even though he wasn't exactly correct. But who could have predicted at that point what would happen to the music industry over the next twenty-five years?

The KISS tour was definitely a blast, but nothing with Anthrax happened without problems. Joey was still drinking and becoming more like Mr. Hyde when he was drunk. On a night off during the KISS dates, he went up and down the halls of a hotel banging on people's doors, looking for someone to fight. He could barely stand, which didn't stop him. He wavered back and forth like a slalom skier shouting, "Open your door! Get the fuck out here," at random rooms. He started kicking the doors, cursing and screaming, so Frankie ran down the hallway and tackled him so we didn't get kicked out of the hotel. "You're going to go to your fucking room and shut the fuck up!" shouted Frankie. We had to walk Joey back to his room, and he finally went to sleep.

By April 1, 1988, the KISS tour was over, and we were running late on writing our next record. Unlike in the past, we hadn't written any full songs on the road. To add to the pressure, Iron Maiden had asked us to open for them in stadiums that summer, but we had to have the new album done and the single out in time for the dates. That was part of the deal. We worked on finishing *State of Euphoria* in April and went into overdrive, not because we felt inspired but because we had to meet a deadline. To say *State of Euphoria* was rushed would be putting it mildly. We were writing, writing, writing, and we really weren't finished by the time we flew back to Quadradial Studios in Miami to start preproduction with Mark Dodson. We chose to work with him because he had engineered Judas Priest's *Sin After Sin* and *Defenders of the Faith* as well as Metal Church's *The Dark*. You can't get much better than that for a thick, powerful metal sound.

We had a few songs finished and the Trust cover "Antisocial." We spent three or four weeks working on another batch of songs that were just not where they should have been yet. They weren't done cooking. I still look at *State of Euphoria* as a half-finished album. We probably needed about four more months to do it justice, but we skimped. We recorded songs that needed more arrangement work and better melodies.

We rushed through the vocals. "Be All, End All" is the best track on the album. It's a lot closer to the songs we wrote for *Among the Living* than anything on the rest of the record, but as a whole the record is a long way from Anthrax at our finest. It's the record that could have been but wasn't because we wanted so badly to tour with Iron Maiden.

On top of feeling shitty from recording a subpar album, I had a health scare in 1988 that weirded me out. We were in the studio, and we ordered out from some Italian place. I had a big plate of shrimp scampi that tasted fine. The shrimp were tender and cooked through and nothing seemed particularly fishy. After dinner, Artie, who was hanging out with us, lit up a big, fat joint. It smelled really good; I've always loved the smell of weed even though I never feel like I've gotten high from smoking it. I figured maybe I had some weird immunity to pot. I turned to Artie and asked him for a hit. He passed the burning joint to me. I held it to my lips, took a big hit, and held it in for a few seconds before exhaling a fragrant plume of smoke and coughing my lungs out. I had a drink of water and my throat still felt a little irritated, but I wasn't in any pain. I wasn't buzzed at all, so I shrugged and continued the conversation I was having with Frankie.

About twenty-five minutes later, I started feeling really strange. At first I thought I had finally done it. I was high! But I didn't feel good. I got nauseated and started feeling like I had the flu: cold sweats, dizziness. Then something crazy started happening inside my skull. The best way to describe it is to remember the scene in *Star Wars* where Luke, Princess Leia, and Han Solo go down the garbage chute. The walls start closing in, and there's a monster called the Dianoga who grabs Luke with one of his tentacles. It was like a wall at the back of my skull was slowly moving forward toward my forehead. All that was missing was the Dianoga pulling me under. When the wall almost reached the front of my head, everything went fuzzy and I saw a cloud of purple dots. There was a loud buzzing in my ears—then I was unconscious. When I came to, I was shaking. "What happened?"

"You passed out," said Artie.

"How long?"

"About thirty seconds."

I still felt like shit, so we called the paramedics. I went to the hospital. They checked my blood sugar and told me I seemed okay. An hour later I felt fine. No one could explain what had happened. I figured I probably ate a bad shrimp and got food poisoning. That happens all the time with oysters. Eating shellfish at the wrong place is kinda like playing Russian roulette.

Chapter 16

EUPHORIA & DESPAIR

We went back to New York, and Mark Dodson and Alex Perialas mixed *State of Euphoria* at Electric Lady Studios, which
is an amazing place and has a great vibe. But even being
there felt hollow since I was convinced we had sold Anthrax short.
When the record came out on September 18, 1988, it was a huge success. We made a video for "Antisocial" that did really well at *Headbanger's Ball* and other outlets, but whenever anyone would praise the
record, I would think, "Oh, you don't fucking understand! This is Anthrax slumming on autopilot."

The only songs we still play from that record are "Be All, End All"
and "Antisocial," and that's not even our song. It's by the French band
Trust. "Now It's Dark" was a cool song and I loved the lyrics about
Frank Booth, the character Dennis Hopper played in David Lynch's
brilliant movie *Blue Velvet*. "Finale" was good, too, and featured some
of Charlie's fastest double-bass playing ever, but four songs don't make
a great album. There was no consistency in the writing because the rest
of the record was rushed. To me, *State of Euphoria* simply didn't hold up
compared to the previous three Anthrax records.

It really fucked with my equilibrium. I can't even listen to it, and
when I think back about some of those songs, I feel sick. It felt like the
first time we made a mistake as a band. Instead of following our creative instincts, we let the music business dictate what we were doing. I
was sure it was only a matter of time until people started realizing how
shitty *State of Euphoria* was.

I actually got paranoid and neurotic and started to think we were
becoming a joke because I had lost confidence in myself. I had always

felt like I was in charge of making the right decisions for Anthrax, and I began to question my judgment in a big way. We were on a tour cycle for an album I hated, and we had to play songs from the album every night. That made me angry.

We'd play "I'm The Man," and I'd think, "Who are we? What is this? You don't see Metallica doing this." I felt like maybe we were becoming a parody of ourselves. I second-guessed wearing shorts onstage and thought, "Oh, no, our image is becoming really goofy. At least we're not still wearing chain mail." But it just didn't feel "Anthrax."

In the video for "Antisocial," Danny Spitz was wearing a fucking Tweety Bird T-shirt with long red jam shorts that came down past his knees with the Jetsons all over them. And he was playing a guitar with Teenage Mutant Ninja Turtles on it. I fucking gag thinking about that. How is this metal? It was more like a promotion for Cartoon Network, even though that wouldn't exist for another four years.

I think I was so thrown and self-conscious because we totally could have put our feet down and told the label we needed more time to finish the record. We even could have dropped off the Iron Maiden tour if we had to. We had said no to offers and demands many times before. We got greedy. That's all there was to it. The brass ring was hanging in front of us—a stadium tour with Iron Maiden—and we grabbed it.

Fortunately, touring with Maiden was a dream come true, so that took some of the sting away from the fact that we had made a shitty record. They were great guys to hang out with—very professional but also extremely friendly and full of advice. And you'll never see a band so consistent onstage night after night. The shows were amazing for us as well. We were playing to sold-out stadiums of people losing their minds to Anthrax. We were selling hundreds of thousands of records and selling truckloads of merch. We had "made it."

The pace didn't let up after the Maiden tour. But Joey was getting more and more unpredictable. He was at the peak of his partying, and we were constantly dealing with his outbursts. When we were playing with another band that partied, he'd wander off to their dressing room to rage with them or members of their crew. I saw him wide-eyed and out of his head, looking like a serial killer, many times onstage and off. I didn't interfere until I felt the indulgences were affecting his performance.

My attitude was always, "Hey, man, I'm not your fucking dad. I'm not gonna tell you how to live, but if what you're doing starts to damage what we're doing onstage, then we have to deal with it." On November 16, 1988, we opened Ozzy Osbourne's *No Rest for the Wicked* tour, and Joey was not singing well. His voice sounded weak. The timing couldn't have been worse. We were on the biggest, most important tour of our career, we were worth 7,000 tickets a night, and our merch was moving better than ever, but our singer was going down the tubes because he was doing blow and not holding up his end of the live performance. We were not about to let Joey destroy everything we had built up.

During a day off in Chicago, we sat him down at the old Days Inn on Lake Shore, which is now a W Hotel. We all got into the room together like it was an intervention, which it basically was. I said, "Look bro, your partying is affecting your voice. When you drink you turn into a madman, and not only are we sick of it, it's hurting the band so it has to stop."

We told him we were there for him, and if he needed help quitting, we'd do whatever we could. We didn't have to do anything. He literally stopped drinking and snorting coke right then and there, and he has been clean and sober ever since. I have an unbelievable amount of respect for him for being able to do that. It's not easy to just stop doing drugs cold turkey, and it's even harder for a problem drinker to lay off the bottle. Joey had incredible willpower and was able to face his problem head-on and say, "That's it, I'm done."

The same tour we convinced Joey he was going over the edge, the rest of us almost got arrested for one of the most pointlessly gleeful nights of drunken destruction of our career. We were playing two nights with Ozzy at Long Beach Arena on December 30 and 31, and Jonny had booked almost a whole floor of rooms at the Hyatt on Sunset. All we could think of was this was the Riot House where Led Zeppelin committed all these crazy antics in the seventies. Nothing much happened after the December 30 show, because we were getting amped up for the second night and we didn't want to risk getting thrown out before New Year's.

Between the band, crew, and all our friends who came out to celebrate my twenty-fifth birthday, we more than made up for it the next night. We had the bathtubs and sinks in two rooms filled with ice and bottles of liquor, beer, and wine. When those were overflowing, we filled garbage cans with more booze. The scene was set for a raging aftershow party. That was one of the few nights in the eighties that I got really drunk. Pretty much everyone else was wasted as well, and we all spun completely out of control. We didn't restrict the shenanigans to pouring water and piss over each other. We were flinging full bottles of beer from either end of a long hallway. Someone could have gotten really badly hurt. The floor was slippery with beer and there was broken glass all over the place.

One minute I was laughing my head off, then out of the corner of my eye I saw someone's arm in a throwing motion and a bottle would whizz by my head and smash on the wall. We eventually got bored of whipping beers at each other, so someone chucked a bottle through a closed window, over a terrace, and down onto Sunset Boulevard. Suddenly, everyone was smashing windows with projectiles. We didn't stop at bottles, either. Room lamps went out the window facing the parking lot along with clock radios and pretty much anything that wasn't bolted down. We yanked a TV off the stand and threw it out the back side window into the parking lot. Even though we were shitfaced, at least we had enough common sense to realize that throwing a TV onto Sunset Boulevard could land us in serious shit; we could go to jail for killing someone—not that we couldn't have taken someone's life with a beer bottle or a lamp—it just seemed like a TV was a lot worse.

It was hard to haul the TV out the open window. Those giant tube sets they had in people's rooms in the eighties were fuckin' heavy. It took a couple of us to toss it out of the hotel to the empty parking lot below. We didn't see it land, but we sure heard it. There was a satisfying crunch as it made contact with the pavement. A few minutes later, the police arrived. We were so drunk and cocky we thought, "What can they do to us? So what, we're throwing bottles and other stuff. It's New Year's Eve. Who cares? What's going to happen? What are they going to do? We have a whole floor of rooms we've paid for. They can't do shit to us! They can't throw us out. We own this fuckin' floor!"

Again, we stupidly felt invincible. We thought we were entitled to fuck with people and make their jobs hard by doing irresponsible shit and assuming we didn't have to face any consequences because we were big-time dudes in a band. It was a terrible attitude to have, and it's the kind of thing that turns perfectly nice people into total assholes. When the cops arrived it was about 3 a.m. I was in one of the party rooms and the door was closed. John Tempesta, who later joined White Zombie and played in Testament, Exodus, and the Cult, was Charlie's drum tech at the time. He was there with me and so was our security guy Billy.

There was a knock at the door, and I looked through the peephole and saw one of the hotel employees. He had already come up twenty times. There were other parties going on at the hotel, so the first few times people came up we'd say, "That wasn't us. We didn't throw any bottles." When one of the more sleuth-like hotel staffers asked why the window in our room was broken, we told him it was an accident and that someone fell against the window. It didn't take much investigation on their part to see that a TV was missing from one of our rooms. Even the Keystone Cops could have put two and two together and realized we had tossed it.

The guy said, "We're going to have to ask you all to leave." By that time, four LA sheriffs had joined him. "You're being kicked out of the hotel."

Tempesta was drunk out of his mind and didn't take kindly to this news. "Fuck you!" he shouted at the hotel manager. "I ain't fucking going anywhere. Fucking throw me out? Fuck you!!"

He didn't see the cops. I tried to warn him. He didn't hear me. Instead of backing down he stumbled up to the manager and flipped his middle finger in the guy's face. "Fuck you, little man! You can't fucking tell me what to do." Then Tempesta poked him, I guess to emphasize his point.

A second later, a cop slammed Tempesta on the ground, jerked him back up, rammed a knee into his back, and cuffed him. Apparently, as soon as John touched the manager, that counted as assault. Billy tried to come to his defense, and a policeman threw him against the wall. Not wanting a giant knee in my spine I said, "Excuse me. This isn't my room. Can I go to my room to get my stuff?"

They let me leave, so I ran down the hallway to Jonny Z's room. He was there partying with Marsha and a couple other people. I told him the cops were here and they were arresting Tempesta and kicking us all out. Jonny was out of his mind and wired as fuck, but he was our Peter Grant—the dude who managed Zeppelin and kept them out of too much trouble—he'd fix this. Jonny went over to the hotel manager and shouted, "What's going on here? You can't throw us out. We have the whole floor of rooms. No band's ever going to come back here again if you make us leave. I'll see to that."

After his theatrical tirade, Jonny walked down the hallway with the manager of the hotel and the head sheriff. They talked for a few minutes while we just stood there and Tempesta lay on the floor in handcuffs, cursing the air. When they came back Jonny told us he negotiated a compromise. The hotel was only going to throw out Tempesta and Billy, which was pretty good considering we basically had destroyed a hotel floor. No one was being arrested; we just had to find another place for the two guys to stay. The girl Tempesta was with said they could crash at her house, and that was that. The rest of us stumbled back to our rooms and passed out.

After the Ozzy tour, we did a short UK run with Living Colour opening, and then we went out on the Headbanger's Ball tour with Exodus and Helloween. We returned to our old routine of throwing buckets of water and pee bombs. We knew nothing could compete with the craziness of the Ozzy tour, so we didn't try. In June we flew to Europe to play headline shows with Suicidal Tendencies opening; it was Robert Trujillo's first tour. Fourteen years later Metallica would hire him to replace Jason Newsted. We toured the UK through mid-July with King's X in support.

I spent so much of 1988 and 1989 on the road or recording with the band that I was never in New York, which meant I never had to see Marge and have the conversation I had avoided for so long. My behavior, meanwhile, had gotten worse, to the point where my marriage vows weren't worth the empty air they were spoken with.

In September 1989 Metallica played three nights at Irvine Meadows on the . . . *And Justice for All* tour. I was in LA anyway, since I was scheduled to be on one of the panels at the Foundations Forum metal convention, which was happening around the same time. Frankie was there, too, and so was my friend Andy Buchanan, who flew over from Scotland to hang out. We had no major commitments waiting for us back home, so we stayed for all three Metallica shows.

During the second concert, Frankie and I met two girls backstage. I was immediately drawn to one of them, Debbie Leavitt, who was a little shorter than me, which is always a plus. She had long, dark brown hair and was thin but shapely. She looked to me like the hot girl next door, and she, too, was Jewish. That's not something I was looking for since I'm not at all religious, but it immediately gave us something in common. It's funny because Huntington Beach, where she was from, doesn't really have a Jewish population. Yet there she was, and I couldn't take my eyes off her. She was eighteen at the time and I was twenty-five, so there was a little bit of an age difference, but it wasn't like I was R. Kelly pissing on teenage girls. I probably had the mentality of an eighteen-year-old at the time, anyway.

Debbie was into rock but wasn't a metalhead. She grew up on KROQ and listened to stuff like the Cure, the Red Hot Chili Peppers, and Depeche Mode. But I could tell she was impressed that I was in a band. We hung out and talked, then I gave her and her friend a ride back to their car, which was in the general parking area of the venue. When I dropped them off, I invited Debbie to come with me to see Metallica the next night.

She said she'd like that and asked if she could bring her friend Kelly. I told her that was cool and figured Andy might hook up with Kelly or at least have someone to hang out with while I figured out if there was anything going on between Debbie and me. Sure enough, we connected at the show. We were talking so much we didn't see much of the band. I decided to stay with her in LA three more days. I changed my flight and gave Marge some bullshit excuse about having to stay on the West Coast for record industry meetings. She worked for IBM, not RCA. She didn't know anything about the music industry, so she just accepted whatever I told her. She didn't like it, but she had no way of knowing I was lying.

During that time, Frankie, Andy, and I had a blast playing basketball with the Beastie Boys in Laurel Canyon all day long. Then I'd go back to the hotel, nap, shower, and meet Debbie for dinner. Nothing happened other than some fine dining and good conversation. We didn't hook up on that trip; I kissed her, that was it. But when we kissed I actually felt something. Being with her was invigorating, exciting. She seemed interested in my war stories, and I wanted to know what was going on in her life. I felt I should find out more about her and see if there could be anything serious between us.

I started to make regular trips to LA. Every time was another lame excuse that Marge should have seen through but didn't want to. The first time I went back to LA, Debbie and I hooked up. Somehow, sex with her was different than it was with all the girls I had been with. Not that we did anything different; it just felt more heightened and intimate. We started sleeping together regularly.

After I flew home, I was right back in limbo with Marge. I didn't like living this much of a lie, but I tricked myself into not feeling guilty because we had become two completely different people. We were like roommates who tolerated one another. Then toward the end of 1989, Marge started really putting the thumbscrews on me about having children. She had mentioned it several times before over the past year, but I acted like I hadn't heard her or told her I wasn't ready yet. I wanted to tell her it was over, but I would just keep procrastinating. Every day I'd tell myself, "You're going to tell her!" Finally at two in the morning one night, I was lying awake because I was too stressed out to fall asleep. Suddenly she woke up and realized I was still up. She said, "Are you okay?"

"No, we need to talk," I sputtered.

"About what? I'm tired. Can this wait until the morning? . . ."

"It's over," I said, gaining more courage. "I can't do this. I'm not in love with you and I'm seeing someone else. I need to move out and figure out where my life is going."

She started crying. She couldn't stop. She wasn't yelling or throwing things; she was brokenhearted and miserable. I told her I wanted a divorce. It felt good to be able to finally get all of this baggage out in the open, but the confession created a mountain of Jewish guilt—she told her parents, I told my parents. Suddenly everyone was involved.

"What's wrong with you? How could you do this to her?" My mom dug into me and so did her parents. My dad was the only one who supported me. He has always had my back.

Marge begged for a second chance and I agreed to go into couples therapy. I figured, "Hey, I'll try it. I owe her that much. Who knows? Maybe this therapist will say something and a lightbulb will go off in my head and we'll live happily ever after."

I sat at couples therapy bored out of my mind, and after a few sessions the therapist said, "You really don't want to be here, do you Scott? You're not working at this." I said, "No, I'm not. I'm telling you, I'm done. I'm not in love with you and I don't want to have kids. I'm being honest. I've been dishonest for years, now I'm being honest, and I have to go. I have to get out."

I moved out of the house and into a studio apartment in Greenwich Village.

Chapter 17

STARTING OVER

I went back to LA soon after breaking the news to Marge, and when I got back to New York in late 1989, Debbie came back with me and moved in. It was nice to have real companionship. Everything was great. We'd eat out, go to movies, and have lots of sex. I guess most new couples do. The mundane becomes the unusual and being with someone is suddenly exciting again. Marge would still call pleading for me to come back. "Please, please, please. Let's try again. I can change!" That was a drag, and my sympathy quickly turned to annoyance. "No, no, no. It's over! Don't you get it? I'm done. Done!"

I always loved New York and I still do, but by the end of 1989 I couldn't wait to get out of the city. There were too many ghosts, too many memories. Going to Los Angeles to make *Persistence of Time* gave me an escape route. Debbie came with me. She was thrilled because, basically, she was going back home and she wasn't in love with New York like I was. To be fair, she didn't have the best experiences there. One night, I convinced her to come with me to see *Henry: Portrait of a Serial Killer*. Looking back, it reminds me of the scene in *Taxi Driver* where Travis Bickle (Robert De Niro) takes Betsy (Cybill Shepherd) to a porno movie and she storms out.

Debbie wasn't thrilled about going to the film to begin with, but she knew I really wanted to see it. The movie is a gritty, realistic depiction of mass murderer Henry Lee Lucas, his sidekick Otis Toole, and the heinous murders they committed in the sixties and seventies. She was already tense when we sat down in our seats. The theater was right in Times Square, and it was old, shitty, filthy, and broken down—the kind with rips in the screen that distract you throughout the film—and the place was pretty empty. About forty-five minutes into the movie, during one of the really violent scenes, we heard a rhythmic noise behind us, like a seat creaking in time, quiet at first, but it gradually became more noticeable. We heard moaning and heavy breathing. Debbie turned around and saw a guy two rows behind her forcefully beating off while he watched the movie. She screamed, stood up, and left in a state of pique. I followed her and apologized, but she yelled at me as if I had planned the whole charade. She was so angry that I took her to such a twisted film she threatened to break up with me. It took some effort, but I was able to talk her down. We were leaving for LA in just a few days, so she wouldn't have to deal with crazy NYC anymore.

We got a free ride to LA because I was able to put all my shit on the gear truck heading to California. First, though, I had to shoulder the weight of another pile of Jewish guilt. A couple of days before I left for LA, Anthrax were at Electric Lady rehearsing songs for *Persistence of Time*. I planned to meet my mom at the studio and have lunch with her. I thought that would be a good time to tell her I was leaving New York and going to LA with Debbie, which I knew she wouldn't be happy about. She had always liked Marge and was heartbroken when our marriage ended. Actually, I didn't know how upset she was until we were coming back from lunch and walking down Eighth Street back to Electric Lady.

In her best Jewish mom voice, she said, "I just have to tell you. I'm very, very unhappy with this decision. I think you're making a huge mistake. This is the wrong choice, absolutely wrong. I don't know how you could do this to Marjorie. It's a horrible thing you're doing. You want my blessings? If I had my way right now, you'd fall in front of a bus and wake up in the hospital with amnesia and not remember any of this, and this girl from California"—she fucking hated Debbie—"you wouldn't know who she was."

I looked at her and said, "You're kidding, right?"

"No, absolutely not," she insisted. "I've wished this every night since you told us you had split up with Marge."

"Ma, that's pretty fucked up. You want me to get hit by a bus?"

"I don't care. This is how I feel," she said.

She was going nuts, practically foaming at the mouth. So I said, "You know what? Go fuck yourself! Go fuck yourself, Ma. Really. Take it back! Tell me right now that you're sorry."

She stood her ground and refused to apologize.

"Go fuck yourself!" I said again. There were no other words to express how betrayed I felt. I walked into Electric Lady, shut the door, and I didn't talk to her for almost two years. My attitude was, "You're my mother. I love you, but I don't have to like you. And I definitely don't have to talk to you."

Eventually my father convinced me to reach back out to her. He said she wasn't going to be around forever and I would regret not remedying the situation or at least having closure. "I know how she is," he added. "I used to be married to her. Just call her. Be there. Be her son. Be civil. Just get back into her life."

I wrote her a letter, because I couldn't call her. I didn't want to hear her voice. I wrote and I told her exactly how I felt. I said, "Apologize or don't apologize at this point. I don't care. But I'd like to have you back in my life in some way, shape, or form."

She was thrilled. But it took a long time for me to feel close to her again. Granted, I was in California and I had a 3,000-mile buffer. That was great. I'd see her once or twice a year when I was in New York with the band, and my obligations as a good son were met. But I don't think all of the ice around my heart melted until recently when I saw how happy she was interacting with my son Revel and how much he laughed when he was with her.

Debbie and I lived at the Oakwood Apartments over on Barham in Toluca Hills, North Hollywood, which is where the band was staying while we were recording. I had a furnished apartment there, so I put all my shit in storage. A few months later we found an apartment in Huntington Beach off the Pacific Coast Highway. In less than a year I went from living in a tiny studio apartment in Greenwich Village to a brand new modern two-bedroom apartment right on the ocean. I had never lived anywhere but smoggy, grimy New York, and suddenly

I'm in a location that looked like something out of *Endless Summer*. It was really a dream come true because I had wanted to be in California again ever since I was there in 1977 to skateboard.

Los Angeles was like a carnival funhouse with no security, a giant playground where there weren't any rules and I could act like a kid all the time. A lot of people from New York have this East Coast–versus–the world mentality. I've never believed in any sort of rivalries between cities. Even when I was a proud New Yorker, I never hated LA. I loved the weather, the geography, the history of Hollywood, the James Ellroy noir weirdness, and the Charles Bukowski excess LA offered. There were great clubs, great bands. California had Metallica, Slayer, Exodus, and Testament. At the time it was everything New York wasn't.

Some of my friends said, "Dude, why do you want to move out to LA? Fuck LA! Fuck the West Coast." And I'd tell them, "Man, every time I go to LA, I have a blast. Come out and see for yourself." My brother Jason and a few of my friends did and ended up moving there not long after. Debbie started introducing me to her friends right away, and I was instantly hanging out with all these old-school punk rock and heavy metal surfer dudes who had been in Huntington Beach their whole life and who all knew me from Anthrax. For about a year and a half it was great, then reality started to take its toll.

Things had changed a lot between 1987 and early 1990, and I wanted our music and lyrics to reflect that. My divorce was getting really ugly. I looked back at my life with new perspective and started thinking about the future. Most of my friends were having kids, and I was still touring in a rock band and about as far from settling down as possible. Even though I was with Debbie and I was faithful to her, I felt an emptiness in my soul. I felt like I wasn't doing anything really meaningful, just repeating the same cycles: shampoo, rinse, repeat. I know a lot of dudes dream of being in a successful rock band and would sell their soul to make it happen. Sometimes I felt like I had already done that, only without being at the crossroads with my guitar and Jack Butler disguised as Gene Simmons. Maybe signing a record contract or a manager's contract is pretty much the same thing as making a deal with the devil. Having toured the world and lived out all the stupid rock and roll mythology, I started to wonder if there was more to life. Don't get me wrong. I had a blast making music and playing shows and being a juvenile delinquent, but I started looking into the future more and trying to figure where I'd be in ten, twenty, thirty years. And that weighed on my mind while I was writing the lyrics for *Persistence of Time*.

Anthrax started seriously working on the album in early 1990, and that's when the cracks really started to show, and that little foul smell I was detecting in our chemistry started to become a garbage dump. Working on that record was not fun. The inflammatory mood of the sessions was foreshadowed by a fire at our practice space in Yonkers. We were renting a room on the second floor of a printing shop. We'd had it for a few years at that point, and it was basically our jam space that we used all the time. I was staying at an apartment on Horatio Street in the West Village, and I got a call early in the morning from Charlie saying, "You don't need to come to the studio today."

I was expecting to swing by and work on some songs, so I asked why, and he said, "There was a fire in the building last night, and it's all gone."

"What?!?" Practically before I could hang up, I got on the train and headed to the studio. We were all there and the second floor, where all our gear was, was smoldering. The fire was out, but the building was still smoking.

No one would let us in while the firemen were there, and we kept asking, "Is there any gear left?" But they just said to stay away and they'd pull out whatever was left the next day.

Once the firemen left we were like, "Fuck this." Everyone in the band and some of our friends climbed up on the roof, got in through a window, and started salvaging what we could. In retrospect it probably was stupid to walk into a building that had just been in flames. The floor could have caved in on us, but we weren't thinking about that, we were thinking about our Marshalls and our Jackson guitars. We literally made a human chain so people inside handed stuff out the window to guys on the roof and from the roof to the ground. There were a whole bunch of us. We pulled out everything that wasn't destroyed, even stuff that was burned but maybe salvageable. In total, it was about half of our equipment. We easily lost fifteen speaker cabinets and a lot of guitars and four track machines. I also lost two Jubilee Series Marshalls that I had gotten in 1987. They were great heads, but they were only two years old, and I was able to replace them. At least I was able to pull out the two main guitars I used back then, my white Jackson Randy Rhoads and my black 1981 Gibson Flying V. The Jackson Rhoads had been in a different part of the room and hadn't been touched by the fire. But the guitar case holding the V was pretty damaged and moderately burned. I opened it and saw the pick guard and knobs were partially melted because it was close to where the fire was, but it looked super cool. It was otherwise undamaged and still, to this day, it has the melty knobs on it—I just left them on there.

Fortunately, we were insured, and we were reimbursed for a lot of the stuff we lost. So it wasn't a total catastrophe, and we were able to move forward without losing any momentum. We knew we didn't want *Persistence of Time* to be a thrash album. Even though less than three years had passed since *Among the Living,* we felt so far removed from that scene. We had grown into something bigger and better than just a thrash band, and we didn't want to be pigeonholed. We wanted to be taken as seriously as Judas Priest and Iron Maiden. We naturally started to change, evolve, and explore other avenues of heavy music.

Thrash burned bright and hot in the eighties, and now everyone was moving on to other things. The same thing happened to the NWOBHM. With the exception of Priest and Maiden, a lot of bands we loved from that era didn't make it past 1985. Where were Raven, Angel Witch, Saxon, and Venom? It wasn't too hard to imagine ourselves in that same predicament. We were still drawing crowds and selling merch and albums, but I knew that if we didn't do something bigger and better, people were going to get bored.

From the point *State of Euphoria* was released, I felt like time was ticking, which might be why time was such a recurring motif in *Persistence of Time.* The truth is, we never made it easy for straight-ahead thrash fans, as thrashy and brutal as *Spreading the Disease* and *Among the Living* had been. We constantly challenged ourselves, and consequently our audience, because we wanted to keep our music fluid and evolving. Maybe that's one reason we're still around. If *State of Euphoria* was *Among the Living II* and *Persistence of Time* was *Among the Living III*, we probably would have gotten bored and broken up by 1992.

The songwriting process for *Persistence of Time* was the same as it had been since *Spreading the Disease*. Charlie wrote the bulk of the music, and Frankie, Charlie, and I worked on the arrangements. I wrote the lyrics. Frankie wrote and helped with the melodies, and then Frankie and I worked with Joey over a period of weeks on the vocal parts. That formula worked great for the first two albums and okay on *State of Euphoria*; we just didn't spend enough time on it. But with *Persistence of Time*, it felt impossible. Our usual process with Joey wasn't working anymore. Even after we started tracking at Conway Studios in Los Angeles at the beginning of 1990, it wasn't happening. I had lost the patience I used to have with him because I had no patience left in my life at that point, and I couldn't come to grips with the idea of my words, thoughts, and feelings being sung by someone else anymore. That balance in my life was gone. It was okay when I was writing about Stephen King stories and comic books, but the lyrics for *Persistence of Time* were extremely personal and to hear Joey misinterpreting songs about my destroyed marriage made me furious. It's not like I could step up to the plate and sing. I couldn't, and that inflamed my frustration even more. I wanted this record to be perfect. After *State of Euphoria* it *had* to be perfect. I wasn't going to settle for just okay. It had to be exactly how I wanted it to be or it wasn't going to get done.

We busted our balls to get those songs right—and to get Joey to learn them. We thought he had it and he sang them, but they didn't sound right. He was getting frustrated as well because he didn't understand what I meant when I said the songs needed a different kind of emotion. He tried to make them sound angrier. He tried to make them more raw. But the core of the problem was that the lyrics weren't his; they were mine. My thoughts, my feelings, and my ideas, and how could he express my torment? Maybe nobody could. The music on *Persistence of Time* was much deeper, denser, and darker than anything we'd ever done. It has more in common with *Sound of White Noise*, musically, than it does with *State of Euphoria*. It was really a bridge in a lot of ways to that record, yet I couldn't hear that grittiness because of Joey's disconnected vocals.

It made me insane. I felt like I had written the best lyrics of my career, and Joey's voice didn't match the words. Every time he sang "Keep It in the Family" he sounded happy. I told him, "Dude, this is not a happy song. This is about racism." "Belly of the Beast" is about the Holocaust, and when he sang it I couldn't feel the weight and passion that those words needed to convey their meaning. The phrasing and timing on the opening track, "Time," were challenging, and Joey had to do take after take to finally get close to the vibe I wanted for the song.

That was especially irritating to me, because "Time" was about aging and it was extremely personal. I was twenty-six, my marriage was over, my world was different, yet for Joey everything was the same. To my mind he hadn't grown with the band, and I couldn't fix that. I couldn't stand hearing him sing my words anymore. I hated it, and at the same time we were pulling teeth, working as hard as we could to get the best we could out of him.

It was a terrible time for me, and it must have been worse for him because he didn't know what he was doing wrong. How could he? On the surface with me everything was business as usual. I was having an internal meltdown over my words, and I wasn't communicating that. I didn't have the tools then to be able to, I just wanted it to be right without having to force it. I kept thinking, "How long have you been in this band now? Sing the parts. Why am I doing your job?" Of course, I never said any of that. I could never be confrontational with Joey because he wasn't combative at all. He's a really sweet, gentle guy, which made it even harder to approach him. Frankie and I were on the same page, and we talked about where we were going with Joey all the time.

Joey could tell I was getting angry, but I never yelled at him. That's not who I am. When I'm pissed I become stone dead fucking silent. I walked out of the room quite a bit because if I didn't, I would have started screaming, and I was determined not to do that. I wanted to be more like my dad, in that respect. In the end, we put a lot of work into *Persistence*, more than any of the previous records, and I was really proud of it. The songwriting for that record showed me a different side of myself and the band that I wanted to continue exploring. I think it's underrated. It sold well. It shipped gold and our fans loved it. We maintained everything we had. But for all the work we put into that record, I feel like it should have been bigger.

It felt like we had been around long enough and this should have been the record that broke everything open, except some people didn't seem to get that we had changed musically as a band and mentally we had grown up. We were darker, the smiles onstage were gone, along with the jams and goofy T-shirts. Anthrax definitely had a darker, deeper vibe. Live, we still played the best songs from *Spreading the Disease* and *Among the Living*, but people shouted out, "Play 'I'm The Man,'" and we didn't want to do that anymore. We did that in 1987, and we felt like we milked it for all it was worth. Fortunately, we had another rap-metal song to play, and it fit our new, dark image. It wasn't a joke. "Bring the Noise" was a cover of a song by my favorite rap group, Public Enemy, and it was heavy as fuck and serious as an IRS audit.

Chapter 18

BRING THE NOISE

One day I was fucking around with a riff and I thought it sounded like the horn part in the PE song "Bring the Noise," which was originally on the *Less Than Zero* soundtrack and also included on the group's 1988 album *It Takes a Nation of Millions to Hold Us Back*. It was a very political song and somewhat controversial since it referred to Nation of Islam president Minister Louis Farrakhan as "a prophet that I think you oughta listen to." I didn't care about Farrakhan; all I wanted to do was work with Public Enemy.

My friends Georges Sulmers and Scott Koenig used to work at Def Jam, and they introduced me to Rick Rubin. I was so into rap, I used to hang out at their funky little office on Elizabeth Street in Greenwich Village. They gave me T-shirts and Def Jam stuff. I still have one of the original Def Jam baseball jackets with my name on it. I spent a lot of time down there picking up rap records and hanging out because the place had such a cool vibe and it really felt like something was happening.

The first song I heard from Public Enemy was "Miuzi Weighs a Ton," and it was like the first time I heard "Rock and Roll All Nite," the first Iron Maiden album, or Metallica's *No Life 'til Leather*. It made me want to run down the fucking street and punch people in the face as hard as I could!

I got an advance copy of *It Takes a Nation of Millions*, and I met Chuck D in the office soon after. We shook hands and he said to me, "Everyone tells me you guys are big fans. Thank you so much. I see pictures of you wearing Public Enemy T-shirts in magazines. That's so cool, thank you."

I was like, "No, thank *you*! You guys are awesome!" And we became friends. He came to see us play for the first time in '87 at the Beacon Theater when Metal Church and the Cro-Mags opened for us. When I found out he was there, I turned into that giddy eleven-year-old again. We actually had a lot in common. He's from Roosevelt, Long Island, I spent a lot of time in Merrick, which is the next town over, and we were into the same shit growing up. Chuck has always said classic rock was just as important an influence on him as soul and funk. I loved Public Enemy. PE were a rap group like no other at the time: they layered their tracks with beats, bass, guitars, horns, noise, and bits of speeches from black leaders like Malcolm X, Thomas "TNT" Todd, and Jesse Jackson, creating a ferocious sonic landscape. Their live show was equally aggressive—much more akin to a metal concert than to a performance by any other rap group of the '80s.

Fast forward to early 1990. I had this riff, and I started playing it along with the "Bring the Noise" track. I thought it sounded really awesome and made me wish Public Enemy had put the part on their song. From there it was a natural leap to writing an arrangement of the song for Anthrax. When Charlie was done with all his drum tracks for the *Persistence* album, I said, "Don't break the drums down yet, I have this idea for a cover." He loved the riff, so we arranged the song and recorded the drums and guitars in about ten minutes. Frankie added the bass, and we had ourselves a monster of a track. I got Chuck's number from Georges at Def Jam, so I called and told him that we recorded a metal version of "Bring the Noise." We wanted to send it to him because we thought it would be great if he and Flavor Flav did the vocals.

"Wow, Scotty," said Chuck. "That sounds really cool, but it just seems maybe kind of redundant, because we've already done 'Bring the Noise.' Why don't we do something together from scratch—something new?"

I said, "Well, we should do that, too, but you just have to hear this."

He agreed to give it a listen and told me to send him a tape. He said he'd talk to Rick Rubin in the meantime and see what he thought. We made him a cassette and mailed it to him, and I called him the next day. He told me he spoke to Rick about my idea, and he felt the same way. The song was already done and on a record. It didn't need to be done again. I convinced him not to make a final decision until he listened to the cassette I sent.

It was already in the mail. We sent it from Los Angeles regular postage, so we figured it would take four or five days to get to him in Long Island. The wait was interminable. About four days later he called.

"Yo, I got the tape," he said. "This is fucking slamming. Let's go! When and where?"

This was way before the Internet. You couldn't just e-mail MP3 files back and forth. We were still in Los Angeles and he was in New York, so there were logistical problems. For almost the past twenty-five years, we've told people that Chuck and Flavor came and did their vocal parts while we were in Los Angeles recording *Persistence of Time,* and then I did my parts for the third and fourth verses. That's not really what happened. We couldn't coordinate our schedules so they couldn't come to LA to do their vocals. We felt like a mouse on a glue trap until we realized we had an a cappella version of the song, which is a track composed only of vocals, with all the instruments and samples edited out. We told Chuck we could use those original tracks and sample them into our version. I asked him if he was cool with it and he said, "Yeah, who cares? We'll just tell people we did it. It's hip-hop. Everybody samples everybody else, anyway. Just send us the track when you're done and we'll make sure it lines up and doesn't sound weird."

Charlie and I went into the studio in New York and line by line, sometimes word by word, we edited the vocals to fit into our track. This was before ProTools, so making everything fit perfectly was, to put it lightly, a grueling exercise in editing technique.

We put the song under a microscope to make sure there was nothing out of place. I can't even say how many times we went back and moved a single word a fucking millisecond forward or backward. It was painstaking and agonizing because the last thing we wanted was anyone figuring out we used a prerecorded track. We had so much respect for those guys, and it meant so much to be able to lie to people and tell them, "Yeah, Chuck and Flav did the vocals." In a sense, they *did,* and the only people who knew the whole thing was done by us were Chuck, Flav, and I think Rick Rubin. Island Records didn't even have a clue.

We finished all this vocal placement and it turned out great. We sent it to Chuck, and he called me back and said, "It sounds like we did it! It's fucking perfect! I've been rapping along to this for about an hour now and it's as if I did it!"

"You did do it. It's your vocals," I said.

"Yeah, but you know what I mean. It really sounds like I came in the studio with you guys and recorded it. Go for it. Put it out. It's all yours. It's incredible and we're going to change the world with this. People are going to lose their minds."

To a certain extent they did. The song influenced a new generation of kids who were listening to hip-hop and metal and showed them how it could be done right. I know it really inspired Limp Bizkit guitarist Wes Borland and Linkin Park as well as a bunch of other bands. But I give Rage Against the Machine full credit for pioneering rap-metal. We were a metal band that loved rap and collaborated with Public Enemy. We stayed a metal band and Public Enemy remained a rap group. Rage created this whole new thing that was absolutely groundbreaking.

As influential as "Bring the Noise" might have been, not everyone understood what we were doing with it at first. When we finished it, we were out of our minds about how good it sounded. After we played it for the new regime at Island Records, there were a few long seconds of silence before someone finally spoke.

"How do we market this?" said an A&R guy. "What do we do with it?"

"What do you mean what do you do?!?" I blurted. "You fucking get it out there. Do whatever it takes to get it on the radio. People are going to love it. It's like Run DMC and Aerosmith but backward. This is a metal band covering a rap song. And it's got Public Enemy on it!"

Public Enemy were at their peak at the time, and we were doing great. We saw no reason "Bring the Noise" couldn't be as big as "Walk This Way." As emotional as I was in that meeting, Jonny Z was going nuts, waving his arms, eyebrows flapping like Groucho Marx. He was in full Peter Grant mode, saying how this was going to be the biggest song of all time.

Island remained on the fence and acted pretty nonchalant. That was a huge bummer. Worse yet, Def Jam owned half the track and had the right to release it as well. Since Island didn't own it outright, they didn't care what happened with it. We were literally shouting that this was the best thing we had ever done and they were idiots for not recognizing that. Jonny Z threatened to release it through Megaforce and tell everyone that Island wanted no part of it. Since Island didn't want one of their main bands badmouthing them, they agreed to release the song on our *Attack of the Killer B's* record, which was mostly covers and live tracks. Public Enemy put the song on their *Apocalypse 91* album. *Killer B's* did great and sold a ton of records, making an otherwise throwaway B-sides disc into a gold record. We wanted to hit the road with Public Enemy, but first we had to prepare for a giant Iron Maiden tour that started in Barcelona, Spain, on October 21, 1990.

In the beginning, it couldn't have been better. We were playing arenas all over the world with Maiden, and rabid metal fans were loving us. Then five weeks in, Bruce got sick and lost his voice, and Maiden had to cancel ten shows. We couldn't do the concerts without them, and all our gear was in Maiden's trucks, so we couldn't play our own club shows. We were stuck and bleeding money. It would have cost us more to fly home and then fly back for the rest of the tour than to stay in Europe. So we decided to find a place with snow and go skiing.

We drove to Innsbruck, Austria, which was beautiful but expensive. Everyone in the crew was on salary. We had hotels booked in every major city that we were losing money on. We hit the slopes every day, which was great. We knew we were fucked, so we figured why not have fun and make the best of it? One day I got back to my room and there was a phone call from Jonny telling me I would have to write a check for $16,000 at the end of the tour. I hadn't made a dime in Anthrax at that point, other than album and merch advances, and those went pretty quickly. We thought we'd actually come home with a little bit of cash from the Maiden dates, and suddenly I was being told we were in the red because of the shows Maiden canceled. We should have made money on that tour, but by the time we headed back on the road with Maiden, we were $80,000 in the hole, and we didn't have concert insurance because we weren't the headliner.

We were flipping the fuck out. We couldn't afford to lose $80,000. Shit, we didn't have that much money between the five of us. Jonny went back to our agent, John Jackson, and Maiden's manager, Rod Smallwood, and tried to figure out a way to minimize or eliminate the damage. He asked if Maiden could add one dollar to the ticket price for the rest of the shows and we could use the money to recoup. Maiden's people said it was impossible at that point to do that.

Basically, we were screwed. For the rest of that tour, as fun as it was playing to Maiden's audience, we were freaking the fuck out. Jonny figured out that we could pay off the $80,000 with merch money, so it wouldn't have to come from our personal bank accounts, but that was supposed to be money we would have made. We resigned ourselves to having to pay the money. Then at the end of the tour when we went to settle our debt, it didn't exist anymore.

We thought there might have been a clerical or computer error and a bill would arrive soon enough. Then we found out that Smallwood and Maiden made up the loss for us. We didn't lose a dime. That proved to us what kind of people Maiden are and what kind of folks they surround themselves with. They understood that it wasn't fair for us to lose money because they took time off, so they made our debt go away. Not only are they one of the greatest bands ever, they're some of the best guys you could ever hope to meet.

In the end, we made okay money on that tour, but most of it went right back into the band. We built these elaborate stages with walkways and ramps, and for the *Persistence* tour we had the giant clock from the album reconstructed in minute detail sitting on top of a platform on stage right; that cost a small fortune. We wanted to look like Maiden even when we weren't on tour with them. Jonny Z said to us, "You realize you could make two hundred grand at the end of this tour, or you could not make any money because you want to ship your stage everywhere around the world."

We were stubborn: "We can't play without our stage. Iron Maiden has their stage."

"Yeah, but Iron Maiden is selling out arenas," Jonny sighed, explaining the obvious. "They can afford to travel with that production. You guys are not able to really afford it. You can *do* it, but you're not going to see a penny."

We didn't care. We were just going for it and doing it. We weren't worried about mortgages or college funds. We figured the success and production would keep getting bigger, so, hey, let's load the giant clock onto the truck and think about what else we could build.

After the European dates with Iron Maiden, we came home for two weeks over Christmas and New Year's and then went out again with them in the States from January through March. Most of the shows went off without a hitch. Then we played Irvine Meadows in Laguna Hills, California, and there was a dude in the front of the stage who kept throwing firecrackers at us. I couldn't see who it was, so I got on the mike between songs and said, "Hey man, whoever's doing that, you'd better stop, because we're going to leave, and there's 15,000 people here that'll be pretty pissed at you."

Then I said to the crowd, "If you see who's doing it, point them out to security, or police that shit yourself." The firecrackers continued to fly, and sure enough when we finished the next song, all these kids started pointing at this one guy about eight rows back on the left side of the stage. They were holding him so he couldn't get away. Security went running over, and I said, "Let's get him out of here so we can finish the show." I was trying to contain my fury and be professional. But when security brought him down the aisle and started walking him past the front of the stage to escort him out I lost it. I jumped off the stage, the security guy let go of him, and I plowed into this dude and started punching him in the face. As I was hitting him, I saw something fly past my head and land on the guy. It was Frankie. He had done a flying dropkick through the air and nailed this kid in the face, like something from a kung-fu movie. Security pulled Frankie off the guy and we climbed back onstage.

After the show, the head of security came into our dressing room and said, "We have the guy backstage."

My heart sank. "Does he want to press charges?" I asked, expecting the worst.

"No," the guard said. "We wanted to know if *you* wanted to call the cops and press charges. What you guys did was awesome. If you want, we'll have him arrested."

"No, let him go. I think he learned his lesson," I said.

It was the first in a series of weird occurrences on that tour. In March 1991 we played in the MTV *Rock N' Jock* softball game, where a bunch of musicians play ball with a bunch of veejays and producers and everyone drinks too much. We were outside all day in the sun, and then that night we played LA with Maiden. Even though we were pretty wiped from our long day, a bunch of us went to a club on Sunset after the show. It wasn't an official after-party, just a bunch of guys going to a bar. At about midnight I was having drinks with Debbie, Charlie, and some guys in the crew. One of them pulled out a joint. I was already buzzed and feeling good, so I took a hit. Within twenty-five minutes I started feeling like I did that night I ate the shrimp. The club was packed, so I figured I was dehydrated and exhausted and needed to go home. Next thing I knew, people were standing around me outside trying to revive me. I had passed out in the club, and Charlie and Frankie had to carry me out to the street. My butt was wet so I turned to Debbie and said, "Why did you sit me in a puddle?"

"We didn't sit you in a puddle," she said, almost frantic. "You peed your pants, passed out, and started shaking. We thought something was really wrong!"

We went home, went to bed, and the next day I felt fine, so I didn't think about what happened again until years later.

keeping üp with the
Kilmisters

Written by: **Scott Ian**
Illustrated by: **Stephen Thompson**

IN THE FALL OF 1985 JOEY BELLADONNA, JON ZAZULA AKA JONNY Z (ANTHRAX'S MANAGER) AND I FLEW OVER TO LONDON SO JOEY AND I COULD DO PROMO FOR OUR SECOND ALBUM; SPREADING THE DISEASE. THIS WAS ONLY MY SECOND TIME OUT OF THE COUNTRY AND JOEY'S FIRST. WE WERE BOTH VERY EXCITED TO BE IN LONDON, THE EPICENTER OF ALL THE NEW WAVE OF BRITISH HEAVY METAL BANDS WE LOVED AND THE HOME OF KERRANG! MAGAZINE (IT WAS STILL A METAL MAG THEN). OH YEAH, AND REAL BEER.

THINGS HAD GROWN CONSIDERABLY FOR US AS A BAND SINCE THE RELEASE OF FISTFUL OF METAL IN JANUARY OF 84 AND THERE WAS A DEFINITE BUZZ AROUND SPREADING THE DISEASE WHICH WAS GOING TO BE OUR FIRST MAJOR LABEL RELEASE ON ISLAND RECORDS. SPREADING THE DISEASE WAS JOEY'S FIRST RECORD WITH US AND HIS VOCALS WERE A GAME CHANGER. WE HAD A REAL SINGER IN ANTHRAX AND THAT SET US APART FROM OUR CONTEMPORARIES IN METALLICA, SLAYER AND MEGADETH.

REMEMBER, WE WEREN'T THE BIG 4 YET. IN 1985 WE WERE ALL A BUNCH OF KIDS SCRAMBLING TO MAKE ENDS MEET AND GET OUR BANDS NOTICED. WE FELT THAT HAVING A SINGER MORE IN THE VEIN OF HALFORD OR DICKINSON WAS WHO ANTHRAX WAS AND IT WAS GOING TO MAKE US A BIGGER AND BETTER BAND AND OPEN MORE DOORS FOR US CREATIVELY.

AND IT DID. JOEY'S VOCALS MIXED WITH OUR NYC THRASH SENSIBILITY CREATED A NEW SOUND AND SPREADING THE DISEASE WAS THE RECORD THAT PUSHED THE DOOR OPEN WIDE FOR US TO BE ABLE TO MOVE FORWARD AND MAKE AMONG THE LIVING. SHIT, THERE WAS ENOUGH EXCITEMENT FOR THE LABEL TO FLY THE THREE OF US TO LONDON AND PAY FOR EVERY-THING AND AT THE TIME THAT WAS INCREDIBLE. IN MY MIND WE HAD "MADE" IT EVEN THOUGH I WAS STILL LIVING IN A 10' X 6' BEDROOM IN MY MOM'S APARTMENT WITH MOST OF MY GEAR AND A MATTRESS ON THE FLOOR.

WE ARRIVED IN LONDON AND JOEY AND I SPENT A FULL DAY DOING PRESS AND THEN WE

WENT TO THE MARQUEE, THE ORIGINAL ONE ON WARDOUR ST TO SEE THE SWEET. I

REMEMBER THE SWEET BEING GOOD BUT I DON'T HAVE ANY SPECIFIC MEMORIES ABOUT THE

SHOW AND YOU'LL FIND OUT WHY SOON ENOUGH.

AFTER THE SHOW WE WERE INVITED BY SOME OF THE KERRANG WRITERS TO GO ACROSS

THE STREET TO A BAR CALLED THE ST MORITZ.

I WALKED INTO THIS CLUB WHICH WAS BASICALLY A DARK BASEMENT WITH SOME TABLES AND I SEE LEMMY STANDING AT THE BAR. I GOT REALLY EXCITED AND I FIGURED THAT THIS IS HOW IT IS IN LONDON, YOU JUST WALK INTO A BAR AND YOUR HEROES ARE JUST HANGING OUT. I ASKED THE KERRANG! GUYS IF WE WENT TO ANOTHER BAR WOULD STEVE HARRIS BE THERE? I WASN'T KIDDING.

I WAS NERVOUS TO WALK UP TO HIM, I MEAN IT'S FRICKIN' LEMMY BUT FOR FUCKS SAKE I WAS WEARING A MOTÖRHEAD SWEATSHIRT SO I THREW CAUTION DOWN MY THROAT WITH THE REST OF MY PINT AND I HEADED OVER TO HIM.

LEMMY ORDERS TWO WHISKEY AND COKES. I'VE NEVER HAD A WHISKEY IN MY LIFE. THE ONLY THING I KNOW ABOUT WHISKEY IS THAT MY GRANDFATHER HAD SOME IN THE SAME CABINET WITH THE MANISCHEWITZ AND AS A KID WHENEVER I'D GET SENT TO GET THE WINE OUT OF THE CABINET FOR THE PASSOVER SEDER I'D SMELL SOMETHING TERRIBLE. MY TEN YEAR OLD JEW* NOSE WOULD SHRINK AND MY EYES WOULD BURN FROM THE HOT CAUSTIC SMELL THAT WOULD PUNCH ME IN THE FACE EVERY TIME I OPENED THAT DREADED CABINET. WHEN I ASKED MY MOM WHAT STUNK IN THE LIQUOR CABINET I WAS TOLD IT WAS GRANDPA'S WHISKEY. AND NOW I'VE GOT A GLASS OF CHILDHOOD NIGHTMARE IN FRONT OF ME AND I AM EXPECTED TO DRINK IT, I HAVE TO. I'M DRINKING WITH LEMMY FOR FUCKS SAKE AND I AM SECONDS AWAY FROM CHEERS-ING WITH HIM AND I'M SWEATING THIS, WORRIED THAT I'M GOING TO MAKE A FACE OR SPIT IT OUT OR EVEN WORSE, PUKE IT RIGHT BACK UP IN HIS FACE. **NOT COOL.** I'M ON THE VERGE OF PANIC WHEN THIS R. LEE ERMEY LIKE VOICE IN MY HEAD SPOKE UP...

LISTEN TO ME JACKASS, JUST CALM DOWN AND LISTEN TO ME. YOU ARE STANDING HERE DRINKING WITH LEMMY. HE IS YOUR FUCKING HERO AND THERE IS NO WAY IN HELL YOU ARE GOING TO ACT LIKE A PUSSY IN FRONT OF HIM! YOU'RE GOING TO DRINK YOUR DRINK LIKE A MAN! LIKE CLINT FUCKING EASTWOOD YOU'RE GOING TO DRINK IT! NO FACES, NO SPITTING, AND NO PUKING! NOW MAN THE FUCK UP AND DRINK YOUR DRINK!!!

MY NERVES STEADIED AND I STEELED MYSELF AFTER BEING RIPPED BY R. LEE ERMEY. LEMMY AND I CLINKED GLASSES, "CHEERS" AND I DRANK AND I GOT IT DOWN WITH A BIT OF A GRIMACE AND A SLIGHT SHUDDER. LEMMY WASN'T EVEN PAYING ATTENTION SO I GOT AWAY WITH IT!

*Jew meaning big

THE NEXT THING I REMEMBER IS BEING WOKEN UP BY JONNY Z IN MY HOTEL ROOM STILL IN MY CLOTHES AND HAVING TO PACK UP BECAUSE WE WERE ALREADY LATE FOR OUR FLIGHT TO MUNICH TO CONTINUE THE PRESS TOUR.

I WAS IN SOME FUCKING STATE OF BEING, MORE THAN A HANGOVER, JUST PHYSICALLY DESTROYED. I WAS HURTING FROM HEAD TO TOE, LIKE JUDGE DREDD WENT AT ME WITH A BATON. I WAS A DISGUSTING SWEATY PUKE COVERED PILE OF SHIT IN TWO DAY OLD CLOTHES. I MANAGED TO PACK MY BAG BETWEEN PUKING EPISODES AND WE HEADED TO HEATHROW. I COULD BARELY SPEAK, IT HURT TO BREATHE. I ASKED THEM WHAT HAPPENED AND THEY TOLD ME I WAS DRINKING WITH LEMMY FOR A WHILE AND THEN I WAS COMPLETELY GONE, JUST OUT OF CONTROL. THEY TOLD ME AT SOME POINT I RAN PAST THEM RIGHT OUT THE DOOR OF THE CLUB, YELLING INCOHERENTLY. JONNY FOLLOWED ME OUT FIGURING I RAN OUT TO BE SICK. HE TOLD ME THAT I WAS RUNNING BACK AND FORTH ACROSS THE STREET, SHOUTING, SWEARING LIKE A MANIAC AND DIVING INTO PILES OF GARBAGE. NOW AT LEAST ALL THE PAIN I WAS IN MADE SENSE. THE ILLUS-TRATION ABOVE DEPICTS THIS PERFECTLY. IT LOOKS LIKE AN OLD IRON MAIDEN 12" EXCEPT THIS ISN'T RUNNING FREE IT'S SCOTT'S AN IDIOT.

THEY GOT ME OUT OF BED AND CARRIED ME INTO A TAXI. I COULDN'T WALK, I WAS TOO WEAK AND TOO SICK. JONNY HAD TO CARRY ME FROM THE TAXI THROUGH HEATHROW. I WAS OVER HIS SHOULDER PUKING BEHIND HIM AND HE WAS SHOUTING AT ME "NOT ON MY BACK! NOT ON MY LEGS!" IN 1985 YOU COULD ACTUALLY GET THROUGH AN AIRPORT LIKE THIS. POST 9/11? FUCK NO. WE GOT TO SECURITY AND THE AGENTS WAVED THE *AMERICANS* THROUGH.

IT'S AMAZING WE MADE IT ON THE PLANE. AND THEN I HAD TO RUN FOR THE BATHROOM AS WE WERE TAXIING FOR TAKEOFF AND I PUKED AGAIN.

I PASSED OUT ON THE PLANE AND WOKE UP IN MUNICH. AT THIS POINT THE PUKING HAD SUBSIDED A BIT BUT BY THE TIME WE GOT TO THE HOTEL THINGS TOOK A TURN AND I WAS PUKING FROM MY ASS NOW AS WELL. I WAS FEVERISH, SHAKING, COULDN'T EVEN DRINK A SIP OF WATER WITHOUT BILE RACING FROM MY BODY.

JONNY HAD THE HOTEL CALL A DOCTOR. ABOUT FORTY FIVE MINUTES LATER THERE'S A KNOCK ON THE DOOR. JONNY OPENS IT AND *THIS GUY* WALKS IN. IN MY FEVERISH STATE HE LOOKED JUST LIKE DR SZELL FROM MARATHON MAN. HE WAS PROBABLY A WONDERFUL HUMAN BEING AND DOCTOR BUT ALL I KNEW ABOUT GERMANY I LEARNED FROM TV, MOVIES AND CAPTAIN AMERICA COMICS. AS FAR AS I WAS CONCERNED AS SOON AS WE LANDED IN MUNICH AN ALARM WENT OFF AND EVERYONE WAS POINTING AND SCREAMING AT ME LIKE LEONARD NIMOY AT THE END OF INVASION OF THE BODY SNATCHERS. ANYWAY, MY JEWDY-SENSE WAS TINGLING AND I COULD TELL THAT THIS DOCTOR WASN'T THRILLED WITH THIS QUIVERING MESS UNDER THE COVERS BECAUSE HE JUST STOOD TEN FEET FROM THE BED STARING AT ME AND THEN AFTER A FEW MINUTES PULLED OUT A HUGE NEEDLE ALREADY FILLED WITH SOMETHING AND SAID "YOU NEED THIS." I SAID "WHAT DO YOU MEAN I NEED THIS? WHAT IS THAT? YOU HAVEN'T EVEN EXAMINED ME, TAKEN MY TEMPERATURE OR ANYTHING, HOW DO YOU KNOW I NEED THAT?" HE JUST FROWNED AND REPEATED, "YOU NEED THIS." HE MIGHT AS WELL HAVE ASKED "IS IT SAFE?" I WAS IN NO SHAPE TO ARGUE WITH HIM, "OK, GIVE ME THE SHOT." HE ASKED ME TO PULL DOWN MY TROUSERS. I GOT OUT FROM UNDER THE BLANKETS, SHIVERING AND SWEATING AND I PULLED MY SWEATPANTS DOWN AND ROLLED ON MY SIDE. THERE WAS COMPLETE SILENCE IN THE ROOM FOR LIKE FIVE SECONDS.

ACH... DISGUSTING!

AT SOME POINT OVER THE PREVIOUS TWENTY FOUR HOURS I HAD SHIT MYSELF.
I HAD BEEN WALKING AROUND WITH PANTS FULL OF POO. THIS GUY WAS
STARING AT WHAT MIGHT AS WELL HAVE BEEN SOME BUMS HAIRY SHIT-STAINED
ASS. I WAS PAST THE POINT OF EMBARRASSMENT. IF ANYTHING I WAS FEELING
THE OPPOSITE OF THAT BECAUSE I REMEMBER HAVING A TINY INTERNAL LAUGH
AT THE FACT THAT THIS HALF A NAZI PRICK OF A DOCTOR HAD TO SMELL MY
FILTHY JEW BUTT. MY REVENGE FOR THE HOLOCAUST. NO, NOT REALLY.

MY FILTH DIDN'T STOP HIM FROM DOING HIS JOB AND THE NEEDLE FELT LIKE HE
WAS PUTTING A CIGAR OUT ON MY ASS. I HAVE TO SAY MENGELE JR KNEW WHAT
HE WAS DOING BECAUSE WHATEVER AUSCHWITZ TESTED POTION WAS IN THAT
SHOT, IT WORKED. ALL THE SHAKING AND SWEATING STOPPED AND IT KNOCKED
ME THE FUCK OUT AND I SLEPT FOR FOURTEEN HOURS. THANKS DOC.

I WOKE UP THE NEXT DAY LIKE A HUMAN. I WAS THIRSTY, I WASN'T SHITTING MYSELF, I COULD WALK. I SHOWERED, ATE, GOT MY LAUNDRY DONE AND ACTUALLY DID MY INTERVIEWS.

AT SOME POINT DURING ALL THIS JONNY HAD ME SIGN A LIFETIME MANAGE-MENT CONTRACT BECAUSE OF HIM TAKING CARE OF ME. HE WROTE IT ON A NAPKIN. I WIPED MY ASS WITH IT. IF YOU EVER WANT TO GET OUT OF ANY DEAL YOU'VE SIGNED JUST WIPE YOUR ASS WITH IT. TOTALLY LEGIT AND WILL NULLIFY ANY DEAL.

CUT TO MAY 1986, ABOUT SEVEN MONTHS LATER. ANTHRAX IS PLAYING THEIR FIRST EVER SHOW IN THE UK AT THE HAMMERSMITH PALAIS IN LONDON. THE SHOW IS SOLD OUT AND WE'RE ALL SUPER EXCITED IN THE DRESSING ROOM BEFORE THE SHOW. EVERYONE IS GETTING READY, WARMING UP, STRETCHING ETC AND THE DRESSING ROOM DOOR OPENS AND LEMMY WALKS IN. NOW EVERYONE WAS REALLY EXCITED. SERIOUSLY, FUCKING LEMMY CAME TO SEE US??? LEMMY IS SAYING HI TO EVERYONE AND THEN HE SEES ME AND SAYS "HOW YA FEELING?"
I COULDN'T BELIEVE HE REMEMBERED THE NIGHT AT THE ST MORITZ. I GUESS AT SOME POINT I MUST'VE TOLD HIM ABOUT ANTHRAX.

I ASKED HIM WHAT HAPPENED? DID I DO ANYTHING STUPID? I TOLD HIM
ABOUT MY TRAIL OF SHIT AND PUKE FROM LONDON TO MUNICH, BECAUSE I HAD
NO MEMORY OF ANYTHING PAST THAT FIRST DRINK. (THAT'S LEMMY'S REACTION
TO MY STORY ABOVE). LEMMY SAID EVERYTHING WAS FINE, WE WERE
TALKING ABOUT MUSIC AND THAT I HAD TOLD HIM ABOUT SEEING MOTÖRHEAD
PLAY IN NYC AND WHAT AN INFLUENCE THEY WERE ON US AND THEN AT SOME
POINT HE SAID I JUST STOPPED MAKING SENSE. HE SAID HE ASKED ME IF I
WAS MUCH OF A DRINKER AND WHEN I SAID NO, HE SAID AGAIN "I CAN TELL."
HE ASKED ME "WHAT DID I THINK I WAS DOING TRYING TO KEEP UP WITH
HIM?" AND I TOLD HIM "YOU'RE LEMMY, WHEN DO I EVER GET THE CHANCE TO
HANG OUT WITH YOU IN LONDON. I JUST FIGURED I'D GO FOR IT." "BAD IDEA"
HE LAUGHED AND THAT WAS THAT. THE SHOW THAT NIGHT WAS AMAZING AND
WAS THE START OF OUR LOVE AFFAIR WITH THE UK.

LEMMY AND I HAVE BEEN FRIENDS EVER SINCE. A FEW YEARS BACK I WAS
ASKED TO GIVE A QUOTE ABOUT MOTÖRHEAD FOR THEIR EVERYTHING LOUDER
THAN EVERYTHING ELSE RECORD. OF COURSE MOTÖRHEAD RULES! IMMEDI-
ATELY CAME TO MIND BUT I FIGURED I COULD DO BETTER. I THOUGHT BACK
TO 1980 WHEN I BOUGHT MY FIRST MOTÖRHEAD RECORD, ACE OF SPADES. I
DIDN'T KNOW ANYTHING ABOUT THE BAND, I JUST THOUGHT THE COVER LOOKED
COOL. I WENT STRAIGHT HOME FROM THE RECORD STORE EXCITED TO HEAR
WHAT THESE THREE BANDITOS HAD TO OFFER. I PUT THE NEEDLE ON THE
RECORD AND THE SONG ACE OF SPADES KICKED IN AND I COULDN'T FUCKING
BELIEVE WHAT I WAS HEARING. I'D NEVER HEARD ANYTHING LIKE IT. THE
ENERGY, THE POWER, THE SPEED, THE ATTITUDE. I WAS SO BLOWN AWAY AND
ALL I COULD THINK OF WAS "WHO THE HELL ARE THESE THREE MEXICAN'S AND
HOW DO THEY PLAY SO FAST???" I TOLD LEMMY THAT STORY AND THEY USED
THAT QUOTE ON THE RECORD. I'M JUST HONORED TO BE A PART OF THEIR
HISTORY!

ANTHRAX HAS TOURED WITH MOTÖRHEAD MANY TIMES OVER THE YEARS AS
RECENTLY AS THE 2012 ROCKSTAR MAYHEM FESTIVAL AND A SOLD OUT
UK/EUROPE TOUR IN NOVEMBER AND DECEMBER OF 2012 AS WELL.
AND IN CASE YOU WERE WONDERING... I NEVER TRIED TO KEEP UP WITH
LEMMY AGAIN.

Chapter 19

TOUR HIGHS AND LINEUP LOWS

After the shows with Iron Maiden, we toured the US leg of Clash of the Titans with Slayer, Megadeth, and Alice in Chains. It was three of the Big 4 thrash groups and one of the best of the new batch of Seattle bands that were about to take over the world. We started to see our first ever tour income—after we were charged with the single most expensive episode of damage in our career. I can't remember who started it, but on days off from the tour, we always stayed at the same hotel as Slayer, which is asking for trouble right there. Megadeth never stayed in the hotel with us. The other guys in Megadeth and their crew wanted to, and they would hang out with us at the hotel, but Dave Mustaine wouldn't allow them to stay there, because he was angry with Slayer at the time. He was angry with everyone at the time except us, pretty much.

When we checked into the Hilton in Indianapolis, Indiana, on June 17, 1991, all hell broke loose. Slayer made sure they started the tour armed with paintball guns, so after a couple shows we all had to have paintball guns to defend ourselves. There were twelve guns between our camp and theirs, and every day on tour there were wars backstage. Someone from Slayer would sabotage us and open fire. These paintballs fuckin' hurt when they hit you. We didn't have warrior vests or helmets. We were in T-shirts and jeans, and there was nothing but cloth protecting us from the blinding sting of a paintball to the back or stomach.

There were two rules: no shooting at the head and no up-close assassinations, but the rules were loose and there was nonstop fucking warfare. Sometimes we'd go onstage with big welts from where the paintballs had hit us in the arms or legs. When we got to Indianapolis everyone got extra drunk—even me—and extra rowdy. I was drinking beer, and Slayer vocalist and bassist Tom Araya introduced me to tequila. I never had tequila in my life, and, let's just say, it clouded my judgment. Someone's hotel room opened up onto this roof area. So we went out his window, walked across the roof, and saw the giant white Hilton sign on the side of this building. We immediately grabbed our guns and opened fire. We shot hundreds and hundreds of rounds for twenty minutes until there wasn't any white left on the sign. It looked like a vomit-colored Jackson Pollock. We were proud of our work and high-fived one another before we went back to our rooms. The hotel didn't share our artistic aesthetic.

The next morning when we were checking out, our tour manager, Rick Downey, and the guy who was on the road with Slayer were having a heated discussion with someone at the front desk. In our drunken state the night before, we all figured the paint would wash off the sign or drip off. No one thought they'd wake up in the morning and the Hilton sign would be 8,000 shades of puke. Rick walked up to us and delivered the bad news. The hotel was charging us for damaging and cleaning the sign. It was going to cost $10,000 and we would have to split it $5,000 per band. We couldn't very well say, "It wasn't us!" Everyone had seen us with our paintball guns. It wasn't a big secret that we were having backstage battles. So you didn't have to be a CSI detective to know what happened.

Every New York musician dreams of someday playing Madison Square Garden. It's one of those things you strive for. MSG is the Mecca of New York venues, and everyone huge played there—Zeppelin, the Who, Sabbath, Alice Cooper. And when I was a kid, that's where KISS made me realize I wanted to rock and roll every night for thousands of people. I also saw legendary shows there by Ted Nugent, AC/DC, Judas Priest, and Iron Maiden before Anthrax got off the ground. Our opportunity to headline the Garden came in 1991 when Clash of the Titans hit New York. The show sold out. We were super stoked and invited all of our friends and family members to come hang out with us backstage. My mom came, though our relationship was still frosty at best; we had only recently started talking again.

She said she was happy for me and hugged me, and I believed her. I took pride in the fact that we were headlining MSG and my parents were there to see it. Our dressing room was packed, and we decided not to have our tour manager clear the room thirty minutes before we went on. It was a moment worth celebrating. Then, five minutes before Anthrax were scheduled to go on, we left our dressing room and started to walk toward the stage. I was so excited to be walking in Gene Simmons's footsteps. Our intro music started playing, and above it I heard my mom's shrill voice, "Scott!!!" I figured she wanted to congratulate me and give me one more hug or a kiss for good luck. I smiled and turned around.

"I left my jacket in the dressing room! I don't know how I'll ever get it. There's all this security back there and everything and I'm not sure which door it is. Will you please get it for me?"

I actually laughed out loud over the ridiculousness of the situation. Here I was expecting a Kodak moment where Mom tells me how proud she is of me, and instead of carrying that extra little victory with me onto the stage, I have to exit my big moment to run back to the dressing room to get my mom's jacket and then make it back to the stage in time for the beginning of our set.

Fortunately, I reentered my moment, and the MSG show was everything I hoped it would be, especially when we had Chuck D and Flav join us on "Bring the Noise" for the first time ever in front of a sold-out New York City crowd. It went down so well we knew we had something huge on our hands.

The Clash of the Titans tour ended in Miami, and we were determined to pull an end-of-tour prank on Slayer. We decided to break their evil façade and make them crack up laughing onstage. Back then there was no smiling in Slayer. They were SLAYER. Their singer, Tom Araya, is like a big smiley grandpa bear now when he plays, but back in the nineties no one in Slayer ever broke character. They grimaced, scowled, and snarled the entire set. Slayer took pride in being the most savage band in town, or at least looking the part, but we knew that offstage they were just a bunch of goofballs who loved to fuck around and laugh all the time.

Slayer's end-of-tour prank was to shoot the shit out of us with their paintball guns during our set. They hid in the wings of the stage like Navy Seals and picked us off. That shit hurt! But we expected nothing less. What were they going to do, run out with water balloons and feathers? Hell no—they're Slayer.

The day of the final show, we sent a crew guy to a fish market to buy the biggest fish he could find. It must have weighed two hundred pounds and it stank. We had the lighting guys put it up in the rigging, and we instructed them to slowly lower it as soon as Slayer started playing their last song, "Angel of Death." We wanted the fish to be right in Tom's eye line as soon as he started his bloodcurdling scream. It couldn't have worked out better. They started the song, and the fish came down super slow and hit its mark at the perfect time. We were at the side of the stage laughing. Their guitarist Jeff Hanneman was head-banging, looking as mean as a serial killer, his long blonde hair matted with sweat and flying everywhere. All of a sudden he saw this fish in his peripheral vision and busted out laughing. Then their other guitarist, Kerry King, saw it and tried to maintain his composure, but he lost it, too. You could see him trying to stop himself from cracking up; it looked like he was constipated. Then the mighty Tom Araya broke and laughed while he was singing. The fish hung so perfectly in front of his microphone, and it dangled there for the entire song.

Two weeks after the Clash of the Titans tour ended, I got a call from our business manager, asking me where I wanted him to send the check. I was confused and asked him what it was for and he told me it was for tour profits.

"We made money?" I said in awe. That's when the lightbulb went off in my head. "Hmmm, maybe Jonny was right. I guess we shouldn't have spent five grand shooting paintballs. Maybe we should stop building bigger stages, because if we did that, we could get a big, fat check at the end of *every* tour."

We got back from the Clash of the Titans and things were happening. Money and tour offers were coming in. But the core of the band was fucking rotten. I was losing my mind, and I felt like I was keeping an important secret away from everyone who really needed to hear it. I don't remember the first time I ever expressed my dissatisfaction with Joey to the rest of the band. Frankie knew quite a bit, and so did Charlie, because through the writing process of *Persistence,* I told them how frustrated I was. Then we'd tour and everything seemed to go well. I can't pinpoint a final moment. It was a slow, slow, slow burn, and maybe the dynamite detonated during Clash of the Titans. Only the explosion didn't happen in the open; it took place in my mind. During a day off in Chicago, we shot the video for "Bring the Noise" with Public Enemy. Boom! The explosion that validated my feelings about the future of the band went off in my head like a nail bomb. Chuck, Flavor Flav, and I were rapping. The rest of the band members were playing their respective instruments. As happy as I was to be rapping with Chuck, in my heart I wished Joey was doing it, that he would've stepped up and got outside his box, but that just wasn't going to happen. So where does Joey fit in that picture? He's running and jumping around, being goofy, and finding something to do to be a part of it. But I was the one rapping and being the front man. That's probably why still, to this day, people who don't know the band well think I'm the singer of Anthrax. Nine times out of ten, that's what they say to me. But we were burning too hot to make a change right away.

After the "Bring the Noise" shoot, we were in this van on the way back to the hotel, and I said to Chuck, "Man, that was a lot of fun, fake-playing that all day long. We should do some real shows together."

"Tell us when and where, and we're in—whatever you want to do."

It was that simple and organic.

We planned to tour together starting in October, and that's when it became obvious to me that four guys in Anthrax wanted to push the envelope and try new things, and we all felt Joey was still in the same zone he was in for *Spreading* and *Among.* By mid-'91, the cancer that was eating at the gut of Anthrax started impacting my home life. Maybe the two sources of friction had nothing to do with one another, but they rubbed together in my head like two pieces of sandpaper. After Clash of the Titans, I was looking forward to having some time at home and being with Debbie. Within a few days, I realized everything was wrong.

She seemed weird, really possessive one moment and then she'd tell me she needed space the next. We didn't have sex for a few days after I had been on the road for a long time. I thought she was being very distant. When I asked her if things were okay, she made it clear they weren't.

"You come home from tour and you expect everything to be normal!" she began. "While you're away, I get to do my own thing. Then you come back and you're just in the way! I wish you'd stay on tour."

"Isn't it good that I'm home and now we get to be together?"

"Yeah, but I like to do my thing and not have to revolve around your schedule," she said.

I got a little angry: "You can do whatever you want. I'm not your boss. But we live together. We're a couple. It would be nice to be a couple, not just live separately as roommates in our house."

We made up and apologized to each other. I was so excited to be home with her, and she was on a different planet altogether. I should have taken that little blowup as a sign of things to come. Instead, I viewed it as a natural reaction to an unnatural situation. Touring can turn normal people into complete basket cases.

We finished up 1991 by making good on our pact with Public Enemy. I always wanted to bridge barriers like that and help open people's minds to new ideas and sounds. Primus came on the tour with us. They were just breaking at the time, so they brought out more people. When we finished our set at the end of the night, everyone would come out, and we'd all do "Bring the Noise" together. We filmed the Irvine Meadows show. There were 15,000 people, sold out. There was a smell of invention in the air that night. Everything we did with Public Enemy was a career highlight. At the same time, there's no question that we alienated a portion of our audience by doing those shows. Some of our fans didn't like it, didn't understand it. They didn't want to come to the show, and they would wait until we put out another record to decide whether they still wanted us on their radar.

People loved "I'm The Man" because it seemed like a novelty. Nobody took it seriously because we didn't keep rapping after that. "Bring the Noise" wasn't a joke. It was something we strongly believed in. No other metal bands were playing with rap groups at that time. Doing that may have opened us up to a new, alternative audience, but that didn't replace what we lost.

Before the tour, I asked Chuck, "What do you think these shows are going to be like?"

"We have different audiences for different tours," he said. "When we were out with Sisters of Mercy, it was all white college kids. Black kids weren't coming to that show. When we're on a hip-hop tour, it's obviously a black audience. But more white people buy our records than black people. This tour is going to be all white people. You'll see."

He was absolutely right. It's not like I thought we would become the first metal band embraced by the black community and this whole giant audience that buys rap records would start consuming Anthrax albums. The white college kids who didn't listen to metal but listened to rap and indie rock—maybe some of them got turned on to us. As symbolically important as that tour was, it didn't change anything, at least not right away. But we weren't thinking about laying the ground-work for a new musical genre at the time. We were having too much fun for that. Back then and even today, people look at Public Enemy as this militant black, super-serious rap group. They used to scare the shit out of white people, and some thought they were anti-Semitic, because one of their members, Professor Griff, made some unfriendly com-ments about Jews. He told one journalist, "Jews were responsible for most of the wickedness in the world." He was sort of fired for that but rejoined the group later.

I just felt bad for him. I was friends with Griff during that whole time, and he knew I was Jewish. I don't think he hated Jews, I think his comments were taken out of context. Was it smart to say whatever he said? No, but we hung out and laughed, and he never had a problem with me. Spitz is Jewish, too. There were two Jews, two Italians, and a part Italian / part Indian in Anthrax. All that was missing was a punch line: "These two Jews, two Italians and a half breed walk into a bar . . ."

The other thing no one mentions is that Public Enemy's label, Def Jam, was co-run by Lyor Cohen, the biggest Jew in the business. Did Griff harbor some prejudice deep down? I don't know; I can only judge by my relationship with him. Chuck D definitely wasn't anti-Semitic.

He's one of the smartest people on the planet and he's very intense, but what everyone misses is he's also the nicest guy you'll ever meet. He loves to have fun and is the first to laugh at a good joke. All those Public Enemy dudes look like such hard-asses onstage, but they just want to have fun and entertain the fuck out of people. And Flavor Flav comes from another planet, entirely. He's like a fucking court jester 24/7.

The really funny thing about our tour with Public Enemy is that, for all the touring they had done up to that point, they never had chicks and groupies hanging out with them. Back then, it didn't happen in rap like it did in rock. So when Flavor found out he could hang out on our crew bus and get girls, he never wanted to leave. The first time he saw girls would come on the crew bus, take their clothes off, and have Polaroid pictures taken of them or even maybe blow someone, he went out of his fucking mind. He was on the bus with the crew in the back lounge every day. You couldn't pry him away with a crowbar. His eyes would be falling out of his skull when these chicks got naked and someone took out the camera and started snapping pictures. It's amazing he didn't quit Public Enemy right there and join our road crew.

It was a perfect matchup all the way around. The two camps got along so well. We used to play pranks on each other, and we always got the opening group, Young Black Teenagers, so bad. Before their set, we had the riggers set up cables like hunting traps so if someone stepped into the circle of wire, the trap sprung and the cable cinched around their leg and lifted them into the air. We got two of their guys. They didn't even step into the trap. A bunch of our guys and Public Enemy's guys and the S1Ws (Security of the First World) grabbed them and wrapped these cables around their ankles. They were hanging upside down from the rigging. Thank God none of them broke their ankles. While they were up there, we all grabbed knotted towels filled with baby powder and beat the crap out of them. I'm sure it fucking hurt, and each time we hit them, a giant cloud of powder burst out of the towel.

The last North American show we did with Public Enemy was in Vancouver on October 24, 1991, and Flavor Flav couldn't get into Canada because of his arrest record. So Frankie dressed up as Flavor. He didn't do blackface, but he zipped up his hoodie so nobody could see his face, and put on Flavor's outfit. He had the giant clock and big sunglasses. When the show started, Frankie had this big grin on, which he couldn't have suppressed if he tried. But that was fine 'cause Flavor was always smiling anyway. Terminator X started spinning up on a riser, and Public Enemy came out underneath it. The S1Ws marched out, Chuck walked out, and then Frankie ran out, jumped up, and went into the Flavor dance, which he had down perfect. None of the PE guys knew it was coming except Chuck. The S1Ws were supposed to stand there looking as serious as Slayer, never smiling, acting as PE's personal army. But they all lost it. Meanwhile, the audience thought it was Flavor Flav and couldn't figure out what was so funny.

Everyone had fun on that tour, but for Public Enemy, touring with Anthrax was also an education. At the time, nobody in rap toured professionally. It was the wild, wild West, and Chuck was determined to break the mold and do it right. They learned how by watching us and soaking up everything. Chuck's lighting guy sat at the board with our lighting guy. Their sound guy stayed with our soundman. They watched everything and everyone so they could emulate what our guys were doing, and I took that as a huge compliment. That's part of the reason they're the only rap group that's been on the road for twenty-seven years.

We got home from the Public Enemy tour at the end of October, and in my mind our time with Joey was up. Either we were finding a new singer or I was out. I didn't want to go through another album with a vocalist who didn't grasp that we had evolved and were no longer just that band that did "Medusa" and "I Am the Law." It wouldn't have been fair to me or to Joey to try to pretend we were still on the same page. We went to Europe with Public Enemy in January and February of '92, and when we got back to the States, the last thing we did with Joey was *Married with Children*, which aired February 23. Everyone flew to LA for the taping. On the show, we performed "In My World." I did the spoken word intro, and we only played the part of the song up to where the vocals came in, so, coincidentally, once again Joey was the odd man out.

Everyone in the band knew we needed to move forward. It's not like I was mad at Joey. It wasn't like with Neil where we hated the guy. We all loved Joey; it just wasn't working creatively anymore. I wasn't thrilled about firing him, but it had to be done. Having him singing my words felt fake, and that couldn't continue. Maybe the band couldn't continue. If I was lying to myself, I was lying to the audience. Everyone from management to the label asked us a million times, "Are you sure? Are you sure? Are you sure?" I understood their concern. Some bands never recover after they change their lead singer. And it wasn't like Joey was hurting our sales. We were doing great. "Do you really want to fuck with the formula?" asked Jonny. "Is this the right time to do this?"

In truth, it was the only time to do it and it was the only thing to do. We all felt like we had exhausted every possibility to make it work. If one of us even had a doubt, it wouldn't have happened. I felt terrible about asking Jonny Z to call Joey and tell him he was out of the band. It was arrogant and shitty of me not to call myself. I had so much else going on with Debbie and the band at that point that it was one task too many. So, Jonny Z fired Joey with a phone call, and that really blindsided him. He had no idea how unhappy we were with him or why there was no way we could grow if he was still in the band. He was oblivious to the depth of the turmoil and took it pretty hard. The timing was crazy, too, because our deal with Island was up, and Elektra and Columbia both wanted us and were willing to pay an obscene amount of money.

Chapter 20

A BUSH IN THE HAND

B ack in the eighties and nineties, Bob Krasnow ran Elektra. He was a visionary and a great record-man as well as a businessman, and he hired a staff of people who were passionate about music. There has always been a division at labels between artistic individuals like Rick Rubin, who come from a love for music, and bean counters, who are there to make sure the label makes money. We talked to Metallica, and they were really happy with Elektra so we sided with them. Bob and our A&R man, Steve Ralbovsky, came to our New York show on the Public Enemy tour. By that time we had decided to fire Joey, but we didn't know how to break it to the label that was about to advance us $4 million. Finally we told Steve and he told Bob. If I said we weren't worried that having a new singer in the band would put the kibosh on the whole deal, I'd be lying. But Steve got back to us and said, "If you think this is going to make the band better, then we back your decision."

What a lot of people don't realize is when we fired Joey he got his share of the Elektra advance—an equal cut as the rest of us. He had worked just as hard as we had for all those years and toured as much as we did. He was a huge part of Anthrax's success. He was the singer in the band that got us to the point that Elektra wanted to offer us a huge amount of money. Of course we felt he was entitled to his share. The timing for the Elektra deal was bittersweet. My divorce with Marge had gotten ugly, and her attorneys were fighting for all they could get. She knew there was a lot of money coming, and she wanted a hefty chunk. Since we weren't officially divorced, I couldn't get remarried yet, which was fine with me because, even though things seemed to be going well with Debbie, I wasn't ready to ask her to marry me. That mistake was soon to come.

We worked with a good team at Elektra. Steve had signed Sound-garden. He was very much on the cutting edge of what was happening at the time. To be honest, Elektra signed us on the back of "Bring the Noise," not so much on our catalog. They were happy that we had all these gold records on Island and a devoted fan base that was going to help them recoup their investment, but to them, "Bring the Noise" was new and different, and it was getting the most amazing mainstream press. Elektra was still known as the "artist's label," and they wanted to have the coolest, most forward-thinking acts. When they started courting us, they confirmed our belief that covering "Bring the Noise" was a groundbreaking move. "Goddammit," said Steve, "if I would have had that song you'd have sold five million copies of that fucking record. Island just had no idea what they had." Steve was familiar with our other music as well. Bob was not.

"I don't know one song from your band," Bob said straight up when he signed us. "But my people tell me you're the best band in the world right now, and you're only going to get better, and I hire these people for a reason."

Once we knew Elektra had our backs, we were already making plans for a new singer. From the start, we knew we wanted John Bush. He was far and away our first choice. There really wasn't anyone else. I loved John's voice from the first time I heard him sing "March of the Saint" in Armored Saint. He reminded me of a heavier John Fogerty, and I've always been a huge Creedence Clearwater Revival fan. Bush has this timeless voice that's more rock than metal. He always seems more Paul Rodgers (Bad Company) to me than James Hetfield. That growl was so gritty and visceral.

There was a time before *Kill 'Em All* came out that James didn't want to sing for Metallica, and he actually asked Bush to join. But John stayed with Armored Saint because at the time they were doing as well as Metallica. When I think about it I'm like, "Thank God John said no." But I have to admit it would have been a great *Fringe* episode. Would Metallica have blown up if John Bush was their singer?

It wasn't just me who was gung ho about getting John. It was unanimous. He was like the hot chick that everybody wanted to hook up with. He had universal respect in the metal world and was considered one of the best singers around. Way back in 1988 when we had that meeting with Joey Belladonna about his alcohol and drug use, Charlie, Frankie, Danny, and I all decided that if he didn't get his shit together we'd ask John to join.

At the same time we wanted to cover our backs. It was kind of like when a company knows who they want to hire for a staff job but they place an advertisement on Monster.com anyway just in case. We auditioned our buddy Death Angel vocalist Mark Osegueda, who has a great voice but was strangely too metal for us. We also tried out this guy from Mind over Four, Spike Xavier, who was cool, but the vibe wasn't right for Anthrax. He later had some success with Corporate Avenger.

Fortunately, we got our first choice even if it took a little arm-twisting. In March 1992 Jonny Z called up John Bush. Now, Bush is a smart guy. It had been years since he had last talked to Jonny, and he knew what was going on with us. So he picked up the phone and said, "Hey, I haven't heard from you in a while. Interesting. You called me once before to join a band you were managing."

"Yeah," said Jonny. "Anthrax are coming to LA to rehearse. They've been writing new songs and they'd love it if you would come down and jam with them."

John thanked Jonny for thinking of him and then told him he didn't want to join another band. My attitude was, "Fuck that shit! There's no way . . ." Nothing against Armored Saint, but by 1992 they were pretty much done, and we were at the opposite end of the spectrum. We kept pressing Jonny to call John back and ask him if he would just come down and hear some of the new songs. We had already written "Only" and "Room for One More," and we wanted John to at least hear them before he ruled out joining the band. I also wanted John to know that we didn't have lyrics or melodies yet and we wanted him to write with us, which is something Joey never did. I didn't want a mouthpiece anymore. I wanted a singer who was going to come in and collaborate. And I wanted to stress to John that we wanted him to be a full member of Anthrax, not just a hired gun. With some cajoling, John agreed to join us in the rehearsal studio. We jammed on some Sabbath and Priest. We even fucked around with U2 and Living Colour. Then we played him demos of our new songs.

"Wow, that sounds different," John said. "It's not thrash." We played him "Only," and he said, "It's really big, anthemic, and epic," and we said, "We need *you*. You're the missing piece right now."

Just in case John still didn't want to join, Jonny Z had an open audition at a club in New York. They had a cover band learn fifteen songs, and people got up and told them what song they wanted to sing. Jonny videotaped the whole karaoke session and sent us the tapes. It was total comedy. Maybe there was one person in two or three hours who could have played in an Anthrax cover band—but certainly not in Anthrax. If John Bush hadn't joined, we would have been back to plan B, which was having me and Frankie do the vocals, and we definitely didn't want that.

After the first meeting with John, he called us back and said, "Let's do this. This is going to be huge."

We all had that attitude. We really felt that John was the right voice for Anthrax at that time. Metal wasn't all about singers that sounded like Bruce Dickinson anymore. It was meaner. We didn't want a growler or a screamer; we wanted someone who could sing his balls off but sounded like he would kick your ass if you crossed him. That was John. The first thing we did together was write the lyrics for "Only." We were so excited afterward. I never knew we could write a song like that. It was Anthrax, but it was a totally different Anthrax. I was feeling really good about our future.

As excited as I had been about *Spreading the Disease* and *Among the Living,* now I had a completely different feeling. I had someone to work with, a writing partner who was on exactly the same musical wavelength I was on. We would sit for hours on end at my place in Huntington Beach and throw ideas around. I'd hand him a verse and he'd finish it. He'd hand me words, I'd finish them. We were like an old married couple that completes one another's sentences.

Having a cowriter took so much pressure off me, and at the same time it was a lot of fun. I loved hanging out with John as a bandmate and a friend. I was friends with Charlie, Frankie, and Danny, but we didn't hang out. Now I had a guy in LA I could go to bars with. He was like a bro. I couldn't have been happier, knowing we made the right decision. We heard what we were coming up with, and we thought this is the *new* Anthrax! At one point, Elektra asked us if we wanted to change the name of the band, because when we played them the demos they said, "This shit's amazing! It's you guys, but it's *not* you guys."

We understood what they were saying and we felt the same way, but we never considered it, not for a second. From a marketing perspective, they figured that since Seattle had blown up and alternative bands were happening, maybe they could market us as something other than metal if we changed our name. We were strongly opposed to that. We felt that if we changed our name, we'd be over. Our fans would feel betrayed and we'd be through.

The working process for *Sound of White Noise* was slightly different from the way we created the other Anthrax albums. Charlie wrote about 90 percent of the music at his place in New York. With me out of the music-writing picture, Frankie, who had always wanted more of a role in the band, saw an opportunity. He came up with ideas and showed them to us. Some of them were really good, but they weren't Anthrax. Charlie and I were certainly very set in our ways and comfortable with how things worked when it came to songwriting. We weren't the Beatles. We didn't all come to rehearsal with full songs. The band collaborated on the arrangements and it worked. People liked our music and each record sold more copies than the previous one. We didn't want to fuck too much with the formula.

Understandably, Frankie had a huge issue with the fact that we wouldn't let him in and he even threatened to walk if we didn't use his ideas. Frankie was very much a part of the writing when it came to melodies; it was the music he came up with that just wasn't happening for us. We encouraged him to write his own songs and sell them to other people or put them out as a side project. But he'd always hold that "I'm-gonna-quit" gun to our heads, which created tension between him and Charlie. John and I avoided most of it because we were doing our own thing, working on lyrics and vocals, and flying back and forth between LA and New York to collaborate with the band. We had rebuilt the studio in Yonkers after the fire, and were back in there. We stored our gear in half of it and the other half was a jam room. John and I would stay in New York for weeks at a time and take the train to the studio every day. We'd write all day there and then come back to the city and go out all night. After a while, we started subletting apartments for three or four months at a time so we didn't have to stay in hotels. We enjoyed being bicoastal. We could write lyrics just as easily in California as we could in New York. Then, when we had a good batch of stuff done, we'd go to Yonkers and start rehearsing. It was the best of both worlds, because I could be with Debbie for a while in LA and then John and I would go to New York and rage every night.

He was single, and when I was in New York I didn't pine away that I wasn't with Debbie. I was having too much fun. We'd get back from the studio at 8 p.m., shower, eat something really quick, and be out until five in the morning drinking. Then we'd wake up at 1 p.m. and take the train back to Yonkers. We did that for months and months. It was the first time in my life I drank pretty regularly for a few months straight. It was like I was making up for all those years I didn't imbibe. We'd drink beer like it was the healthiest beverage on earth and there was only a limited supply. By the time we'd get to the studio, we were usually hungover but ready to work.

Of course, I can't say that was always the case. Sometimes we were hurting bad and less focused, but there was no rush and no deadline. We didn't feel we had to be clear headed and laser-beam focused *all* the time. We wanted the process to be fun *and* productive. Drinking with John was definitely fun.

We took our time writing *Sound of White Noise* because it was important to get it perfect. Charlie was a little bummed because he was doing most of the heavy lifting when it came to writing the music and we were out partying like idiots. But even though John and I were hungover as fuck a lot of the time in New York, we weren't raging 24/7. And when we were in LA, we were determined and dedicated. More important, we were writing great stuff.

I think I felt I had earned the right to loosen up and drink because I was the one who kept the lights on in the factory for years. I didn't want to be the head supervisor anymore. But the main reason I was drinking so much was because I was still trying to get over my divorce and deal with the fallout from another relationship I probably shouldn't have been in. My divorce from Marge had pretty much bled me dry. I lost my apartment in Queens and a whole bunch of cash, and I had to make alimony payments for a couple of years. When the dust settled I didn't even own a spoon. I was starting over again from scratch. At one point, I tried to get back boxes of my comics that I never picked up after Marge and I broke up. It was my cherished silver-age Marvel collection, complete runs from inception to the mideighties of *The Incredible Hulk, Thor, Fantastic Four, Spider-Man, X-Men, Daredevil,* and more. These were books I had collected since I was a kid in the late sixties. It wasn't the most pristine Mile High–type collection; I had read and reread most of them. Then I found out Marge's dad had put them in storage and insured them for a lot of money and didn't pay the bill for two years. When I called the storage place, a guy told me I had to pay over $20,000 if I wanted them back. I had no way to get the cash in time, so they all ended up in someone else's collection.

It was a real dick move, his petty revenge for me divorcing his daughter. The collection was worth a lot more than $20,000, but it wasn't the monetary value of the comics that I cared about. It was the books themselves. They had been a part of my life for so long, my only connection to my childhood, and now they were gone. I was angry about it for a few months but was able to move on because my freedom was worth anything and being angry about that was just holding me back. That being said, sometimes I'll see books I had in comic shops or online, and I see what they sell for now and I just have to laugh. Maniacally. Like the Joker . . .

When John joined Anthrax he was in a tough emotional place as well. He had just broken up with a girl he had been with for more than five years, and he was still hurting. In that sense, we had a lot in common. He was bummed and I was starting to be bummed, so a lot of *Sound of White Noise* addressed personal and introspective subject matter. I had touched on my marriage to Marge on *State of Euphoria* and *Persistence of Time,* but only from a distance. I didn't want to bum out our fans, and at the time I still felt more comfortable writing about comic books, Stephen King, and a little about history and politics. Now, I needed to write songs that were more personal, painful, and real.

It was therapeutic to work with John on "Room for One More," "Only," "Black Lodge," and "Invisible." In some ways it was catharsis in action because there was still drama all around us. On April 22, 1992, we went to see Pantera and Skid Row at the Felt Forum in New York. During the after-party, I met a model named Lynne through a friend of a friend. We started talking, one thing led to another, and within days we were having an affair. Lynne was connected to the world of fashion, and I started going out with her to all the clubs where celebrities hung out—the real hotspots. John and I instantly fell in with that scene. Every night, we went to these fancy-pants clubs. We got in free, never had to wait in line, and didn't have to pay for drinks. And there were beautiful girls everywhere. These were tall, thin, gorgeous models, not overly made-up, slutty groupies. I had never experienced this before. It was nuts and I went all-in. I was so hot and heavy with Lynne that I started staying in New York and didn't come home.

I wasn't monogamous with Lynne, either. How could I be? There were all these hot women around, and she didn't seem to care. I was just a lucky guy getting lots of play. I still didn't have the game of someone like Sebastian Bach or Bret Michaels, who would have had orgies with these chicks on a nightly basis. I had to settle for one at a time, but that was good enough for me. There's always room for one more. And then I always had Lynne. Living in that dreamworld almost took over my life.

At the same time I was basically living with Lynne at her apartment in New York, I was talking to Debbie about buying a house for us. Again, the girl I was with at home had no idea what was going on when I wasn't with her. It started to feel like a serious case of déjà vu, and I didn't want to make the same mistake I made with Marge. I couldn't live that lie again. Yet there I was, sneaking out of the house in California all the time so I could find a pay phone to call Lynne. Eventually it became too big a secret to keep, and I decided to break off the engagement with Debbie and move in with Lynne.

I told Debbie I had been having an affair for months and that's why our relationship had gotten so shitty. I apologized and told her I just couldn't be dishonest with her anymore. It wasn't fair.

She freaked out and screamed and cursed at me. She cried and slammed doors, then yelled at me some more. But somehow over the next two weeks of me being home, we reconciled the situation. I started thinking with my brain instead of my dick, and I asked myself, "Do I really want to go back to New York and live with this crazy model chick?" As unstable as my relationship with Debbie was, with Lynne life was fucking nuts. She was really into cocaine and pills and shit that I knew nothing about. I wasn't doing any drugs, just drinking. That scene was over-the-top crazy, and I thought, "Do I really want to walk away from what I have going on here, which seems more solid? Is that the best move? Maybe what's happening in New York is just a phase."

I decided that being with Lynne was just a way to escape the pressure I was under and to get my rocks off without all the baggage that goes with a real relationship. The more I thought about it, the clearer it became that it would be a real mistake to get serious with Lynne. So instead of ending it with Debbie, I broke up with Lynne.

Chapter 21

NO MORE ROOM

Anthrax recorded *Sound of White Noise* with Dave Jerden, who had worked with Jane's Addiction, Alice in Chains, and tons of bands we loved. We stayed in LA; we did the drums at A&M Studios and tracked everything else at Eldorado and Cherokee recording studios. We had spent so long working on the album that we all had our parts down cold, and before we knew it we were done. It was the closest we had come to the final recording being exactly what we had imagined. Elektra sent out tons of advances of *Sound of White Noise* to journalists and radio programmers, and the reactions were phenomenal.

John and I went to Europe to do interviews a few months before it came out, and people were fucking pumped. They loved it. I don't remember any negative reviews from anywhere that had previously supported us. The media ate it up, but I didn't know how fans were going to react until it was released and we went on tour. The first indicators were good. "Only" was the first single. We shot a video for it that MTV played, and the song was on the radio. It was a completely different experience than what we were used to. Elektra Records had invested a large amount of money in the band and was putting the full power of their company behind it, just like they promised. *Sound of White Noise* came out May 25 and debuted at number 7 on the *Billboard* album chart. The album sold almost 100,000 copies our first week, which was more than double any of our other records.

Debbie and I found a nice house in Huntington Beach down the street from the beach. I was able to get a mortgage for the place because I carried a copy of *Billboard* magazine into the bank that included a chart showing how high the album debuted. The loan officer literally said, "Oh, you have a top 10 record. You obviously have enough money for a mortgage."

It's a good thing they accepted the chart as proof of income. Despite this big advance check for the album, my first divorce bled me dry and I still owed Marge about $50,000. I couldn't prove from my tax forms that I'd been employed at a certain location for a certain amount of time and earned a regular income. I also had my cut of the money from the Elektra deal, but that was gone in fifteen minutes. I had a check for $508,000, and it felt like I had won the lottery. But I put aside 40 percent of it in an account to pay taxes, I wrote Marge a check, and I put a huge down payment on the house and set up a mortgage. By then I only had about $50,000 left for living expenses. Granted, I bought a house, but it was scary that so much money could be gone so quickly.

The whole band was excited about the chart position of *Sound of White Noise*. We felt like we had beaten the odds and everything was going our way. We changed singers, and we survived and came back stronger. What else could we possibly think at the time but that people were stoked by our decision? Later, we found out that wasn't entirely true. At the time, the majority of our fans still supported us, but there was a certain percentage, maybe as much as 30 percent, that couldn't accept Anthrax without Joey Belladonna singing. I understood that gut reaction because I felt that way when David Lee Roth left Van Halen. I didn't buy anything they put out or go to any of their shows until Roth came back. Their 2012 album, *A Different Kind of Truth*, was the first Van Halen record I bought since *1984*. So I know how it works. Did I buy the Judas Priest records with Tim "Ripper" Owens? No, and I love Ripper. He's a fucking awesome dude and an incredible singer, but Priest only has one real singer. We understood that we had crossed some of our fans. We insulted them and fucked up their world. We changed from something they loved into something they didn't want anything to do with.

That didn't matter though, because we loved the record and we were still a great live band. There were a lot of highlights that came from the album. There would also be some huge disappointments. We came out of the box really strong. The record went gold in about six weeks based on the success of "Only." We had a big summer tour with White Zombie and Quicksand lined up, and most of it sold out right after the tickets became available. Everyone wanted to get a second single out to radio and a new video to MTV in time for the tour. We wanted to go with "Room for One More." We thought it was a fucking kick-ass track, and people were really reacting to it live. We thought it was our "Enter Sandman," and it would take us over the top. It's heavy, it's got groove, it rocks. And it's super catchy as well.

We went to Elektra and told them our plans, and they came back to us and said that they thought we should release "Black Lodge" instead because it was more of a ballad. We all thought that was a really bad decision. We understood that it was the least "heavy" song on the album, and we knew bands usually broke big with videos for ballads, but it was still dark. We didn't feel like it was a summer song that would have fans jumping up and down. I thought I could convince them to go with "Room for One More." So I went to a meeting at the Elektra building and explained how we all felt. "Black Lodge" was too moody to come out in the summer. It seemed more like a song for October or November. I told them we should hold it until then and have it be the third single. I said, "For now, let's keep rolling with the heavy shit and then in the fall we'll tone it down a bit, and 'Black Lodge' will be like our 'Unforgiven,'" another Metallica ballad that went gangbusters.

The Elektra team didn't agree. They strongly believed "Black Lodge" was the smash that we needed to release right away. They said we would quickly go from 500,000 records to 1.5 million, and once that happened we could do whatever we wanted. We never had this kind of discussion with a label before, and we'd never had the kind of success we were having, so we figured they knew what they were doing. They told us they would get Mark Pellington to shoot the video. He was the biggest video director in the world at the time. He did Pearl Jam's "Jeremy," which had become the gold standard for other directors. They said they'd spend $400,000 on the video for "Black Lodge," and it would be our "Jeremy."

Our contract with Elektra gave us creative control; we had to agree with what they wanted to do. So we said we needed a couple days to mull it over. Charlie, Jonny, and I had a meeting and decided to go with Elektra's decision. Even though it wasn't what we felt in our gut was the right move, their machine was well oiled and running like a fine Swiss timepiece. Who were we to argue with success?

We told them to go for it, and they assured us we were making the right decision and that Pellington was in. There was only one hitch. He was tied up with a documentary and wouldn't be available right away. We asked them if we could get another director, and they said it had to be him. He had already done a treatment for the video, which they loved, and he was "the best."

So we started the tour with White Zombie without a new video. Rob watched us every night from the side of the stage, and one day he asked me, "Why isn't 'Room for One More' your single? That song fucking rules." I told him it was supposed to be, but the label decided to get Mark Pellington to shoot a video for "Black Lodge," which the label thought had more "bang for the buck." He was supportive. "That sounds great! Mark Pellington's awesome."

For all of Rob's outrageous music, videos, and films, he's the most levelheaded, down-to-earth guy ever. And he's an astute businessman. Our radar should have blipped when he asked why "Room for One More" wasn't the single, but we went with the program. As wild as Rob Zombie was during White Zombie's show, he was the exact opposite of the guy he was getting compared to at the time, Ministry's Al Jourgensen.

I first met Al when Ministry were touring for their 1992 album *Psalm 69: The Way to Succeed and the Way to Suck Eggs* because Jonny Z was managing his band as well as ours. I was already a big Ministry fan so I knew a lot of their songs. When they played Lollapalooza in Jones Beach, New York, they invited me to come up with them and play their cover of Black Sabbath's "Supernaut." Then, when I was back in Los Angeles, I went onstage with them, and Al just handed me his guitar. I did "So What," "Thieves," "Supernaut," and a couple other songs. It was nerve-wracking because his guitar is, by far, the loudest thing on the stage, and if I screwed up, it would mess everyone up. But I pulled it off, and it freed him to run around like a lunatic with his giant microphone stand decorated with cattle bones. The thing was built on wheels so he could ride it around like a scooter and crash into things.

When we got to Chicago on the first leg of the *Sound of White Noise* tour, Al joined *us* onstage at the Aragon Ballroom, and we played "Thieves." Afterward, he took me for a ride in his brand new, insanely fast Nissan. He told me it was the fastest street-legal car in the United States, and it sure felt like it. He was driving a hundred miles per hour from the club to whatever bar we were heading to. He was a maniac behind the wheel, and a far from sober maniac. I was clinging to the side of the seat for dear life, like that would protect me if we plowed into a brick wall. Al told me how, a year earlier, he had Eddie Vedder shitting in his pants (like I was) in his car, and he played him *Speak English or Die*, which was, apparently, a huge inspiration for Al to add thrash metal guitars to his electronic music. At the end of the night, he said, "Maybe I'll see you guys tomorrow. Maybe I'll come to Detroit."

I said that would be awesome but figured there was no way in hell he was going to drive from Chicago to Detroit to see us play. The next day we were hanging out at the venue after sound check, and Al drove up in his Nissan in the late afternoon. I said, "Dude, you drove to Detroit?!?"

"Fuck yeah. Let's hang out!"

We had another wild night, and at the end of the evening he said he'd see us the next night in Cleveland. We were flattered and we were having fun, but it didn't take a lot of intelligence to realize that if he kept driving this high-octane rocket engine from city to city after long nights of drinking, he was likely to become a statistic.

"Dude, why don't you just ride in the bus with us?" I said.

"Nah, nah, nah. I'm having a blast driving this car."

Sure enough, he showed up in Cleveland. We were playing an outdoor venue called the Nautica Stage. At that time we had two buses, one for the band and one for the crew. All the partying happened on the crew bus, which enabled us to keep the band bus nice and clean. That's the night Al tried to pick a fight with Rob Zombie. Maybe they exchanged words over something that had gone down over the past couple days and the confrontation came to a head in Cleveland. At the time, Al was seeing White Zombie's bassist Sean Yseult, and she and Rob had been a couple for years. Whatever. Al was standing outside White Zombie's bus banging on the door, calling Rob a pussy and screaming for him to get off the bus and get his ass kicked. Rob had no intention of leaving the bus and did the smart thing by just ignoring Al. After about ten minutes of banging on the door, Al gave up and staggered to our crew bus.

Later that night, I was back on the band bus. The TV was on in the background, and I was eating a chicken sandwich when the front door burst open and Al came storming in and ran through the bus, wild-eyed, gesticulating, and screaming. "That fucking bitch! That fucking whore! That fucking cunt!"

"Dude, dude," I said. "What's wrong? Calm down."

"That fucking bitch!" he repeated. "I went in the back room of the crew bus with this fucking pig. She started going down on me, and the next thing I know she fucking straddles me and slips my cock in her pussy!"

Al was apoplectic at this point: "I screamed 'Goddammit, you fucking bitch!' and threw her off of me, and I ran off the bus trying to pull my pants up. I came over here. Who knows what fucking disease that whore has?"

"Dude, calm down," I said, trying to chill him out before he started smashing things on our bus. "Don't worry. I'm sure you're fine. Why don't you go inside the venue? Maybe you can find a shower and rinse off."

Al looked at the table where I was sitting at the front of the bus and there was a stack of unopened Domino's pizza boxes waiting for the band and crew. He walked over, opened the top box, raked his hand across the pizza, dragging cheese and piping hot sauce under his fingernails. He put his hand down his pants and started rubbing his cock and balls really hard with the steaming cheese and sauce. He screamed and looked at me with frantic desperation.

"Dude, what the fuck are you doing?!?" I said. "Seriously, are you tripping?"

He looked at me and said, "I read somewhere that the acid in tomato sauce will kill any STD. That's right, isn't it? Didn't you hear that?"

Of course, I hadn't heard any such thing, but I figured I'd go along with him. "Right, Al. Yeah, I think you're right."

He calmed down right away, sat down, had a drink, and got back off the bus and wandered into the night to find another party. Pizza cheese and sauce were dribbling over the front of his pants. After that show, we told Al he needed to lose his car if he wanted to stay out with us. He could either leave it in Cleveland, and then maybe fly back there at some point and drive it home, or we could figure out another plan because it wasn't safe for him to be driving long distances in the condition he was in after shows. He wanted to drive to New York next, and that was a long haul. We convinced him to go home to Chicago on a day off, and then we paid for him to fly to New York to hang out with us. As far as I know, he went to bed that night in the hotel with his pants filled with cheese and sauce, and God knows how long it stayed down there. He wasn't big on hygiene, so I doubt he showered at the hotel, and I'm sure he drove with it to Chicago. He probably figured the longer he left it in there, the better chance he had that it would kill any possible disease he might have contracted from this girl.

A day and a half later, there he was in New York. We stayed at the Parker Meridien on Fifty-Seventh Street. They had an indoor basketball court. A bunch of us were there shooting hoops, and in walked Al, black cargo shorts, black tank top, and big black motorcycle boots, and he ran around and played basketball with us. Years later, he told me that the week he spent with us was probably the healthiest week of his life as a musician because no one on the bus was doing coke and none of us did heroin, so there was nowhere for him to score.

The whole tour with White Zombie and Quicksand was great. Zombie were right on the verge of breaking. *Beavis and Butthead* was playing the shit out of "Thunder Kiss '65," and when those animated characters got behind something, it was destined to explode. It's such a weird concept that a cartoon show where moronic high school kids almost arbitrarily ranked videos by saying "that's cool" or "that sucks" had such an impact on the American public, but it did. Type O Negative got big thanks to Beavis and Butthead, and their undiluted praise for Danzig sent him over the top as well. White Zombie quickly became bigger than us, but the timing was good because it brought tons of people to the venues. I got up and played "Thunder Kiss '65" a bunch of times with Zombie; they would close with it. Charlie and I chose Quicksand as an opener because we loved those guys. Our audience didn't know them, and I don't know that they converted much of our crowd. But having them on the road with us was our personal, selfish indulgence because we were in a position to say, "Hey, we want Quicksand out with us, and we don't care what the promoters think."

We were pumped when we got back home from the tour, but we had been so busy playing shows we hadn't kept track of sales. When we looked at the numbers, we realized that while we were on the road our chart position had slipped considerably. Nothing new had gone to radio, and Mark Pellington still hadn't started shooting the video for "Black Lodge." We went to Elektra and asked what was up, and they said that it didn't even matter what was happening at the moment because when Pellington did the video for "Black Lodge," it was going to hit and hit hard.

"Can't we just do something really quickly for 'Room for One More' in the meantime," I asked, "just so we have something out there in the interim?"

They wouldn't go for that, and within weeks everything ground to a halt and there was nothing out there to help us build back our momentum. "Only" had already been out there for three months, and it was done, dropped, finished. We needed something new and we had nothing to offer. Pellington finally made the video for "Black Lodge." It came out in the fall and didn't impact. We weren't even in the video except for these quick, weird flashes of our faces. I love the video. It's conceptual and artistic. I think it's the best video we've ever made visually, but it had nothing at all to do with Anthrax and it didn't connect with the millions of people who were listening to Pearl Jam and loved the "Jeremy" video. They didn't see it and rush out to buy *Sound of White Noise*.

We were stuck. We had 600,000 records sold, and we could sense Elektra starting to panic because of the amount of money they had invested in us. We kept a good attitude. We felt like we could still do our thing and tour and we'd still draw crowds and build back up organically. Then we'd go out with "Room for One More," and Elektra would realize they should have listened to us in the first place. Before they convinced us that they should go with "Black Lodge," they said they could see five singles coming from the album, so we figured we still had time to turn *Sound of White Noise* into at least a platinum album.

Chapter 22

WE THOUGHT YOU WERE DEAD!

ome strange shit happened during the *Sound of White Noise* cycle. It seemed like a giant ball of rope had started to unravel, and the psychic debris that resulted from that was taking its toll on my life. We did a great tour of Japan in October of 1993, and after the last show we had to fly from Tokyo to LA and then from LA to Dallas and connect to a flight for Tampa, where we were finally shooting the video for "Room for One More" with George Dougherty.

That's a crazy amount of flying. I had already been up almost two days straight in Japan, then I was traveling for twenty-two hours between Tokyo and Tampa. By the time we got there, all I wanted to do was grab a cheeseburger and go to bed. Then I found out a bunch of my friends from Huntington Beach were flying in to be in the video and hang out for a couple of days. I met them in Tampa and told them I was fried and wanted to crash.

Apparently, that wasn't an option. Cypress Hill and House of Pain were playing right down the street, and everyone was going. I'm friends with all those guys, so I agreed to go as well. My plan was to be out of there by 11 p.m. so I could get some sleep before our shoot. My friends Bobby, Billy, and Rich went with me to the venue, found House of Pain's tour bus, and knocked on the door. They let us in and we hung out for a few minutes.

All of a sudden a six-foot-long bong appeared, as you might expect on a House of Pain bus. My friends were all taking hits off it, and so were the guys in the band. It smelled good, and I was really wired because the only thing that had been keeping me awake for the past day was cup after cup of coffee. I thought a hit of weed might calm me down and perk up my appetite before we went out for dinner. Then I'd be able to sleep without being hungry.

I climbed up to the bong, which I had to hold like a cello. Another guy loaded it from the bottom while I braced it from the top. I breathed out, put my mouth over the top lip, and inhaled with all my might. About three inches of smoke rose up the bong. I had to take another huge breath, inhale, and then cap it with my hand and try again. The smoke moved maybe another two inches. Everyone else was able to pull the smoke all the way to the top in one shot. Old iron-lung Ian had to repeat this process five times, until finally the smoke got to where my mouth was. I took a tiny little hit because I knew that I was dealing with straight-up Hulk weed, not some Bruce Banner shit. I had never smoked weed like this before. It was West Coast chronic, the same shit Snoop Dogg, Dr. Dre, and all those big-time rappers were smoking. Instantly I realized my mistake.

I sat down in the booth in the front of the bus. I was instantly bathed in cold sweat, and the walls in my skull started to close in on my brain again. That fucking Dianoga was coming back. I looked around and said, "I'm going to pass out, and I might even have a seizure because this has happened to me twice before now."

I may not be a fucking genius, but I put two and two together and finally realized that maybe I didn't have bad shrimp or dehydration the last two times I passed out smoking. Maybe it was the weed. Meanwhile, everyone was high as fuck in the bus. House of Pain rapper Everlast told me just to relax and I'd be fine.

The solid wall in my brain kept sliding toward my face. "I'm going to pass out! I think I have a problem with the weed and I feel like I'm about to lose consciousness," I said louder.

Everlast gave me a bottle of water and told me that the weed was really strong and I didn't have anything to worry about. He told me I should sit down and just chill out.

Nobody was listening to me, and the wall was turning my brain to soup faster than ever, probably because the weed was more potent. I found my friend Rich, who used to do security for Anthrax, and I convinced him to find a paramedic right away.

As he ran off the bus, I pictured my brain exploding and my body collapsing dead in a pile on the dirty floor of the House of Pain tour bus. I imagined two metal Beavis and Butthead–type dudes having a conversation in the future: "Hey, whatever happened to that Scott Ian guy from Anthrax?"

"Oh, didn't you hear?" answered his friend. "He was smoking chronic with House of Pain and died on their bus." Yep, that's what happened to me. So fucking lame.

The last thing I remember was standing up and being face-to-face with Everlast. Then I woke up on the floor of the bus, and my friend Bobby was leaning over me, pounding on my chest. I looked up at him.

"Ow, ow, ow! What the fuck are you doing?!?"

"We thought you were dead!" he blurted. "We thought your heart stopped."

I got up and sat on the couch, favoring my bruised ribs.

Everlast explained, "You stood up, and next thing I knew, you just dropped, and I caught you before you hit the floor. Then you started shaking. You had a full-on seizure. Your eyes rolled back in your head and everything."

After I had been shaking for about thirty seconds, they put me on the floor. Then they placed me on the couch. Then back on the floor. They were all high as fuck and didn't know what to do. That's when Bobby put his ear up to my mouth to see if I was breathing. He didn't think I was, so he started pounding the shit out of me. Right then, Rich showed up with paramedics, and they took me away in an ambulance. Thank you, good night.

We started toward the hospital. My blood sugar was insanely low, so they gave me a tube of some gel to squeeze under my tongue, and I popped up like Popeye after a can of spinach. I asked the paramedic, "What the hell was that? I feel great! Can I get a prescription for that stuff? I'll take it before every Anthrax show!" He looked at me like I was the dumbest person on the planet and said, "It's glucose. You can get it at any drugstore. We were just boosting your blood sugar. You could have gotten the same effect from eating an Oreo." They dropped me in the emergency room, and after a couple hours one of the doctors saw me. He took my temperature and my blood pressure. Everything seemed normal. I told him I had been traveling and I hadn't slept—oh, and that I was smoking weed.

He told me I was dehydrated and exhausted, so my blood pressure dropped, which was why I passed out. He told me to go back to the hotel, eat some dinner, and then go to sleep, which I did. I felt better in the morning and we made the "Room for One More" video. When I got back to LA, I saw my doctor and told him about my experiences with weed and seizures.

"There's something going on there," he deduced with the acumen of Sherlock Holmes. "Weed is the only common denominator in this equation." Over the next week he took a bunch of blood and ran tests. They even tested me for epilepsy. I had to sit in a dark room with a strobe light in my face. It sped up, slowed down, and sped up again over the course of about twenty minutes. I asked my doctor if they could at least put some Maiden on while I sat there in front of the strobe so I could feel like I was at a concert. I'm surprised my insurance picked up the cost for that one because, clearly, having been in a metal band for ten years at that point and having strobes flashed in my face every night, epilepsy wasn't the problem.

About four days later, they still hadn't called with my test results, and I was extremely nervous. I was worried they were going to tell me I had a tumor or an embolism. At the very least they'd say I somehow had a giant pothead tapeworm wrapped around my cerebellum, and it went wild every time it was exposed to weed. I was sweating this big time.

Finally my doctor called me. I went to his office and he said, "Scott, I have good news and bad news." I thought, "Fuck, that's what they tell you right before you find out you have a terminal disease that's going to take more than a year to kill you so you still have a little 'quality time' left."

"The good news is you're not dying. Your brain is fine, your blood is fine, and you're not allergic to anything except for one thing—THC."

I asked him why I never passed out when I was a kid and smoked weed. He said I probably had a minor allergy to it back then, if any, but that I developed a severe allergy over time. He explained how some people eat shellfish their whole lives, and then suddenly they have lobster and they go into anaphylactic shock. He said I had two choices: I could either stop smoking pot or I could do it again and risk another seizure or maybe even a brain hemorrhage. Maybe even death could show up at the party next time. I decided to stop smoking weed.

But that didn't stop me from trying psychedelic mushrooms. I was in New York City hanging around with some girl John Bush was dating, her sister, and some of their friends. After hitting a couple bars, there were four or five of us hanging at someone's apartment in the West Village. I was planning to meet my friend Dominick, who was deejaying old metal songs that night at L'Amour in Brooklyn. We had a couple more drinks then someone took out a bag of mushrooms. I knew about mushrooms, but I had never done them before. I was curious because mushrooms grow out of the ground. They're not man-made, so how bad could they be? I asked, "What do they do? What is a mushroom trip like?"

One of the girls said, "It's fun. It's mellow. You may feel a little sick at first. You may even throw up, but generally it's a pretty mellow thing, depending on how much you eat."

I said, "Fuck it," which was so out of character for me. I'm *never* the guy that says fuck it, but I was intrigued by these weird-looking things. I took a couple of pieces of mushrooms and chewed them. They tasted like bitter metal mixed with dried turds. "No wonder people throw up," I thought. I washed the 'shrooms down with a beer. Ten minutes passed. Twenty. Thirty. Nothing. I took another two little pieces, and fifteen minutes later the drug started to hit me. I was sitting there watching other people tripping, and I didn't realize I was also high at first because the logical part of my brain was still there and I started having an inner monologue with myself.

Then it got really intense. I started receiving the answers to all the questions that mankind has ever asked about God and the universe. It was like a window had opened and everything was so obvious. All this stuff was flooding in. I was sitting in a chair with a broad smile, and I was cracking up laughing. I thought, "Man, I have to write all this stuff down so I remember it afterward. Everyone's problems will be solved and I'll be a hero!" Of course, I was fucking high and in no condition to answer even simple questions like "Where do you live?" or "What's your favorite color?" let alone write down the answers to all the world's problems. The "logical" part of my brain kept bothering me to get up and find a pen and paper, but I was having too much fun laughing at all the lesser beings around me to get up. At some point, I wandered out on the fire escape on the second story of this West Village apartment right across from John's Pizza on Bleeker Street. I sat there laughing at people in the street. Then it dawned on me that not only did I know everything there was to know but I could fly.

I yelled at people that I was going to swoop down like the Human Torch and pick them up and take them for a ride. Someone at the party saw what I was doing and convinced someone else to drag me back inside before I jumped. What a cliché I had become.

Suddenly I blurted out, "Brooklyn! L'Amour!! We've got to see Dominick. It's going to be the greatest thing of all time. Wait until we get there!!!"

Of course, it was just my friend Dominick spinning metal records in a club, but in my head it seemed really important to go. Somehow I called a limo. No idea how I did that. I had never called a limo before, nor did I have the number of a limo company. Mushrooms may not give you the power of flight, but apparently they do enable you to call a limo.

Everyone else was tripping as well, so they were excited. At that point I was thinking mushrooms were the greatest thing ever—way better than weed. The car came, and six of us got in, four girls, one other dude, and me. As soon as the driver hit the gas, I started to feel like a character in a mob film who's asked to get into a car and "take a ride." Something was way wrong. Two of the girls were looking at me and whispering to each other. It was dark and lights from outside were splashing into the car and then disappearing. I started feeling paranoid even before one of the girls across from me coughed and then slumped over, dead.

I started freaking out and yelling at everybody. "What the fuck? She's dead, she's dead!!!"

They tried to calm me down and convince me that she just fell asleep because she was stoned and tired.

"No, she's dead, you fucking maniacs!" I screamed. "You killed her and now you're trying to kill me, too!" The mushrooms had definitely turned on me, and everything that was great about the drug contorted into a horrible nightmare. I started throwing up. I didn't just puke; I projectile vomited on everyone across from me. Then I started screaming because I was still sure I was the victim of a sinister murder plot. The barrier between the front seat and the back was all the way up so the driver had no idea what was going on. He kept going. "He must have heard me," I thought. I wondered if he was in on the plot. By this time we were in Brooklyn, and I was still yelling, "There's a dead girl in the fucking car! What are we going to do with her body? I'm not going to jail for you motherfuckers!" In my mind the dead girl had now come back as a zombie and was going to try and turn me, too. I tried to roll down the window to jump out of the car, but they pulled me back in.

Then I remembered I had called the car so the driver had to do what I wanted. I was still convinced there was a hit on me. I was sure the girl across from me was a zombie. But at least I had a plan that would allow me to escape unharmed. I tried to placate the killers the way doctors talk to a psychotic mental patient.

"Okay, fine, she's not dead, and you're not trying to kill me. I get it. I'm okay. But I feel really bad. I think I'm in trouble, so I'm going to have the driver drop me off at a hospital in Brooklyn, then he'll take you all back to Manhattan and drop you off wherever you want to go."

"Scott, you don't need to go to a hospital," one of the girls said. "It's just the mushrooms messing with your head. You took too many. Now relax and . . ."

I wasn't about to fall for that. "Don't tell me. . . . It's because you're trying to kill me!"

I rolled down the barrier and screamed to the driver, "Take me to the nearest hospital. I'm sick!"

We were five minutes from Prospect Park Hospital, and it was 1:30 in the morning. The driver dropped me off and left. I was safe! But I was still tripping hard, and by the time I had walked ten feet I couldn't remember where the fuck I was. I wandered in circles around the hospital parking lot until an EMT saw that I was dazed and had puked on myself. She figured I had been in a car accident and led me to the emergency room. She helped me check in. When they asked me what was wrong, I wanted to shout that a girl was dead and she was a zombie and we all might be next, but I stifled the urge because a tiny voice in the back of my head told me that maybe that's not what was happening at all.

"I'm sick. I've been throwing up," I told the woman at the check-in desk. Prospect Park Hospital in Brooklyn is much different today than it was back then. There were crazies screaming, babies crying, people coming in with stab wounds. It wasn't the best place to be tripping on mushrooms. I sat on a chair in a tight fetal position for a solid three hours. During that time I had an epiphany. I had eaten poison mushrooms and died in the hospital, and now I was in hell. I was surrounded by bleeding people and elderly ladies coughing and some dude who had collapsed on the floor and was shaking. There was evil laughter in my head. I wouldn't have been surprised if Pinhead from *Hellraiser* walked through the wall and chains with hooks at the end shot out of the ceiling and into my flesh.

I was shaking uncontrollably, too. Then I snapped out of my imagination and back into my head. I realized I was in a hospital emergency room and I wasn't dead. I knew I took mushrooms and had a really bad trip, but I was finally coming down. It was 5:00 a.m., so I got up and started to walk out when they called my name. I saw a doctor and told him I had eaten mushrooms. He laughed and then examined me quickly and told me I was fine. He asked if I had health insurance, and I said, "Yes, I do. Here's my card." He told me that Blue Cross probably wouldn't cover an ER visit for eating psilocybin, so he wrote up the diagnosis saying I had gotten food poisoning from bad mushrooms. Thanks Doc!

I walked out of the hospital into the early Brooklyn morning, and all I wanted to do was get some food and go to bed. I was supposed to go to Long Island and hang out with my dad and see my brother Sean (born from my dad's second marriage) play soccer. I must not have been completely lucid because I made another great decision. I walked to the nearest pay phone, called my dad, woke him up, and asked him to get me.

"Hey Dad . . ."

"Why are you calling so early?" he interrupted. "Are you okay? Is everything alright?"

I explained to him everything was fine but that I was at Prospect Park Hospital and I needed him to pick me up.

"Why are you at the hospital? Are you alright?"

I told him I did mushrooms and had a really bad trip and that I'd give him the details later. Everything got really quiet for a few seconds. Then he burst out laughing. "How fucking old are you?" he said. "Do you think you're still eighteen?"

"Dad, I'm thirty-three. You *know* I'm thirty-three." I felt ashamed. He laughed again then said he'd get up and come get me. An hour later he picked me up and drove me to his place. I changed my puke pants, and we had lunch and went to my brother's soccer game.

During my one time tripping on mushrooms, I had almost killed myself twice, once on the fire escape and again when I tried jumping out the window of the car. It turned out the only one who was trying to kill me was me. Standing there sober, I shivered and decided I never wanted to be out of control like that again. The drunkest I've ever been, I was always under my own power. When I couldn't control myself anymore, I blacked out and I was sleeping. That wasn't the case with mushrooms. I wasn't there. Scott was gone and *they* were in control. I'd never do that again.

Chapter 23

THE LAST REGRET

On October 30, 1993, I got a message from Al Jourgensen saying he was going to be in town to play this all-star show at the
Viper Room in LA on Halloween, and he wanted to invite
me. The band was called P, and they featured Al, Butthole Surfers vocalist Gibby Haynes, Red Hot Chili Peppers bassist Flea, and Johnny
Depp. I was at my house in Huntington Beach, so it was easy enough
to make the show. I asked Everlast and my friends Bobby and Rich to
come. We all met out front of the club and squeezed our way inside.
The place was packed way beyond capacity. We had our backs to the
bar, we couldn't move. We decided to give the band five minutes and
then get the fuck out of there unless the music was really incredible. P
took forever to come on, and we'd already been there an hour. I noticed
a lot of people at the bar were acting really weird and were definitely on
something heavy. All of a sudden, there was some commotion in the
crowd near us. We couldn't even get out of the way. All we could do
was lean. Some dude pushed through with a guitar case, trying to get
onstage. People surrounding him were yelling for everyone to get out of
his way. It smelled like someone had shit their pants.

"Fuck this," I said. "If the band isn't on in the next five minutes
we're out of here. I don't care if we see Al or not."

Right as we were about to bolt, the lights came on and the dude
who had poo pants walked on with a guitar. The lights were dim, but
I could tell it was ex–Red Hot Chili Peppers guitarist John Frusciante.
Everyone knew he was a major junkie, so it made sense that he stunk
like a bum. He walked up to the mike, a dazed expression in his eyes,
and smiled a toothless grin. He mumbled that he was gonna play some

songs, but he was really hard to understand. He slurred indecipherable lyrics and picked at his guitar like he was trying to remove scabs. It was fucking awful. After the second song he started to say something, then turned and threw up on Gibby's leg.

We had already suffered through eight minutes of this, and it was like watching a super-slow-mo video of someone spontaneously combusting. He played one more song, then P came on, and it was almost worse than Frusciante because now there was a whole band onstage making incoherent noise. They played some cover songs, but they were so bad you couldn't tell what they were. One of the only details I remember from the actual performance is Al stepped on his own guitar cord and unplugged himself. He spent the next four minutes leaning over and trying to find his cord. I zoned in on this because it was a real feat of gymnastics. The way he was bending and stretching trying to reach his cable on the floor while holding a guitar was gravity defying. The song ended, and Al found his cord and plugged it in.

A screech of insanely loud feedback shot through the room. Gibby was singing something, and he turned around to Al and shouted, "Shut up! Stop making noise!"

It was a disaster. My friends and I looked at each other and gestured that it was time to leave. We walked out of the club and onto the corner of Sunset Boulevard.

"Why don't we go back to my place?" Everlast said. "I got booze and we can play pool."

I thought that was a good idea. As we were about to bolt, the back doors of the club flew open, and a bunch of people came out and lay some dude on the ground. We figured someone got really fucked up and his friends were leaving him there so he could sober up. Then I realized there was no more sound coming from the club and Flea was outside staring at this guy. Other people started coming out, including Johnny Depp. Five minutes later an ambulance pulled up, and paramedics got out. They worked on the guy for five minutes.

"Whoever that is, he's in bad shape," Everlast said. "He's obviously not breathing. He's probably dead."

"Fuck, this is getting really weird," I said. "Let's go."

Before we had a chance to leave, Christina Applegate walked up to me. "River's dead," she sobbed. It took me a second to realize who she was talking about, because I didn't see River Phoenix in the club and I had never met him before. She repeated, "River's dead."

"River? . . . Oh, River Phoenix," I said.

"He's dead! He's dead!" she cried then took off.

We agreed that we should get the fuck out of there before the TV news crews showed up. As we were walking away, some paparazzi asked me and Everlast to take a picture. River's body was on the sidewalk just behind us, in the shot. Paparazzi are annoying at the best of times; this was seriously not fucking cool. Everlast exploded at the guy, "YOU WANT TO TAKE A PICTURE OF US WITH THAT DEAD KID ON THE STREET BEHIND US YOU SICK DISRESPECTFUL FUCK? SHOW SOME FUCKING RESPECT MOTHERFUCKER!" Everlast grabbed the guy and was going to take his camera and smash it when Rich got between them and pulled Everlast off the guy, saving him what would have been a big lawsuit and maybe jail. Everlast thanked Rich for stepping in, and we went to his house and turned on the TV. Sure enough, within five minutes of watching CNN, they reported River Phoenix had died.

As crazy as my little thrash metal world was, that was a different scene entirely. You could tell there was some bad mojo when you walked into the room that night. It felt much safer in our sheltered circle of chaos. As much schism as there was in Anthrax, no one ever overdosed. Still, we weren't REO Speedwagon. Sometimes shit would blow up when we least expected it to.

One night, Debbie and I went to see Danzig at Irvine Meadows, and we bumped into this guy who started talking shit to me. "Hey, Mr. Anthrax guy. You fucking suck!"

I didn't care. It's funny that people think I'm going to get mad if they tell me my band sucks, like their opinion means so much to me I'm willing to fight them. Idiots. So I ignored him. This guy followed me all night everywhere. I was there with Debbie and my friends Billy and Bobby trying to have fun and watch the show, and this guy was six feet away, busting my balls, trying to start something. Before Danzig went on, we walked down a flight of steps to go backstage, and there's this guy again coming up the stairs. "Fuck you Mr. Anthrax! You fuckin' suck."

I just laughed. Then Debbie yelled at him, "Why don't you shut the fuck up already?"

"Fuck you, bitch! Why don't you suck my cock?!?" That was it—fuck with me fine, but fuck with my family or friends? No fucking way. I snapped.

I saw red and charged toward him. Bobby grabbed me in a full nelson and dragged me back down the steps. I was at the bottom of the stairs, and this dickhead was at the top. "I'm gonna fucking kill you!" I shouted.

People turned around and stared. Nobody knew this idiot, but everyone knew who I was. The guy laughed at me and shouted something. Billy was at the top of the stairs talking to him. I wondered what the fuck Billy had to say to this asshole. Then Billy shrugged and the guy charged down the stairs. As soon as he got to the bottom, Bobby let go of me. The guy took a swing at me, but it was a sloppy, drunken hook. I'd been taking boxing lessons for three years, and I dodged his punch with ease, and then I landed a full-on straight right as hard as I could to the side of his head. He went down like a sack of potatoes and was out cold. I instantly felt terrible. As much as I wanted to pummel this moron, I was bummed that I knocked out a drunken idiot, and now I felt like the idiot. The guy's friends came running over, and I braced myself to fight them, too.

"Dude, we've been telling him to shut up all night," one of them said. "We're really sorry. He fucking deserved it." They picked up their friend and all walked away. I was shaken. I'd never hit someone like that outside of a ring.

Not long after decking the moron at the Danzig show, I asked Debbie to marry me, which triggered an avalanche of other unpleasantness. It wasn't Debbie's fault, surely, but sometimes all it takes is a crack in the foundation to realize your walls are about to crumble. Looking back, getting engaged to Debbie was a mistake, but it had nothing to do with what happened afterward with Anthrax. Elektra finally released the "Room for One More" video. It got decent airplay on MTV, and we figured radio would take to it as well. But Elektra decided not to push the song to radio because they thought we were done. We had released two singles, and now radio was through with us because "Black Lodge" wasn't a hit. That was perplexing, since our fans were stoked on "Room for One More," as we knew they would be.

We stayed on the road all the way into the summer of '94. Rob Halford's Fight opened for us on the last leg of the tour. By that point we had sold around 700,000 copies, which, other than the "I'm The Man" EP, was our best-selling record. We felt bittersweet because this was the record that was supposed to go double platinum and beyond. I'm convinced it came down to the fact that we caved and let Elektra make the decision about "Black Lodge." Had we gone with "Room for One More" first, I'm sure *Sound of White Noise* would have done for us what *Countdown for Extinction* did for Megadeth. If we had done what we felt was right in our hearts, we would have sold millions.

That's definitely the biggest business mistake we've made in the history of the band, and it cost us big time. If I could use a Tardis and change one thing, that's it. That would be the single event I would alter in my whole professional life.

On July 10, 1994, Debbie and I got married. A few days before the wedding, some of my friends threw me a bachelor party in the club-house of an apartment complex on PCH, and there were strippers and booze . . . and Gene Simmons. He fucking drove down from Beverly Hills to Huntington Beach to come to my shitty little party. He walked in and everyone lost their minds. No one could believe it was him. At first everyone thought it must be a Gene impersonator. The strippers immediately lost interest in me, and within seconds one of these girls was doing a handstand with her back to Gene and her legs up over his shoulders. Gene went with it and obliged by sticking out that famous tongue of his. The room literally exploded.

Afterward, we went to some shitty café on Main Street in Huntington Beach to have something to eat with Gene Simmons. "You came to my bachelor party?!?" I blurted.

In that unmistakable Gene voice, he said, "You invited me, I came."

I asked Gene if he wanted to come over to my house and hang out, and he said, "No thank you, I'm going to go home now."

So me, my best friend Andy Buchanan, who was living with me in LA at the time, and Guy Oseary, who ran Madonna's label and is now her manager, crossed Pacific Coast Highway to get more booze from a convenience store before it closed, and Gene went with us to get a water for his drive home. We walked into a convenience store I had been to a thousand times because it was right in my neighborhood. I went to the back of the store where the beer was, and I heard raised voices. I walked back to the front, and Guy was arguing with a seventeen-year-old kid who was the son of the owner. They were yelling at each other, so I said, "What the fuck is going on?"

Turned out, the store owners were Palestinians, and the kid got mouthy when he saw Guy's Star of David necklace. "You're wearing a Jewish star!" the kid said. "To my people, that is what wearing a swastika is like to your people."

"What the fuck are you talking about?" Guy said.

"You fucking Jews!" the kid snarled.

Guy is Israeli and doesn't take kindly to anti-Semitism. He's a hardcore Jew—unlike me. I was all drunk and happy. I said, "C'mon guys! Gene Simmons is here!"

Gene looked at what was going down, dropped his water bottle, said goodnight, and walked out of the store, disappearing into the fog on PCH like a real-life Demon. He didn't need this shit.

I was trying to calm everyone down. I said, "Hey, you know me. I'm in here all the time. I'm Jewish. Did I ever want to kill you?"

"Fuck you, too!" said the kid. Suddenly, my mood went from cheery to black. I reached across the counter, grabbed the guy, and started pulling him toward me. "You fucking punk! What's your fuckin' problem, motherfucker?!" I shouted. "I come in here and spend money in your fuckin' store. My friends spend money in your fuckin' store. What the fuck?!"

"Fuck you! I kill you motherfucker!" the kid screamed.

The dad and uncle started yelling, defending the kid. The uncle started to run toward us, and Andy grabbed the guy—who must have been fifty—and slammed him by the neck against the beer fridge, choking him. I let go of the kid, figuring it would diffuse the situation and we could all go home. Wrong. He reached under the counter and pulled out a gun. With hands shaking, he waved it at me and Guy. "Fuck you! Fuck you! I'll fucking kill you! I'll fucking kill you, you Jew fuck bastards!"

I was really drunk and not thinking clearly. We were unarmed, so the fact that this kid pulled a gun on us was a total pussy move and only made me angrier.

"Yeah? You pull a gun, you fucking pussy! You need to pull a gun? Come on, motherfucker! You're bigger than me. I'm just a little fucking Jew! Come on, motherfucker, let's go right now. I'm gonna fucking kill you!" Then Andy slapped him in the face.

"Fuck you! Fuck you! I kill you! I kill all of you!"

Luckily, that was when we heard sirens. Someone else who had been in the store called the cops. "Let's get the fuck outta here," Guy said.

We turned around and hightailed it back to my house. Once we were inside we all busted out laughing, partially from the absurdity of what we had been through, but also because we had made it out alive.

Guy said to Andy, "Dude, you're an idiot! What the fuck were you doing? The guy pulled a gun on you and you slapped him?!?"

"I'm Scottish" was all Andy said and all he had to say. Fucking crazy Scots. And then he added, "I'm lucky I didn't get my fucking head blown off!"

After that, the wedding was seriously anticlimactic. It wasn't a big Jewish fiasco like my first wedding. This one was completely nonreligious. It was more like a gigantic party with tons of friends. We held it at the Hilton in Huntington Beach. Debbie handled most of the planning, but there wasn't a lot. A couple of weeks before the wedding, I met Debbie and her mom at the Hilton to talk to the caterers. While we were there the famous O.J. Simpson police chase happened. We watched him drive the white Ford Bronco down the highway in front of a sea of cop cars. He was running for his life. I should've been as well. Two weeks later we were married.

STOMPED OUT

D ebbie and I celebrated our marriage by taking a honeymoon to Bali. It was relaxing, beautiful, and inspiring. By the time it was over, I couldn't wait to get back to LA to start writing songs for *Stomp 442*. At first, life was great for me both personally and professionally. Then everything turned to shit.

Our label viewed us as a huge disappointment; they were never going to take any blame for making the wrong decision about the way they promoted *Sound of White Noise*. It was the second time in our career that we got greedy and made a bad call, and we vowed it would never happen again. We were determined not to let anyone make decisions for us from then on, and for better or worse, that's the way we've been ever since.

We were looking to point our finger at someone and blame them for not helping to push us over the top, and that's one of the reasons we fired Jonny Z. We were mad at him for not standing up to Elektra. We felt he should have known they were going to lose faith in us and taken control of the situation before it went south. Looking back, there was no way he could have known what would happen. We were all equally responsible. But that's just what happens with managers. Most of the time they probably get fired for the wrong reason. It's the same way in sports. If a team underperforms, the manager or head coach is the first to go.

The truth is, Jonny's heart just wasn't into it anymore. We came a long way and he was an important part of our growth, but he made his money and he wasn't the same after that. He used to call fifty times a day with ideas. Maybe forty-nine of them were stupid, but one of them was usually good and we'd run with it. That was the great thing about Jonny. He had this fire in his belly that never went out—until it did. He had made a ton of money for what he did with Metallica. They left him and went to Q Prime, and Jonny sued and won. He maintained his commissions for the first four Metallica albums. He was already getting massive royalty checks, and by the time *The Black Album* came out, he didn't need to work so hard managing bands.

We hired Steve Barnett and Stuart Young, who managed AC/DC, and then we started writing, figuring the next album would make up for whatever we didn't accomplish with *Sound of White Noise*. We thought everything was okay. We were still on Elektra, and we were determined to give them something they couldn't ignore, take control, and make the right marketing decisions.

John and I were still raging every night and often arrived later to writing sessions than ever. So the rest of the guys decided we should move to a place in White Plains, New York, that was just a few miles from the Anthrax studio in Yonkers. Since there was nothing to do in White Plains, they figured we'd stay out of trouble and be more responsible. We acquiesced because we knew we were guilty of being late or showing up hungover to sessions when we did *Sound of White Noise*. We reluctantly agreed to stay in this crappy furnished apartment. It was like an airport hotel with a small desk, a couch, and a TV. It sucked big time and it was mind numbing. There was no way we could be creative in that place. But we had a rental car to drive to the studio, so after a few days John and I began driving forty miles to the city at night and hanging out in SoHo. We'd go to these hotspots like Spy and Wax, where you had to know someone to get in. We'd party, get insanely drunk, and then drive back to White Plains at 4:30 or 5 in the morning.

John's nickname back then was the Phantom because he'd get to a point of severe drunkenness and then he'd just disappear. No one would know where he went. When he was living in the city, he'd somehow find his way back to the apartment and get back into bed or crash on the couch or the floor. He'd never tell you when he was leaving. He'd be there one minute, the next he'd be gone. But I couldn't rely on him getting back to White Plains by himself. We had to drive back together. I don't know how I never got pulled over or drove the rental car off an overpass I must have driven shitfaced at least a dozen times, which I don't recommend to anyone. It's a great way to end up a cadaver. But somehow I always got lucky.

Once, the only thing that saved me was a blizzard. John had Phantomed out. I couldn't find him anywhere. I finally stumbled out to the street, and he was sleeping on the still-warm hood of a parked car. I got him into our car and he immediately passed out. The snow was so heavy I could barely see out the windshield. I was practically seeing double because of how much beer I drank. Fortunately, the storm was so bad it was impossible to drive faster than ten miles per hour. It took a long time to get back to White Plains that night, but if the weather was better and the roads were clear I probably would have crashed. The next day we were having coffee and I said, "We're moving to the city. If we don't, we're either going to jail or we're going to kill ourselves." The idea of getting arrested was almost worse.

We told the rest of the band we were leaving White Plains and moving to the city. They said that was fine as long as we kept our shit together. And we did. For the rest of the album cycle, we made it to rehearsal on time and always delivered. Being back in the city meant we could go out at night. But it was also a way to unite us more as a band. But right as I was striving to make Anthrax a cohesive unit, Danny Spitz became more of a phantom than John.

The whole time we were writing and rehearsing for *Stomp 442*, Danny was hardly ever there. He popped in at most once every two weeks. He wouldn't stay, either. He'd grab a cassette from the eight-track we'd done demos on, take it home, and then show up again two weeks later with his solos added to the songs. When we listened to what he recorded, it sounded like he hadn't paid any attention to what we had done. His solos were almost unrelated to what we were playing.

Maybe we should have seen it coming. Some of the solos on *Sound of White Noise* were melodic ideas Charlie came up with and then showed to Danny. I think he pretty much checked out at some point on the *Sound of White Noise* tour, maybe because Joey wasn't there for him to hang with anymore, and they had been pals. Whatever the case, we wrote all of *Stomp* without Danny then decided to kick him out of the band. He didn't know what we were doing, he didn't know the songs, and he didn't seem to care. It was like he was telling us he didn't want to be there.

We knew we could continue without Spitz, no problem. Charlie and I were coming up with lead ideas, and Dimebag Darrell had already told us he wanted to play on the record. We also had Paul Crook, who had been Danny's tech for years. He knew all of Danny's parts, and he was an insane guitar player on his own. Still, we kept procrastinating because none of us wanted to be the one to hand Danny his walking papers. It was hard enough to fire Joey. Danny had been with us almost since the beginning of the band.

We got to Philadelphia to start making the record with the Butcher Brothers, and we called Spitz and said, "Don't come to Philly, we've made a decision and you're out."

It seemed like he knew it was coming, but then he sued us for all kinds of money he knew we didn't have. That's just the way lawsuits work. You go for millions and hope you get something. He lost everything—every lawsuit he filed against us.

He even tried to file a copyright suit against us, which was ridiculous. He claimed he wrote all the songs on *Stomp 442*. His attorney sent us a list of the song titles, half of which weren't even songs. One of them was "A Splendid Time Is Guaranteed for All," which is a line from the Beatles song "Being for the Benefit of Mr. Kite." Charlie had written that on the demos that we made for everyone in the band. Danny assumed that was a song on the album.

The copyright infringement case went to federal court, and it was so shoddy the judge threw it out and berated Danny's lawyer. He said, "If you ever bring a lawsuit like this in front of me, I'll start disbarment procedures." But the fiasco still cost us $80,000 in legal fees. We should have taken that out of Danny's cut when he rejoined Anthrax for the reunion tour we did in 2005 because that money came right out of our pockets. We didn't hold John responsible for any of the legal expenses because he was in Armored Saint for practically the whole time Danny was in Anthrax.

Looking back, it dawned on me that Danny had a wife and kids by that point and they took priority over the band. We had done this eighteen-month tour and then we got home and went straight into writing mode for *Stomp 442*. He didn't want to work on a new album. He probably wanted to be home with his family and hang out with his kids. I can't blame him for that, especially now that I have my own son. But he should have tried to work out a schedule with us so he could spend more time at home. He never did that. He just cost us eighty grand.

While we were working on *Stomp 442,* Time Warner cleaned house. Bob Krasnow, Steve, everyone who was on our team was washed away by this corporate tsunami. The company brought in Sylvia Rhone to run Elektra. She was previously the CEO and president of East/West Records and made her name by discovering R&B and rap acts. At the time, we didn't worry about it. We were bummed that the people we liked working with were gone, but we were still signed, and we figured we'd make friends with the new crowd that came in. We knew nothing about Sylvia Rhone, other than that she had Pantera, who were starting to make a lot of noise. *Vulgar Display of Power* had broken, and they were on the verge of becoming huge. And she had worked with AC/DC, so we figured we were cool. Then we heard from our new manager, Steve Barnett, "You'd hope that she'd know something about metal, but I know her from dealing with AC/DC, and she's a fucking nightmare."

Steve arranged a meeting with Sylvia to discuss our future plans. He walked in her office. Our contract was sitting on her desk, and as soon as he sat down she said, "I never would have signed this band in the first place. I never would have done this deal."

"That's a good start, Sylvia," said Steve. "Hi, how are you, and what do you mean you never would have done this deal?"

"I never would have done this deal with this band, ever," she repeated. "It never would have happened on my watch. What's happening? What's the plan?"

"You *do* owe the band $1.6 million in advance for the record," he reminded her.

"I'm well aware of what they're getting paid!"

Steve told her we were in Philadelphia working with the Butcher Brothers and we were expecting full cooperation from the label. We had a lot of specifics in our contract about marketing dollars and video budgets. It was ironclad and the best record contract we'd ever heard of for a metal band—$10 million for three albums. Of course, people assumed it was $10 million in our pockets, and that was far from the truth. The money went into video budgets, marketing, and promotion as well as the $4 million advance for *Sound of White Noise.*

Our relationship with Sylvia started out bad and got worse. We made *Stomp 442.* Dimebag Darrell played lead guitar on "Riding Shotgun" and "King Size," and we thought that was an awesome selling point. The record started with a flurry of punches and didn't let up. It wasn't thrash, but it had that energy and anger. "Random Acts of Senseless Violence" ripped. The song was an indictment against anyone who would use a gun to commit a crime. "Fueled" was a great radio track, and the whole vibe was summed up by the chorus: "What doesn't kill me makes me stronger."

Marcos Siega shot the video, and we thought we had everything going for us . . . until the record came out. We understood that Elektra didn't believe in us, and we tried everything we could to change their minds. I pointed out that our last album sold 700,000 copies and Pantera had a number 1 album. I said, "Look, if 15 percent of our audience goes out and buys this record, it will sell 100,000 copies in its first week. All you have to do is the minimum amount of promotion to let those kids know that the new Anthrax record *Stomp 442* is out there, and they'll buy it!"

Elektra did less than nothing. They did what they were contractually obligated to do, but they used every means at their disposal to find all the loopholes in the deal. It's like they wanted us to fail and were trying to sabotage us. We sort of saw it coming and wrote songs like "Riding Shotgun," the lyrics of which expressed our discontent with the company: "Two steps forward, one hundred steps back." Elektra didn't spend a dime at radio and didn't promote the album at all. It felt like they held up the memory eraser from *Men in Black* to make people forget we were ever a band. We went from selling over 100,000 the first week in 1993 to selling under 25,000 copies in our first week two years later. It seemed impossible and made no sense.

It was hard to believe that all those fans of *Sound of White Noise* were listening to Soundgarden, Alice in Chains, and Nirvana and wanted nothing to do with Anthrax anymore. Metal had dipped, but it wasn't dead. Pantera were selling tons of records, Metallica had *Load* and *Reload*, which both did well. Elektra just dropped the ball. Dropped it down the sewer.

Far worse—our audience didn't seem to care about us, either, anymore. We played venues one-third the size of the places we were booked at in '93 and '94, and they weren't packed. It was completely demoralizing. It felt like after all the increased success we had over the years, we had run face first into a wood choppper. Steve Barnett flew out to a show at this club, Trees, in Deep Ellum, near Dallas. There were six hundred people there. He hadn't seen us live before, and after the concert he said, "You guys are fucking amazing. We're going to turn this ship around. It's a big ship, but you deserve to be cruising back the other direction."

He agreed it was crazy that we weren't selling records and that Elektra was fucking us every way we turned. They had pretty much closed the Anthrax file and thrown it in the fire. We went from being a band that went gold with every record since 1987 to a group that could barely sell 100,000 records on a major label. We were done. Nobody gave a fuck. Then Steve, Mr. "We're going to turn this ship around" Barnett, got an offer from Sony to become the head of their international department. So he jumped ship, too. Nobody had our backs. Nobody wanted to book us, nobody wanted to promote us. We weren't selling tickets. Those tours for *Stomp 442* lost money. The world totally changed, and to this day I don't have an answer for where 600,000 people went.

By the end of '95 going into '96, my personal life was mirroring my career. I had this big monthly financial nut that I couldn't afford anymore. I was starting to panic because I could see my income stream drying up and I didn't know what to do. As that became more of a disaster, so did my marriage. I was blindsided. I never thought of myself as a rich guy. But for a few years there I *did* have a lot of money. Then, when I didn't, everything went into the toilet. I was spending most of my time in New York because that's where we were working with the band. God knows what Debbie was doing back in our house in Huntington Beach.

There was virtually no communication between us anymore. When I was in California, we lived together but we weren't partners. We'd sleep in the same bed without ever having sex. I thought she was still my friend. I still had feelings for her. I still wanted us to have a relationship; I just didn't know how to fix it. I'd try to be romantic and I'd always run into this wall. I'd make moves on her, and she'd say, "No, no, no, not in the mood." It was exactly what I used to do with Marge, and I couldn't accept that because I really didn't want my second marriage to fail. My head was screaming: "Oh my God! You're going to be divorced twice. You suck! You're really bad at being married."

I tried. Between 1994 and 1997 when we were married, I never cheated on her. I still partied; I just didn't sleep with anyone. I had already fucked up one marriage by being unfaithful, and I wasn't going to go down that road again. I was in love with Debbie, and I wanted to prove it to her. But by the end of '95 going into '96, when *Stomp* was dead, my marriage was in its final gasps as well.

I was looking at about $8,000 a month in expenses. Our record bombed, and I realized, "Hmm . . . I have money in the bank, but that's not going to last too long."

We were all anxious and frustrated in the beginning of 1996 because we didn't know what was going on with our career. Regardless of what Elektra decided to do, they owed us $1.6 million for a third album, whether or not they put it out, so we knew there would be money coming in. We had to use some of it to make a new record, but there would be cash left over that would provide income and that provided some relief.

It was a hollow victory, though, because my personal life was miserable and my band life was just as shitty. I felt sorry for myself, which I despised. I will forever see the bright light at the end of the tunnel. Regardless of some of my angry lyrics, I'm not a negative guy. I've always seen the glass as half full, even in 1996 when that half-full line was nearly impossible to detect. At one point, I had my band American Express taken away from me because I was using it for personal expenses. I wasn't stealing; I had every intention of paying back every penny. I just didn't want to put anything on my own credit cards. So I'd use the AmEx, knowing that our business manager would get the bill at the end of the month and see that I put some restaurant charges on it that certainly weren't a band expense, and he'd say, "I need money for that; you need to write a check."

Every month I asked, "Don't we have any band money coming in?" And he'd say, "No." So I wouldn't send a check. Then another month would go by, and there would be a bunch of dinners on the card. Finally, I got the call from Charlie.

"This is the hardest call I've ever had to make in my life," he said.

"What?"

"You need to stop using your AmEx. We're turning it off because you're abusing it and costing us money. It's not our responsibility. These aren't band expenses."

I was so embarrassed. "I'm sorry, dude," I explained. "I'm starting to flip out because I've got these expenses and I don't know what's going to happen in the next few months financially."

"I understand," he said. "But you can't do this anymore. We're turning the card off, and you have to pay back what you owe when the money comes in."

They took it right off the top of any money I was owed, and it was done, but I'd never been so ashamed. I felt like one of those politicians who gets caught abusing campaign funds. At least I wasn't voted out of office.

Chapter 25

BROTHER, CAN YOU SPARE A DIME?

Nineteen ninety six was a pretty shitty year. Elektra didn't want another record from us and paid a ton of money just to get rid of us. They even let us keep our masters for *Sound of White Noise* and *Stomp 442*, which shows how much faith they had in those records as valuable titles in their catalog. The band had a lot of expenses and unpaid bills at the time, so a large chunk of the money they paid us got eaten up, and we split the rest. At least we had *that*. But Elektra didn't care about Anthrax anymore, and that stung. And now we had to look for a new record deal. We got Walter O'Brien and Andy Gould to manage us. They worked with Pantera and White Zombie, two of the hottest metal bands at the time. It wasn't easy and we were desperate. I went to New York to have a meeting with Walter. I said, "I'm here to ask you to manage the band. You should have been managing us for the last ten years."

"Wow, I'm flattered," he said, "but I have to tell you, I just don't know. I can only do this if I can do it right for you guys, and truthfully, I'm unbelievably busy with Pantera. They're a fucking handful, and I'd hate for you guys to have to suffer for that."

I was dying inside. I felt like Walter was our last hope. Everyone had given up on us. Our business managers, who were the biggest in the business, couldn't get anyone to touch us. Nobody would take meetings with us, and our lawyer was out trying to find us a record deal. It was like we were toxic to the touch—like real Anthrax.

The first question every label executive asked was, "What did your last album do?" And when we told them it sold 100,000, they immediately lost interest. They didn't want to know how the record before *Stomp 442* did. We were only as good as our last album. We were dead in the water. I left that lunch with Walter feeling decimated. We had no label, no manager. We might as well have had no band. Then Walter called the next day.

"You know, I thought about it last night," he said. "Why the fuck wouldn't I manage Anthrax? It's a fucking honor. Count me in 100 percent."

I felt a wave of elation. It was like I was adrift at sea and a boat appeared out of the fog and threw me a life preserver. I was convinced Walter would help save the band. My marriage was another story. I started to stay in New York a lot again, because every time I was at home, Debbie and I would fight or just coexist. Eventually she moved out of our house and in with some guy friend of hers because she "needed her space." It was a mess, and truthfully, as much as I hated the idea of getting divorced again, I knew I couldn't go on like this. I was supporting her, and it seemed like she had no respect for me at all. When I was in New York, I'd stay at the rehearsal place the band was paying for or with friends because we couldn't afford a hotel. Manhattan was my escape, and John and I were raging again.

I was reckless. I took stupid risks, and I developed an obsession with snowboarding, which isn't particularly bright when your world is unraveling and you sometimes feel like a leap into the abyss would be preferable to another day in hell. I attacked slopes like I was an Olympic champion, only I wasn't. I was an overachiever. I'd go down sheer drops with no fear. In Austria I went snowboarding on a show day with Joey Z, the guitarist from Life of Agony. I came out from this tree run, and there was a blind drop I couldn't see. I figured I would traverse right back onto the trail and head down, but there was a two-foot lip I didn't know was there. It looked like the trees just continued into the flat. So I came flying out of the trees, hit the lip, and pitched forward, and my head smacked right into the hardpack of the trail. I was unconscious for a minute and there was a big welt on my head that was bleeding through my hat. I got back up and continued riding for the rest of the day, and I played a show that night. I was super dizzy from the fall and felt like shit. Blood was running down my face during the show; it was very black metal.

I saw a doctor the next day in Warsaw, and it turned out I had a full-on concussion. I felt like crap for the next three days then I had a headache for another week. But we didn't cancel any shows. For five gigs blood dripped down my face when I headbanged. The crowds loved it. After the snowboard accident, I started wearing a helmet when I rode. That protected my head from injury, but the shit going on in the rest of my life—there was no protection from that. Debbie started calling me in the middle of the night: "You're off having fun and I have to deal with all this bullshit! There are bills coming in and I don't have any money. Why am I dealing with this crap?"

Finally, I came back from New York, and we had one of our rare adult, civil conversations. It was one of those discussions that starts with, "We need to talk," just like the one I had years earlier with Marge, only Debbie initiated this one. I opened the door and sat down, and she said, "We have to separate. We need to see what it's like not to be a couple anymore."

By that time, I was fine with that. Our relationship sucked and reminded me of being a kid and hearing my parents fight all the time. We didn't have kids, so there was no reason to stay together. The only thing we shared anymore was a house, and I was hardly ever there. I had a mortgage of $3,800 a month I was throwing away for a symbol of the American dream. I told her I needed to sell the house. We put it on the market. Not only would it put the final nail in the coffin of our shitty marriage; when someone bought it, it provided some much-needed income.

Before the house sold, we stayed in different bedrooms down the hall from one another. If I knew she wasn't going to be home, I would bring chicks to the house, which got really uncomfortable. We weren't officially divorced, but we might as well have been, so I didn't feel bad about living this other life. At the same time, when couples are no longer together, they shouldn't have a window into one another's lives anymore. I knew she was dating people, and I certainly suspected she had already been cheating on me. She never brought anyone home, but I saw her go out. The whole scenario was just fucked. I couldn't afford to get my own place, and I was stuck sharing the house with someone who didn't want to be with me but I was still supporting. Good times.

That's around the same time I went to Tampa and got arrested for trying to steal the on-deck circle at the Yankees spring training stadium. It all seems stupid and funny now. I was on page 6 of the *New York Post,* and my mug shot was in *Rolling Stone,* but Yankees owner George Steinbrenner wasn't amused. He pressed charges for breaking and entering and grand theft, since the thing was worth over $1,000. Those were both felonies, so I had to hire a criminal lawyer. It cost me $25,000. Luckily, money had just come in for the next record, so I had the cash, but my stupid shenanigans cost me money I needed to live on. During that whole summer going into the fall, I had this case hanging over my head, and I had no idea how it would play out. There's a saying that any press is good press, and oddly enough my drunken stupidity turned into positive publicity for Anthrax. I would walk down the street in New York, and people would say things like, "Hey, Scotty, where's home plate? Yeah, right on, man!"

Fans were stoked about this stupid fucking prank that I pulled in Florida. A lot of people thought I broke into the actual Yankee Stadium. If I had done that, I'd probably still be in jail. I'd smile at anyone who made jokes, but I was freaking out inside. My lawyer told me I wouldn't go to jail since it was my first offense. He said I'd probably have to pay a decent-sized fine and I'd end up doing a hundred hours or so of community service. I'd probably have to put on an orange jumpsuit and clean up shit on the side of the road. But the big problem was that the charges were felonies, and I couldn't get visas and travel around the world if I had felonies on my record. It was a real concern and my lawyer didn't have any answers. Then Gary Dell'Abate, the executive producer of *The Howard Stern Show,* called and said, "We read about you on page 6. Howard wants to know if you want to talk about it on the radio."

I'd been a huge Howard Stern fan for years, so I said, "That would be awesome. I just have to check with my lawyer and see what I can talk about."

"You absolutely cannot appear on the show and make fun of this situation in any way, shape, or form," my attorney said. "This is serious. If Steinbrenner's lawyers get wind that you're not taking this seriously, things could get worse."

I was bummed out. I called Gary back and told him what my lawyer said. The next day Gary rang me back. "Listen, we weren't going to tell you this, but we already spoke to Steinbrenner, and he's going to come on the show, and you're going to get to apologize to him if you do this."

Steinbrenner was a semiregular guest on *Stern*, and if he was willing to talk to me, I would be more than happy to apologize on the air. I told my lawyer what Gary said, and he said the plan sounded good, but he'd look into it further and get back to me. Fifteen minutes later he called me and told me he had just gotten off the phone with Steinbrenner's lawyer, who didn't know anything about Steinbrenner going on *Howard Stern*. "I don't know what these people are trying to do to you, but you'd better call this guy back and tell him you're not coming on."

I was pissed. I called Gary and said, "Why are you fucking with me? My attorney just told me Steinbrenner doesn't know anything about this. This is my life, dude."

"Scott, I swear to you George is calling in tomorrow," Gary insisted. "Howard wants you on at 7 a.m. You call in at 6:55. I'll put you on with George, and if you're not satisfied that it's him, hang up."

I called my lawyer back, and he said to go ahead with it but not to say anything that might get me in worse trouble. That meant no jokes. I was fine with that. I just wanted this to go away. I called at 6:55 the next morning and Steinbrenner was there. They put us on the air. Howard gave a synopsis of what had happened. He talked to George about the Yankees making the playoffs. Then Howard busted my balls a little bit. Finally he said, "All right, Scott. The reason we have you here is so you can apologize to Mr. Steinbrenner about what you did in Florida."

I had spent the previous night writing, "Dear Mr. Steinbrenner, I am very, very sorry," like a fuckin' sixth grader who was caught shooting spitballs and has to go to the principal's office. But I put down my scribbled notes and apologized from the heart because I'm a huge fan and I never meant any harm. I certainly wasn't trying to besmirch the name of the Yankees.

"Sir, this was an anomaly," I said. "I've never been arrested in my life, I'm not that person. I drank too much and I made a big mistake. I didn't hurt anybody. I had no malicious intent. I swear this will never happen again. I'll never be in trouble with the law in any way, shape, or form for the rest of my life."

"Scott, you sound like a nice young man, and most importantly, you're a Yankee fan," Steinbrenner said. "The playoffs are coming up and we need all our fans. We can't have our fans in jail, now, can we?"

He told me he would talk to the Yankees' lawyers and see what he could do. I thanked him and apologized again. Two weeks later, his lawyers called my lawyer and said they were dropping all charges because of lack of evidence, even though they had the videotape of me running around the bases like a lunatic and trying to steal the on-deck circle. Steinbrenner had found it in his heart to let me off the hook. Not only did they drop all the charges; my record was expunged like it never happened. It was a good day in Mudville.

I stayed true to my word and never got arrested again, but I definitely didn't walk the straight and narrow. And when we went on tour with Pantera in November 1997 for two months, I kind of jumped off the cliff. I had known Dimebag since 1986, and we had many nights between then and 1997 when I would have a few beers while Dime went wild on bottles of whisky and beer. He had a trademark drink, the Black Tooth Grin, or Black Tooth, or just Tooooth, which was a shot of Crown Royal and a splash of coke. He'd down those all night long. Dime made that drink famous.

Every night with Dime was a party whether I was drinking heavily or not. I always felt like I was in the eye of the hurricane when we were hanging out—like everyone else was moving around me at high speed and I was in the center of it, nursing a beer, people-watching, and pointing shit out. "Ha, that was funny. They just blew up that guy with firecrackers." Or "Shit, that looked expensive. Someone smashed a soda machine with a sledgehammer." Or "Boobs!"

Dime was always hysterical, paying people to do stupid shit. He'd find kids who were working for an opening band and not making any money and get them to do disgusting things. Once we played a show with Pantera for 6,000 people, and afterward the floor was covered with empty beer cups and cigarette butts. Dime told this guy, "I'll give you $20 for every cigarette butt you pick up with your tongue. The kid fuckin' picked up about thirty of them, and Dime just laughed and handed him $600. Some people made good money off Dime. He didn't care. It was the price for entertainment.

When *Jackass* became popular on MTV, Darrell was irate. "*Jackass*. Fuck that shit, I'm the original *Jackass*. They're just following in my boots. Give me their money, give me their fucking lawyers. I'll show them a jackass!"

One time Type O Negative and Biohazard were playing with Pantera, and Biohazard singer Evan Seinfeld came up to Dime at a show and said, "How come you never give me a chance to make any money?" So Dime said, "Well, what do you want to do?"

"I don't know. Whatever."

Halfway through Pantera's set that night, Dime had to pee. He always had a bucket behind his amp stacks where he would piss during shows. He went back there between songs and then saw Evan standing by the side of the stage. Instead of peeing in the bucket, he asked his tech to get him a cup. The guy came back with a red Solo cup, and Dime peed into that, went up to Evan, and said, "You wanna make some money, hip-hop? $200 if you drink this cup."

"No way," Evan said. "$1,000."

Darrell said, "Fine," and handed him the cup. Evan drank it and instantly threw up. But he did it! I would have asked for $83 million to do something so gross. Dime told me his piss isn't clear and watery like healthy urine. He described it as "fluorescent yellow, thick, and glowing."

Dime always amused everyone around him. He took pride in it. He was also insanely generous. One time he was wearing some kind of western shirt, and Charlie said, "Cool shirt, Dime!" The next day we showed up at the show, and Dime had bought not just the shirt for Charlie but boots, pants, and a hat to go with it. It was the kind of thing you would wear to go line dancing. Dime had a heart of gold. He was the ultimate host and went out of his way not to disappoint anyone.

He was so grateful that he was getting to do what he wanted with music, and all he ever wanted to do was give back. He would tell me, "I'm going to end up fucking broke on the street with a guitar case open with people throwing money in. I know that's where I'm ending up because I'm going to spend every fucking thing I ever make on stupid shit. As long as I'm playing guitar, I don't give a fuck."

"You could always stay at my house," I told him.

At the end of 1997, Pantera invited Anthrax to spend two months on the road. It was them and Coal Chamber. I knew touring with Pantera meant upping my game when it came to drinking. Beer wouldn't cut it anymore. I had to prepare myself for the hard stuff, so I made an adult decision to let Darrell teach me how to really drink. I was at another crossroads in my life. My second marriage had failed and I needed a change. More importantly, I needed to really let loose for the first time—just let go and have fun, and being on the Pantera tour was a crash course in losing all inhibitions. When I told Darrell about my decision, he asked me if I was sure and if I understood how hard it would be. I told him I did. I wanted him to be my Yoda, and I would be like Luke learning from the Jedi master of partying. He didn't get the reference at all. He said, "A yo da what?" He thought it was some "Yo, yo, yo rap shit." But he told me if I put in the time and effort the shit would pay off. I said, "Never mind Yoda. I'm all in. See ya in a few weeks."

The only other time I drank whisky was in England with Lemmy, and I got alcohol poisoning. I knew I'd have to up my game big-time. I did my first Black Tooth Grin on the Pantera tour—the first of many. I put myself on a drinking schedule because I knew if I was going on tour with those guys, I was gonna do shots with them, and I couldn't play guitar drunk. Dime had this muscle memory where he could do the most amazing shit totally wasted. Me, I could barely play "Louie Louie" after a few beers. I had only tried to perform wasted once in my life, at the Megaforce party in 1989 at the Ritz in New York. We only played four songs, but I was literally looking at my hands saying, "Why won't you work?"

I wasn't going to fuck up the shows with Pantera, so my one caveat was that I stayed sober until 7:00 p.m., which is when Dime usually showed up with a shot. I would do one shot, then I'd do another right before we went on, which was about 8 p.m. after Coal Chamber. Then during the show, Dime would stand on the side of the stage and feed me between three and five shots. I'd be seven shots in by the time we got offstage, but I wasn't drinking it all at once so I was able to keep my shit together. After we got offstage I'd hang out with Pantera in their dressing room for thirty minutes leading up to their set and we'd do shots the whole time. Then, while Pantera was onstage, Dime and I would do another two hours of endless shots. There was no escape, which was kind of the point. I was going to become a heavy drinker even if it killed me.

By then I was hammered, and Pantera hadn't even started drinking backstage after the show yet. Dime used to live by a code he called "drink it or wear it." If he poured you a Black Tooth, you had a choice. He'd say, "Shot, Baldini?" Baldini was just one of the many names he had for me. He came up with it when he was driving by a store in New York City on Third Avenue in the Fifties. There was a shop called Dino Baldini Men's Clothing. Somehow Baldini became my nickname from that. Sometimes it was Dino Baldini, sometimes it was Jew Baldini—whatever he felt like at the time. I didn't care. I loved the guy.

He'd hold this shot, and if I didn't want to drink it, he'd say, "Okay," and splash the shot on me. He didn't do it to be a dick; it was just the way he was. It was part of the game, and that game had rules, just like baseball. If you hit the ball to second base and the second baseman throws the ball to first before you get there, you're out. That's the rule; it's not the second baseman being an asshole. Drink it or wear it. After the first time I wore a shot I decided I didn't want to spend the rest of the tour with my clothes smelling like Crown Royal. If I was gonna smell like whiskey, it was gonna be because it was seeping out of my pores from doing so many shots.

Pantera turned me into a real drinker. No more of this beer bullshit. Those first two weeks were brutal, straight-up booze boot camp. I was puking a lot and Dime would say, "Get back on that horse Baldini!" I always thought that after you puked you were done. That was your brain and body telling you that you can't drink anymore. I have memories of being on the bus with Darrell after the shows because I wasn't allowed to just escape to my bus. No, I'd ride with him and Vinnie Paul, and we'd drink and listen to KISS and talk about KISS and watch KISS videos all night. I was in the moving bus bathroom puking, trying not to mess up their bathroom. I was worried about that. Ever the good Jewish boy. I came out of the bathroom thinking I was done, it's time to go to bed, and there was Dime with this look of mischievous expectation holding out a Black Tooth for me. I told him, "I can't drink that. I puked, I'm done." I thought only crazy people kept drinking after they vomited. And if you did have another drink, your brain would go, "Oh yeah, well fuck you then, how do you like this? ANEURYSM. Dead." I said this all to Dime, and he just looked at me with that Cheshire Cat grin and said, "Ya ain't gonna die Baldini, you just have more room in yer stomach now!"

Two weeks into the tour, I was polishing off a bottle of Crown and endless beers and wine every night on the bus. Somehow I pulled that off. If I tried to do that today, it would kill me, but back then it was mind over matter. They would keep a separate bottle of Crown for me and mark it off with a Sharpie to keep track of how much I was drinking. The night I was about to finish my first whole bottle of Crown, everyone was chanting, "One more shot! One more shot!" and I'd be chanting along, but in my brain I was saying, "You're an idiot! Your liver is fucked!"

Every night toward the end of Pantera's show, I'd go onstage with them and we'd play "A New Level." Their singer, Phil Anselmo, would grab me, tilt my head back, and pour wine down my throat like fucking Caligula.

It's not like I was keeping up with those guys either. If I did a shot, Dime and Vinnie did two. And Phil drank an insane amount, as did their bassist, Rex Brown. After those first two weeks, I started to settle into the routine. I stopped puking and craved my next shot. I was drinking like a maniac, and most importantly, I was having a blast. The adult decision I had made was paying off just like Dime said it would. I wasn't worried about shit, I was just going with it.

The hangovers were pretty intense, and one day I shambled into the venue around 5 p.m., and Darrell saw me and asked, "You on the skids Baldini?" I could barely open my eyes, my head hurt so badly. He whipped a Coors Light from out of nowhere, handed it to me, and said, "Get a good pull off of that, it'll get ya off the skids." I had never tried "hair of the dog," but I figured at this point anything that would stop the two monkeys sitting on my shoulders from hitting my head with hammers would be worth a try. I hit the beer and I started to feel better right away. I sucked the whole thing down and Dime said, "Ya feeling a little better?" I told him I did and I remember thinking, "Jesus Christ, I'm a fucking hobo now."

I had become a professional drinker. I had made it from the minor leagues up to the show, and I was excelling, I was an all-star. It was the most fun I'd had in my life up to that point, and I had Darrell to thank for that. After pulling that off for two months, I felt a strange sense of accomplishment. It was like passing an initiation rite or earning a doctorate in drinking.

When I got home from touring with Pantera, my friends didn't know about my decision to flirt with alcoholism, and I was excited to show off my newfound talent. I didn't realize I was about to use my powers for evil. The day after I got home from the tour, I called a few of my friends to come hang out at our favorite dive bar, the Coronet Pub, on La Cienaga in LA. Four of my buddies showed up, and I headed to the bar saying, "First round is on me." I ordered thirty Irish Car Bombs. It took a few minutes to offload all the pints of Guinness and Jameson shots from three different trays. My friends looked confused at all the booze in front of them, and finally one of them said, "Are you expecting more people?" My eyes flashed red, and with a Dr. Doom-esque flourish, I quickly and sternly replied, "No. Why?" I could see my friends were getting nervous. "Well, uh, who is going to drink all this booze then?" he asked.

"WE ARE!" I roared. "NO ONE DARES LEAVE THIS ROOM UNTIL EVERY DROP OF DOOM'S PRECIOUS AL-COHOL HAS BEEN CONSUMED, YOU VILE CLODS!" So we drank, and after a few weeks of me thinking I was the Lord of Latveria, they had enough and wouldn't hang out with me anymore, so I went back to New York.

Chapter 26

VOLUME FADEOUT

After we finished touring for *Stomp 442*, we took a few weeks off and then went right to work on our next album, *Volume 8— the Threat Is Real.* I was still in a bad place mentally because of my failed second marriage. I'll take the hit for fucking up the first one. We never should have got married; I wasn't in love. I was twenty-three and that was too young. This time, I felt like it could have worked, but I wasn't taking the blame. I didn't think it was my fault, and it took me a little while to see that maybe it was never meant to work out.

After I sold the house, Debbie and I moved into an apartment in Hollywood where I barely spent any time. I was paying the rent and all the bills, and she was living there. I allowed that to happen long after we separated, which was fucking weak, but I was a sucker; I let her take advantage of me.

I don't know if having two shitty marriages short-circuited my brain or if something inside burst out of its cage while I was on tour with Pantera, but from 1997 to 2000 I was tearing it up in a way that made my dalliances with models and scenesters with John in the early nineties look like I was a fucking altar boy. You hear all these stories about young bands that get some attention and suddenly they're out of control, doing blow, dropping acid, shooting up, driving drunk. If they survive their wild years, they mellow out by their third or fourth album. I was just the opposite. I wasn't doing narcotics, but I was drinking enough to get cirrhosis of the liver. John leveled off a bit, but not me. Maybe after my career peaked and then plummeted, I thought I'd never make it back to the top. Or maybe I cared too much in the beginning to screw up, and once I tasted fame and realized it wasn't as sweet as it looked, I didn't care anymore. Whatever, I started living like there was no tomorrow. It was very much *Bright Lights, Big City* without the cocaine or *American Psycho* without the murder, or mostly like Charles Bukowski without the whores.

In New York I was hanging out with a lot of shitty people and fucking around with a lot of shitty girls. I didn't want to be alone because I was depressed. As insanely fun as it sometimes was, the whole thing was fucking pathetic, and I would wake up every day feeling empty and hungover. So I'd have a beer in the morning to make the headache go away. Thanks, Dime.

When I was in LA, I'd usually get together with our neighbor Tracy, who I'd known for years, and her boyfriend, Jesse. He worked at a bar called Daddy's over on Vine. I'd drive with him to work at about 5 p.m. and begin drinking at 5:30. The bar closed at two, and that's when the bartenders started drinking. First came Irish Car Bombs, and we'd keep going until God knows when.

Anthrax worked hard during this whole time, and I was somehow able to switch off between drunken delinquent and dedicated band member. I'm still proud of the songs we wrote for *Volume 8—the Threat Is Real.* They were really diverse and heavy, modern sounding with a crushing metal groove. Nineteen ninety eight is the year that nu-metal took over but we were definitely not a part of that scene. If anything we were old metal, so getting anyone to support us was proving difficult. Since we didn't have a deal, we recorded the album at our studio in Yonkers, and Paul Crook produced it. We worked on *Volume 8* for a year and must have done a hundred revisions on the songs "Killing Box" and "Harm's Way" before we got them right. We put everything under a microscope because we didn't know if this was our last chance. Since we were all so anxious about making this our comeback record, we second-guessed ourselves and argued about everything. There weren't any full-on fistfights, but at times we came close.

John and I lived together and worked through our real-life trauma in the lyrics. A lot of the album is about my shitty marriages and the hedonistic lifestyle I had adopted. "Catharsis" is about being miserable with someone and being unable to let her go even though you know being free would be the best thing for both of you. I wrote it on the plane home from Florida after I got arrested. I had an epiphany. I realized I had hit rock bottom in my relationship and my personal life, and by reaching that low I knew everything would work out and I'd be able to climb back up. "Inside Out" mirrored where we were with the band. We used to be on the inside, now we were on the outside looking in, and no matter what we did, no matter how hard we worked or tried, we were shut out and it hurt: "It's in my stomach like fire, in my stomach like cancer, / in my stomach like a knife / I've been gutshot." We worked with Marcos Siega again for the "Inside Out" video, which was an homage to the "Nightmare at 20,000 Feet" episode of *The Twilight Zone* with William Shatner. It's a great video. Nobody saw it. At least people can see it forever on YouTube now. Dimebag played the sick solo on "Inside Out" as well as the solo on "Born Again Idiot."

I was reading a lot of Charles Bukowski, and in some ways I was modeling my life after his. I love his motto: "Drink, fuck or fight." At some point, they're all completely the same—emotional releases that leave you dizzy and breathing hard. Bukowski was truly free. All he cared about was his art, women, and booze. As long as he had those three elements in his life, it didn't matter if he was living in the slums or hanging out with Hollywood snobs selling books out the ass. For a while, that's what I aspired for as well, whether I had $10 million in the bank or I was back at home living with my mom. It's so different from the way I am today.

I was blinded by rage and felt like a failure, and since I couldn't make either of my marriages work, I became the opposite of the responsible husband. I was all about drinking and fucking. I treated a lot of people like shit, and I'm not proud of that. I was living for myself and only aware of my own needs. In that respect, *Volume 8* was about as real, raw, and dark as I could get. We did it without a label because we needed to make a record—not for financial reasons (although we were all getting a little fiscally desperate)—but because we're musicians and that's what we do. We knew we made good albums and it was time to create another. We weren't ready to throw in the towel just because we got fucked over by Elektra. We had a lot left to say.

When the album was done, Walter talked to a bunch of labels. Ignition was a new rock division started up by the rap label Tommy Boy. At that point, they were the only game in town unless we decided to sign with an indie like Metal Blade or Century Media. Looking back, that might have been a better career move, but our egos were too big to leave the major-label playground. At least Ignition was part of that world. They had money. We were their biggest rock act, and they promised to market and promote us.

Volume 8—the Threat Is Real came out in the summer of '98, and "Inside Out" started impacting at rock radio. People were sick of alternative, and they were ready to listen to really aggressive music again. We sold around 70,000 copies between July and early December, and everyone thought the next single, "Catharsis," which was scheduled to come out in early 1999, would help us maintain upward momentum. Maybe we wouldn't go gold, but heading into the holidays we felt positive that we'd sell at least 400,000 copies. Then at the end of the year Walter called me.

"We've got problems."

"What do you mean?" I said.

"Ignition is out of business. Tommy Boy's not funding them anymore. They're done. In a month you won't be able to find your album on the shelf."

That was that. Ignition stopped printing *Volume 8,* and Walter was right. It literally disappeared. It was like we were cursed. That was the knockout punch for me. We had worked so hard on the album in the most adverse conditions. We bled for it, and now everything was gone. We were starting over—again—and nobody gave a shit.

Going into '99, we were essentially done with Anthrax. The thought of spending eighteen months writing and recording another record after what we went through on *Volume 8* was not an option. We didn't just have a bad taste in or mouths. It was like we had eaten shit and all the mouthwash in the world wouldn't rinse away the nauseating flavor. We were really happy with *Volume 8.* Of all the records we did with

John Bush, it's my second favorite. I like it better than *Sound of White Noise*, and it was devastating to have it thrown into the garbage by a parent company that was making decisions based on an inane call to scrap all of their rock releases to try to remain afloat. The crazy thing about that whole arrangement with Ignition was we didn't get an advance for the album. It was strictly a distro deal, yet they owned the masters. We financed it with our final payment from Elektra. We kept a lot of money for our living expenses and put the rest into the album and touring costs. By the end, we were flat-out fucked. All we had was the money we had in the bank. There would be no royalties or advances. We had nothing physical that we owned and could sell to another label. It was like *Volume 8* never existed. We tried to make deals with Ignition to buy the masters or at least put it back out, and they wanted ridiculous amounts of money.

There was no way Anthrax could continue as a functional band without taking a break. John Bush went back to Armored Saint to work with them on *Revelation,* and Charlie and I got together with Dan Lilker and Billy Milano and did the S.O.D. reunion album, *Bigger Than the Devil.* We had the time, and I was going stir-crazy sitting around trying to figure out what Anthrax were going to do next. Plus, we needed money. Nuclear Blast wanted to release an S.O.D. record and put us on tour, so we thought, "Why the fuck not?" We spent a year writing and putting out the record and playing some shows. It was a welcome distraction. Fourteen years after we released *Speak English or Die,* Sgt. D rose up from the grave to lead S.O.D. through another set of hilariously stupid, politically incorrect crossover metal. We had songs like "Celtic Frosted Flakes," "Free Dirty Needles," and "The Crackhead Song," and we ripped through them in an effort to offend everyone who didn't get the joke.

It was cool to get back together with Dan and Billy after all that time, and we joked around in the studio and had fun throughout the writing and recording process. That first tour for the album was great. It felt good to get out and play places that never got to see S.O.D. People forget the band only played seven concerts before 1999. Six of them were way back in 1985, and then we did the reunion show in '92 that we filmed for the *Live at Budokan* concert video. So the idea of going out and playing European festivals, getting to go to Japan, and doing a proper run through the States was exciting. The tour started, and we quickly turned into a brutally fierce band, tight as fuck and grinning through every song. There's nothing quite like 30,000 people screaming "You're dead" during "The Ballad of Jimi Hendrix." The shows turned out great, and I definitely felt satisfied with what we had done with the album and tour.

But after a while, it became too much like a real band, which is what it was never meant to be. We shouldn't have done a second leg of the tour in 2000. We didn't draw as well because it was our second time around in a short amount of time and we started having baggage. It became like a job. I said from day one that S.O.D. was only ever supposed to be about having fun. I already had a "day job" with Anthrax.

I started questioning why we were still on tour when it wasn't good for laughs anymore. I didn't want to tour those songs anymore. I felt like I was exploiting my child, selling him into zombie slavery. Sgt. D was not happy. It wasn't too long into that second leg of shows in the US that Anthrax were invited to tour with Mötley Crüe and Megadeth in the summer of 2000, essentially ending S.O.D.'s "comeback." That was a huge relief for me because I didn't want to do S.O.D. anymore and the Mötley tour seemed like a great opportunity for Anthrax. Win-win. Hahahahahahahaha. If only I had a crystal ball.

In the aftermath of the *Bigger Than the Devil* tour, Billy got really angry at me and Charlie, and blamed us for what seemed like everything that was wrong in the world. 9/11? That was me and Charlie. The Florida election debacle in 2000? Me and Charlie. The rise of nu-metal? Definitely me and Charlie. I get it, though. If we had left Anthrax in 1986 and made S.O.D. our full-time band, then we all would have reaped the benefits of that. But we didn't, and our paths went in different directions. I've always considered Billy a good friend, and we've had some amazing times. Those are the things I like to think about, not the fights and the arguments.

We recently reconnected with Billy over some pending S.O.D. business. We got ripped off for a shit-ton of publishing money. (Shocking, right? Yay to the music business.) We're trying to figure out how to get the cash back. Through the drama, it was good to be on the same page again with Billy because there was a time when his yelling bothered me to the point where I had to cut off contact with him. Every time I talked to him, he'd verbally abuse me for ten minutes. I didn't need that in my life anymore. I had already been married twice. (Rim shot, please!) Besides, I never called him up and yelled at *him*. He and Charlie definitely had a falling-out as well. Billy said a lot of shit to Charlie that he could never take back, and that's why Charlie will never work with Billy again. It's kind of too bad and all unnecessary, but I don't lose sleep over it because I have no desire to make a third S.O.D. record or play any more shows with the band—unless of course someone wants to back four trucks of money up to our respective houses. Until then I can sit in my house and play "March of the S.O.D." and write Sgt. D comic strips. S.O.D. FTW!

At the beginning of 2000, Anthrax received an offer to play a headline tour with Fu Manchu opening. We didn't want to do it because the money wasn't that good and we had nothing new to promote. But we knew if we played the shows, we would all come home with something in our pockets, and that was definitely an incentive. At the same time, the idea was kind of demoralizing. I thought, "Why slog it out in a bunch of shitty half-filled clubs? That won't help the morale of the band."

Our agent at the time, Dave Kirby, talked us into doing the tour, and it went well. It started a little slow, but as we went along the crowds got bigger and bigger and pretty much every show was full, which took us by surprise. We thought it would suck, but we ended up doing good business, whereas the year before was terrible except for the small window when *Volume 8* was actually out and people came to the shows. When we finished the tour, we thought, "Well maybe we should get back together and write a new record." A fresh start could be just what we needed. It felt like the nineties were finally over and our curse was broken. The pendulum seemed to be swinging the other way.

Touring went well, and it wasn't long before Allen Kovac, the manager, contacted us about recording for his label, Beyond. We started working on a compilation for them, *Return of the Killer A's*, which was a spin-off of the *Attack of the Killer B's* odds-and-ends record we did for Island. *Return of the Killer A's* was pretty much a greatest hits album that spanned our career and included a cover of the Temptations' "Ball of Confusion," which featured both John Bush and Joey Belladonna singing. What's even weirder is Dan Lilker played bass. Frankie wasn't available when we were recording it, so we asked him if it was okay if Lilker played on it. It was fine with him and Lilker said he'd do it, so we went with it. Paul Crook produced it, and we recorded it at Big Blue Meenie studios in Hoboken, New Jersey—the same place S.O.D. recorded *Bigger Than the Devil*.

Someone at Beyond came up with the idea of having both John and Joey on the song and asked me if I thought they'd both do it. I said probably not but we asked them anyway, and they were into the idea since the rest of the record featured songs from each of them. Joey came to New York and hung out with us for a while. We joked around and got along really well—no tension at all. And then he recorded his parts perfectly. I don't know why Beyond chose that song, but we all liked it; the Temptations were an amazing and groundbreaking band, so we were happy to do it. The track itself is not one of our best songs. The singing was good and I made some cool guitar noises, but I was a little disappointed when we were done. The real coup is that it's the only recording that features both John and Joey.

Next thing I knew, Beyond wanted to do a full studio record with us. Suddenly, we had a deal again. We couldn't start working on the record right away because of the upcoming shed tour with Megadeth and Mötley Crüe. We hadn't gotten an offer like that in a while, so it definitely seemed like the boat was turning around. In the back of our minds, we were thinking, "Madison Square Garden, here we come."

Chapter 27

THE PERFECT PEARL

was editing the S.O.D. home video with this guy, Kevin, in a suite at the Beyond Records offices in the spring of 2000, and I was talking about the upcoming tour with Mötley. "You're going out with Mötley?" Kevin said. "My wife is one of their backup singers. Her name is Pearl, Meat Loaf is her dad."

It was just a conversation point. I didn't think anything of it. Kevin and I started off on friendly enough terms, but while we worked on the S.O.D. video, we started having problems. He claimed Nuclear Blast agreed to pay him $5,000 more than he had received. I went to bat for him because I was about to go on tour with his wife and I didn't want it to be awkward. The last thing I wanted was for her to think I was trying to rip off her husband. I asked Nuclear Blast to pay Kevin the money because they were going to recoup on the DVD whether they paid him or not. And it didn't seem like something that should turn into a sticking point that might delay the release date. So they paid him and Anthrax headed out on tour.

The first show with Mötley was June 24, 2000. We were backstage in catering on an outdoor deck at the Sacramento Valley Amphitheater, and Pearl came over to where I was sitting and introduced herself. I had seen her picture, so I knew what she looked like. She said, "Hi, I'm Pearl, nice to meet you." I shook her hand, barely looked at her, and replied, "Hi, I'm Scott," but that was it because I was sure her husband had been talking shit about me and I thought she hated me. I definitely was concerned about being on tour with someone who had heard negative things about me. I thought she'd tell everyone on the tour that I was this total stingy, egomaniac asshole.

During the first few days of the tour, we'd play our set, get cleaned up during Megadeth's show, and then go to the side of the stage to watch Mötley and drink. I never loved their music overall, just a few songs, but they sure put on a show. Mick Mars is a great guitar player with a sick tone, and there were hot girls on the stage, so why not? When the show was over, Pearl and the other backup singer, Marty, would change out of their stage clothes and get wasted with me, John, and Frankie. During the first week, we all became drinking buddies. I figured either her husband didn't tell her I was an asshole who owed him money or she figured he was full of shit.

Against my better judgment, I developed a major crush on Pearl almost instantly. And I found out she didn't know anything about the tiff I had with her husband. After a few days of getting wasted and laughing our asses off together, she said, "The first two days of the tour I thought you hated me."

"I thought you hated me!" I replied, smiling.

"Why would I hate you?" she said.

I told her the whole story. The mood got a little darker for a moment. I thought she might have figured out that I was the guy her husband had bitched to her about, and my stomach rose into my throat.

"Yeah, Kevin," she said with distaste. "He and I are getting divorced. We're separated. Our relationship is awful."

I couldn't have been happier if Elektra had dropped another $500,000 check in my lap. "Oh my God! Me, too! I'm separated, too!"

I told her about my last marriage and the toll it took on my psyche. We were both in the same exact place in our personal lives. We had both struggled through three years of hell and somehow made it through to the other side—with the help of recreational beverages.

Actually, she was raging even harder than I was. Her tolerance for booze was amazing, so every night we'd drink and talk for hours. I hadn't made a move yet because I was really into her and I didn't want to fuck up everything. She was smart, funny, talented, beautiful, and there were never any awkward pauses in our conversations. We'd talk about family, relationships, music, movies, books. I enjoyed her company so much, I felt like if I crossed the line and tried to kiss her, I would ruin everything. You don't do that on a tour. You're in a vacuum with everyone else you're hanging out with, and if something awkward happens between two people, it compounds itself tenfold. So, buds, buds, buds. We hung out every night.

We never even held hands, but everyone thought we were fucking. We were in the Salt Lake City Hard Rock on a night off, and I went back to her room. There was a big party and I ended up staying over. It would have been the perfect place to bust a move, but no. We got hammered, I crashed in a chair, and she slept in the bed.

When we got to Houston after the third week of the tour, Mötley asked us to cut our already-small guarantee in half because they were losing money. Tommy Lee hadn't rejoined the band yet. Former Hole drummer Samantha Maloney was playing with them, and while she was okay behind the kit, she didn't have Tommy's star power. Mötley fans didn't exactly flock to the shows, and we wound up playing in these big sheds to between 3,500 and 5,000 people a night. No one in Anthrax was willing to cut our guarantee in half, so we got kicked off the tour. We were in Six Flags riding rollercoasters the day we found out we were going home. I didn't really care about not playing the last five weeks of shows. What bummed me out was that I wasn't going to be able to hang out with Pearl every night. I was going home and she was still on the road.

Not only did I have to leave this totally rad girl, I had to go back to my apartment where my fucking not-yet ex-wife still lived. I felt like I had blown my chances of ever making anything happen with Pearl. She was going to meet someone else and I'd become a distant memory. Just the thought made me queasy.

I went back to Daddy's every day with Jesse. For five weeks straight I was a total barfly. When everyone left, I'd be so fucking drunk I felt like the only thing that would keep me from dying would be the five-mile walk back to my apartment. If I drove home and made it without crashing, I'd be home in ten minutes, and I'd still have so much booze in my system that there was no way I would be able to get to sleep, and I'd probably end up spinning until I puked.

This way, I was moving the whole time and I didn't feel sick. Those walks were amazing because Hollywood is a weird fucking place, but at 5 a.m. it's even weirder. You see a lot of crazy shit, whether it's trannies giving each other blowjobs, junkies shooting up, or hookers arguing with their pimps. I got to see the underbelly of life, which I had written about before but never experienced quite like that.

During those walks home I usually called Pearl. We'd talk for three hours, out of our minds drunk. She was on the bus in the middle of nowhere, and I was metaphorically nowhere, wasted. It didn't matter what we talked about. Just hearing her voice made me feel better. I finally decided I had to tell her how I felt about her, because if I didn't and she wound up with someone else, I'd be devastated. This way, if I at least tried and she turned me down, I wouldn't live the rest of my days wondering what if. . . . I handwrote her a five-page letter, and I spilled my fucking guts out about how much she meant to me, how our conversations were the highlights of my day, and how much I wanted to kiss her. I wrote about how much fun I had with her on tour, told her I wished we were in a relationship, and I felt like I was falling in love. I ended the letter by saying, "You may not feel the same way at all, but that's fine. Either way, I just have to let you know because I can't let this opportunity slip by."

I put the pages in a FedEx box with a bunch of goofy Anthrax stickers and a Sgt. D figurine from Japan and sent it to her. I knew she'd have it the next day, and I even told her, "I sent you a FedEx package. You'll have it tomorrow."

The next day I talked to her and she didn't say anything about the package. Another day passed. We talked a couple more times. The conversations weren't awkward at all, but she never said anything about the letter. After four or five days I figured, okay, that's it. Just friends.

We kept talking, and I didn't bring up the letter because I was already crushed. I knew how she felt. I didn't have to make her tell me. By not saying anything, she'd already told me she didn't share my feelings. And I still loved talking with her anyway.

Finally, the Mötley Crüe tour ended and she got home. I called her and said, "Hey, you're home. Let's go do something."

My friend Kenny and I planned to go to the Troubadour to see Nebula and High on Fire. I invited her to join us, and she said she'd meet us at the club. When I saw her we hugged and watched the bands. Then after a few drinks I decided I'd go for broke. "Did you ever read my letter?"

"Yes, of course I read it. It was wonderful, it was beautiful, it was unbelievable."

"So, why? . . ."

"I tried to reply to you," she said, looking me in the eyes with the warmth of a fireplace. "I must have started so many times writing you back to tell you I felt exactly the same way, and every time I did it, it sounded terrible. It didn't match what you wrote me, and I just felt I couldn't send you something like that. It didn't express how I felt."

I was pretty buzzed, not really from the booze—more by her response. I was as happy as when we were hanging out on tour and physically lighter. The weight on my heart had lifted. I asked her why she never said anything at all on the phone for five weeks and told her I was really tormented. Pearl felt the same way, but she said she didn't want to talk to me about something so important over the phone, and she figured we'd see each other when she got back and we could talk then.

That was September 9, 2000, and we've been together ever since. I had found my true love. I think I knew it from the second day we were hanging out on the Mötley tour. I'd never felt that way about someone so quickly. The connection we made was so strong that nothing else in my life was as important. I felt like I was in love with her and I was only getting to know her. And the more I knew, the deeper I fell. I never really loved Marge. I *thought* I knew what being in love was with Debbie. But it was nothing compared to this. The only shitty thing was I was head over heels with Pearl, and I was still living in an apartment on Orange Grove with Debbie, and Pearl was living in Brentwood with her parents.

Meat Loaf and Leslie G. Edmonds hadn't split up yet and the atmosphere at their house was pretty tense. After Pearl and I were dating for a while, I started going over to her parents' place for dinner. I met her mom before I met my future father-in-law. Leslie was friendly, nutty, and nice, and we got along really well. Before I met Pearl's dad the first time I asked her, "What do I call him?" I had no idea. "Mr. Loaf" just didn't sound right, and I wanted to get off on the right foot with him. Pearl said, "Call him Meat. That's what everyone calls him." The first time I met him was just a short "Hi, hey. Nice to meet you." Then he went back into his office and closed the door. He wasn't in a good place. He and Leslie were right at the beginning of what became a brutal divorce.

There was a lot of dysfunction in the house. He definitely intimidated me at first because I had *Bat Out of Hell* as a kid and I saw Meat Loaf play at Calderone Concert Hall on Long Island in '78. Obviously, he was a massively huge rock star, and I was this fucking weird, bald, goateed, tattooed heavy metal guy dating his daughter. I was in *his* house watching *his* TV and eating *his* food. I understand the pecking order. I was definitely determined to be extremely respectful whatever happened.

The first real interaction I had with him was on Christmas Eve of 2000. Pearl and I were on the couch watching TV. The plan was that I would stay over with her that night and we would all be together the next day for Christmas. At around 8:30 a car pulled up and Meat Loaf came walking through the living room. Pearl said, "Hi, Dad." He grumbled, "Hi." Then he went straight to his office. He didn't say anything to me. I was okay with that. Pearl and I returned to watching TV. Five minutes later, he walked out without saying a word and went back outside. Then we heard his car peel out of the driveway. We didn't think anything of it. It wasn't so out of the ordinary.

Pearl and I were lying down, and I had my arm around her. It was completely innocent. A few minutes later her mom called down from upstairs and said, "Pearl, pick up the phone." She picked up the receiver and said, "What? What? We weren't . . . huh? Okay, okay, okay."

"What?" I said.

"That was my dad, screaming at me, telling us that we've got to get the fuck off of his couch and get the fuck out of his house. Who the fuck do we think we are? He said we better be the fuck out of there before he gets back."

Our friend Kenny was having a Christmas Eve party, so we went over there. Everyone (including us) thought it was pretty funny that we got thrown out of Meat Loaf's house on Christmas Eve. After the party was over, we went back to my apartment, where Debbie was still living and stayed over in my room. We went back to Meat Loaf's place the next morning, and it was like nothing happened. We certainly didn't bring up what he said the night before, and we all had a great time. Meat was stoked that it was Christmas. And we all had a great meal.

I figured that things were pretty crappy for him and Pearl's mom, and when weird shit happened I shouldn't take it personally. He wasn't angry at me, he was just angry. Once, he threatened to punch my teeth down my throat. He didn't say it to me. He said it to Leslie or Pearl, and to this day I have no idea why. He never yelled at me directly. It was just that, in the beginning there when he was going through his own personal hell, I happened to be in the wrong place at the wrong time, and I got some fallout. Maybe he didn't want some new character hanging around while all that bad shit was going on in his life. Pearl was still singing in his band at the time, and he knew she really liked me, so he tolerated me as a human that existed in his daughter's life, but there was no real relationship between Meat and me. Then something happened that totally broke the ice.

In early 2001, Metal Shop, the eighties hair metal spoof band that evolved into Steel Panther, were doing a Monday night residency at the Viper Room. Pearl and I used to go every week from the first few times they ever played. They fucking ruled. I hate hair metal, but when they covered Bon Jovi and Ratt songs, I actually liked it because they injected humor into the show. Their presentation was ironic, their whole shtick was amazing. Pearl and I told her dad about it a few times in passing. We told him how much fun it was and said, "You should come out with us one Monday night and check it out. Steven Tyler came and got onstage with them, and it was really great."

That was the big thing at the time. All these musicians would do impromptu guest performances with them, and it was obviously massive. Steven Tyler was the first big, big dude to do it. One night Pearl and I were out to dinner, and while we were eating we were talking about going to see Metal Shop like we had for the last six weeks in a row, and we decided to skip a week. We had been out for a couple nights straight, and we figured we'd go home and take it easy. We were walking into the house around midnight when my cell phone rang.

"Scott!! It's Meat!!"

"Hey Meat, what's happening?"

"Where the fuck are you guys?!?" he shouted. He was clearly someplace where there was lots of noise, and I could barely hear him.

"Oh, well we're walking into the house right now. We just got back from dinner."

"Well, what are you doing?!?"

"Nothing. We're probably just going to go to bed."

"Well, I'm at the fucking Viper Room to see this Metal Shop thing that you guys have been talking about for all these months. Where the fuck are you?!? You better get your asses down here right now!!"

I got off the phone and said to Pearl, "Guess what? We're going to Metal Shop. That was your dad. He's there and wants to know why we're not."

We turned around, got back into the car, and drove to the Viper Room. As we were heading there, Lonn Friend, the author who used to edit *Rip* magazine, texted me that he was hanging out earlier with Meat Loaf at the Grand Havana Room smoking cigars and having some drinks, and now they were at the Viper Room. "Meat's in rare form—he's had about sixteen margaritas—no exaggeration."

We got there, and he was a different Meat Loaf than I had ever seen—all smiles and having a fucking ball. He was totally into the show. I had never seen him like that before, so it was really fun for me. Obviously, Pearl had been with him when he was in that state. For me, I was like, "Wow, this is a new Meat Loaf!"

Metal Shop called him onstage, and they did Bon Jovi's "Livin' on a Prayer." Meat didn't really know the words; he just did whatever he did with Ralph Saenz, their singer. But even though he didn't know the lyrics, Meat fucking owned it. Then he did a Whitesnake song with them that he didn't know at all. And he owned that, too! He just had so much charisma, it didn't matter what he sang or how he sang it. The crowd went nuts. Then Meat came over and sat down with us.

At the end of the night, everyone was leaving and I said to Meat, "Hey man, give me your keys. I'm going to drive you home."

"You are not! What are you talking about? You're not driving me home," he slurred, then laughed.

So I said, "Dude, seriously. You gotta give me your keys. I don't give a fuck what you think or anything. You're giving me your keys or you're taking a cab. You're not driving home."

So he handed me his keys. We left our car there at the Viper Room, and Pearl and I got in his big black Mercedes. I was driving, Meat was in the front, and Pearl was in the back. I drove Meat to the house he moved into after he and Leslie split. I was a little worried he'd be mad at me for insisting on being the designated driver, but I didn't care. I didn't want to see a story about him on CNN later that night. I didn't have to worry. During the whole ride to the house he was thanking me. Then he said, "I know things have been strange, but I fucking love you! You're fucking awesome—I fucking love you, man!"

He was putting his arm around me and leaning into me. Then he kissed me on my cheek and on my neck.

"I love you, man. I love you! And you're so good to my daughter!"

It was this really great moment between the two of us—a total bonding experience. And from that point on, we were totally bros. Over the years, Meat has gone above and beyond for me, Pearl, and Revel.

I introduced Pearl to my circle of friends, and we'd all go to Daddy's. Pearl would keep up with me drink for drink. Actually her drink at the time was double vanilla Stoli straight, so if anything she was drinking way more than me! We kept raging hard for at least that first year of our relationship—but for a different reason. Neither of us was drinking to stop feeling bad. We were drinking because we felt good. It was a happy, in love, go out, get drunk, come home, have sex all night long kind of partying. It was the best.

It was truly a miracle. I really thought I'd never meet the right person and never be happy. I figured I'd always have to compromise. Then within a matter of months I was happier than I ever was or realized I could be. It made me think that there really is someone out there for everybody. I was on this path of self-destruction when I met Pearl, and she was on a parallel path. She has told me a million times that I was her savior. She'd say, "If we didn't meet, I don't know where I would have ended up, certainly in rehab. Maybe dead." Once we started hanging out, everything changed.

The closer I got to Pearl, the weirder Debbie became. Pearl and I would be lying in bed, and Debbie would walk into my room naked under a completely see-through nightgown with her boyfriend in the other room. And then she'd ask me for cash: "Can I have $20 to buy a magazine?" It was fucking crazy, and I enabled her because I was afraid that if I told her I wanted a divorce, she'd get a lawyer and go after me like a shark, and I'd be financially fucked for the rest of my life.

I didn't even see how I was letting her manipulate me until Pearl threw down the gauntlet. "You're still kowtowing to her like you're married. You're still enmeshed in this." I tried to assure her that wasn't the case. But when Pearl opened my eyes to what was going on, I was dumbfounded. Then I just felt dumb. I paid the rent, expenses, and food. I sold the house, found a way to manage month to month, and the whole time I was busting my ass she didn't have a job. Then, after we broke up, she started dating other people and I was bankrolling *them*.

I was so scared Debbie was gonna sue me for alimony that I allowed her to emasculate me. Then I grew my balls back. One day Debbie tried to pull some shit with us and got rude with Pearl. When she saw that things were real between Pearl and me, that the two of us were deeply in love and about to do our own thing, Debbie became threatened. I confronted her because I wasn't afraid anymore.

"You need to fucking shut the fuck up and mind your own business," I told her. "You are not a part of my life anymore. We are over, done. You're not the magic witch who once blinded my eyes. You've been taking advantage of me for years, and it's over! No more free ride. I'm moving out and we're getting divorced."

Chapter 28

THE OTHER SIDE
OF THE MIKE

Thank God I had Pearl in my life because aside from my relationship with her, everything else seemed to be going down the shitter. I was barely getting by, which is why I knew Pearl wasn't with me for my money. That was a small consolation. I literally had nothing and was almost fucking broke. The band wasn't making any money. I had enough to pay my rent and feed myself, but for all intents and purposes, I was living month to month. And everyone in Anthrax was counting on the Beyond record to get us back on our feet.

Even before our divorces were finalized, Pearl and I moved in together, and it was like a sea change had taken place, which only backs up my theory that my professional life is often a direct reflection of my personal life. I got the hell out of the apartment with Debbie, stopped paying her bills, and moved in with Pearl, and that immediately brought bliss back into my life. Days later, I got a call from VH1 asking me if I wanted to host *The Rock Show*. They decided not to renew Cane's contract and wanted me to fly to New York to host the show on a trial basis.

The producers told me I'd be introducing rock and metal videos, reporting metal news, and interviewing guests. My gut did a bit of a flip when they told me I'd have to do interviews. I'm not a talk show host, and I definitely was not comfortable being the guy asking the questions. They wanted me to interview my peers—my friends. Just the thought gave me douche-chills. I asked if we could do the show without guests. They said no, so I sucked it up and prepared for the worst.

The first shoot was really easy. They offered me a teleprompter, but I had already memorized my script. I didn't know anything about TV. I learned fast. All you need to do is read and make it look like you're *not* reading, and you've got it nailed. I got really good at not reading. I shot a few weeks with no guests because they wanted me to get comfortable being the host. Then they told me the Cult were coming in to the studio, which made me nervous. I could talk to the camera no problem. They let me improvise and make jokes. They wanted me to be myself, and that's why the show was working. Now, I suddenly had to become a journalist and ask all the lame questions that I hate being asked: "Tell us about your new record. What are your greatest influences? What's the wackiest thing that happened on the road?" Then there were all the other mind-numbingly boring pearls of journalistic wisdom like "How's the tour going?" and "How do you get along with your bandmates when you're on the road?"

I couldn't be that guy. I was sweating it to the point that I was ready to quit the show rather than look like some asshole. I couldn't reconcile that I was in Anthrax, yet to do the TV show right I'd have to interview other bands. I didn't belong there. I belonged on the other side of the mike. Looking at myself in that position, I became so self-critical that it was incapacitating. I was convinced that if I started interviewing bands, my career *in* a band was over. Who would ever take me seriously again as an artist?

No disrespect to journalists. I've had the pleasure of talking to many fine writers and deejays over the years. There's a big difference between people asking cookie-cutter questions scribbled on a sheet of paper and professionals who actually do their research and involve you in a conversation enough to get something back from you that you weren't expecting to give. A good interview can be inspiring. A bad one makes you never want to answer another stupid question again. It reminds you of the precious minutes of your life you're wasting with some idiot who went on Wikipedia for ten minutes and rewrote well-worn facts in the form of questions. Hey, we're not playing *Jeopardy* here. I can't tell you how many times I've wanted to punch someone in the face through the phone line for wasting my time.

The day of my first interview as *The Rock Show* host, the producers handed me a list of questions for the Cult, and just as I had feared, they sucked—unless the objective was to bore both the band and audience to death. I didn't know what to do. I knew the guys in the Cult—friends since the eighties—and they are as Britishly razor sharp and dry as you can get. I figured I'd be lucky to come out of this sane, considering the blank stares I'd be getting from their guitarist Billy Duffy. To make things worse, backstage before the shoot, they were all being really nice to me. In my neurotic state I figured it was because they felt sorry for me. "Poor Scott. Look at what his career has been reduced to. He had such promise once. Let's be really nice to him. He has it hard enough, having to do this now." It kind of felt like a pity fuck.

I took a deep breath and swallowed my humility. The stage manager set us all up and the cameras started rolling. Then, at the last second, an inner voice told me to go off script and talk to the Cult like I talk to my friends. Why ask a scripted question that I already knew the answer to when we could just shoot the breeze? The conversation was natural—lots of ball-busting, lots of commiserating about shared band experiences—and it became a situation where I wasn't a TV host interviewing my guests. We were a bunch of friends hanging around telling stories. It wasn't me against them. We were on the same team, and that made everyone less guarded, and in the end it made for a much better segment.

During the conversation, I made sure to touch on the things the band was there to promote. The producers were happy and so was the band. I had found a winning formula. The guest segments became my favorite part of hosting *The Rock Show*. Over the forty-eight episodes I shot, I got to hang with Ozzy, Pantera, Rob Halford, Megadeth, Stone Temple Pilots, Tenacious D, Alice in Chains, Deftones, Godsmack, and more.

So what secrets did people let slip because they felt so comfy talking to me? I don't know. I didn't ask questions I would be uncomfortable answering, nor did I bring up personal things I may have known about some of my friends I had on the show. In the end, people wanted to be on the program because they knew they were sitting down with me and I wouldn't cross a personal line.

When I interviewed Sully Erna from Godsmack, he told me a story about how they got their name. As he explained it, one of the guys in the band came to rehearsal one day with a big zit, and Sully made fun of him. The next day Sully had a zit as well, and someone said, "God smacked you for making fun of him." Voila! Godsmack. It had nothing to do with the Alice in Chains song "Godsmack" or the fact that they used to cover Alice songs. Total coincidence. There were a few times I had to interview bands I knew nothing about because their music wasn't for me. Three Doors Down and Nickelback come to mind. I went into those interviews not knowing what the fuck I was going to talk about, and I was worried the whole time that my expressions would give me away (that's where I learned my poker face). As it turned out, they were all really cool guys, and a lot of them grew up listening to Anthrax. That's when I started making my list of nice guys, bad bands. It's a long list.

Of all the *Rock Show* episodes I did, my favorite was the Halloween interview I did with Ozzy Osbourne. Ironically, it started as a disaster. The fact that we got him was a major coup. It was fucking huge! He was in town doing promo for his *Down to Earth* record, and I was his last interview of the day. He started at 6 a.m. on *The Howard Stern Show* and did interviews all day up to the point where he got to our set at 4 p.m. I could tell he was exhausted. The set was decorated for Halloween. I was dressed as Gene Simmons in full makeup and costume but with a bald head and a goatee.

Ozzy and I had been friends since we toured together in 1988, and I was totally looking forward to hanging out with him and telling stories. Having had dozens of guests at this point, I felt confident about my "interview" skills. The producer said Ozzy was told in advance that I would be in Gene Simmons makeup for Halloween. But as Ozzy walked in with Sharon, I could see him across the room looking at me with a serious shit-smell face. We reached the interview segment. Ozzy walked on and I could tell something was wrong. He grimaced at me and then looked off set to Sharon. He was fidgety and it seemed clear he didn't want to be there.

We started the interview, and I asked him the most basic questions about his new record—what the recording process was like—real simple stuff. Ozzy was giving me short, curt answers and staring at me like I was someone he didn't know. At that point I was freaking out that I was fucking blowing it with Ozzy Osbourne. All the excitement of my biggest interview was sweating away right through my Demon face paint. The director yelled "Cut" and told everyone to take five so they could reset for a different shot. That left Ozzy and me sitting there in a palpably uncomfortable silence. The makeup girl came over and touched up my widow's peak, and I was trying not to show that I was stressed, but I literally didn't know what I was going to say next.

I just didn't know why Ozzy couldn't be bothered with me. The director said, "Action," and before I could stammer out another question I noticed Ozzy staring intently at me, moving his face closer to mine to get a better look. Just when I thought he was going to head-butt me, he smiled and said, "It's you . . . it's you, man. Scott, is that you? It *is* you. Hey, it's Scott!" I was so relieved and said, "Yeah Ozzy, it's *me*. I thought you knew."

I could hear Sharon yelling, "Ozzy, I *told* you it was Scott Ian under the makeup," and then Ozzy said, "I thought you were some wanker dressed like KISS, and I couldn't figure out the bald head and I didn't know why I was here to do some stupid interview." He gave me a big hug and said, "Let's start over." Fifteen minutes later we were done. We had a great time, and I was thrilled to have had the chance to sit and talk to one of my idols on my show—even as a wanker in Gene Simmons makeup.

Thanks to the *Rock Show* gig, I went from practically being broke to having a regular paycheck, something I hadn't had since I worked for my dad. I was on Viacom's payroll! That was a definite morale booster. One thing I've learned in life, though, is right when you think everything's going your way, something can happen that can leave you feeling helpless and speechless. That's what went down in the middle of my gig with VH1 when one of my best friends, Jennifer Syme, died.

I met Jennifer in '91 at Irvine Meadows, backstage at a Beastie Boys concert. She worked for David Lynch, and Charlie and I were massive *Twin Peaks* fans; the song "Black Lodge" was a *Twin Peaks* reference. We used to ask Missi Callazzo at Megaforce to call David Lynch's office all the time to try to get us *Twin Peaks*–related swag. Jen was the person Missi would talk to.

One night, I was backstage at a Beastie Boys show, and a girl walked up to me and said, "You're Scott, right? I'm Jennifer from David Lynch's office. Your management calls all the time looking for stuff."

We immediately became great friends. She was literally like my sister and became a big part of my life. She had a wicked, extremely politically incorrect sense of humor. Most of the years through the nineties, when I was having fun, Jen was there. When Pearl and I first started dating, Jen couldn't wait to meet "the love of my life." They hit it off immediately and became very close as well.

Jennifer was Keanu Reeves's girlfriend, and in 2000 she got pregnant. I remember Keanu moved Jen out of her place and into a house to help shield her from the constant paparazzi hassle. She was thrilled about having a baby, and everything in her life seemed to be working out. So when she came full term only for the baby to be stillborn, it was terrible—just fucking horrible and tragic. Having my own child now, I can't even imagine what that would do to your heart and soul. We all came together for Jen and Keanu and did our best to help them through it. Sadly, the tragedy didn't end there. The rest of the story was well reported by the tabloids.

Jennifer was at a party at Marilyn Manson's house. She went home and then decided to drive back to his place. She was already fucked up, and when she reached Cahuenga Boulevard she lost control and crashed into a bunch of parked cars. She wasn't wearing a seat belt and was thrown from the car out onto the street and killed. I couldn't believe it. I had lost my closest friend. And of course it wasn't just devastating to me but for a whole circle of friends that Jen was the center of. Her death was tragic and shockingly avoidable. I always imagine what could've been for her because she really was a special person, a rare human, and I still miss her.

I was devastated by Jen's death, but I knew I couldn't let it slow me down. If she found out that happened, she would have let me have it. Fortunately, the stability of a day job with *The Rock Show* and the ability to save some money set me up to the point where I was excited about going back in the studio with Anthrax to work on another record.

Once again, we had to find a guitarist before we started tracking. Paul Crook did a great job playing with us for almost seven years. He was a sick guitarist and a good friend, but for some reason we never made him a member of the band. We just couldn't commit. We even did photo shoots as a four-piece; I guess we never considered him an actual member, which sucked. Maybe we always felt like he wasn't really the guy. Granted, it was the worst period of time in our history business-wise, so he was better off not being a member of the band. He was too good of a friend to put through that hell. So around late 2001, when we really started focusing again on writing new music, we decided we needed to find a new guitar player. Someone who was aggressive and felt "Anthrax."

Pearl and I got Paul a gig playing with Meat Loaf, and he's way better off now financially than he was in Anthrax. Then we asked Rob Caggiano if he would audition for us. We knew Rob from a New York band called Boiler Room. He came to Yonkers and learned a bunch of songs. He knew most of them already, since he was ten years younger than the rest of us and was an Anthrax fan growing up. Boiler Room wasn't doing anything, and he was happy to have a new gig. He blew us away at his audition. He played great, looked great, and was easy to get along with. At the time, Rob had a production team with Eddie Wohl called Scrap 60, and they produced *We've Come for You All*, which meant we didn't have to work with someone we barely knew.

We wrote *We've Come for You All* in a more copacetic environment than we had been in for a while. I think everyone was psyched to be back together and just be a band again with what seemed like little or no pressure on us because, fuck, what did we have to lose? There was nowhere to go but up. As we wrote, we could tell it wasn't going to be a thrash album, just a great metal record with equal amounts of grit and melody. Plus, we experimented with some styles we had never tried.

There's a lot of groove in songs like "Cadillac Rock Box" and "Superhero." "Taking the Music Back" is midpaced and heavy, but the guitars are jagged and off-kilter. "Think About an End" has these tribal drums and cool vocal harmonies, and "Safe Home" is one of our best songs ever, my first love song, written for Pearl, telling the story of what she meant to my life. Then there's "Black Dahlia," which has some of the fastest drumming Charlie's ever done, and "What Doesn't Die," which could have been on *Among the Living*. Rob Caggiano played great on all of the songs, and we got Dimebag to play leads on "Strap It On" and "Cadillac Rock Box." The biggest surprise on the album, though, is that we got Roger Daltrey to do guest vocals on "Taking the Music Back."

While we were writing that song, the chorus reminded us of something by the Who. When I mentioned that to Pearl, she said that her mom knew Roger and his wife, so she arranged a dinner for the four of us. There I was with the lead singer of the band whose guitarist inspired me to pick up my first guitar, drinking bottles of wine and laughing. We were there for about four hours, and Roger told us amazing stories about the Who. Then we started talking about Anthrax, and he volunteered to do guest vocals. I didn't even have to ask him.

He came into the studio with me, but when he heard the song we wanted him to sing on, he was a little confused. He said, "This is heavy, heavy stuff," over and over. I was like, "Man, this is like a pop song for us," but I understood that he was coming from a different place. The Who's songs are heavy, but they don't have that kind of distortion and propulsion. But he kept listening, and after about forty minutes he was able to separate the parts and come up with a vocal for the chorus.

John did most of the vocals, but for the chorus Roger came in with that trademark scream and just killed it. He did a take, and then he asked me if I thought it was good. That was completely surreal, sitting there critiquing the vocals of one of the greatest singers in rock. I felt like I was in Pete Townshend's chair, thinking, "How the fuck did I get here?" So of course I answered Roger with, "Yeah, that was alright, but why don't you do it again with a little more energy?" Not.

When Pantera broke up, Walter retired, so we needed to find new management. Rob was friends with Larry Mazur, so he told Larry we were looking for a new manager. We talked and Larry took over and started shopping for a deal. None of the majors were interested, but at that point we didn't care. The industry had completely changed, and the majors were all trying to figure out how to stay in business. Their answer, it seemed, was to look for more pop and hip-hop. Artist Direct, which was funded by this billionaire, Ted Field, called Larry and offered us an unbelievable deal—$250,000 for the album, and we would get to keep our own masters (which in the old days was unheard of). We'd also make a large percentage of cash for every record sold and have a healthy marketing budget. We negotiated the contract and signed the deal.

The record was already done and ready to come out, so we figured we were all set and that it was time to plan the tour. Then out of nowhere, Will Pendarvis, who runs Sirius in LA now, called Larry and told him Ted Field had pulled all funding, and the Artist Direct label was done. The head of the company hadn't signed the deal yet, so he was tearing it up. We had nothing. At least they didn't own the album, so we were free to find a new home. A day later, Larry called us and said he had talked to Sanctuary Records, which was offering us the same money and would put the record out on schedule. We didn't have the same distro deal, so we wouldn't own the masters, but our backs were against the wall, so we agreed to the terms.

The Sanctuary deal was only for the US, since we were already on Nuclear Blast in Europe. They did a good job with *Bigger Than the Devil* over there, so I figured they'd have that part of the world covered with the new Anthrax album. *We've Come for You All* came out in March of 2003, and the press said it was the album fans had been waiting for. The fans agreed, and it seemed like we were back on track again. We toured the US with Lamb of God and Lacuna Coil opening, and the shows sold well. We played all the big European festivals and destroyed. We supported Judas Priest, Mötorhead, and Dio, and everyone said, "Anthrax are back!" Then Sanctuary folded.

Universal swallowed up the label, so the record was still available, but there was no label to support it and no money to keep us on the road. Once again, it was almost like someone had reached down from the sky, grabbed the masters, and threw them in the garbage. The music industry had fucked us in the ass for the third straight time, and while we didn't have a strict three-strikes-and-you're-out rule, tensions in the band were escalating. It felt like something was about to blow.

Chapter 29

TOTAL SCHISM

We stayed on tour as long as we could because we didn't want to face the reality of what Anthrax should do next. We had no idea. After a sold-out show at Irving Plaza in New York, we turned to Larry Mazur in our dressing room and said, "Okay, where do we go from here? What's the plan?"

He looked at us, shrugged, and said, "I have no fucking idea."

"You're our fucking manager!" I said. "You better help us figure out what to do."

Nothing. Days went by. Nothing. Finally, we fired Larry. It was a bummer to be changing managers again. We didn't want to and we all liked Larry a lot. The reality is, at the time we needed more than a manager—we needed a miracle worker.

We brought in our buddy Tim Dralle because he loved the band and he'd do anything to help us out. Instead of writing a full new album, which we weren't ready to do after the Sanctuary debacle, we decided to rerecord a bunch of songs we'd written before John joined the band and have John sing them. We asked fans to vote for the songs on our website and used their selections for the track list. We called it *The Greater of Two Evils,* and started working on it at Avatar Studios in New York.

We played a whole set live in front of an audience in the studio. Little did we know it was going to be the last thing we recorded with John Bush. After one of the sessions, we had a meeting with management in the studio's big live room. Charlie, who had decided to move to Chicago, told us he was building a studio there and thought we should move our gear from Yonkers to his place and make Chicago our home base. Frankie didn't like that idea. He had already called Charlie's hood "the Poughkeepsie of Chicago." But I thought it was worth thinking about. I had all the facts and figures from our business manager about how much we'd be saving on a monthly basis by not having to store our gear and pay rent on the studio space in New York. Plus, it would be cheaper to all be in Chicago than it was for me and Bush to fly to New York and stay in Manhattan. It was going to save us thousands of dollars over a year's time, which was pretty appealing since we basically had no label or band income. That's when Frankie lost it.

"Fuck that shit! I'm not going. I will never set foot there. If you want to work there, do it without me!"

He started screaming and yelling because that's how he gets when he's worked up. He can't hear or see anything. He's a self-proclaimed "hothead." I can't remember his exact words, but it was something to the effect of "I don't need to come out to Chicago and be involved in your fucking scene."

Charlie, who is the opposite of Frankie in temperament and had been calm the entire time, said, "Oh yeah? What's that supposed to mean?"

"Whatever the fuck you think it means!" Frankie snapped.

"Yeah? Fuck you!"

"Well, fuck you!"

They had been on opposite sides of this big room, and they charged each other like two rams about to butt heads.

Rob and I ran in to try to stop them, but we were too late. They collided and started throwing punches. We grabbed Frankie, dragged him into the vocal booth, shut the door, and locked him in. We told him we wouldn't let him out until he cooled down and promised he wasn't going to start up again.

Charlie was across the room sitting on a road case. "You're fucking dead, motherfucker!" he screamed.

"No, you're dead!" shouted Frankie from behind the locked door.

I started laughing. I couldn't help it. It was like a scene out of *Goodfellas*. It was real greaseball shit.

Finally we let Frankie out and we had a band vote. Everyone else voted to move our base to Chicago. Frankie refused. We never fired him, and he never actually quit, but he sure didn't come to Chicago. There was this weird, gray area when Frankie was out of the band and joined Helmet. He was gone for about eighteen months. Even though he was playing with another band, he wouldn't quit Anthrax. Because of the legalities involved, he told us we would have to fire him if we wanted him out. If you fire someone, they can make all kinds of legal claims against you, whereas if you quit, you get nothing. We didn't want Frankie out of the band, that wasn't the case at all, so we just let it float, and we got Armored Saint bassist Joey Vera to fill in for us all through 2004. Tim convinced Sanctuary to put out *The Greater of Two Evils*. Although the label had stopped signing new bands, they held on to the catalog and put out select releases, so at least we had something to tour behind.

John was not psyched about doing those shows because he had gotten married and he and his wife were about to have their first baby. She was due while we were supposed to be out on tour. He didn't want to miss the baby's birth. We had to really push him and force him to go out with us. We were playing packed rooms, making some money, and we felt like we needed to keep the momentum going. Finally he relented because he knew it would be best for the band and it was keeping us active. We felt like as long as we were out there working, we didn't have anything to worry about. If we were out there being a band, we had a purpose. But if we stopped and came home, we didn't know what the hell we would do next.

The last tour we did for *The Greater of Two Evils* was opening for Dio in the fall of 2004. The guys that managed Mudvayne, Zen Media—Jonathan Cohen and Izzy Zivkovic—came to see us at the Beacon Theater, and they loved us. Our agent, Mike Monterulo, had played them "Safe Home," and they couldn't believe it wasn't a radio hit. They wanted to be onboard, so we started working with Zen Media, and they suggested we do a reunion tour with Joey Belladonna and Dan Spitz.

"That could get you out of every deal you've gotten into," Jonathan said. He told us he had gone over all of our contracts with a fine-toothed comb, and we still owed Sanctuary a record even though they weren't a label. If we did a reunion tour, we'd be in the clear. "This reunion tour is an asset that you have held back all these years, and with that asset I could clean house and get things moving forward again."

It made sense. We could do a reunion tour DVD and CD and give it to Sanctuary, take the nooses off our necks, and walk away. We didn't *want* to do the tour, but from a business perspective it was a good idea. Charlie and I talked about it, and we asked Jonathan and Izzy if we could do a tour where both John and Joey came out with us and Anthrax would play songs from both of their catalogs. We were dead set against doing a reunion tour that left John hanging out to dry.

Jonathan and Izzy agreed that would work, so we went to John and explained the financial and business position we were in and how this would be a way for us to move forward. At that point, we couldn't make another studio record and just see it disappear up Sanctuary's ass again. That would have killed us.

"I know it seems like a step backward, but people will love seeing you and Joey together," I told John. "And then after it's over we can make another Anthrax record the way we want to."

John understood what I was saying, but he didn't want to do it. He was a veteran singer. He wouldn't share the stage with another vocalist. "I understand if you have to do it," he said. "But I can't be a part of it."

Maybe it was wishful thinking, but when he said, "I understand if you have to do it," we figured he was giving us the thumbs-up to tour without him. Maybe that's not what he meant. We certainly didn't have his blessings, but it's easy to talk yourself into doing something that's advantageous, especially after you've been swimming up a river of shit for years. If we didn't do the reunion tour, we would have broken up. It was that simple. But John clearly realized that if the tour went well, there would be a big demand for us to do another studio album with Joey, and it would be hard for us to say no. That would leave him out in the cold. It was an ethical dilemma, for sure.

I thought about it for days. I felt like the band had a good run and had accomplished everything we ever set out to do. We had traveled the world, released great records, and lived out our rock and roll fantasies and then some. Finally, I got to the crux of the matter and asked myself, "Okay, am I going to do this reunion tour to keep the band together and be able to move forward, or not do it and break up the band? Am I finished with Anthrax?"

Fuck no! I wasn't ready to walk away. I couldn't. I had spent almost twenty-five years working with the band through thick and thin, and I knew someday the ship really was going to turn around and we'd be back making albums and playing sold-out venues. We'd be on a real label that would support us, and we'd make money doing what we loved. Plus, I still had something to say. If that meant losing John Bush, I was ready to make that sacrifice. My life in Anthrax and my career were bigger for me than losing John as our singer, as great a friend as he always had been.

It wasn't an easy decision. It was a horrible, shitty place to be in. Not only would we be leaving John behind; we'd also be touring without Rob since doing a full reunion tour meant getting Dan Spitz back. Rob didn't find out he was out of a job until we were already making plans for the tour. Literally, a couple weeks after the Dio tour, he was out.

Aside from the business reasons for the reunion, there was one other factor that contributed to Charlie and my decision to reunite the old lineup. On December 8, 2004, Dimebag Darrell was shot and killed onstage in Columbus, Ohio, while he was playing with his new band, Damageplan. Pearl and I were on our way to visit her grandmother in Lancaster, Pennsylvania, when I found out. We had flown from LA to New York, rented a car, and were driving from JFK airport to Lancaster, which took a few hours. We got to the hotel at about 11 p.m., exhausted from traveling all day. I went to shower before we went to bed, and when I came out of the bathroom Pearl said, "Your phone has been blowing up nonstop."

I checked it and saw I had missed calls from Charlie, Adrenaline PR owner Maria Ferrero, who worked with us in the early days of Megaforce, and all these other people. They were all calling at 11:30 p.m. on a weeknight, which was weird. So I called Charlie back and he said, "Did you hear?"

"Hear what?"

"Darrell was shot."

"What?"

"Dime, Dime was shot and killed at Alrosa Villa at a Damageplan show."

I couldn't fathom it. Dime being shot onstage seemed even more unreal than Cliff Burton getting killed in a bus accident. How could someone be shot onstage? That's never happened, ever. Even in the sometimes volatile and violent world of rap, no one has ever been shot onstage. There was no precedent for this. It just seemed so fucking beyond my imagination.

I got off the phone and told Pearl, and we sat there in shock. I turned the news on, and within minutes it was on the CNN ticker: "Rocker shot and killed in Columbus, Ohio." We were completely shocked and stunned and didn't know what to do. Here we were in this tiny hotel in Lancaster, Pennsylvania, and we had to visit Pearl's grandma the next day. We weren't going to cancel that, so we spent a couple of hours visiting her, then we got right back in the car, drove back to New York City, and flew to Dallas.

We stayed there for a couple of days for the funeral and memorial. It was completely surreal. Some of my best friends were all in one place at the same time, and we were all in mourning. There was no joy.

I kept expecting the whole thing to be some fucking giant Darrell wind-up because he was the king of that shit. I half thought he would pop up and yell, "Gotcha, motherfuckers!" and we'd all laugh. I still can't fathom what happened to Dime, and every time I think about it I get angry. There was no rhyme or reason to it at all. I already distrusted most of humanity, but that made me really want to close my circle of friends even more. I'm generally an optimist about my life, but to this day I hate people and I don't trust anybody. After something like that happens to one of your best friends, how can you ever feel safe, anywhere, ever?

I think about what happened to Dime every time we play a show. The few times that kids have made it up onto the stage, no matter how friendly the scenario, the first thing I think is, "Dude, you should not be on this fucking stage. You should know better." Everything changed after Dime was killed. The stage became off limits for everyone but musicians. I don't give a fuck how much fun you're having. Stay the fuck off the stage.

Yes, my friend, you have turned me on to a lot of cool shit over
the years, as well. With Kirk on tour a few months after Cliff died,
Netherlands, February 1987.

With my dad and Uncle Mitch circa 1987.

Maiden was the biggest influence on Anthrax, and Steve has always been a true friend to the band. Up the Irons!

Showing my Ramones influence. *Among the Living* tour, 1987. Photo by Gene Ambo

"Antisocial" video shoot, late 1988. I wonder where that stage is now. *Photo by Gene Ambo*

Persistence of Time. Everything was perfect, everything was sick. *Photo by Gene Ambo*

I am a better man for knowing Chuck D.
Bring the Noise tour, late 1991.

Dad and little bro Sean around 1992.

Ladies and gentlemen, John Bush.

Merry X-mas, 1994.

Yep, that's Madonna. You'll have to read my next book to find out what happened.

Tracking *Stomp* in Conshohocken, early 1995.

July 13, 1994

Mr. Scott Ian
c/o Zazula/Crazed Mgmt
210 Bridge Plaza Drive
Manalapan, NJ 07726

Dear Scott,

This note is just to personally let you know how much I've enjoyed working with you over the past years.

I'm sorry to have to say goodbye and I do hope that somewhere down the line we will work together again. Throughout the past years you've made me look great and I want to take this opportunity to thank you for that.

Wishing you continued success and all the best in the world. I leave you in good hands.

Warmly,

Bob Krasnow

"I leave you in good hands." HAHAHAHA HAHAHA. The downward spiral of the nineties begins.

The love of my life when we were just drinking buddies.

HUSTLER

With my future
father-in-law and
his future lead
guitar player.
Los Angeles,
July 2000.

I know the where (Nassau Coliseum), I know the when (2001),
I just don't know the why.

Halloween with Ozzy on *The Rock Show*, 2001.

Jumping Jew! Opening for Judas Priest at the Palace of Auburn Hills, early 2002. *Photo by Pearl Aday*

With Mom and Jason in LA.
Photo by Pearl Aday

Geezer and Tony. I will never be able to wrap my head around the fact that I know these guys.

At Metallica's Hall of Fame induction. First time we heard about the Big 4 and we hung out with this guy. What a night!

My Jimmy Cricket.
Photo by Pearl Aday

Just think, he was (almost) our singer! With Corey at the *Kerrang!* awards.

Stan Lee helped create a world that led me down the path I chose. Like meeting your maker.

We're back! The first Big 4 show in Warsaw, Poland, and the second rebirth of Anthrax. *Photo by Andy Buchanan*

I am a lucky man because . . .
Photo by Angela Boatwright

. . . I married the love
of my life! (Not Elvis.)

**The day before
Revel joined us.**
*Photo by Andy
Buchanan*

With two-week-old Revel, watching Anthrax play with Andreas in Germany live on the Internets!

The photo shoot I left my wife and two-week-old son for. *Courtesy of Guitar World*

Revel's first show was the Big 4! *Photo by Andy Buchanan*

Yankee Stadium: the high point of my career. *Photo by Andy Buchanan*

Charlie was the one who brought up Dime's death before we decided to reunite with Joey and Spitz. We questioned whether Pantera would ever have gotten back together if Dime hadn't been killed, and I absolutely believe at some point they would have. Then we talked about all the newer fans who had never seen us play with Joey and Danny.

"Look, we're all still here," Charlie said. "Not a lot of bands can say that anymore. And we're being offered this chance to relive history. This opportunity may not last forever."

It wasn't the best-case scenario, and maybe we were rationalizing because we certainly weren't dealing out of strength, we were dealing out of desperation. It was either do this and piss some people off really badly or break up. The choice was pretty clear.

Once we made peace with our decision, we tried to make it a triumphant comeback. In the beginning it almost was. Danny and Joey were both excited to play in Anthrax again. And Frankie came back. He wasn't going to miss this! There was a lot of interest. We were selling out shows and playing bigger venues than we had in a long time. The Download Festival in England booked us for the slot right before Black Sabbath and Velvet Revolver. And the press was out of control. Everything was perfect, everything was sick. It all happened too fast. The first time the five of us were back in a room together, we were sitting in this loft in downtown New York with Danny and Joey and Juliya from Fuse, doing an interview for the DVD that was scheduled to be shot at our first show in Sayreville, New Jersey.

There was no preparation, no get-together before the interview, no time to hang out and catch up, no time to talk about the past and what we wanted out of this moving forward, no time to reconnect as friends. Nope. We jumped in headfirst and didn't even look to see if the pool was full. The first month was fun. It was cool to be *that* band again, and we played those old songs better than we did in the eighties. But it didn't take long for all the old shit to start surfacing again, mostly with Danny, who had been out of the business for a long time and had no clue how things ran anymore.

He thought we'd still be able to ship tons of gear all over the world. I told him that's not how it works anymore. The gear companies we endorse can get us gear in every city. I said, "We don't spend a dime to ship stuff so we can put the money in our pockets."

He didn't get that and wanted to use his whole giant rig everywhere we went. That was the least of our hassles. The tour was a fucking nightmare from the first day of the second month, and we were out for eighteen months. We were right back where we were in 1990. Anthrax was a total schism. Frankie, Charlie, and I were on one side and Joey and Danny were on the other.

The biggest blowup was in Milwaukee, where the digital console took a shit thirty seconds before we walked onstage. The monitor man rebooted it, and all the settings that were made at sound check were erased. All the sounds were coming out of the wrong monitors, and for some reason Danny's guitar came up through everything louder than an F-111 taking off. Before that, nobody had Danny's guitar anywhere in their mix. Frankie lost his fucking mind. He kicked all the sound monitor wedges off the stage. His face was red, his teeth were clenched, and I could tell he was going to go postal after the show even though the monitor man had the mix fixed by the fourth song. To add salt to the laceration, Frankie found out that Danny had turned down the bass in the monitor wedges because he couldn't hear his guitar.

For ten minutes straight, Frankie laid into Spitz. The dressing room door was closed, but you could hear it from down the hall. "Who the fuck are you?!? Who do you think you are? You're not even fucking human!!!" It was brutal, personal, and nonstop. Frankie was ranting and kicking tables over, and Danny just stood there unable to get a word in. The rest of us hid and laughed. Still want to be in a band?

Chapter 30

MY KINGDOM
FOR A SINGER

The reunion tour was pretty depressing. It helped us financially and cleared up our business problems. We delivered *Alive 2: The DVD*, the greatest hits CD, and DVD *Anthrology: No Hit Wonders 1985–1991* to Sanctuary. They put them out but failed to properly promote them. Go figure. At least we were out of our contract. Everyone assumed we'd do a record with the *Among the Living* lineup when we got back home, but there was no way we could move forward as *that* band because we were all at each other's throats. It was 2006, and I was thinking that, unless we could somehow miraculously get John Bush to come back, this really was the end of Anthrax.

I was angry because this was the reunion tour everyone had been waiting for and everyone loved it but us. I had wanted so much for it to work and for us to part as great friends again. We parted ways alright, but we were more like feuding college roommates.

I can't put all the blame on Joey and Danny. It would be very easy to point the finger and say they were difficult and wanted everything their way, so it didn't work out. I could say that we were the ones fighting to keep Anthrax alive all those years, and those guys weren't. So when they came back they should have listened to us. The truth is, you could very easily argue their side: "Look what you did to Anthrax over all those years while we were sitting at home. Maybe if we weren't pushed out of the band, Anthrax would never have been in this position in the first place. Maybe you should listen to *our* ideas."

I couldn't see that in 2006, but I can see it now, having had some time to reflect on the situation. I talked a lot of shit in the press because I was so frustrated and I could only see one side of the picture. I said we couldn't move forward because Joey didn't want to and kept putting up obstacles. That was true to some extent. We told Joey and Danny we wanted to make a record, and Joey kept coming back with more and more demands, mostly about firing managers and cleaning house. It turned out he was right about all of that, as we ended up having issues with all the people he had a problem with. A lot of journalists reported that Joey didn't come back right away because he wanted too much money. That wasn't true. He wanted his share of the cut, and we had always had a five-way split. He never asked for more than that.

Ultimately, the decision not to work on a new album with Joey came from us not being on the same page. We were set in our ways and weren't willing to budge. I certainly was curious about what a new Anthrax record would sound like with Joey, but my curiosity was outweighed by my ego and my inability to give up any kind of control. Funny how things happen for a reason. In reality, that would've been the wrong time for that record to happen. Maybe somehow we all sensed that?

Still, we were hamstrung without a singer. In our sweetest pipe dreams, John Bush would have come back and made a new album with us, now that we had new managers and had cleared the decks of some bad business deals. We hoped he would realize we did what we needed to do for the sake of the band, and now we could move on like we were simply following up *We've Come for You All*. But we knew that wasn't going to happen. John was hurt that we did the reunion tour with Joey, and he's a very prideful guy. The last thing he was going to do was forgive us for dicking him over and jump right back in.

In addition to the emotional chasm, he was in a different place in his life. He had young children and didn't want to be on tour all the time. He wasn't ready to drop everything this time just because we asked him to. He didn't want to do what was best for the band; his priority was his family. Once it was clear we weren't doing a record with Joey and Danny or John, the band dissolved down to two men standing. At the end of 2006, Charlie and I got together in the room at his house in

Chicago and started writing new material. We were pissed about what had happened, so we naturally wrote some really fast, aggressive stuff with crushing double-bass beats and really crunchy stop-start riffs. It felt good and we knew we were on to something. When we had a batch of solid songs, we tried working with a vocalist who had been recommended to us, but that didn't work out. For more information, feel free to check out Wikipedia, as accurate or inaccurate as it may be.

During that time, we called Frankie and said, "Hey man, shit's happening. We want you in on this." The first thing he did was insist on being a part of the writing process. I told him we had already written five songs we were really happy with, but the rest of it, who knows? Frankie jumped back in and helped rework the stuff we had already written. Frankie was back, but again there was an uncomfortable amount of fighting and arguing, mostly over melody ideas for the vocals. That's actually where Frankie has always shined, writing-wise. He's great at coming up with melodies. But a lot of times Charlie would come up with something different, and it would be a better fit for the song. Frankie would say, "Well, who are you to say it's a better fit? Of course you like yours more, you wrote it. But mine is better." I would try to use both of their ideas, plugging in my lyrics to their melodies, sometimes adding my melody ideas as well, and when that worked we would get the best of all worlds and the songs would benefit. When it didn't work and one person's idea was clearly better, well, then we'd get back to that fucking age-old argument of who knows what Anthrax really is. When that happens, Charlie and I always say, "Look, we know what's right." That wouldn't end the fight—far from it—but we would just move forward, and usually the best ideas would be so obvious they'd make themselves undeniable.

We tried to move forward as a band just like we had done after we fired Neil Turbin and were working on writing *Spreading the Disease* without a singer. But the idea of not being able to make it work out with John or even Joey hung over our heads. We didn't *want* to find someone else. We wanted Anthrax, and Anthrax have only ever had two singers that mattered.

Around the time we were trying to figure out how to keep the band going, I started copromoting an acoustic rock lounge night at this

New York club, Retox. I was working with my friend Mike Diamond, who was a big club promoter. We decided to have a showcase one night a week. Whenever anyone I knew would be in New York, I would fly in and we'd do acoustic sets. I booked a diverse variety of artists, including Cypress Hill, Sebastian Bach, Whitfield Crane, Bo Bice from *American Idol,* and Corey Taylor from Slipknot and Stone Sour.

The night Corey came in, we had dinner before we went to the club. It was me, Corey, Frankie, and Pearl just hanging out. Corey asked us what we were going to do about our singer situation, and we told him we didn't know, but we had a bunch of new songs that were really great.

"I'll do it," he said.

We laughed. We figured he was joking. He was already in two successful bands, and it didn't seem realistic for him to sing for Anthrax as well.

"I'm serious!" he said, voice tinged with excitement. "It would be a fucking honor to sing with you guys, and you already know I've been into you since I was a kid. I would be thrilled to write songs with you and be a part of your history."

We talked seriously about how we could make it work. We agreed to send him what we had already written, and he would start writing vocals after his current tour with Stone Sour was over. He had a large window of time before he had to start working with Slipknot again. He figured he could take at least a year to make the record with us and tour. It seemed like an amazing solution to a serious problem. Frankie was into the idea right away and I was sold.

That night at the club was incredible. We played a bunch of cover songs with Corey and had a blast. I woke up the next day remembering the conversation about Corey singing for us, and I just chalked it up to booze and fun; I really didn't take it seriously. Stone Sour played Roseland Ballroom the next night, and we were backstage. I walked into the dressing room, and Corey's manager, Cory Brennan, said, "Hey man, congratulations on your new singer."

"What? Huh? Uh, he told you about that?" I said.

"Yeah, he told me immediately," Brennan said. "I already called the rest of Slipknot and Roadrunner Records, and it's a go. It's on. He has the approval."

I gave Corey a big hug. I told Frankie and Charlie and they were stoked. We sent Corey preliminary arrangements for six songs. He loved them and told us he had ideas for vocals. We put together a schedule based on when his tour was going to end. Corey was going to put his parts together for a couple weeks after the tour ended and then drive to Chicago to spend three weeks at Charlie's, and we would work out the songs. I thought it would be a good idea to keep our plans to ourselves for a little while, but Corey went online and spilled the beans. He didn't even call me and tell me he was going public with the news, which was fine. He was just that excited. We started telling interviewers it was happening, and everyone was congratulating us. It seemed like a new chapter was about to begin and it was gonna be a good one.

I flew to Chicago to start working with Taylor Thrax July 9, 2007, after spending a few days in London to see Metallica at Wembley Stadium. To say I was on an adrenaline high would be an understatement. I was so inspired to get back in the room and write the greatest Anthrax record of our career. When I landed at O'Hare airport, I turned my phone on and it was filled with messages. I saw our agent (and my good friend), Mike Monterulo, had called, so I called him back from inside the terminal, and he said, "Did you talk to anyone?"

"No, I just got off the plane."

"Corey's not coming," he said. The words didn't exactly sink in.

"Well, I'm already in Chicago. So, I'll just stick around here, and if he can't come for a few days, that's fine. I'm not flying home and then coming back again."

"No, he's not coming, period. He can't do it."

Corey's label, Roadrunner, had put the kibosh on the whole thing at the eleventh hour. They had looked at their release schedule for the upcoming year, and some major project they thought they were going to have—I think it was a Nickelback record—wasn't going to come in when they expected it. And now they weren't going to get a Slipknot album, either. The label heads looked at their bottom line and decided they couldn't allow Corey to take a year off from Slipknot. The band members had already taken advances for the record, and the label threatened to take back that money if he worked with Anthrax. Corey asked them why they waited until the day before he was leaving for

Chicago to work with us to drop this bomb on him, and their answer was, "We didn't think you were actually going to do it." Corey let them have it, but he was between a rock and a hard place, and the music business is, to quote Hunter S. Thompson, "a cruel and shallow money trench, a long plastic hallway where thieves and pimps run free, and good men die like dogs. There's also a negative side." Had Corey not caved, it would have financially affected all nine members of the band, and he couldn't and wouldn't make that call. He was pissed but he had no choice. It sucked for us, and it sucked for Corey as well because not only was he looking forward to working with us, he had already written songs and was 100 percent ready to go.

Standing there in O'Hare, I felt like I had been punched in the stomach. It was like a scene in a movie where a character is moving in real time and everything else is zipping by. I felt nauseated, disoriented, devastated. For a second it seemed like someone had sucked all of the air out of me, and nothing we did could possibly go right again.

I stumbled over to the American Airlines desk and said, "I need a flight to LA, the first one out."

The woman at the counter looked at my itinerary in the computer and said, "You're not supposed to fly back to LA for three weeks."

"I know, but I need to get home immediately." Clearly, she heard the pain in my voice and made it happen. I was empty, over, finished, gone, done. I got on the plane, downed a couple of Maker's Marks, and passed out.

One day I'll get to hear what Corey wrote for us. He told me he has all the lyrics in a book at home. I told him recently that we can get together and play the songs, a private concert for just the two of us. As crazy as all of that was, in the end it's better that it didn't happen. Of course in the moment I couldn't see or know that, but three years later when Joey rejoined, it all made sense. After the Corey Taylor fiasco, I had to get away from Anthrax for a little while. I wasn't ready to let it go, but I definitely needed a break. Pearl was starting to launch her solo career after having performed as a backup singer with her dad for a number of years. She put together a group with the guys from Mother Superior, Jim Wilson and Markus Blake—who both played in the Rollins Band from 1999 to 2003—and started writing songs. I was the rhythm guitarist because I had an inside connection—and because Anthrax were in a state of flux. I worked with Pearl from 2007 all the way through 2010. She recorded an EP, which she sold at shows, and she did a whole bunch of tours, two opening for her dad in the States and two more with him in Europe. I was multitasking the whole time, driving the van, selling merch, acting as the tour manager, being the travel agent. I wore many hats, which was a blast because I was getting to be out on the road with my wife and taking a backseat to her and watching her shine. I got to play rhythm guitar and live out my Malcolm Young fantasies, just being this guy who hangs out in the back with the rhythm section.

Obviously, we weren't playing metal, and it was far removed from anything I've done in Anthrax, but it was right in my wheelhouse because I grew up on seventies music. That's how I learned to play guitar. So getting to play songs like "Rock Child," "Love Pyre," "Nobody," and the Tina Turner cover "Nutbush City Limits" was great. It was hugely liberating to be able to get onstage and just play and hold a big fucking "A" chord sometimes. I didn't have to do all the right hand palm-muting and super-fast down-picking, which I call "fascist guitar playing." In the context of Anthrax, that's my style. It's extremely tight, there's no room for improvisation. It is what it is, and there's no fucking around—the fucking train is running on time. Whereas with Pearl I was able to sit back, do these big rock chords, and have a blast.

Before Pearl released her debut album *Little Immaculate White Fox,* I got her a tour opening for Velvet Revolver on their last run of dates in the UK. I e-mailed Slash and said, "Hey man, Pearl's making this great fucking rock record. I can't think of a better band for her to open for than you guys."

He asked me to send him the record, and two days after he got it, he e-mailed me back saying, "Tell your agent to expect a call." Sure enough, two days after that, their agent called our agent and offered Pearl the UK run of the Velvet Revolver tour. It was so cool of Slash to make that happen. He even got us enough money to make it viable, and we earned bonus cash by selling merch and copies of the EP. The shows were amazing. Pearl played to a sold-out Brixton Academy in front of 5,500 people. The audience didn't know who she was. They were there to see Velvet Revolver. Maybe some people saw me and said, "Hey, I recognize that guy," but the crowds didn't know her music. And by the second song she fucking owned it.

During the set she would invite the crowd to come to the merch stand and say hi after the show. And every night there would be as many as two hundred kids there, and they would all buy the EP. These were seventeen- and eighteen-year-olds saying, "I've never heard of you, but you were fucking awesome!"

She proved that she belonged where she was. It wasn't like she had some sense of entitlement, "Oh, I'm someone's daughter and I'm gonna be a singer, too!" She worked her ass off, and it was really inspiring to get to see her do that every night—even in front of her dad's crowd, which in a sense is a built-in audience. But even then she had to win them over. They might have known who she was, but they were there to see Meat Loaf and weren't going to go crazy just because his daughter's band was opening. The audience would usually be quiet and polite for two or three songs, and then she would just get them fucking revved up, so by the time her forty-five minutes were over, people were on their feet clapping. She's a great, great front woman.

We worked on *Little Immaculate White Fox* after she got off tour, and it came out in January 2010. Ted Nugent guested on the song "Check Out Charlie." He e-mailed over his tracks for that, but Alice in Chains guitarist and vocalist Jerry Cantrell came into the studio to record the solo for "Anything," which was awesome. I've always loved Alice in Chains ever since we played with them on the Clash of the Titans tour. They got spat at and pelted with coins and bottles of piss, and they totally stood their ground. Jerry is an extremely talented musician and an amazing songwriter. We didn't have to give him any direction. He just sat down, listened to the song, and came up with these guitar lines that were very David Gilmour-esque, which is exactly what we were looking for.

Almost eleven months after Pearl's album came out, the side project I put together with Fall Out Boy guitarist Joe Trohman, the Damned Things, released its record, *Ironiclast*, which was criminally overlooked and which I'm still extremely proud of.

I met Joe in 2008 through a mutual friend, David Karon, who worked with both of us at Washburn Guitars. David and I were good friends and hung out all the time. He was sure that Joe and I would get along even though we played very different music, so he introduced us and we hit it off. I'm old enough to be his dad, but he wasn't just some douchey kid from a band. Joe is a serious musician, great guitar player, super smart, and funny, and we were into a lot of the same shit. We became fast friends.

Whenever I was in Chicago or Joe was in LA, we'd get together and hang. I even went to see Fall Out Boy a couple of times just to check out what he was doing. One night he was in LA for the day, and he asked me if I'd be into jamming. Fall Out Boy were leaving to go to Japan the next day, and were spending the night at the Renaissance Hotel in Hollywood. He asked me to come over if I wasn't doing anything and to bring a guitar so we could jam. I figured he'd want to do some Thin Lizzy covers because we'd talk about them all the time—but he told me he had some riffs he had written that he wanted to show me.

I brought an acoustic, and after a couple of beers he played me the riffs he had talked about; they were really good and doomy in a way vaguely like Down or Kyuss.

"Are those for Fall Out Boy?" I asked.

"No, they're way too heavy for Fall Out Boy. Why don't we use them and write some songs together?"

I thought that was a cool idea, since Anthrax were kind of in limbo. I told Joe I'd learn the riffs and start coming up with new ideas while he was in Japan. I was in Chicago soon after Joe returned, and we started getting together to work on songs. We had both come up with some ideas, and before we knew it we had three or four song skeletons. They were dark and moody like the first riffs he showed me, and two of them, "Ironiclast" and "Grave Robber," eventually made it onto the Damned Things album, but they had different names at the time. Those songs are pretty representative of what we were doing at the beginning, and they convinced me that we could actually make a record together.

Joe called Fall Out Boy drummer Andy Hurley, who's a total metalhead. Before he joined Fall Out Boy, Andy only played thrash metal and hardcore, and he's a great drummer. We rehearsed in this crappy basement at Johnny K's studio building in Chicago; he let us use the place for cheap. We had a bunch of gear down there, and we went down to rehearse and write. Our buddy from Washburn, David, was playing bass, and we were rehearsing these songs.

We had five solid ideas together, but we didn't have a singer. It was a common dilemma for me. One night we were driving around Chicago listening to Every Time I Die, and Joe and I both agreed, "If we could get Keith Buckley to sing for us, that would rule."

"I know him," Joe said. "Let me text him right now."

Joe told him he was our first choice for a singer for our new band and asked him if he had time and was interested. Keith was flattered that we thought of him and asked us to send him some songs right away. We found out after the fact that Keith really didn't think it was ever going to happen so he may as well just say yes. At the time we thought we would call the band Methuselah; that didn't stick. Keith listened to our demos and wrote back to tell us that he loved the songs, he was in, and he'd start writing immediately.

Not long after, we were all in New York at a bar across the street from Irving Plaza with Pearl, Joe's girlfriend, Marie, and Rob Caggiano, who was back in Anthrax. I felt like it would be great to have Rob in the new band. It made sense for us to have three guitarists because the music we were writing had all these Thin Lizzy-esque guitar parts.

"We need Rob in this band," I said to Joe when Caggiano stepped out to go to the bathroom. "Imagine the harmony possibilities. We'd be able to do everything live, and you guys get along great. His playing, writing, and production skills would be a real asset."

Joe agreed, so when Rob got back I asked him if he wanted to be in Methuselah. Back then, he jokingly referred to it as Mejewselah since Joe and I were Jewish. Rob was surprised I asked him, but he was also stoked. He liked the songs we were writing and wanted to be a part of it. When the band started to get serious and the songs were really coming together, we realized that David, the one who had introduced us, wasn't the right bass player and there was no way he was going to be able to track the record and tour with us. He just couldn't keep up. It really sucked.

The band started out as a goofy project between a bunch of friends, and all of a sudden it became serious and one of the founders no longer cut it. Joe told him, and David was understandably upset. I didn't talk to him for a couple of years. I've reconnected with him since, but our relationship was definitely strained for a while.

Mejewselah was rechristened The Damned Things by Keith, taking the name from a lyric from the song "Black Betty." We were having fun and the songs seemed to be writing themselves. We'd listen to something like "We've Got a Situation," and Rob would say, "Hmm, it doesn't have a chorus." So I'd pick up a guitar and say, "What about this," and play a riff off the top of my head, and it would be perfect. Joe had really stepped it up as well, writing the bulk of the music and coming up with killer riffs for songs like "Handbook for the Recently Deceased" and "A Great Reckoning." Even though The Damned Things' songs gelled easily, the record took longer to make than anyone expected, mainly because Joe and Rob were meticulous about everything. We experimented with tons of gear and tones and sounds on *Ironiclast* because they wanted to be sure all of the ideas worked as well as possible.

Fall Out Boy's label, Island Def Jam, had the right of first refusal on the album, and they wanted it. Then they completely dropped the ball, as we knew they would. But we had no choice, which fucking sucked. We thought we had a fighting chance because Bob McLynn from Crush Management, who manages Fall Out Boy, took on The Damned Things as well, and he knew all these people at Island Def Jam. We figured he'd motivate them to love the record and promote it properly. But once again, as it is with record companies, the guy who was running the label for a while, L. A. Reid, left and someone else was hired. Or maybe it was vice versa. I can't keep track of all these executive shifts. I just know all kinds of shit was happening on a corporate level, and budgets were frozen. The word of the day became no. No, we can't do that; no, we can't do this. Maybe one out of fifty things they said they'd do actually came to fruition.

Fans of Fall Out Boy, Anthrax, and Every Time I Die who had read about the project were interested at first, but a lot of people didn't even know there was a record out. We figured we had a platinum album with four strong radio hits. They sure sounded like radio hits to me. But when *Ironiclast* came out in 2010, Island did nothing. If we had someone on the team who was really behind it, we could have sold a million copies based on the pedigree and the quality of the music we wrote. Fuck, we gave them such a no-brainer, and they found a way to screw it up. At the worst, I figured we'd sell at least 100,000 records, and we didn't sell half that.

That being the case, touring for The Damned Things was great. We got to experience the excitement of being a new band starting out. The fact that we were all already friends made it that much better, because under normal circumstances, with our bands' schedules, I would never get to hang out with Keith that much. Now, we got to travel the world together and really become friends. We did a Jägermeister tour, a headline run in the US, festivals in Europe, a US tour with Volbeat, the Soundwave Festival in Australia, and the reaction was really good. If we had the time after all the touring to write more songs and go back into the studio to record another record, I think we could have broken the band. But we only had a certain window before everyone had to go back to their day jobs.

We'd all still like to do a follow-up to *Ironiclast* one day, but who knows when that could happen because you're dealing with guys in four active bands. Fall Out Boy are doing really well right now, and Anthrax are coming off our biggest album since *Sound of White Noise*. Even if we could write a new The Damned Things record in the next year or so, when would we be able to tour it? It's not like we could ever spend a year traveling around the world. It would have to be three weeks here, four weeks there, every once in a while. That's possible, but who knows? The one thing I do know is it wouldn't be on Island.

Chapter 31

BELLADONNA AND THE BIG 4

For a while, I was double-shifting between The Damned Things and Anthrax. In 2009, when Anthrax were still in the writing phase for *Worship Music*, we were invited to do a bunch of Sonisphere shows in Europe. We couldn't believe we were going to lose our opportunity. We thought about who we might be able to get to sing with us, and we figured why not at least ask John Bush to fly out to England with us and do this one show August 1 in Knebworth. I had been in touch with John the whole time he was out of the band. I'd see him here and there, so it wasn't like we had this ugly rift. We figured the worst he could do was say no. Charlie and I got on the phone with him and asked him if he would play Sonisphere with us.

"I can't leave today to go . . ."

"No, no," I interrupted. "We're blowing off a couple weeks of shows. We're hoping to just go over and play Knebworth; it's such a historic place. We just wanted to put it out there and see if you might be interested."

John paused, which I took as a good sign. He asked if he could have the weekend to think about it. We told him that was fine. Then he called us back on Monday and told us he would do it. The hope, of course, was he'd have such a good time and realize how much he missed being in the band that he'd rejoin. I wasn't expecting it, but that would have been ideal. We flew to England and rehearsed the day before the show at a studio in London. It was like no time had passed. It felt awesome and the show was incredible.

There was so much emotion in the air when we hit the stage. Pearl was standing on the side crying. I was so overcome after the show that I was dizzy and had to sit down in the dressing room. I almost passed out, and I hadn't even smoked any weed. Everyone in the band was euphoric, and we were hoping John felt the same way. Maybe we were kidding ourselves, but we honestly felt like that experience might be enough to show him that he needed to be back in Anthrax.

I tried exerting my magical powers of persuasion. "Don't you want to be doing this again?" I asked, trying to be gentle, not pushy. "Your kids are a little older now. We can tour less, and you can bring the family on the road when you want to."

He wasn't into it. He loved playing the show, but he wasn't ready to be back in the band. Early the next year we asked him if he would play the Soundwave Festival shows in Australia with us, and to our surprise he said he would. That's when we started talking more seriously to him about doing a record. *Worship Music* was almost finished. The preliminary guide vocals were done, so we told John we were going to send him the music.

"I don't really know about making an album," he responded. "Doing shows once in a while is one thing, but recording an album is a huge commitment. I'm not there. I'm not ready to do that."

We sent him MP3s of stuff we had done anyway, and I said, "Just give it a listen and let us know what you think."

Soon after, he came back to me and said, "This is really good. But what if we can't top *We've Come for You All*?"

"I'm telling you, with the songs we have, we're going to top *We've Come for You All*."

I thought John was actually going to come back. My guarded optimism was taking off its jacket. "Yeah, I really like it. Do you want to start writing to it?"

"Well, I have some stuff I'm really happy with lyrically and melodically, but I'll scrap the whole thing if you want to start from scratch."

"No, if you like your ideas, I'll listen to them."

It seemed like everything was slowly moving forward. It was all about baby steps. We were reeling him in. Eventually he wouldn't be able to help himself. He's John fucking Bush. We felt like it was in his blood to do this. We played five huge festival shows in Australia, and they were amazing. John sang with the enthusiasm and aggression of a gifted kid who had just joined his first band, and we were at the top of our game. When we flew back home, however, there was a lot of tension and irritability. It was time to shit or get off the pot.

Finally, John said he would do it. He asked us to send him all the music we had, and he was ready to formulate a plan with us to make it happen contractually. Our manager was Mark Adelman from CAM, part of Irving Azoff's empire. He was the guy who got Dave Ellefson back into Megadeth. He was insanely confident, and we trusted that he'd be able to seal the deal with John. We set a meeting at Adelman's office in LA. It was me, John, Charlie, and Frankie. Everyone was under the impression that we were going to walk out of the meeting with John Bush back in Anthrax. Then we would finish *Worship Music* and take Anthrax back to the top of the metal heap. We all sat down and in no time we were shooting the shit and busting one another's balls like we've always done. Mark started talking about an eighteen-month plan during which the record would come out and we would play all these headline tours in big places. We were all listening intently when John spoke up.

"I'm sorry to interrupt, but I can't do this."

The room went dead silent. I had spoken to John on the phone the night before, and he was still in. Sixteen hours later and the world was upside down again.

"I can't do this," he repeated.

"We all came to this meeting to make plans," I said. "You said you were back in. You said you *wanted* to do this."

"I know," he said. "But I spent last night really, really thinking about it, and the reality of it hit me. I can't be the guy you want me to be. If it was just going out and playing shows every couple of months, big festivals, etc., etc., then fine. I'd love to play shit like that every once in a while. But you guys need a singer who's going to go out and work."

He knew we needed to play 150 shows or more to support our next record, and he couldn't do that. He didn't want to be away from his children for that long. He said his heart wouldn't be in the right place, and we needed someone who was 100 percent there and wanted to be on the road.

"I'm just not that guy anymore," he added. "I wouldn't be happy. I have no animosity about anything that happened in the past. I love you guys. The shows we just did were fucking awesome, but I can't do this unless you tell me we're only going to do thirty shows next year. And if you tell me that, I'll know you're lying."

We were stupefied, speechless. We looked around the room at John, at each other, at the ground. We were so close . . .

After way too long, Mark asked if anyone had any ideas. I said I wasn't going to audition a new singer we didn't know. And that was when Charlie suggested bringing back Joey. Frankie, Mark, and even Bush agreed that made the most sense and it was a great idea. It was weird to have John's blessings, since bringing Joey back in the band for the reunion tour was the wedge that drove Bush out and caused such bad blood.

"Remember what happened at the end of the reunion tour? How do we know Joey would even want to come back? We didn't exactly make things easy for him. How is this possibly going to work?"

From that point, the discussion was on the table, and it was the upcoming Big 4 tour that made the idea of Joey coming back make all the sense in the world. The chance to be part of a celebration of the birth and longevity of thrash metal with some of our best friends and the singer who was with us when it was all happening was definitely appealing. I decided that if Joey wanted to try again I was all in.

I was on tour with Pearl, just after the release of *Little Immaculate White Fox,* and we were playing New York at the Studio at Webster Hall. Frankie was in town, and Charlie happened to be in New York as well, so we asked Joey if he would come down from upstate and meet with us. Charlie called him and told him about the Big 4 shows we had coming up. He told Joey that he really wanted him to play the concerts with us since he was a big part of the evolution of thrash as well. Joey agreed to meet us in the city, and they all came to the Pearl show.

It was good to see Joey, and we all went out for coffee the next day. It was probably the shortest business meeting ever. I said, "We want you back, we want to be a band again," and Charlie added, "Is everyone on the same page? Do we all want to do this and move forward as a band? Can we finish *Worship Music* together, whatever it takes?"

Everyone, including Joey, gave an enthusiastic yes.

"All I ever wanted to do was be in the band," Joey said. "Let's do it again."

It was as simple as that. I can pinpoint April 29, 2010, as the day everything turned back around for Anthrax. The ship was back on its proper course. Or, to use a reference from Greek mythology, instead of us pushing this giant boulder up a hill like Sisyphus, it started to roll downhill for the first time in a long time.

The Big 4 shows played a major role in reintegrating Joey into Anthrax. We were celebrating the legacy of thrash with Metallica, the band that first brought it to the masses. It was only natural that we had Joey playing those concerts, since he was the singer for Anthrax when we were indisputably one of the four bands that created thrash metal. We had done our share of shows over the years with Slayer and Megadeth, but there was always this idea that it would be awesome to get the Big 4 together for a tour. We all waited for Metallica to come up with the same idea, but they never even came close. There were never any talks between them and the other bands before it happened. The first time I got an inkling that the Big 4 tour might actually happen was when Charlie and I got invited to Metallica's Hall of Fame induction in Cleveland on April 5, 2009. We were at the bar at the aftershow party, and Lars came up to the two of us. We congratulated him and hung out for a little while shooting the shit, and then, kind of in passing but out of the blue, he said, "What would you guys think about doing Big 4 shows?"

"Huh? What do you mean?" I said. I didn't even register what he was talking about because it was so far from what we were discussing and the possibility had never been mentioned before. He repeated, "What'dya think about doing Big 4 shows?"

Again it was like, "What? Big what?"

"You know, Big 4 shows—us, you guys, Slayer, and Megadeth."

When we understood what he was saying, Charlie and I both said, "Yeah, of course! That would be fucking awesome! But that's never gonna happen. When are we gonna do that? That's what you guys wanna do?"

Lars didn't answer that question. He just shrugged, smiled, and left the idea hanging in the air.

Cut to late 2009, and we started to hear rumors. There were rumblings in the music community, and then we finally got an official call from Metallica's management asking us what our availability was for these certain dates in the summer of 2010. They were putting together the Big 4 shows and wanted to make sure everyone was going to be around. That's when it actually became a reality. Before that it was all speculation. The whole period leading up to those shows was super exciting, knowing that this was going to happen for the first time ever. The concerts went on sale really early. The public knew they were happening, and it blew their minds. All these shows were far away— Poland, the Czech Republic, Bulgaria, Romania. People were chomping at the bit, waiting for Metallica to book some Big 4 shows in the States and the rest of Europe. The excitement was electric. Holy crap! The Big 4's coming. Metallica hired a team to film the fourth show, in Sofia, Bulgaria, and simulcast it in theaters across the world. And then they released it on DVD. There was definitely a lot of planning that went into these concerts.

The first show was in Warsaw, Poland, and Metallica invited all the bands to a party the night before at an Italian restaurant. Then we got word that wives, girlfriends, and tour managers had to wait until three hours into the party to attend. We all thought, "Huh?" We all know each other's wives, so it seemed weird they would make the party this exclusive event. But they really just wanted the guys in the bands to be able to hang out, catch up, and feel the vibe of what was about to happen without any distractions.

That night we all showed up at this restaurant—seventeen dudes in the four bands—and I gotta hand it to Metallica. Everything they do is planned with such military precision. The way their business is run and operated takes every contingency into account before making any decision. Looking back, this was the right thing to do. The vibe was so cool and special. All of the band dudes who had been there since 1981 were starting to hang out with each other again, and it was amazing to look around the room and see the conversations that were going on. Dave Mustaine and Kirk Hammett were hanging out and talking. I had certainly never seen that before. I knew Metallica when Dave was in the band, and then I was there when Dave was out of Metallica and Kirk came in, but I never saw the two of them in the same room together, let alone hugging, smiling, and talking. There were no distractions and it was a great reintroduction for a lot of people. Then later on, when everyone's wives, girlfriends, and friends came in, it turned into a big party.

It was a great idea for Metallica to put the dinner together the way they did because it broke the ice between all of us. Going into the show the next day, everyone was comfortable. There were no awkward moments, we were all happy to be there. That set the tone for the whole tour, and at that point we all knew the Big 4 shows were going to be incredible because we all really wanted to be there.

Joey Belladonna was as excited as the rest of us to play those shows. He was on fire, performing better than ever, singing with more range, clarity, and confidence than I'd heard from him in a long time. Performing with Joey in the summer of 2010 and on the fall 2010 Jäger tour with Slayer and Megadeth helped solidify our relationship again because we did so well at those concerts and all the bands were having a blast. It became clear, once again, that Joey was our guy, which gave those tours this triumphant spirit and opened the door for the future in a way we hadn't experienced in a long time.

I love all the guys in Metallica and Slayer, and I have a good relationship with everyone in Megadeth as well, so we've always had fun when we went out with those guys. Over the years, a lot of people have had friction with Megadeth front man Dave Mustaine, but he has always been cool to me. I knew him way back when he was in Metallica when they first arrived in New York from San Francisco. He came to the first Country Club show Anthrax played with Raven in Los Angeles. He had only been out of Metallica a little while at that point, and he already had demos for what became Megadeth's first album, *Killing Is My Business . . . and Business Is Good.*

After the show we sat in some girl's car, and he played me "The Skull Beneath the Skin," the title track, and "Last Rites / Loved to

Death." I said, "Dude, this is amazing!" And he joked, "Right, right, I fucking rule! Those guys kicked me out of the band, I'll show them!"

Like I said, Dave has always been a friend, even going above and beyond, like when we played on the Maximum Rock tour with Megadeth and Mötley, and he always made sure our backdrop got hung up when he went to check the stage as well as taking our gear on their truck back to New Jersey for us after we left that tour. The only time there was any weirdness between Dave and I was a few years ago, and I wasn't around when it happened. Pearl and I were on vacation, driving around with our friend Joe Bastianich in Friuli, in the beautiful northeastern part of Italy. We were heading to a restaurant in the countryside when my phone rang. Our manager said, "Have you seen [the metal news website] Brave Words?"

"No, I'm in the middle of nowhere. I'm lucky I even have a phone signal."

"It's all over the place," he continued. Mustaine is telling these stories about how you told him in 1986 before Cliff died that Metallica were going fire Lars when they got home."

I don't know if I ever told Dave that. I don't know why I would, but maybe I did at some point. The story wasn't a secret. People knew it and Lars knew it. My manager went on, "Well, Dave's promoting something, and in every interview he does he seems to be mentioning that you told him this story."

That night when we got back to the house where we were staying, I called Dave and said, "Hey man, what's going on?" I told him what my manager told me and asked why he was bringing that up in interviews.

"Yeah, yeah, I figured I'd get your name out there and get you in the press to help you promote your book."

"Dave, I don't have a book," I told him. I have no idea why he thought I did.

"Huh? You don't have a book?"

"No, Dave. No book, nothing. No record coming out. There's nothing happening right at this moment. Next time you want to do something to promote me, run it by me first, please." (Hey, I have a book now . . .)

I quickly got hold of Lars. I texted him and said I didn't know why Dave was telling twenty-year-old stories. He didn't really seem to care. It was just weird. But that's the only time I've had anything approaching a bad experience with Dave, and compared to a lot of people he's come in contact with over the decades, that's pretty good.

In September and October 2010 on the tour with Slayer and Megadeth, we went back and started carefully listening to the songs for *Worship Music*. We needed to figure out what was good and what had to be changed, what we still loved and what could go in the scrap heap. We sat in the dressing room every day and listened to the songs and went over them with a fine-toothed comb. We focused on the arrangements and made sure that every part of each song was the best it could be. Understanding Joey's strengths as a singer—which are considerable—really helped lift the music from good to great. By the end of the year, we had all the arrangements for the record ready to go. The band was working together in a way we never had before, and it was clear that this time Anthrax really were back as powerful as ever!

Some of the tracks for *Worship Music,* such as "Fight 'Em 'til You Can't," came together really easily. It was one of the first songs Charlie and I wrote in late 2006. Charlie had the main riffs, I had the idea for the middle bridge part, and the arrangement came together immediately. I wrote the words in the backroom of the old house in Beverlywood where Pearl and I lived. The idea of using a zombie holocaust as a metaphor for the band never dying instantly came to me. But the title came from a line in the new *Battlestar Galactica* TV series. I always wanted to write a song with that title, but as nerdy as I am, I couldn't figure out a way to actually write a song about the story of two of the show's characters, Chief Galen Tyrol (Aaron Douglas) and Kara "Starbuck" Thrace (Katee Sackhoff). They were fighting the Cylons until they couldn't. That was simple enough. But the title was more about us as a band—Charlie, Frankie, and I—never stopping, never giving in, and never letting anything kill us. Literally, we will fight until we can't. There were also lines in that song inspired by the Steve Niles comic *30 Days of Night.* "The darkest devil nightmare blacker than their evil souls, you gotta fight 'em / God save us prayers fall on deaf ears" comes from a part in the comic where someone's praying to God, and the vampires are like, "There is no God!" On the surface, it's the nerdiest song I've ever written, which, as a sci-fi and comic book freak, I'm extremely proud of.

Some songs were harder to nail than others—much harder. "In the End" took forever to get right. It went through so many different revisions, and it still wasn't quite there even when we worked it through the demo stage and I started the lyrics. I knew I wanted to write a song about Dimebag Darrell, not necessarily paying tribute but about the loss of our friend and how much we miss him. Only, I felt I wasn't doing him justice. I'd read back ideas I came up with, and they sounded so cheesy. I'd throw them away, write something else, and it seemed just as bad. As hard as it was to come up with the lyrics, the melody was maybe even harder. We all had ideas—me, Frankie, Charlie, and Rob—and we were trying to make it cohesive, but nothing was working. We'd give it a rest and come back three days later with other ideas, and they still weren't strong enough.

At some point, I realized I could write the song about Darrell and Ronnie James Dio. They were both close to us and they were both heroes. That's when the lyrics started coming together better because it didn't have to be all about this one person. I could make it a little more general but just as reverential. Then, when Rob and I were on tour with the Damned Things in early 2010, we were in the car in Detroit, and Charlie sent an MP3 to both of our phones. He wrote, "I think I've got it!"

We listened to the file, and it was this whole new arrangement with a completely different chorus that elevated the song to where it needed to be. Rob and I were cranking it in the car and digging this new guitar harmony part and the solo. We called Charlie back and said, "Dude, that's it! Finally!!"

Worship Music is filled with great tracks. It's the most complete album we've ever made. "In the End" is my favorite song on the record and my favorite to play live. I'm so proud that we stuck with it and hammered away at it and IN THE END we got it right.

I knew I wanted to write some different kinds of lyrics on *Worship Music*. I had done a lot of songs about bad relationships, my divorce, and questioning my place in life. I wanted to write about everything on *Worship Music*—from comic book science fiction to real-life politics. For "I'm Alive" I combined ideas about religion and politics. I'm fine with religious people. They can believe what they want. But when it comes to fanaticism from any religion, things get scary. Some religions have the ability to brainwash people, and I expressed that with lines like "Look into my holy eyes / An empty smile and you're hypnotized." Then I really wanted to put a strong message in there about what the Republican Party has become.

In my lifetime the Republican Party has changed so drastically from what it was in the age of Ronald Reagan in the eighties. A lot of Republicans look at Ronald Reagan as a hero. But I feel like they have no idea, other than the fact that he was a famous and popular Republican who came into office after Jimmy Carter. He took the power back for the party. That's true. But if they went back and looked at his policies and what he represented—especially tax-wise—it went drastically against everything the Republicans have been saying since the year 2000. They quote this guy all the time as being their Jesus, yet at the same time everything they want to do is the opposite of what Reagan did. It's become all about money, and they'll kowtow to the religious Right or any special-interest group that's got the cash regardless if they actually feel that way.

These people are so fucking hard up for votes, they would do anything and sell their souls to anybody. If the fucking Phelps' church—the fucking "God Hates Fags" people—had enough power and money, you can bet the fucking Republicans would've sided with them to win a House or Senate seat. It just sickens me that this once-great party aligned themselves with the hardcore religious fanaticism that exists in America, thinking that's what was going to save the country, and it certainly didn't.

Not to get on my political soapbox here, because people like Bono and Tom Morello do it much better than I ever could, but there's stuff in that song as well about Dick Cheney and Donald Rumsfeld leading America to war. As a nation, America is a child compared to the rest of the world. We're not even three hundred years old, and we're led like children by these people into war, over and over. These hawks prefer military conflict to peace because they only care about money. What are people going to look back on when they examine the 2000–2010 era? What is history going to say about that decade, with the wars we got into and the weapons of mass destruction we declared were in Iraq but didn't exist? When the government starts to create laws by sucking up to the religious Right, that starts to affect me. That's where I feel I have to make my voice heard through my music and stand up and protect my right as a free American, because their policies go against everything that I believe in and take away freedom.

Look, I'm not some whiny liberal either. I'm a human being who has his own opinions. Turn off the TV. Get off the Internet. Go outside and live.

Chapter 32

ROCK-A-BYE BABY

When things are going well, that's when the bottom sometimes drops out. From the time we released *Stomp 442*, I had gotten used to that happening. I can't say I ever became immune to it—being an optimist in general means every disappointment still feels like a knife to the gut—but the old scars healed over time, and the anticipation that life is destined to improve kept me going. Since 2010 the ground has been pretty solid under my feet, and with each step I've been able to reach a higher personal plateau.

In January 2011, Pearl and I decided to get married. We had been together ten years and had talked about it for ages. Since we had both been married before—me twice—neither of us felt the need to have a piece of paper drawn up just to prove that we were a couple and we were in love. We would fantasize about it happening somewhere down the line, but Pearl never pressured me to get married, and I never felt the need to do it until she got pregnant. It just made sense at that point, and why not? We were completely in love, we were best friends, and we were about to start a new chapter in our lives together. I knew that getting married wouldn't change us.

We had talked about children a lot over the years, and we'd always say, "When the time is right." Well, there really never is a right time, so in 2010 we just decided to stop worrying about it. We weren't trying to have a baby, but we weren't trying *not* to, either. We pretty much knew what would happen; we just didn't think it would happen so fast. We're pretty sure our son, Revel, was conceived in Louisville on the Jäger tour with Slayer, Megadeth, and Anthrax. Megadeth had a bowling party on a night off, and Pearl and I got pretty tanked up, went back to

the hotel, and made a drunk baby. Based on when she took the pregnancy test and when her obstetrician predicted her due date, we were
able to trace it back to around that time. We were both unbelievably
excited. A baby! Holy crap!!! I knew I always wanted a child and always
imagined that moment of realizing it was happening. The reality was
even bigger and better than anything my brain could conjure up. Pearl
and I were ecstatic and so were our families.

A few months later my dad had his seventieth birthday party in
Las Vegas, and we decided to surprise him by setting up a surprise
wedding to go along with his party. Nobody knew what was going on.
My dad was there with his wife, Rhea, my brothers Jason and Sean,
Jason's wife Tina, and our friend Brian Posehn and his wife, Melanie,
who happened to be in Vegas at the same time.

I invited my mom as well, but she was in Florida then. I waited
to invite her because the wedding was such a secret and I didn't want
my dad to find out at all. Nobody knew anything. By the time I told
her, she felt like the trip was too much to handle so she didn't come,
but everything was fine. I wasn't mad and she was happy for me. Her
firstborn was having a child. What could be better for a Jewish mom?

Pearl and I planned all the logistics, getting our license, booking
the chapel, around my dad's birthday plans. My dad got tickets to see
the Cirque du Soleil show *The Beatles Love*. We were all going to go to
the performance and then have dinner. Pearl told my dad she planned
for a limo to come pick us up from *Love* and take us to the restaurant so
we wouldn't have to deal with cabs.

We all got in the limo, which was stocked with champagne. We
were driving and driving. Everyone thought we were going to the Cos-
mopolitan. No one was paying attention to how long the drive was because we were all having drinks and talking about how great the show
was. And then I saw the chapel and smiled.

The limo turned into the parking lot, and my stepmom said,
"Where are we going. . . . Oh my God! They realized what we had
pulled off, and it was fucking awesome. My dad was so happy. We had
an Elvis impersonator marry us, then we got back in the limo and went
to dinner. It was the ideal way to get married rather than have months
of planning and inviting three hundred guests. I'm sure if we had done

that, it would have been a fucking fantastic party, but in its way this was so much cooler.

When Pearl and I got back to LA, we had to start preparing for the baby. We needed to find a new house because the place we were renting at that time didn't have heat. There was a woodburning stove that'd heat the place and we had space heaters, but we had a baby coming and we're not pioneers. Also, I was back and forth on tour with the Damned Things. I started coming home early from those tours to be with Pearl as much as I could while she was pregnant.

Before long, the sonograms started coming in, which were really cool. We'd come home with fifty pictures of the baby and video. Pearl's doctor was nuts for that, and to him it proved the baby was fine and we had nothing to worry about. But still you worry. That seems the main role of a parent—to worry. That's all my mother ever did. And Revel wasn't even born yet.

All in all Pearl had an easy pregnancy. Now that is not taking anything away from how hard it is for a woman to be pregnant no matter how "easy" or "smooth" things go. For the man, the stress of his lady going through pregnancy may be bad, but for the woman it's unfathomable. As guys, we can never really know.

I'll never complain about the birth of my son, because it's the greatest thing that's happened in my life, but the timing could have been better. Anthrax had done the first seven Big 4 dates in 2010, starting June 16 in Warsaw, Poland, and ending in Istanbul, Turkey, June 27. Since that went so well, Metallica lined up seven more Big 4 shows, mostly in Europe, but including two shows in the US, April 23 in Indio, California, at the Empire Polo Club and September 14 at Yankee Stadium (we'll get to that later).

Pearl was due in June, which presented a dilemma. I had never missed an Anthrax show in the history of the band. As sick as I'd been with the flu or as delirious as I was from exhaustion or heatstroke, I always took the stage. Up to that point the only concert we canceled was in Dusseldorf, Germany, in the late eighties because Charlie was too sick to play. There was no question in my mind that I was going to be there with Pearl for Revel's birth and that I was going to have to miss some of the Big 4 shows. There was nothing that would've taken me away from that. That was obviously my biggest priority. But the idea of not playing those shows was really weird. I made it perfectly clear to everyone that I had to take three months off when Revel was born, and no one had a problem with that. At the same time, we didn't know what to do.

The first person I thought of to fill my spot was Andreas Kisser from Sepultura. Well, James Hetfield was my first choice, but that wasn't going to happen. So, Andreas was perfect. I've known him forever. He's a great rhythm guitar player and he understands the aggression of the music. And he's a name, a personality. That was important to me. If I couldn't be there, I wanted to make sure that whoever was onstage in my place was someone people knew and would be psyched to see. Andreas is a fucking icon. Everybody in the metal world knows who he is, and he's universally respected. He wasn't like some unknown dude that we've never hung out with. We've played with Sepultura and been fans of Sepultura forever.

We sent him everything he needed to learn. I e-mailed him once a week and wrote, "Hey, do you need me to make any videos of how the riffs go?" He always wrote back, "Nope. I'm all good. I got it." He never asked for help and he didn't need it. I loved his confidence, but I couldn't help but be nervous because there was going to be someone onstage in my place.

As these things go, Pearl's delivery was normal and fast, considering it was her first baby. Her doctor, Dr. Paul Crane, started the maternity ward at Cedars-Sinai in LA in the early seventies, so she was in the best hands in the best hospital. They took such great care of her, we didn't want to leave! I can't tell you how important it was to feel safe in that scenario. As first-time parents we didn't know shit, so trusting the doctor and nurses was paramount. There was a moment when Pearl's doctor had to manually break her water, and that caused her some intense pain. She was writhing on the bed, and it took every bit of self-control I had to not tackle the doctor off the bed onto the floor to stop her pain. She went to sleep not too long after that, and when Dr.

Crane came back in the morning, he checked her cervix and said, "Are you ready to have a baby?"

At 10:19 a.m. on June 19, 2011, Pearl and I became parents. The second I saw Revel's head come out, my whole life changed. I cut the umbilical cord, which seemed like a revelation. Everything I ever thought I knew was different. It was insane and amazing. It was like a switch was flipped, and suddenly this infinite amount of love filled my heart for this baby, this person I didn't even know yet but I would take a bullet for. All of that profound emotion, and I hadn't even eaten any 'shrooms.

A week after Revel was born, I was as happy as I've ever been and just as sleep deprived. Meanwhile, Anthrax were in Germany rehearsing before the first show of the run. Since I couldn't be directly involved, we set up a FaceTime session. Revel was only a week old, so I was sitting there with my tiny, tiny baby, feeding him a bottle, and watching Anthrax rehearse without me. They were jamming in the rehearsal room with Andreas, and it was so surreal, yet at the same time it was perfectly right because I was exactly where I wanted to be. I didn't feel, "Oh God, I'm missing this." If it wasn't Andreas, maybe I would have been more freaked out by the whole thing, but Andreas really saved me and made it okay for me not to be there. The shows started, and I got reports back that Andreas was a perfect fit and everything was going well. The guys were telling me I should relax and enjoy being a dad. And then I got a call from our manager.

He said, "You're gonna wanna fucking shoot me, but we need you to fly to Italy for the show in Milan on July 7."

"You're outta your fucking mind!" I said. "I'm not going anywhere. I've got a two-week-old baby here. This is where I need to be."

And he said, "Well, *Guitar World* is shooting the Big 4 cover. It's you, Mustaine, Kerry, James, and Kirk. And we just really feel like you would rather be there than not be there."

I was irate. "Who's thinking that? I'm not thinking that! I'm not getting on a plane from LA to fucking Milan."

They literally wanted me to fly in, do a photo shoot, and then fly home, which meant twenty-eight hours of flying just to go take a picture. I asked them why the photographer, Ross Halfin, couldn't shoot me in LA and then composite the shot. Magazines do that all the time. And they said, "*Guitar World* doesn't want a composite. Ross doesn't want to do it that way. *Guitar World* said they want you guys in the room together, at the same time, because they're doing the interviews backstage that day, and it's happening with or without you."

I talked about it with Pearl, and she was the one who said, "Look, you really should be there. It's okay." But in my heart, it wasn't okay. It was fucked. They were really putting the screws to me, and finally I said, "Alright. I'm gonna fucking do this. I'll leave my wife and my two-week-old son to go take a picture for fucking *Guitar World*." My voice dripped with venom, like, "You motherfuckers owe me."

I got into Milan late at night, and the next day was the show. So I got driven over to the venue site, and I saw everybody. It was so weird because the tour had been going on for a few weeks already, and I just came walking in. It was like I had entered the Twilight Zone. I wasn't on the tour, but suddenly I was there. It was great to see everybody, and they all asked about the baby. We did the photo shoot and the interviews, and then the question was, do I play the show?

My right hand was in no shape to do it. My chops were nowhere near where they needed to be to properly play an Anthrax concert. And I truthfully didn't want to do it. I felt weird about that, because we all sat there—me, Charlie, Frankie, Joey, Andreas, and Rob—and I said, "You know, it's strange that I would just come and show up and play the show and have Andreas sit out." I didn't think that was cool, and that's when we came up with the idea of having the band start with Andreas, and three or four songs in, when they got to "Indians," I would walk out at the part where I scream "War Dance!" every night, and then play the show out from that point. It would be a special surprise for the audience because no one knew I was there.

So the show started. They opened with "Caught in a Mosh." I was standing stage left by the monitor board watching. And I had my guitar on because I wanted to play along unplugged to warm up and get my hands ready since I hadn't played guitar in months. I was standing next to Kerry King. He looked at me and then looked at the stage and said, "Wow. This is pretty fucking cool, huh?" And I said, "Actually, it is!" And he went, "Yeah, I never get to see Slayer!" It was a special moment because I really watched them up there, and they were kicking ass. I thought, "Yeah! Anthrax are fucking great!!" I thought, "When do I get a chance to stand and watch my band? Never." And Andreas was fucking awesome. His tone was ripping, and he was tight as fuck with the rest of the band.

Finally, they got to "Indians." I walked out, the crowd saw me, and the place went fucking bananas. It was so fucking cool playing with two rhythm guitars on stage left, because Andreas and I were so tight even though we had never gotten together to work on the songs. For those next five songs, it sounded like one massive brutal fucking guitar coming off of stage left, and with the two of us doing the backup vocals together, it was so good to the point where I thought, "Man, we should just have him join Anthrax!"

The experience was so rewarding I didn't feel that mad about having to fly for twenty-eight hours straight to make it happen. To do the photo—whatever. That was a jerk-off. But to get onstage and have that musical experience with my band and another rhythm guitar player and just have it be so mind-blowingly cool and sound so great, that actually rectified it in my brain, like, "Okay, I did the right thing."

After the show, the guys were all trying to get me to come on the bus because they had a day off in London and then the next show was the big Knebworth concert, which was going to be in front of 75,000 people. Everyone was saying, "Just get on the bus! It's one more day!" and although I was tempted I put my foot down. "It's not one more day. It'll be two more days and then the flight home which makes it three more days." So I said, "Fuck that shit, I'm getting on the plane and I'm flying home." I couldn't wait to get back in the house and see Pearl and Revel. That meant more to me than anything.

I truly believe Pearl and I were meant to save each other because we were both on terrible paths when we met. Whoever is pulling those strings certainly pulled the right two at the right moment, and our lives have only gotten better with the birth of Revel Young Ian. You think you can't have any more love than you do in your life, and then your child comes and everything amplifies. My love for the both of them has increased dramatically. Pearl and I are going on fourteen years together, and it's the best. As they say, third time's a charm. I just hope we both live long enough to be two old crabs sitting on a porch somewhere, yelling at kids cutting across our front lawn. I was never able to picture that in my other relationships, but I absolutely envision us together when we're eighty, ninety, one hundred to infinity.

Fortunately, I'm thirty years from that now, and Anthrax still have a lot to accomplish before then—not that we'll be jumping around the stage in our seventies like the Rolling Stones, but *Worship Music* definitely injected new hope and life into the band, so I think we'll stick around for a while.

I don't know if it has anything to do with having kids and learning patience or getting older and being more tolerant, or just growing the fuck up and putting my ego in the backseat. But I feel like I understand Joey more now than I did in the past. Since he's rejoined I think we've gotten closer as friends and bandmates. I have his back. In the eighties I never put the time in to get to know Joey as a person; we didn't hang out at all. We spent a lot of time together when he came back for *Worship Music,* and the experience was enlightening. Everyone in Anthrax has a distinct personality, and instead of fighting with someone whose interests and abilities contrast with mine, I've learned to accept them. We're all people. I've learned to let people be people instead of trying to control them. And maybe I have Pearl and Revel to thank for that.

Joey is a great front man. He just has that "thing," that ability to hold an audience in his hands for two hours and take them on a ride. His spot-on vocals and maniacal energy are what put him in the rarified air of great front men. Seriously, the only other guy that moves as much as Joey and hits every note is Bruce Dickinson. That's good company. We put our trust and our faith in him because we know he's going to get onstage and kick ass every night, and that's good enough for me. These days I'm not sweating the little things; I'm celebrating his greatness as a singer and performer.

Anthrax used to be a dysfunctional family, and there's still some of that, but now I live by one of Dimebag's favorite mottos: Don't sweat the small stuff. Now, Joey will text me if there's something he needs to know because he understands I will get back to him right away. I'm pretty insane about returning texts promptly because I hate when I send someone a question and it takes them three days to get back to me.

Once Joey was back in, everybody's big question was, what's he going to sound like on the new record? How will he fit in with these songs? That was a huge unknown. The first time we heard him was when Jay Ruston sent us an MP3 rough of Joey singing "I'm Alive." Charlie, Frankie, Rob, and I were waiting around our computers for this thing to arrive. We all got the e-mail file at the same time and hit play right away because about six minutes later everyone hit "reply all" at the same time.

"Holy shit! Oh my God! He sounds incredible!" we all enthused. It was such a huge relief. I don't know what I was expecting, but when I heard it I thought, "That's the voice of Anthrax!" It sounded like the old Joey but with this depth, warmth, and maturity he didn't have in 1990. From there, everything got better. We barely had to send Jay any notes with suggestions for how Joey should sing something another way. They were nailing it song after song.

"This is amazing. It couldn't have worked out better," Charlie said.

"Dude, you're a fucking monster," I said to Joey. "You're destroying on this record. People are going to lose their fucking minds when they hear this!"

Joey modified some of the phrasing and melodies while they were recording. He knew how controlling I could be about the songs, so he asked what I thought, and I told him, "Keep going! Whatever it is you're doing, keep doing it because it's working. The stuff's fucking great!"

We thought we had a good record—suddenly we had a great record. It was like an act of fate or a prophecy fulfilled. It felt like what we were supposed to be doing, so much that I started rethinking the decision that we made in 1991 to get rid of Joey. At one point he said to me, "You know, I could have done this before. I could have sung on *Sound of White Noise*."

I told him he was probably right, and we were just happy to have him back. That's when I started to wonder, "Did I make a mistake back then? Could he have done those songs, and what would have happened differently if he had? Obviously there's no way to know what career path the band would have taken had Joey never left Anthrax. But at the time, I wasn't in a place, nor was the rest of the band, for him to stay. What happened had to happen, and now it's history. All I know is that Joey gave the performance of a lifetime on *Worship Music,* and if he hadn't I think Anthrax probably would have broken up.

We released the record on Megaforce, which might seem weird considering that's where we started out with Jonny Z back when I was living at my mom's place and Anthrax were rehearsing at the Music Building. But Jonny sold the label to his former employee Missi Callazzo around twenty years ago. It was a good decision to go with Megaforce, but we didn't enter into it blindly. Jonathan Cohen and Izzy split up their business, and we stayed with Izzy, who shopped the record. Roadrunner was interested in putting out the album, as was Nuclear Blast, who were already handling us in Europe. But we took a leap of faith and went with Megaforce.

First of all, they made an incredible offer: a distro deal in which the label would put up all the money up front to make the record as well as handle marketing and promotion, but we would own the masters. Not only that, we'd make close to seven dollars a copy. Second, we trusted Missi because when we worked with her in the past when Jonny was in charge she always went the extra mile. The timing for *Worship Music* couldn't have been better. We were coming off the Big 4 concerts in Europe, which were a big success, so our profile was higher than it had been in years. Joey was back in the band, which gave us extra marketing value and perked the ears of a lot of people. And the pre-album hype from those who had heard it was amazing. Also, it seemed like metal was becoming popular again—not like Jay-Z or Pink popular—but metal bands regularly were debuting in the top 50 on the *Billboard* album chart, and bands like Lamb of God, Mastodon, and Disturbed were drawing really well and helping to resurrect the genre.

The release date for *Worship Music* was September 13, 2011, and we were playing the New York Big 4 show at Yankee Stadium the next day. It was the perfect record release party—50,000 people screaming for us at The House That Ruth Built. It wasn't the same house, of course. They tore the original stadium down and built a new one across the street. But the place is beautiful, filled with every amenity you could want in a venue.

Anthrax played Jimmy Fallon the same week, which was surreal. Programs like that wouldn't even take calls from metal bands years before that. But now it was cool to rock a national nightly TV show. For some reason Anthrax had the ear of the nation again. Why, I don't know. Maybe it had something to do with Joey coming back. Maybe we stayed around so long we outlasted all the bullshit. We lived through the nineties alternative scene and the nu-metal phenomenon and the indie-rock explosion, and all the cynicism and negativity that came with each. We outlasted everything, and now we were considered a legendary band—members of the Big 4. Perception is everything, which is fucking crazy, but it's true, and for the first time in years, people perceived us as contenders. I could live with that.

The Big 4 show at Yankee Stadium was the greatest moment in my life as a musician, hands down. The place was practically a second home to me, at least in spirit. Anthrax still haven't won the World Series of metal—Sabbath, Metallica, Maiden, and Priest still hold those honors—but we've gotten damn close. In my mind, we're like the Yankees that I grew up with. We had great years and shitty years, but we kept fighting. We've lost players and made controversial decisions. We switched managers and got burned by bad business decisions. But we're still here and so are our fans.

That day, we really felt like we were the home team and this was our house. *We* were the fucking New York band on the bill. Sure, we didn't want to be the first band to play, but that was out of our hands. It was Metallica's show and a tour they painstakingly put together. Coordinating the schedules of four touring bands was no easy task. But we were all eager to do it. Even Megadeth understood the promotional value of opening a tour for Metallica, and while Dave Mustaine was suffering from severe neck and back pain at the time, he knew he had to make the show.

A couple of weeks before the concert, I texted Lars and jokingly wrote, "Listen, for Yankee Stadium we want to flip-flop with

Megadeth. They should open and we should go on second. We're the New York band. We just feel like it's the right thing to do in New York."

That kind of freaked him out. He wrote me back and said, "Uh . . . Okay, well, I'll make a call," meaning he'd call management, which was organizing the whole event. I let Lars sweat it out for about twenty minutes, then I wrote him back and said, "By the way, I'm just kidding. I'm only fucking with you. We can't wait to play."

"Oh, thank God!" Lars wrote back. "I really didn't want to make that call, because do you know what fucking can of worms that would have opened?"

"I know, I know. That's why I made the request—just to bust your balls."

We had special jerseys made for us that had Yankees pinstripes but said Anthrax. We looked the part, but as we took the electric carts from the dressing room to the stage, I'd never felt so nervous about playing a show. We walked up the back of the stage. I was with Pearl and Revel and the rest of the band. Our old friend, veteran deejay, and *That Metal Show* host Eddie Trunk was standing behind the stage with Randy Johnson, the baseball player. He pitched for the Yankees between 2005 and 2006 and for six other teams during his tenure in the major leagues. He ended his career with the San Francisco Giants in 2009, having won five Cy Young Awards. After he retired from baseball, he started taking photos professionally. Randy is a big metal/rock fan, and I'd met him a bunch of times, so as we were standing there and he was snapping away, I asked, "What would you do in a World Series when you were on the mound and you were in some super-high-pressure situation and had to get a man out? You must have been nervous, right?"

"Out-of-my-mind nervous," he said. "But you do your job. You shut everything else out, and you do what you've got to do. Why, are you nervous?"

"Dude, I'm kind of losing it right now," I admitted. "I'm so wired and amped, I'm literally cramped up, my hands don't even feel like my hands; playing this show, it's so important to me."

"You're a professional," Randy answered. "You know what you're doing. Go out there and do your thing."

The intro tape was rolling. What choice did I have but to follow Randy's advice—I couldn't not go onstage. As soon as I turned the corner and walked out there and I felt the energy coming from the crowd and I looked up at that historic façade, all my anxiety melted away. And when we ripped into "Caught in a Mosh," I started crying. I was crying from the sheer weight of what we were doing and what it meant to me as a kid from New York. I was crying from the intense happiness of the moment and the release of years and years of emotion from my brain to my heart to my hands to my guitar to the ears of the best fans in the world. For the next hour I felt like my feet weren't touching the floor. I had so much energy and excitement. It was like a great reward, which, in effect, it was. But more than being just recognition of what we'd achieved as pioneers of thrash, it seemed like a gift for sticking it out and persevering against the odds. We had faced and overcome adversity so many times, and it was all played out that moment in a sixty-minute set of explosive heavy metal.

As soon as we finished the show, I had a new answer to the boring, age-old lazy journalist question, "What was the highlight of your career?" It's all downhill from here, motherfucker. We could be playing the Taj Mahal for the next record, and I'd be like, "Who gives a fuck? We played Yankee Stadium."

EPILOGUE

When *Worship Music* came out, I was so worried about how the record was going to do. Everyone puts so much focus on a band's first-week sales, and since nobody buys records anymore, you just have to hope your songs connect with your audience and the label does its job marketing the record so people actually know it's out.

Missi didn't want us to be disappointed, so she told us not to worry about our first week, that it was the first six months of sales or even the first year's worth that would indicate the success or failure of the record. Still, I cared about the first week. I couldn't help it.

We had so much going for us, with the Yankee Stadium show and the Fallon performance. "The Devil You Know" was all over active rock radio. So I thought, "Okay, I'll be happy if we sell 12,000 copies the first week." That's what *We've Come for You All* did eight years earlier. Three days after the record came out, Missi told us the numbers were good and the projections were coming in high, but I told her I didn't want to know anything until we had a concrete Soundscan figure. A few days later I woke up, turned on my laptop, and there was an e-mail saying we sold 28,000 copies and entered the *Billboard* album chart at number 12. I couldn't fucking believe it—almost two and a half times the number I had in my brain. I couldn't help having a tinge of longing for the past. Without the Internet, the album would have sold 280,000 copies first week. Back in the eighties, bands that sold 30,000 records their first week would be number 115 or something. But still, I was thrilled.

Reorders were coming in, and within three weeks we had sold more than 50,000 copies of the record, and it kept selling. Missi knew what she was doing. The record passed the 100,000 mark soon after and is still selling. Our song "I'm Alive" got nominated for a Best Metal Performance Grammy, our fourth nomination. Megaforce had gone to bat for us. The covers EP, *Anthems,* which included "Crawl," another single from *Worship Music,* debuted at number 52, which is great considering it was a promotional vehicle for the single. It also earned us another Grammy nomination for Best Metal Performance for our cover of AC/DC's "T.N.T." *Worship Music* was a huge comeback for Anthrax, and now we're just eager to keep the momentum going. We all still have goals, mainly to keep writing the best songs we can and to keep being a great live band. That's all we've ever wanted to do. We'd love to play more Big 4 shows, but that's mostly up to Metallica. And one day it would be great to be in the Rock and Roll Hall of Fame, just so we can not show up. Maybe that's a stretch, but right now it feels like anything's possible, and we're planning to keep spreading the disease until it's not fun anymore.

These days, the only drawback to being in Anthrax is that I have an amazing family and I have to spend so much time away from them. It's the hardest thing in the world. It's a lot easier to spend six months straight on the road when you don't have anything at home that's better than what you're doing. The *only* thing better than touring with Anthrax is being with Pearl and Revel. It took years of setbacks and struggles (most of which I've documented in earlier chapters), but I can honestly say I'm happier than I've ever been. The bitter irony is, that's what makes it so much harder to leave. It's always the same. The first couple of days are tough enough—leaving the house, getting on a plane, and flying somewhere—and then the brutality begins. There are a few days of trying to adjust and getting into this tour frame of mind. It's kind of like getting the flu. I'm miserable, my body aches, I don't want to do anything.

I'm like that until we start the show. I don't carry that shit onstage with me. I'm not Robert Smith of the Cure. It doesn't affect what I do as a performer. The second I step onstage, I'm in another zone. I can't help it. I'm doing what I've dreamt of since I first saw KISS. That's what keeps guys like me doing what we do for years and years. There's definitely a timelessness to being in rock and roll. If you talk to addiction professionals, they say that heavy drug or alcohol use stunts people's growth. Their maturity stops from the time they start using heavily. I feel the same way about being in a band. When I am onstage, it's like getting to be twenty years old forever, as long as you're in the band.

There's a scene in *Indiana Jones and the Last Crusade* where Harrison Ford finds the Holy Grail and discovers that he can remain immortal, but he has to stay within a small zone, away from the rest of society. I feel like I'm in that situation sometimes. In the band, you're in your element, making music, playing shows. You're the same dude you were when you first started, and you feel that same rush every time you make a great song or play a killer show. It keeps you mentally immortal. When I look out into the crowd and see a sea of young kids reacting the same way to our music as fans did in the eighties, I feel ageless. Rock and roll really is a fountain of youth, but that fountain only stretches from one side of the stage to the other.

As soon as I step off, I'm back in that annoying limbo of between-show apathy. The glamour of globe-trotting wore off a long time ago. Alice Cooper once said, "They don't pay me to play, they pay me to travel." That time offstage is so mind numbing. Every day, day in, day out, I'm stuck in a venue or some cookie-cutter hotel. I do what I can to be constructive and stave off the boredom: write and catch up on reading, TV, and movies. I'm fifty now so I'm not gonna start doing drugs to pass the time. But most of the time I just long to be with my wife and my son. Hey, I know this sounds whiney, but it's how I feel. I know how lucky I am to still be doing this, and I NEVER take it for granted.

Now, I'm fortunate enough to have them fly out to be with me so we haven't been apart longer than two weeks. But Revel is getting older and more aware of his surroundings, and pretty soon he'll need to be in school and won't be able to come out on the road as much. I'm dreading that, and it makes me cherish my time with him even more and hate being away from him even more than that. It's a catch-22. Despite my griping I still love being in the band, and when it comes down to it, I'm not ready to give up Anthrax. I've worked so fucking hard for so long to do this and to be where I am now. Who the fuck knows what's going to happen next month, next year, or two years from now? All I know is, after all I've been through, I'm going to do everything I can to keep it going because this is my band. This is my gig. And whenever I feel like I need some extra motivation, I think of what Randy Johnson said: "Go out there and do what you do."

INDEX